# ASIAN SECURITY HANDBOOK 2000

# ASIAN SECURITY HANDBOOK 2000

Samina Ahmed
Henry S. Albinski
Maureen Aung-Thwin
John C. Baker
Victor D. Cha
James Clad
Paul C. Grove
John B. Haseman
Dennis Van Vranken Hickey
Peter R. Lavoy

Satu P. Limaye
Robert A. Manning
Sean M. McDonald
Michael J. Mitchell
Larry A. Niksch
William J. Olson
Lewis M. Stern
Robert Sutter
M.A. Thomas
Bruce Vaughn

William M. Carpenter
and David G. Wiencek
editors

An East Gate Book

*M.E. Sharpe*

Armonk, New York
London, England

An East Gate Book

**Library of Congress Cataloging-in-Publication Data**

Asian security handbook 2000 / edited by William M. Carpenter and David G. Wiencek.
    p. cm.
"An east gate book."
Includes bibliographical references and index.
ISBN 0-7656-0714-X (alk. paper) — ISBN 0-7656-0715-8 (pbk. : alk. paper)
    I. Carpenter, William M. II. Wiencek, David G., 1958–

UA830.A8415 2000
355′.03305--dc21                                       00-041021

# Contents

# Foreword

East Asia has changed substantially since our last *Asian Security Handbook* was published almost four years ago in 1996. These changes have affected the security balance, economic prosperity, and the future role of the United States in this area.

The Asian economic meltdown that started in Thailand in 1997 rippled through the region. South Korea spiraled downward into crisis—crony capitalism, corruption, conglomerate arrogance, and poor fiscal policies all pulled the rug out from under South Korean smugness about its booming prosperity since the mid 1960s. There are new signs of economic recovery but systemic problems remain unsolved. Indonesia went into a tailspin for some of the same reasons. South Korea, however, elected an extraordinarily talented and democratically inclined leader, while Indonesia's corrupt despot fell and a chaotic transition ensued.

The meltdown affected all countries in the area—the least affected were Taiwan, China, and Singapore with their industrious and well-disciplined workforces, high productivity, and some capital controls.

The second and perhaps potentially more ominous phenomenon was the continuing rise of the power of China. China's economy still boomed, but there were increasing signs of strain. China was a responsible economic partner, holding the RMB (the Chinese currency) steady and granting some financial aid. But at the same time it vigorously pursued a military modernization program, including power projection capabilities and a more advanced strategic weapons force, and flexed its military muscle in the Taiwan Strait in two live fire and missile exercises in 1995–1996. China also strengthened its outpost in the Spratly Islands. The ASEAN countries' reaction to China was much weaker than in 1995, and will probably embolden China in the longer term.

In North Asia, the U.S. administration used the questionable tactic of buying off a rogue state, North Korea, with huge sums of money, food, and heavy oil to limit its development of weapons of mass destruction. Despite this, North Korea remained hostile and threatening. Its conventional power is still formidable, though eroding, its nuclear weapons program was probably being carried out secretly, and it continued to develop and export long-range ballistic missiles, although it has temporarily halted testing. North Korea, dangerous as it is, had to compromise because of its desperate economic situation, including massive starvation and an almost total breakdown of its industrial establishment. South Korea's president, Kim Dae Jung, started an enlightened sunshine policy, which reached out to the North with economic aid and expanded contacts. This combination of North Korean economic weakness and South Korean magnanimity led to the historic summit between the two Koreas in June 2000. But the Korean Peninsula unfortunately remains the region's most volatile hot spot.

Japan emerged as a more prominent military force but remained in the throes of economic recession. The Sino-Japanese relationship was less stable and more competitive, as the Chinese recognized clearly that a strong U.S.-Japanese security alliance was the greatest single obstacle to China's achieving its manifest destiny—in the East China Sea, against Taiwan, and in the South China Sea.

The future role of national missile defense and theater missile defense in East Asia is becoming a major political and security issue. China is strongly opposed to the development and deployment of NMD and TMD, especially in Taiwan, and yet continues its priority emphasis on modernizing its own ballistic missile threat to the U.S. forces, Japan, and Taiwan.

Reports of Chinese espionage in Los Alamos and clumsy attempts to influence the American elections, combined with the U.S. accidental strike on the Chinese Embassy in Belgrade, poisoned the atmosphere between China and the United States, and made progress on China's entry into the World Trade Organization more tortuous and confrontational than necessary. In the end an agreement was reached between China and the United States, but with the serious challenges to the WTO after the 1999 Seattle meeting, passage in Congress of permanent trading status could become more contentious.

This set of comprehensive essays written by the best in the business approaches the security environment in Asia from all angles. China, as Bob Manning points out, is a key actor in all three major potential flash points. David Wiencek covers the important issues of missile strategy. The South China Sea as a center of potential conflict gets close attention by John Baker, who stresses the long-term simmering and cyclical nature of this unpredictable area. The Philippines, Burma, Cambodia, Australia, India, Japan, and Indonesia are all part of the changing Asian environment and must adjust their policies to this evolution.

Taiwan and Vietnam face Chinese pressure—the U.S. deterrent role in Taiwan remains critical to preserving the peace. How the United States acts in Vietnam, India, and Australia will be important in how China emerges in the next millennium.

In the end economic cooperation and competition in a new world order should lead the way into the next century, but the oxygen of a strong and stable security environment will be essential if Asia is to prosper.

Ambassador James R. Lilley

August, 2000

*James R. Lilley is resident fellow and former director of the Asian Studies program at the American Enterprise Institute. He has also served as founding director of the Institute for Global Chinese Affairs at the University of Maryland, College Park. He formerly served as ambassador to the People's Republic of China and the Republic of Korea, as well as serving as director of the American Institute in Taiwan. He also served in the Central Intelligence Agency, on the National Security Council staff, and as Assistant Secretary of Defense for International Security Affairs. He has published articles in* The Washington Post, Foreign Policy, *and other journals and newspapers in the United States and Asia. He previously co-edited* Beyond MFN: Trade with China and American Interests and Crisis in the Taiwan Strait *(1994) and* China's Military Faces the Future *(M.E. Sharpe 1999).*

# Editors' Note

This is the second edition of *Asian Security Handbook*. Our first volume was published in 1996.[1] Since that time, Asia suffered a major financial crisis, which precipitately halted positive growth rates around the region. Some two years later, the signs of economic recovery are beginning to appear. The 1997–98 financial crisis also had an impact on political stability in several countries in Southeast Asia, most notably Indonesia, where the Suharto regime ultimately gave way to the powerful forces of democracy.

The intervening years since our previous edition also have witnessed high tensions in the Taiwan Strait between Taiwan and the People's Republic of China (PRC)—an unfolding security situation with major potential regional consequences that has yet to play itself out. We have also seen in recent years the dramatic effects of the spread of weapons of mass destruction (WMD) in North Korea, China, and between India and Pakistan. The missile and nuclear weapons capabilities of these countries will play an increasingly significant role in shaping the Asia-Pacific security landscape for years to come.

This edition of *Asian Security Handbook* addresses these and other important political-security topics. It updates our previous assessment, looking at regionwide security concerns, the elements of political stability, and conflict potential. We also examine specific issues seen from the perspective of individual countries, now expanded to twenty, covering a huge expanse of geography stretching from Ulan Bator to Wellington and from Islamabad to Manila. We believe our country profiles make a unique contribution to the existing literature, particularly in that our coverage extends to many of the smaller countries in the region and an emerging nation like Mongolia; their concerns are often omitted from security surveys or regionwide analyses. This coverage enables us to provide a comprehensive picture of the region's overall security setting.[2]

As such, this book can be properly placed in the field of comparative security studies.

Our analysis offers regional breadth, with the intent of striving for a handbook or primer that is relevant and accessible to a general audience, including students and the business community, as well as specialists in Asian studies and international security affairs.

In doing so, we would place this volume in the analytical area of the literature that lies between highly specialized academic works and some of the annual reviews produced by organizations like the *Far Eastern Economic Review* (*Yearbook*), the London-based International Institute for Strategic Studies (*Military Balance* and *Strategic Survey*), or its Tokyo-based counterpart, the Research Institute for Peace and Security (*Asian Security*), which produce year-end political, economic, and security analyses and compendiums.

The chapters presented here bring together the insights and expertise of our contributors, a diverse group of international security analysts and Asian affairs experts from government, academia, and the private sector. They bring significant experience and insight, as well as a variety of perspectives, to the book. They have written sharply focused essays that are designed to be analytical and interpretive. Our frame of reference is essentially twofold: First, the larger regional context is viewed through the prism of overarching strategic relationships between the nations of the region based on traditional measures of power (primarily military strength, political influence, and economic potential) and enduring geographic realities, as well as new types of security concerns and challenges that are taking on greater salience as we enter the new millennium. Second, the country profiles contain risk assessments highlighting key internal and external political-security problems and issues. We believe this overall approach allows us to illuminate well the main factors that have a bearing on the Asia-Pacific region's future stability.

A short bibliographic list for further reading and reference appears at the end of each chapter. The views expressed in each chapter are those of the individual author or authors. Taken together, we believe the essays contained here will give the reader a useful overview and assessment of the current and future political-security environment and important security trends in the Asia-Pacific region, from which judgments can be drawn about future developments and the directions the region may take.

As with the previous edition, this book is a collaborative effort between the editors and the contributors. We thank all our contributors for generously donating their time and expertise to this project. We are extremely grateful for the efforts they put into preparing the individual chapters. We also thank the editors and staff of M.E. Sharpe, Inc., for their superb professional assistance in putting this book together.

## Notes

1. William M. Carpenter and David G. Wiencek, eds., *Asian Security Handbook: An Assessment of Political-Security Issues in the Asia-Pacific Region* (Armonk, NY: M.E. Sharpe, 1996).

2. Although we have attempted to be as inclusive as possible, our coverage is admittedly selective and does not include every Asia-Pacific nation. For example, Russia's role in the region is discussed at several points in the text, but there is not a separate chapter on Russia.

Burma is officially named Myanmar, but in this book we use the former and more familiar name.

# List of Tables, Maps, and Photograph

## Tables

## Maps

## Photograph

# ASIAN SECURITY HANDBOOK 2000

# Introduction

## William M. Carpenter and David G. Wiencek

Asia sits on the eve of the new millennium a region of great potential—and of great potential danger. It has recently weathered serious financial storms, with an economic recovery now beginning to take shape. The main security threats and challenges to stability are generally agreed to, but how they will be resolved or managed is not. Thus the nations of the region tread warily toward an uncertain future, on the one hand hopeful of regaining economic momentum and on the other hand worried about serious potential political-security crises.

The situation today is indeed more complicated than when we prepared the first edition of this book in 1996. At that time, strong economic growth was taken as a given. Few analysts cautioned about the potential for an economic downturn.[1] Fewer still imagined the impact that sharp economic reversals would have on political stability in the region, particularly in Suharto's Indonesia.

At the same time, the security uncertainties of the late 1990s have not abated, and in fact are intensifying as we enter the twenty-first century. What has changed in the security arena? In brief, there have been several key developments. First, the U.S.–China dynamic has become more pronounced, and the competitive nature of the relationship between these two major powers is growing. In addition, the status of Taiwan continues to be a major focal point—and potential flashpoint—of this relationship. Second, the Indian and Pakistani nuclear tests of 1998 and North Korea's 1998 Taepo Dong missile launch heightened concerns about the spread of weapons of mass destruction (WMD). Nuclear and missile capabilities are increasingly altering the strategic landscape of the Asia-Pacific region, and considerably raise the stakes in future crisis situations. Third, recent developments in the South China Sea indicate that this vital maritime passageway will remain an area of contention for years to come. Finally, political stability has been tested in several countries recently. Indonesia is the most notable example. It is a vitally important country, yet it is not entirely clear how Jakarta will manage to move what is now the world's third largest democracy peacefully into the new millennium.

3

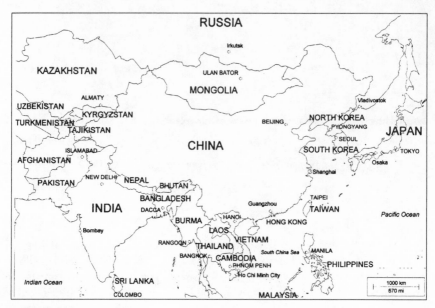

**The Asia-Pacific Region**

This book addresses these and other issues by assessing the current and prospective security setting in the Asia-Pacific region. The chapters that follow identify the key near- and longer-term political, military, and security forces at work in the region and analyze security perspectives and threats on a regional and country-by-country basis.

**Financial Meltdown . . . and Recovery**

In our first edition, we noted the dramatic economic successes realized in the region over the last two decades. By almost any measure, Asia, particularly East and Southeast Asia, appeared to be an economic powerhouse, poised for long-term growth and increased prosperity. But the economic good times came crashing down in mid-1997. In July of that year, the Thai currency (the baht) suddenly collapsed. Quickly enough, systemic economic flaws were exposed. Banks closed. Stock markets fell. And currencies sharply lost value. The financial meltdown in Thailand rapidly spread around the region and beyond, with the "Asian flu" or "Asian contagion" eventually touching the entire global economy.

Table 1 shows the precipitous drop in regional growth rates by 1998, as measured by the key yardstick of gross domestic product (GDP). At least six economies contracted that year, while the important Japanese economy (not shown) turned stagnant as well, experiencing a GDP contraction for much of the entire 1997–99 period. The Asian Development Bank has noted that, during this crisis, "for many countries

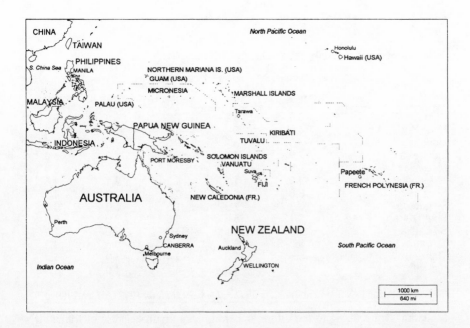

the economic hardship has been similar to that suffered during the Great Depression [of the 1930s]."[2] Major international aid packages were required to help restore economic stability, including upward of US$17 billion for Thailand, some US$43 billion for Indonesia, and some US$58 billion for South Korea.

Gradually, growth rates have climbed back into positive territory, as indicated by most 1999–2000 economic forecasts. Association of Southeast Asian Nations (ASEAN) ministers meeting in Manila in November 1999 declared the crisis essentially over and the recovery in full effect.

### Crisis Exposes Economic and Political Weaknesses

But much remains to be done. In the economic sphere, the crisis exposed underlying weaknesses in many countries, prominently including lack of economic and financial transparency and the debilitating effects of favoritism (or "cronyism") and corruption. Addressing these and other specific concerns will take years.

In the political sphere, the crisis revealed a tenuous underlying stability in many countries, including Indonesia, Malaysia, South Korea, and Thailand. Two of these countries—South Korea and Thailand—were tested, yet likely have emerged stronger politically. Both worked with international authorities and implemented difficult but necessary reforms. Malaysia too was tested, but results there to date are mixed. Short-term stability has been restored, particularly in the wake of the November 1999 elections giving a vote of confidence to long-serving Prime Minister

Table 1

**Asian Economic Growth (GDP) Outlook**

|  | 1996 | 1997 | 1998 | Forecast | |
|---|---|---|---|---|---|
|  |  |  |  | 1999 | 2000 |
| China | 9.6 | 8.8 | 7.8 | 6.8 | 6.0 |
| Hong Kong | 4.5 | 5.3 | −5.1 | −0.5 | 1.5 |
| India | 7.8 | 5.0 | 6.0 | 7.0 | 7.0 |
| Indonesia | 7.8 | 4.9 | −13.2 | 2.0 | 4.0 |
| Malaysia | 8.6 | 7.7 | −7.5 | 2.0 | 3.9 |
| Pakistan | 5.2 | 1.3 | 4.3 | 3.1 | 4.5 |
| Philippines | 5.8 | 5.2 | −0.5 | 3.0 | 4.5 |
| Singapore | 6.9 | 7.8 | 1.5 | 5.0 | 6.0 |
| South Korea | 7.1 | 5.5 | −5.8 | 8.0 | 6.0 |
| Sri Lanka | 3.8 | 6.4 | 5.3 | 5.0 | 6.2 |
| Taiwan | 5.7 | 6.8 | 4.8 | 5.5 | 6.3 |
| Thailand | 5.5 | −1.3 | −9.4 | 3.0 | 5.0 |
| Vietnam | 9.3 | 8.2 | 4.4 | 4.0 | 4.5 |

*Source:* Asian Development Bank, *Asian Development Outlook 1999 Update*, 1999, p. 47.

Mahathir. But looking to the future, uncertainties remain because of Mahathir's questionable handling of the crisis and lack of genuine reform. He displayed a strong anti-Western attitude, placed a heavy blame on foreigners, and implemented currency controls, which hurt and discouraged foreign investment. More crucial was the manner in which Mahathir clamped down on dissent in the form of his main rival, former Deputy Prime Minister and Finance Minister Anwar Ibrahim, who was jailed on charges of corruption and indecent personal behavior. This action launched a "Reformasi" (Reform) movement, with demonstrators taking to the streets of Kuala Lumpur en masse. Those demonstrations eventually died out.

Unlike its neighbors, however, Malaysia went against reformist trends necessitated by the financial crisis. But the battle is not over and will likely resurface at a later time, as reform-minded opposition forces grow stronger. At a minimum, there will be acute political tensions. Beyond that, there is a potential for violent outbreaks as the old order in Malaysia clashes with the new in this ethnically complex society.

**The Case of Indonesia**

But nowhere were the effects of the financial crisis more severely felt than in Indonesia. By early 1998, the rupiah had declined over 80 percent against the U.S. dollar, inflation grew to triple-digit levels, and unemployment soared, ultimately culminating in one of the sharpest economic reversals experienced by any nation since World War II. Rising food prices led to mass riots, a surge in crime, and ethnic violence. Students took to the streets, and President Suharto, a leader who had exercised a tight grip on power for thirty-two years, was suddenly threatened.

By May 1998, Suharto's position proved untenable. He was forced to step aside in favor of his vice president, B.J. Habibie. Although the transfer of power occurred within the country's constitutional framework, significant economic and political turmoil continued, with the Habibie interregnum lasting only through 1999. By late 1999, the forces of democracy had prevailed and the country, in its first free and fair elections in forty-four years, elected a new parliament and eventually a new president, Abdurrahman Wahid. As a result, Indonesia overnight became the world's third largest democracy (after India and the United States).

But ethnic and religious tensions remain palpable. The long-festering situation in East Timor came to a head in 1999. Jakarta consented to an independence referendum in the province, which was approved by a large margin. But violence broke out and international peacekeepers, led by Australia, were forced to intervene to help restore order. At the end of the day, East Timor emerged as a battered country, but nevertheless was on its way to true independence. Looking to the future, the Aceh and Ambon regions, with their ongoing ethnic and religious conflicts, are among the political-security challenges that continue to face the Wahid government. The international community urgently needs to embrace and assist Indonesia's new leaders. Efforts to withhold aid and investment or military assistance, based largely on the East Timor fiasco, are unwise and shortsighted. Indonesia is a nation of immense strategic importance and every effort should be expended to see that it remains a good regional neighbor and valuable friend of the West.

## Military Implications

In addition to the economic and political dimensions, the Asian financial crisis had an immediate impact on defense spending around the region. In virtually every country, military modernization programs ground to a halt for lack of funds.[3] Ambitious equipment upgrade plans were frozen. Some countries were even forced to cut back on patrols, exercises, and various training activities. The one major exception appeared to be China, which pressed ahead with its defense buildup. China's continued defense modernization, at a time when most of its neighbors were forced to substantially curtail military spending, exposed a regional security vacuum that Beijing seemed eager to fill at its neighbors' expense.

In sum, the 1997–98 Asian financial crisis had a major impact on the region. The long cycle of economic growth was broken, creating major hardship and necessitating difficult reforms. Underlying political and economic weaknesses were exposed in several countries, but most notably in Indonesia. Within two short years, the world's fourth largest country—and largest Muslim nation—went from politically oppressed, but economically vibrant, to economically depressed, but politically free. Yet the turmoil in this critically important nation is far from over. Given the widespread drop in military spending, the Asian financial crisis also reinforced China's growing military advantages vis-à-vis its neighbors—a situation that will have long-term strategic implications relative to the region's power equation.

**Near-Term Issues**

Against the background of general economic and political volatility that we have seen recently, four overriding regional security issues stand out: (1) the military threat from North Korea; (2) China's military buildup and the potential for conflict in the Taiwan Strait; (3) the potential for conflict in the South China Sea; and (4) the spread of WMD. Each of these concerns poses considerable risks and, as such, will have an important bearing on stability in the Asia-Pacific area.

• **North Korea** remains our most immediate concern. Pyongyang continues to engage in reckless behavior and continually defies the international community. In 1998, it provocatively test launched a long-range ballistic missile over Japan into the Pacific Ocean, claiming the move was an attempt to orbit a satellite. But the test fit a clear recent pattern aimed at enabling North Korea to proliferate nuclear-capable missiles to other sensitive regions of the world and to enhance its own capabilities for nuclear and missile blackmail against its neighbors and adversaries, especially Seoul, Tokyo, and Washington. In 1999, it threatened another test of an even more powerful missile. Furthermore, in the past two years, Pyongyang has sold missiles and missile technologies to Pakistan and Iran, adding to security concerns in South Asia and the Middle East.

Separately, in another provocation, in March 1999 two North Korean spy ships entered Japanese waters, leading to rare retaliatory naval gunfire from pursuing Japanese vessels and bombs dropped from Japanese surveillance planes. The spy ships were apparently supported by four MiG-21 fighters, which fortunately broke off during the incident and returned to North Korea.

Other recent disturbing reports reveal that the Kim Jong Il regime is engaged in drug smuggling, currency counterfeiting, and related criminal activities.[4] As with its missile sales, this regime is prepared to engage in any illegal or threatening activity that will earn it hard currency to stay solvent.

The United States and South Korea have pursued a policy of engagement with North Korea over the past several years epitomized in the so-called Agreed Framework of 1994, and in the 1999 policy review conducted by former U.S. Defense Secretary William Perry, a follow-on measure aimed at containing North Korean WMD capabilities. This policy approach did not bear real fruit and had the side effect of allowing Pyongyang to wring concessions from the United States to the point that "North Korea has [now] become the largest recipient of United States foreign aid in Asia."[5]

For these reasons it necessary to assess cautiously Pyongyang's moves. On the surface, the tense situation on the peninsula seemingly changed for the better following the summit meeting in June 2000 in Pyongyang between South Korean President Kim Dae Jung and Kim Jong Il. After a half century of separation and hostility, the historic meeting between the two leaders held out the prospect of potential reconciliation and could presage a brighter future. But it remains to be seen whether the high hopes created by the summit will be translated into tangible results. It is possible that North Korea's apparent willingness to engage Seoul may be a tactical shift aimed at disarming public opinion in the South with the intent of maintaining the status quo without undertaking real reforms.

Exactly how the summit and its aftermath will affect U.S.-North Korean relations will have to play out in the web of multilateral relations among the two Koreas and the regional powers. There are many problems ahead—political, military, economic, and humanitarian—to work out before anything resembling Korean reunification takes shape. As events evolve, the United States and South Korea should maintain their strong security capabilities in the peninsula, and strengthen them where necessary, including by the addition of a Theater Missile Defense (TMD) system to help blunt the North's nuclear missile threats. At some future stage of developing union between North and South, the arms competition across the border may begin to decline, although it seems prudent for the longer view that the United States should keep a military presence in Korea, even assuming the initiation of a reunification process.

• **The Taiwan Strait** has been a potential security flashpoint for many years, but the situation started to become more dangerous in 1995–96 and since then has grown even sharper in intensity. In 1995, Taiwanese President Lee Teng-hui visited his alma mater in the United States in a personal capacity. For a variety of reasons, that visit touched a nerve in Beijing, ultimately leading to People's Liberation Army (PLA) military maneuvers and missile tests off Taiwan. In 1996, on the eve of Taiwan's first democratic presidential election, this pattern was repeated. Beijing unveiled Exercise Strait 961—military exercises designed to practice an invasion of Taiwan, with the intent of intimidating and threatening the people of Taiwan during this important political period. PLA "test" missiles were again fired into two areas that bracketed the island, driving home the point about Taiwan's vulnerability to attack. The United States deployed two carrier battle groups to the region as a warning to Beijing. Despite China's heavy-handedness, President Lee was voted back into office, winning 54 percent of the vote; this was a greater percentage than was expected before the missile firings.

Then, in July 1999, President Lee raised Beijing's ire again when, in an interview with Germany's *Deutsche Welle*, he indicated that Taiwan is a de facto separate nation and that the People's Republic of China (PRC) and Taiwan are engaged in a "special state-to-state relationship, rather than an internal relationship between a legitimate government and a renegade group. . . ."[6] Beijing authorities quickly deemed the remarks an indication of Taiwan's attempt to achieve independence. They warned that President Lee was "playing with fire" and that Taipei had moved to the "brink of the precipice."[7]

In subsequent days, Taiwanese officials tried to soften President Lee's comments and calm rising cross-strait tensions, which they in fact did. But now Taiwan has a new president, creating a new kind of relationship across the Taiwan Strait. President Chen Shui-bian, elected as the head of the Democratic Progressive Party (DPP) in March 2000, ended half a century of rule by the Kuomintang

(KMT) party. Although the DPP was founded on the premise of seeking independence for Taiwan, Chen has been careful to assure the mainland that he and his
party have no intention of declaring independence. Beijing did all it could before
the election, with loud threats to the voters of Taiwan not to elect Chen, but the
voters were not intimidated.

This change creates a dilemma for Beijing, in that the leaders there can no
longer call for "party-to-party" negotiations, as a dodge to avoid "state-to-state"
negotiations. All the political and historical baggage of the KMT is now gone,
replaced by a new government in Taiwan, democratically elected and with full
freedom to set its own terms for cross-strait talks. Beijing, although clearly dis-
pleased by Chen's election, and not fully reassured by his policy statements to
date, nevertheless appears to be holding back to reevaluate its approach to the
"Taiwan question."

For Washington, the Taiwan Relations Act (TRA) remains in effect, as a symbol of U.S. support for Taiwan and of U.S. adherence to the principle that any
future reunification of China must be by peaceful means. Under the TRA, the U.S.
is able to supply arms for Taiwan's defense, and can even proceed with plans to
provide an upgrade of Taipei's TMD capabilities. Beijing will continue to object
to the U.S. supply of arms to Taiwan, and especially will protest against TMD, but
if Washington remains firm and calm, there is little the PRC can actually do about
it. Taiwan needs such support to assure its freedom and security until it can reach
a future settlement with China.

• **The South China Sea** is another potential security flashpoint, involving principally the contested Spratly Islands. The Spratlys constitute arguably the most
complicated territorial dispute in Asia, involving five or six claimants directly, and
affecting the interests of many other key regional states, such as Singapore, Indonesia, Thailand, Japan, Korea, and Australia. One main reason is the sheer volume
of trade shipments that travel through the important maritime passages of the South
China Sea. Such shipments have been estimated to be approximately US$568 bil-
lion, or 15 percent of all global cross-border trade.[8] Some 75 percent of Japan's
oil, for example, is shipped through these sea-lanes. Another key reason this area
is so important is the potential for oil and natural gas exploitation and access to
other valuable maritime resources.

As John C. Baker points out in Chapter 8, this dispute has been of a cyclical nature,
with periods of confrontation followed by lulls. This pattern has helped distract attention from this important issue and create a false sense of security, which suggests that
the conflict can be contained or a negotiated solution easily arrived at.

But diplomacy is not working; it is not working because this issue has come to be
dominated by political-security considerations, which have been infused with a strong
dose of nationalism. As a result, there is a danger that the Spratlys dispute could come
to resemble the 1982 crisis in the Falkland Islands, where a dispute over what were
initially perceived as some very remote islands quickly led to conflict.

The main problem relative to the Spratlys is the position of the PRC, which as-

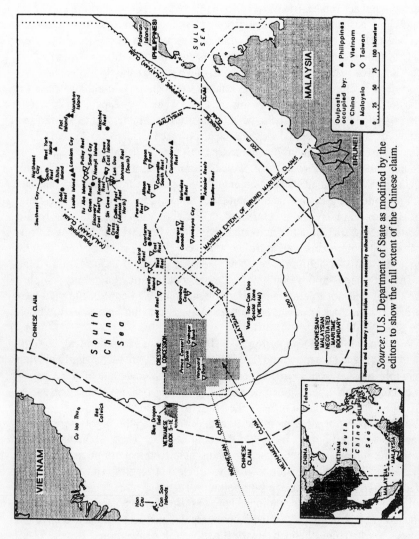

*Source:* U.S. Department of State as modified by the editors to show the full extent of the Chinese claim.

Names and boundary representation are not necessarily authoritative

## South China Sea: Claims and Outposts in the Spratly Island Region

serts a claim to the entire South China Sea. In the first instance, this *mare nostrum* approach threatens the interests of all trading nations whose goods must traverse these important sea routes. But more fundamentally the Chinese position highlights Beijing's long-term intention of asserting political-military dominance over the South China Sea. China is clearly pursuing a strategy of expanding its sphere of influence to include strategic waypoints in the Paracel Islands in the northern portion of the South China Sea (particularly Woody Island) down through the Spratlys. This Chinese strategy is closely linked with its enunciated goals of moving away from a coastal defense orientation and more toward a blue water navy capable of dominating the so-called First Island Chain, which runs from the Spratlys up to Taiwan and the Ryukyus, and then eventually extending its power to reach to the Second Island Chain, which it sees running out to the Marianas, Guam, and Palau.

To date, the major powers have played a limited role in the Spratly dispute. The United States issued its last major policy statement in May 1995 and has effectively adopted a neutral stance and takes no position on the various claims. But it is becoming increasingly clear that, over the long run, U.S. interests would be jeopardized were China to dominate the Spratlys. For this reason, greater support from Washington, as well as Tokyo and other powers, is needed and will be essential in terms of helping damp down conflict potential in the South China Sea. The U.S. needs to develop new and more robust policy guidelines, emphasizing that it will not tolerate an attempt by any nation to control the vital sealanes of Southeast Asia or pursue any actions inconsistent with a peaceful resolution of the Spratlys dispute.

• **Weapons of Mass Destruction (WMD)**, that is, nuclear, chemical, biological, and radiological weapons and their delivery systems, are increasingly playing a major role in Asian security calculations. This issue, explored more fully in Chapter 5, is of considerable importance because any future crisis involving the use of WMD holds the potential to inflict wide-scale damage and destruction.

WMD concerns became particularly salient following the highly sensational nuclear tests carried out by India and Pakistan in 1998. These countries clearly signaled the importance they attach to being able to threaten one another with nuclear weapons. Their decision to embrace nuclear strategies is a recognition of the fact that WMD capabilities are important for reasons of national prestige and highlighting scientific and technological prowess. In addition, the decision reflects a conclusion by policymakers in both countries that they are unlikely to have the resources to challenge their adversary directly with conventional forces. Thus, nuclear weapons and long-range missiles offer a cost-effective means of redressing military imbalances.

WMD concerns have also flowed beyond South Asia, into East Asia, where China and North Korea are involved in significant buildups. Pyongyang has a sizeable force of short-range ballistic missiles. It is also developing medium and longer-range missiles to threaten other adversaries. It may have some nuclear capability as well, and is selling its WMD technologies around the world.

Beijing, meanwhile, has concluded that high-technology precision weapons (as demonstrated by the United States in the Persian Gulf War and by NATO in the 1999 Kosovo intervention) are vitally important to success in conflict situations and implementing a strategy of coercive diplomacy in order to influence the behavior of its adversaries. Chinese strategists have outlined warfighting doctrines that emphasize preemption and long-range attacks against adversaries. Thus, China increasingly perceives WMD capabilities, particularly ballistic and cruise missiles, to be important tools for achieving its political aims and warfighting goals. Missiles can be used to threaten and intimidate an adversary, strike at long distance with precision, and achieve a range of objectives all along the conflict spectrum from conventional to nuclear attacks. As such, China is now engaged in an across-the-board missile buildup.

The upshot of these developments is that nuclear missile races may emerge in South and East Asia in the early part of the twenty-first century. India and Pakistan are clearly engaged in an action–reaction cycle to gain improved capabilities. New Delhi also sees the need to balance Chinese capabilities over the long-term. In East Asia, growing nuclear missile arsenals in China and North Korea are posing new political, military, and economic challenges and raising immediate security dilemmas for the three democracies of Japan, Taiwan, and South Korea. Indeed, rapidly expanding missile threats are sparking a critical reappraisal of security and defense requirements. The hands of all three democracies are being forced and they are now looking to counterforce capabilities and responses in-kind to counter their opponents' growing missile forces. The three democracies are doing this partly for symbolic reasons, recognizing the importance that responses in-kind have for maintaining an adequate level of deterrence. They are also pursuing this path because, in their view, defensive options in the form of TMD systems may not be coming on line quickly enough to meet their urgent security requirements. In addition, China and others have effectively stigmatized TMD, thus helping to lessen its political attractiveness.

In this context, Beijing's anti-TMD propaganda initiative is highly disingenuous. First, Beijing is developing its own anti-missile defense systems, so what is good for Chinese security is apparently unacceptable for the security of others. Second, China's massive missile buildup is in fact the root cause of the problem. And third, and most important, this campaign is counterproductive and dangerous. By making the case to deny TMD capabilities to surrounding states, it is pushing those states to develop new offensive capabilities, which could be used to retaliate against China. TMD, by contrast, is stabilizing in that it is a purely defensive capability. Nevertheless, Beijing's insistence on dominating the regional security environment, and ensuring that its missiles can penetrate unimpeded to their targets, will create new instabilities and heighten the possibility that a nuclear missile race will emerge in Asia.

For this combination of reasons, WMD programs are rapidly undermining the Asian security environment. In East Asia, a new nuclear missile race will mean that the three democracies would move away from their historically low-key, defensive military postures to a form of offensive-based deterrence. New offensive-oriented strategies would place a premium on preemption, creating new types of pressures on political and military leaders in deep crisis situations. In short, WMD programs in Asia are dramatically reshaping the security landscape and have set in motion a dangerous trend that cannot easily be reversed with arms control or other forms of diplomacy. It is a trend that will likely play itself out in the arena of hardware development, new acquisitions, and increased defense spending.

Policymakers and defense planners, as well as the business community, will need to pay greater attention to this evolving situation because the risks are high. Even threats or small missile "test" firings can quickly undermine economic security and investor confidence and contribute to wild stock market gyrations.

## The Future Power Balance in Asia and the Growing U.S.–China Competition

Aside from these near-term concerns, important unanswered longer-term questions exist about the shape of the future power balance in Asia. Perhaps no question is more important than that of how the relationship between the United States and China will evolve. Four years ago, in the first edition of this book, we assessed this relationship to be one of a growing competition and diverging interests in key areas. As we wrote at that time:

> [there] are signs that a new competition is arising between Washington and Beijing. This competition will be unlike the old U.S.–Soviet Cold War rivalry, which was dominated by ideological considerations. Instead, the new U.S.–China competition is likely to be marked by a somewhat more complex mix of political, economic, and security challenges.

That basic assessment is still valid. We do not foresee a new Cold War emerging. China, unlike the former USSR, has no universal ideological claims. Nor is it supporting guerrilla or insurgency movements around the world to advance a political-ideological agenda. What we do foresee is a strategic competition that will be played out initially in Asia, and over the very long term, perhaps globally. On one hand, China will increase its economic integration with the rest of the world. It will be a member of the World Trade Organization (WTO), embracing global trade norms. In this context it will be a key market and important trading partner. On the other hand, China will remain a politically repressive communist dictatorship. It will not tolerate political dissent, not even from a social group like the Falun Gong spiritual/exercise movement. (Although Falun Gong does not have any political basis, Beijing authorities reportedly felt compelled to detain some 35,000 Falun Gong members between July and October 1999 alone). From a human rights/ political openness standpoint, therefore, the Chinese communist regime will remain an anathema to the United States. Thus, economic and political forces will pull the relationship in different directions. The two countries' interests will be compatible in one area, and collide in another.

As already noted, Taiwan, the South China Sea, and WMD concerns will be additional points of contention.

## The Critical Security Dimension

In fact, it is the security dimension that will be the critical part of the strategic competition, and a significant source of tension. Beijing is currently embarked on a major defense modernization effort to position itself as the dominant military power in Asia and eventually a superpower capable of challenging U.S. and Western interests on a global scale. As such, it sees the United States as an impediment to achieving its rightful place in the family of nations. It also perceives a U.S. policy of encirclement or containment, and worries that what happened in Kosovo in 1999, where U.S.-led NATO forces intervened in an internal dispute, could happen to China, perhaps in Taiwan or Tibet.

Chinese perceptions have been strongly influenced by a deterioration in U.S.–China relations in 1999, abetted by such developments as the inadvertent U.S. bombing of the Chinese Embassy in Belgrade during the Kosovo crisis and by the U.S. congressional report detailing charges of Chinese espionage against U.S. nuclear weapons laboratories (report of the Select Committee on U.S. National Security and Military/Commercial Concerns with the People's Republic of China— also known as the Cox Committee).

The United States, meanwhile, sees important indicators of China's intent to build up its military power projection capabilities, including new long-range, mobile, multiple-warhead missiles, new nuclear submarines, advanced cruise missiles, ballistic missile defenses, an anti-satellite (ASAT) capability, and an aircraft carrier to be built in the next decade. The PLA also intends to exploit the Revolution in Military Affairs (RMA). Chinese military commentators speak with increasing frequency about RMA and asymmetric warfare strategies designed to attack an opponent where it is weak, for example, by using ballistic or cruise missiles with a high degree of target penetration to carry out precision strikes, or using ASATs to degrade or disable communications or reconnaissance satellites, or using jammers against Global Positioning System (GPS) receivers. In addition, the PLA has shown a keen interest in recent years in information warfare designed to attack an enemy's decisionmaking capability by employing deception strategies or conducting various types of electronic warfare.

In this respect, U.S. analyst Dr. Michael Pillsbury has noted:

> The Chinese argue each of America's high-technology weapons is flawed in one way or another and can be defeated. They point to American over-reliance on satellites for targeting, reconnaissance and battle damage assessments. They believe the United States relies on satellites for 90 percent of its combat information and communications and that asymmetric warfare targeting these assets could cripple the United States at low cost to China.[9]

China's embrace of new defense technologies is designed principally to give the PLA an edge over other regional powers, particularly looking toward China's interests in Taiwan and the South China Sea, as well as creating a counterweight to India. The notion that China may be able to deploy enough high-tech weaponry to leapfrog from its current equipment to the point of being a formidable regional or strategic power is evident from its foreign acquisitions, particularly from Russia. The Chinese reportedly have purchased military equipment worth about US$6 billion from Russia since 1991. Key purchases have been for off-the-shelf, front-line systems that can contribute quickly to China's military punch. These include Su-27 and Su-30 fighter aircraft, Kilo-class diesel submarines, two Sovremenny-class destroyers equipped with high-performance cruise missiles, and SA-10B anti-aircraft ballistic missile defense systems.

### Role of the United States

Overall, then, there is a clear pattern of hardware acquisition, force modernization, and doctrinal development that points to acquiring the tools and strategies for power projection and exercising a high degree of strategic influence in Asia and beyond.

This puts the two powers squarely into a mode of strategic competition. For the United States is a Pacific power also, having sacrificed its resources and personnel in three past Asian wars in the twentieth century to defend democratic freedoms and economic openness. Washington rightfully, then, must play the role of ultimate guar-antor of peace and stability in Asia. It is the only power that has sufficient military capability to deter and defend against an act of aggression that would threaten U.S. and allied interests. U.S. power is critical to assuring that an equilibrium is main-tained in the Asia-Pacific region, particularly as China's power grows. Fashioning a modus vivendi in light of what will be a basically competitive relationship is the critical challenge facing policymakers in both Washington and Beijing.

### Other Powers

Over time, we see India's power growing and with it a competition between Beijing and New Delhi, as the two Asian giants jockey for power and influence throughout the region. Japan will remain a critical nation, despite recent economic weaknesses, and could rapidly move to become a more formidable military power should it feel its security threatened. A reunited Korea is another possibility over the long term, and could become a significant political-military actor were the economic, scien-tific, and military resources of the South combined with the missiles and military know-how of the North.

### Looking Back, Looking Forward

At the beginning of the new century, it is important to look back. The twentieth century in Asia will be remembered as a violent period, with three major wars:

World War II, Korea, and Vietnam. China was wracked for decades with internal civil strife, and widespread economic and political turmoil resulting from Mao's failed policies. Other nations also experienced prolonged internal conflict and terrorism, which in many cases persist or have taken on new forms, such as the pernicious drug trade felt around the region. (See, for example, William J. Olson's essay in Chapter 7.)

At the same time, it is important to mention the substantial economic successes achieved over the latter decades of the twentieth century in many parts of Asia. A new middle class has been born, and more people have experienced the fruits of prosperity. New technologies, like the Internet, are sweeping across Asia, as they are elsewhere. Democracy has taken root in many places, including Mongolia and Indonesia, but with distinctly Asian characteristics. However, pockets of despair remain in such places as Burma, Cambodia, and Sri Lanka. Moreover, future stability will be threatened until such time as the key holdouts of China, North Korea, and Burma change their political orientations. How these nations will be transformed remains a critical, yet unanswerable, question at this moment.

The Asian financial crisis reminded us that economic progress can be quickly knocked off track. The industrious people of Asia, however, are rebounding from that crisis and working hard to rebuild their economies and political structures.

Looking to the future, we must hope the next century will be more peaceful. Asia has many human, capital, natural, and technical resources to achieve great success in the century ahead. But major challenges loom large, and the indicators we see point to great potential dangers. The rise of China is certainly foremost in many minds. We have identified other key security challenges in the preceding pages. The chapters that follow point up others in more detail and provide a guidepost to thinking about future political-security challenges on a regional and country-by-country basis.

**Structure of the Book**

This book is organized into three main parts. Part I, the Regional Security Framework, examines the broader interplay of regional security issues and the evolving security environment. It contains chapters on security in the subregions of East Asia, Southeast Asia, South Asia, and the South Pacific. Part II, Multilateral Security Issues, addresses four specific issue-areas of concern that affect the regional security environment: nuclear and missile proliferation, maritime piracy, illegal narcotics, and conflict potential of the South China Sea disputes. Part III, Security-Oriented Country Profiles, analyzes political-security conditions on a country-by-country basis. Our comprehensive treatment of country-specific concerns covers twenty individual countries. Each profile describes the country's framework for assessing political-security issues and contains a risk assessment of the key internal and external security problems facing the country. The profiles highlight the role of the armed forces, military force structure, and defense policy issues. Suggestions for further reading are included at the end of each chapter. Finally, the Epilogue wraps up our survey and assessment of political-security issues in the Asia-Pacific region by summarizing the salient themes made in the preceding chapters.

## Notes

1. In the first edition of this book, Robert A. Manning was in fact thinking of such a situation when he wrote, "One can only speculate what the impact on regional security perceptions would be if suddenly the region's dynamism experienced several years of negative [economic] growth." See Robert A. Manning, "Security in East Asia," in William M. Carpenter and David G. Wiencek, eds., *Asian Security Handbook: An Assessment of Political-Security Issues in the Asia-Pacific Region* (Armonk, NY: M.E. Sharpe, Inc., 1996), p. 31.

2. Asian Development Bank, *Asian Development Outlook 1999 Update*, 1999, p. 22.

3. See, for example, Gregor Ferguson, "Economic Woes Stall Asian Revamp Efforts," *Defense News*, April 20–26, 1998, p. 18.

4. See, for example, Kevin Sullivan and Mary Jordan, "U.S. Wrestles with Policy on N. Korea," *Washington Post*, March 13, 1999, and North Korea Advisory Group, *Report to the Speaker, U.S. House of Representatives*, November 1999, at website http://www.house.gov/international_relations/nkag/report.htm.

5. See *Report to the Speaker, U.S. House of Representatives*.

6. "Responses to Questions Submitted by Deutsche Welle," Lee Teng-hui, President, Republic of China, July 9, 1999, (mimeo). President Lee's remarks are reprinted in *The American Asian Review*, Winter 1999, pp. 165–172. For a further elaboration, see Lee Teng-hui, "Understanding Taiwan: Bridging the Perception Gap," *Foreign Affairs*, November/December 1999, pp. 9–14.

7. Quoted in Gus Constantine, "Taiwan Abandons One-China Doctrine," *Washington Times*, July 13, 1999, p. A1.

8. John H. Noer with David Gregory, *Chokepoints: Maritime Economic Concerns in Southeast Asia* (Washington, DC: National Defense University Press, 1996), p. 4.

9. Comments of Michael Pillsbury in Hans Binnendijk and Ronald N. Montaperto, eds., *Strategic Trends in China* (Washington, DC: National Defense University, 1998), p. 77.

# Part I

## Regional Security Framework

# 1

# Security in East Asia

### Robert A. Manning

*There is great disorder under heaven, and the situation is excellent.*

—Zhou Enlai, 1960

## The Three Concerns: An Overview

That comment by then Chinese Prime Minister Zhou, uttered in a very different era four decades ago, still sums up the promise and peril of the East Asian security environment as it enters the twenty-first century. The region's remarkable economic dynamism—despite the hiatus of the economic crisis—has generated a coming of age, with China and Japan emerging as multidimensional great powers (historically unprecedented), the prospect of a unified Korea 70 million strong, and an industrializing ASEAN (Association of Southeast Asian Nations) of some 500 million Southeast Asians, all increasingly prosperous, but uncertain about the future. Moreover, the region's economic modernization has also spawned a similarly unprecedented military modernization with the spread of advanced weaponry, ballistic missiles, and nuclear and other weapons of mass destruction.

East Asia has thus far not seen the historic ethno-nationalist antagonisms long suppressed by the Cold War erupt into conflicts such as those that have beset other regions. However, its historical suspicions and grievances, along with unresolved civil conflict frozen by the Cold War (North–South Korea, China–Taiwan) remain a source of tension. Such anxiety has both near-term and long-term sources. In the near term, the two potential regional conflicts that could transform the geopolitics of the region are the divide on the heavily armed Korean Peninsula, and tensions over the status of Taiwan that could produce an armed conflict engulfing the region. Conflict in either scenario could put at risk the U.S. alliance network in the region and foster a new

21

polarization, altering the U.S. strategic profile in the Asia-Pacific. Even a peaceful reunification of Korea will likely alter the geopolitics of the region. The proliferation of ballistic missiles is another new factor that could put at risk U.S. forward-based forces. The overwhelming long-term concern, however, is about the emergence of China as a major economic and military power, one that may become dominant in the region by the second quarter of the twenty-first century.

This "China concern" informs all three of the key bilateral relations whose positive dynamism or volatility are decisive in shaping stability—or the absence thereof—in East Asia: U.S.–China, U.S.–Japan, and China–Japan. This concern increasingly drives international relations in the Asia-Pacific beyond the three core relationships—Korea and Japan, between ASEAN and the United States, and the United States' ties to China. U.S. declarations of engagement and rationales notwithstanding, the removal of the Cold War certainty behind the U.S. forward-deployed presence and adjustments in its forward-deployed presence have led to lingering doubt, less about U.S. staying-power than in the early 1990s, but more about the relevance and expected behavior in a crisis. As the U.S. forward-deployed presence and network of alliances and access arrangements has been and remains the region's de facto security system, this concern animates East Asian thinking about security across the board.

The Asia-Pacific region has no regional economic, political, or security institutions comparable to those in Europe: no North Atlantic Treaty Organization (NATO), no OSCE (Organization on Security and Cooperation in Europe), and no European Union (EU) single market. Indeed there are no pan-Asian or trans-Pacific economic, security, or political institutions of major operational consequence whatsoever. Thus, it should not be surprising that concurrent with the end of the Cold War we have seen a growing search for new Asia-Pacific security mechanisms, assertive military modernization efforts, and in the economic realm, the development of the Asia-Pacific Economic Cooperation (APEC) forum aimed at managing the region's burgeoning economic interdependence. APEC has provided a political and economic forum for Pacific Rim leaders and lent its collective political weight to a free trade agenda, but as an institution it has become unwieldy. this has led to a new effort, the "ASEAN + 3" (China-Japan-South Korea) discussing EU-like regional trade and financial mechanisms of their own. The ASEAN Regional Forum (ARF), an inclusive security dialogue that began in 1994, is a tentative process of uncertain relevance whose main virtue thus far is to provide a political forum to discuss security issues.

This tentativeness that characterizes Asia-Pacific institution building reflects a bias toward informalism in the region's political culture, as well as the amorphous nature of regional fears and suspicions along with a lack of immediate, specific threats (apart from the Korean Peninsula). It is most likely that new patterns of relations and new political/security institutions will grow out of efforts to address concrete problems rather than by adapting grand schemes, or vague processes of "dialogue," the conceiving of which has become a cottage industry, and which mostly tend to be variants of European models.

## Security Challenges

In terms of security problems, there are several sets of issues, ranging from those most immediate and likely to result in armed conflict and/or chaos, most prominently, the Korean Peninsula, and second, China–Taiwan tensions, both of which are a measure of the most important question: defining China's role in the regional and global system. While Korea and the China–Taiwan dispute remain dangerous flashpoints that could erupt at any time, the most controversial of the region's welter of territorial disputes—the disputed Spratly/South China Sea problems—are more of a medium-term (five to ten years) time line in terms of the likelihood of conflict. The Spratly dispute is also less likely to be a geopolitically transforming issue, and less likely to spark a major conflict.

Moreover, there is a plethora of territorial disputes that are far less likely to generate armed conflict. Most prominent in this category would be the Northern Territories dispute between Russia and Japan, which reflects the pathology of their relations, and the Sino–Japanese dispute over the Senkaku/Diaoyutai Islands. In addition, there are a host of territorial issues between the various ASEAN countries and what are often referred to as the new transnational security concerns, chief among them piracy, immigration, and environmental degradation.

## The Korean Question

Despite the new atmospherics resulting from the unprecedented June 2000 North-South Korean summit, most pressing and potentially destabilizing source of conflict is the armed standoff on the Korean Peninsula, in which the much-publicized nuclear issue is a subset. Though being overtaken by the development of three generations of short- and intermediate-range ballistic missiles, the North Korean nuclear weapons program has been the most urgent aspect of the problem. It has also been an admission ticket to addressing the longer-term concern, the process of North–South reconciliation and ultimately, reunification, which will require major conventional arms reduction efforts. The October 21, 1994, U.S.–North Korea "Agreed Framework" accord froze Pyongyang's nuclear weapons program and offers the prospect of terminating the program by roughly 2003–4, with Light Water Reactors replacing North Korea's gas-graphite reactors. But even if it is strictly implemented, the accord allows North Korea to maintain its opaque nuclear status for perhaps a decade before Pyongyang is committed to cooperate with the International Atomic Energy Agency (IAEA) in clarifying its past nuclear activities.

Moreover, six years after the nuclear deal, political realities in Korea began to change. A North Korean "charm offensive," whose centerpiece was the Pyongyang summit, altered the political situation, offering new hope of reconcilation and a gradual "soft landing." The public "coming out" of Kim Jong Il, visiting China, meeting Russian President Putin, and the North's normalizing ties with an array of nations in Asia and Europe disarmed critics. Clearly, a major North Korean tactical shift was underway that began to reshape security perceptions. Yet not a single instrument of war had diminished. Nor was there yet evidence that Pyongyang was prepared to implement needed economic reforms.

The North's recent maneuverings aside, in regional terms, the nuclear issue is bound up in the issue of Korean reunification, the scenarios for which run the spectrum from implosion and a Romania-type collapse to explosion and a second Korean War. Korea is key to the regional balance as the interests of the four major powers in Northeast Asia intersect on the Korean Peninsula. How reunification occurs may have major implications for the regional balance, particularly on the future of the U.S. forward-deployed military presence in the region. In the case of either implosion (e.g., regime or state collapse—the two are not necessarily identical) or explosion (armed conflict), the result would be a rapid unification by absorption and a resulting new dynamic to subregional Northeast Asia strategic competition.

But any German-type reunification would almost certainly lead to a reassessment of the U.S. troop presence in Korea, and would raise new questions about the U.S. force presence in Japan as well. Such a Korean scenario could precipitate a qualitative change in the U.S. forward-deployed presence in East Asia, and thus alter the geopolitics of the region. In any event, the character of any U.S. security relationship with a reunified Korea will in some measure be shaped by Seoul's and Washington's assessments of China, and the state of U.S.–China relations.

### South China Sea

Events in early 1995, particularly the Chinese occupation of Mischief Reef in the Spratlys (and new Chinese construction there in 1998–99)—real estate that is some 120 miles off the coast of the Philippine island of Palawan, well within Manila's 200-mile economic zone—reflect palpable concern about China's modernizing military force: if it is acting in an aggrandizing fashion now, what will Beijing do twenty years from now when it does have a largely modernized force? Similarly, heated tensions with Taiwan spurred by former President Lee Teng-hui's unprecedented visit to the United States, and in 1999, by Lee's bold statements about "special state-to-state relations," casting doubt on the longstanding "One China" policy on which relations between the U.S., China, and Taiwan have been based, have also raised fears of confrontation. In regard to the Spratlys, there are competing claims among China (and Taiwan), Vietnam, Malaysia, the Philippines, and Brunei. The Spratlys dispute is the most likely source of armed conflict in Southeast Asia in the medium term, though it is more likely to only be of a skirmishing character. These reefs, most of which are under water much of the time, are widely believed to contain a treasure trove of oil and gas resources. Yet there are precious few authoritative surveys confirming that this perception accords with reality.

The dispute reflects emerging nationalisms asserting themselves more than a conflict driven by resources, whose existence in significant commercial quantities is dubious. The real and projected military capabilities of claimants and geography suggest a time line offering a decent period for diplomacy before more than minor military confrontations are likely to occur; geography is likely to limit military engagement to air and naval warfare for control of the disputed areas. But the South China Sea may be viewed as a measure of how China defines itself both regionally and globally: Will it integrate itself into the international economic and political system or will it seek to write its own rules of the road, much like post-Bismarck Germany in the late 1870s? And what if Beijing's behavior is thoroughly ambiguous, joining the Comprehensive Test Ban Treaty (CTBT) and the World Trade Organization (WTO), yet acting provocatively in the South China Sea?

## China–Taiwan

In May 2000, defeat of the long-ruling Kuomintang party and the ascent to the presidency of Chen Shui-bian and the Democratic Progressive Party, whose charter advocates formal independence, added to the uncertainty about cross-strait relations. Recent tensions between China and Taiwan have forced many to rethink the relationship of economic interdependence and political behavior. These tensions have occurred despite massive trade and investment flows from Taiwan into the mainland since 1988—in excess of US$35 billion and some US$20 billion in annual two-way trade. In broader strategic terms, the specter of confrontation has forced the region to contemplate a U.S.–China conflict that could polarize the Pacific, forcing actors to make geopolitical choices not contemplated in recent decades.

Thus, economics and politics appear to be pulling in opposite directions. The Taiwan Strait remains a potent source of regional conflict, one that could easily draw in U.S. military involvement. Thus far there has been incremental progress in resolving this dilemma, such as both Beijing and Taipei attaining membership in the Asian Development Bank, APEC, and both being in the process of joining the World Trade Organization, along with intermittent cross-strait dialogue. How these competing trends play out will be a measure of the degree to which geoeconomics is reshaping political behavior. Yet as the sense of a separate "Taiwan identity" grows, an impulse toward recognition as an autonomous political entity renders the current framework for managing the Taiwan issue—the "Three Communiqués" (1972, 1978, 1982) and the Taiwan Relations Act—increasingly problematic.

## Other Territorial Issues

There is a welter of regional territorial disputes, which are listed in Table 2. Many of these are in a different category than those discussed above, as they are, in regional perceptions, judged to be more bilateral irritants than disputes likely to spark military conflict. The potential for armed conflict resulting is remote in these cases. Most prominent of these is the Northern Territories dispute between Russia and Japan, and the Senkaku Islands, which are claimed by both China and Japan. In both instances, this real estate is of little intrinsic value to any of the claimants except as an enduring symbol of nationalism. In the case of the Northern Territories, they are a symbol of a century-old Russo-Japanese enmity, embedded in the pathology of the relationship, and will only be resolved over time as nationalism matures on both sides and is transcended by a mutual need to remove the issue from the bilateral agenda. The

Table 2

**Sovereignty, Legitimacy, and Territorial Conflicts in East Asia**

- Competing Russian and Japanese claims to the southern Kurile Islands, referred to by the Japanese as the Northern Territories (namely, Kunashiri, Etorofu, and Shikotan Islands).
- The unresolved dispute between Japan and South Korea over the Liancourt Rocks (Takeshima or Tak-do) in the southern part of the Sea of Japan.
- Divided sovereignty on the Korean Peninsula where some 1.4 million ground forces of the Republic of Korea and North Korea remain deployed against each other across the Demilitarized Zone (DMZ).
- Competing sovereignty claims of the Chinese regimes on mainland China and Taiwan.
- The unresolved dispute between Japan and China over the Senkaku (Diaoyutai) Islands in the East China Sea.
- The armed communists and Muslim insurgencies in the Philippines.
- The continuing claim of the Philippines to the Malaysian state of Sabah and its adjacent waters.
- The separatist movement in Sabah.
- Competing claims to the Paracel Islands (Xisha Quandao or Quan Doa Hoang Sa) in the South China Sea, contested by China and Vietnam.
- Competing claims to the Spratly Islands in the South China Sea, contested by China, Vietnam, Brunei, Malaysia, Taiwan, and the Philippines.
- Border disputes between China and Vietnam.
- Boundary dispute between Indonesia and Vietnam on their demarcation line on the continental shelf in the South China Sea, near Natuna Island.
- Boundary dispute between Vietnam and Malaysia on their offshore demarcation line.
- The Bougainville secessionist movement in Papua New Guinea.
- The Organisasi Papua Merdeka (OPM) resistance movement in West Irian/Irian Jaya.
- The Aceh independence movement in northern Sumatra.
- The dispute between Malaysia and Singapore over ownership of the island of Pulau Batu Putih (Pedra Branca), some 55 km east of Singapore in the Straits of Johore.
- The competing claims of Malaysia and Indonesia to the islands of Sipadan, Sebatik, and Ligitan, in the Celebes Sea, some 35 km from Semporna in Sabah.
- Border dispute between Malaysia and Thailand.
- Continued fighting between government and resistance forces in Laos.
- Residual communist guerrilla operations along the Thai-Lao border in northeast Thailand.
- Border conflicts between Thailand and Burma.
- The Shan, Kachin, Karen secessionist, communist insurgent, and pro-democracy rebellions in Burma.
- Insurgency in Bangladesh.
- Hostilities along the Burma–Bangladesh border.
- Territorial disputes between China and India.

*Source:* Adapted from Ball, "Arms and Affluence," pp. 88–89.

Senkakus are tangential to the Sino-Japanese relationship, and it is difficult to envision conflict over the islands unless a climate of strategic rivalry evolved such that they became a spark to start a fire waiting to happen. Much the same could be said for the rest of the laundry list of conflicting territorial claims, such as that between Malaysia and Indonesia over Ligitan and Sipadan.

## "The Three Concerns"

### Concern 1: The Emergence of China

The uncertain future of China in the post-Deng era is one case where potential instability inside a country would likely have major regional impact. For much of the first decade of the twenty-first century, China's leadership is likely to be somewhat collective/technocratic, insecure, and increasingly prone to using nationalism as a source of legitimacy. Historically, the danger of an unstable China has been that it tends to become a magnet for outside intervention—the volatility in U.S.–China relations and palpable fears that the United States seeks to contain, weaken, and divide China will almost certainly affect the calculations and behavior of Beijing's political and military leadership.

Of greatest concern in the region are China's intentions. Thus far, Beijing appears to be pursuing a two-track strategy of calculated ambiguity. At one level it is integrating itself into both international and regional economic and political institutions: the GATT (General Agreement on Tariffs and Trade/WTO), Nuclear Non-Proliferation Treaty (NPT), CTBT, professing adherence to the Missile Technology Control Regime (MTCR), APEC, and the ARF. Moreover, China has been cooperative—or at least pursuing largely parallel policies—if highly idiosyncratic in operating style, on the most pressing regional security issue, the North Korean nuclear problem.[1]

Yet at the same time, China appears intent on preserving maximum autonomy of action and continues its military modernization despite a relatively peaceful security environment. China's most dramatic gesture was the February 25, 1992, passage by its National People's Congress of a Law on Territorial Waters and Contiguous Zones that proclaims Chinese sovereignty over vast swathes of the South and East China Seas. Not only does the law assert Chinese sovereignty over the Spratlys, Paracels, and Senkakus, but it defines all of the South China Sea such that even right of passage (beyond that of straits), in theory, requires permission from Beijing. Apart from the fact that Chinese claims are based on questionable historical grounds, its own law is inconsistent with some provisions in the Law of the Sea (LOS) Treaty, which it has signed but not yet ratified, though then Foreign Minister Qian Qichen pledged during the August 1995 ARF in Brunei that China would adhere to the LOS.

Perhaps more important than the enactment of the law is the political context. It occurred amidst rising concern about the Spratlys, and during a period (which persists) when China's defense spending more than doubled since 1988. Moreover, China is actively acquiring force projection capabilities such as air refueling, a blue water navy, and a more modern air force. It is also pursuing high-tech weapons, such as lasers and cruise missiles. China has developed an extensive supply relationship with Russia, acquiring some 150 Su-27 fighter jets, apparent help in improving its missile accuracy, Sovremenny class destroyers equipped with Sunburn anti-ship cruise missiles, and may be acquiring S-300 anti-missile systems as well. Moreover, it is modernizing its still rudimentary nuclear forces, and is expected to deploy two new long-range mobile nuclear missiles, the DF-31 and DF-41, within roughly the next decade.

PRC policy toward Burma may also be seen as emblematic of concerns that Beijing may seek to reestablish a twenty-first century version of its premodern role as the predominant force on the Asian mainland. Beyond serving as a major arms supplier to the State Law and Order Restoration Council (SLORC), China reportedly has access to a naval base at the mouth of the Irawaddy River, a monitoring station on Burma's Coco Island, and is upgrading roads and rails near and across the Sino-Burmese border. While this is of greatest concern to India, it fits a pattern of preparing a forward defense.

Against this backdrop, Beijing's reluctance to pursue active multilateral diplomacy to resolve the Spratlys issue—even though its official position is that the resources should be jointly developed by claimants—appears part of a strategy of maintaining ambiguity to maximize its freedom of action. China clearly underestimated the regional response to its actions. ASEAN issued an unusually strong statement after Beijing's occupation of Mischief Reef in early 1995, and subsequently held an unprecedented meeting between the ASEAN foreign ministers and their Chinese counterpart strongly registering their protest. Similarly, in May 1995, the U.S. State Department issued a statement adding a new concern, by underscoring the importance of freedom of navigation to U.S. interests, and calling for behavior consistent with the LOS Treaty.

Filipino pressure on China, after minor skirmishes in 1998–99 in response to elaborate new constructions by Beijing (with obvious military purpose) on Mischief Reef, renewed efforts at serious diplomacy.

### Concern 2: Japan's Role

Japan's emergence as a major economic power in the 1980s, its quest for a global role commensurate with its economic weight, its systematic denial of its history during the 1931–45 period, combined with regional concern that the U.S.–Japan alliance may be short-lived are elements that have tended to raise concern about Japan's intentions. Concern, most evident in China and Korea, that a Japan uncoupled from the United States may somehow harbor hegemonistic ambitions in the Pacific, continues in latent form to be part of the pathology of East Asia.

However, nearly a decade of recession and near zero economic growth have diminished the historical concern about Japan and generated a new concern about "Japan passing," becoming less equipped to play a major role in the Asian balance.

What is remarkable, and emblematic of apparent declining concern about Japan, as it is displaced by fears of China, is the lack of regional response to a more assertive Japanese defense role since 1995. Japan's Diet, in May 1999, finally passed enabling legislation on new Defense Guidelines, specifying what roles Japan's military forces would play in support of the U.S. in the event of a crisis. Morever, as North Korea has developed new missiles and China, as was evident in the October 1998 Obuchi–Jiang Summit, has sought to pressure Tokyo, it has developed more of a "security consciousness." Emblematic of this was Diet legislation in July 1999 officially restoring the Rising Sun flag national anthem. Yet apart from China, there have been few signs of discomfort in the region.

## Japan's Nuclear Program

Against this backdrop, Japan's nuclear, space, and new reconnaissance satellite programs should be viewed. While Japan claims that nonproliferation is a key foreign policy goal, it has not (at least until very recently) even begun to view its continuing accumulation of plutonium as contradictory. But in the region, Japan's development of the H-2 rocket (which provides reconnaissance and missile capability) and accumulation of some 80 tons of plutonium despite no economic rationale for the commercial breeder reactor program plant seeds of doubt about Tokyo's intentions. Sino-Japanese relations—which are likely to become the most important bilateral relationship affecting stability in the Pacific by the second quarter of the twenty-first century—continue to be haunted by suspicion and mistrust based on Japan's past behavior. One historic analogy that may be a useful prism to view regional stability through is a comparison of Sino-Japanese ties to the evolution of Franco-German relations: For much of the century prior to World War II, Europe was unstable and engulfed in conflict, as the two major powers had adversarial relations. After World War II, France and Germany finally came to terms with each other, permitting the emergence of NATO and the evolution of the European Community. The analogous relationship in the Pacific, particularly over the coming two to three decades, is the Sino-Japanese relationship. Whether it moves from being a dependent variable (shaped by U.S.–Japan and U.S.–PRC relations) to an independent variable will be an important indicator of power realities in the Asia-Pacific. Until that historic stage is reached, an underlying sense of suspicion will likely plague Japan's ties to China and perhaps to Korea, particularly a post-reunification Korea.

## Concern 3: The U.S. Role

One of the principal reasons there is so much concern and uncertainty about the emergence of China and Japan is the relative decline of the United States in the region. This is true in both the military and economic spheres, though in absolute terms, U.S. trade and investment in the Asia-Pacific continues to grow significantly. And U.S. military capabilities remain substantially greater than any other Pacific power—and its technological advantages appear to be growing—though they are increasingly challenged by lower-tech asymmetrical warfare possibilities. The net effect of these trends is likely to be a process transforming the United States from the predominant power to a major power in the region over time. But the explosion of intra-Asian trade and investment in recent years had begun to overshadow that of the United States in much of the region. In the aftermath of the late 1990s economic crisis, however, U.S. business significantly enhanced its economic and financial presence in much of the region.

While in the short term the resultant access strategy (in shorthand, "places, not bases") has sustained the U.S. bilateral alliance network, Asian perceptions in regard to the longer term are less certain. The U.S. logistical presence in and access to Singapore, use of ship repair facilities in Malaysia, and perhaps in Indonesia, as well as enhanced bilateral military cooperation between the United States and ASEAN nations (and among ASEAN nations)—underscored by the new U.S.–Philippines military cooperation accord—have reinforced the continued U.S. commitment to security engagement in the region. But longer-term Asian concerns are palpable. Indeed, rising interest in security dialogues and new multilateral mechanisms is a consequence of the regional perception of the need for a hedge against a diminishing, albeit gradually, U.S. security commitment to the region.

The Clinton administration's policies toward East Asia added a whole new dimension to Asian misgivings about the United States—from complaints of benign neglect under the previous administration to resentment at the type of attention it now receives. Moreover, NATO expansion and the Yugoslav war reflect what is perceived to be an increasingly Eurocentric foreign policy. There is also concern about the limits of U.S. military commitment. The "immaculate coercion" model of airwar demonstrated over Yugoslavia has raised some concern about the role of U.S. forward-deployed forces in Asia in the future. Similarly, the notion of the "Blair Doctrine," of Western intervention to promote its values, is also not well-received, even among democratic countries in the region.

### Asian Arms Race?

The amorphous fears about China, the United States, and Japan discussed above help explain a sustained military buildup in the region, which some have characterized as an "arms race." Certainly the military procurement that has been under way for the past decade in some cases is divorced from any impending direct threats. And it is true that Japan has the third largest defense budget in the world (US$44 billion), and China's (estimated at some US$28–$36 billion, though a lack of transparency leaves much to guesswork) is also significant.[2]

There is, however, not a Cold War–type arms race in the sense of a cycle of action–reaction, or even overtly adversarial relations among the respective powers in Asia. (The Korean Peninsula is the exception.) But there are growing expenditures financing military modernization programs, which by 1998 may amount to more than US$131 billion for East Asia and Australasia, making the region the second largest importer of arms after the Middle East.[3] Apart from a hedging against uncertainty, this phenomenon is explained by several factors. There are supply-side pressures from the end of the Cold War and arms industries in the United States, Europe, and Russia in some desperation, making for an appealing buyer's market. At the same time, the region features the world's most dynamic econo-mies, with some newfound wealth, and in many cases military establishments with substantial political influence. However, in no country in East Asia is military spending increasing as a percentage of gross national product (GNP). In addition, the LOS Treaty gave countries 200-mile Exclusive Economic Zones (EEZs). This helps explain why many, particularly ASEAN, countries have been acquiring air and sea capabilities over the past decade.

In sum, China's quest for modernized force projection capabilities, Japan's impressive acquisition of dual-use capabilities, the dangers of nuclear and missile proliferation by North Korea, and ASEAN procurement patterns, however, do provide cause for concern. There has until very recently been no multilateral po-litical or security dialogue and there remains a complete dearth of any regional political institutions. This underscores a perceived need for transparency and more discussion of threats, doctrine, and broad security concerns in the region.

One issue that holds promise for new forms of regional cooperation is civil nuclear energy, an increasingly important electricity source in Japan, both South and North Korea, Taiwan, and if current plans are realized, China. Issues such as managing spent fuel, nuclear safety, and monitoring radiation suggest themselves as a common agenda that embraces both energy and security, in light of the prolif-eration potential involved.

Japan's stockpiling of plutonium, considered principally an energy-related is-sue, not a security matter, is a significant regional concern. The regional security environment in Northeast Asia offers Japan as compelling a security rationale for rethinking its plutonium policies as the economics of the fuel cycle do. Viewed from Tokyo, Northeast Asia is highly volatile. Against the background of a century of animosity, Japan faces a Russia likely to evolve in a nationalist direction even as it consolidates democracy and privatizes its economy. Japan's accumulation of plutonium offers an excuse to China, as it continues to plan fuel cycle activities. Moreover, regardless of the fate of the North Korean nuclear issue, if Japan con-tinues its commercial breeder reactor program, a future, reunified Korea will be tempted to reprocess spent fuel, and perhaps even to pursue an opaque nuclear program. Conversely, a deferral or suspension of Japanese plutonium plans could lead by example toward a new regime of regional cooperation.

## Conclusions

While the focus of this chapter is on security threats, in the interest of placing them in proper perspective it is important to stress that the overwhelming emphasis of virtually all the players in the region is a shared priority accorded to economic growth. Moreover, there are two important trends that are unprecedented in the region: the degree and character of burgeoning economic interdependence—both trans-Pacific and intra-Asian—and democratization. While it is impossible to quantify the importance of either of these trends, both are increasingly critical determinants of the nations' international behavior.

To date, intra-Asian and trans-Pacific economic interactions have created a synergy that is essential to sustaining economic growth in the Asia-Pacific, has become an engine of global growth, and has enlarged common interests. But what are the political and/or strategic ramifications of this economic colossus for bilateral and multilateral relations in the region? And how does it affect broader international behavior of Asia-Pacific actors? In the near term, the character of the U.S.–Japan, U.S.–China, and China–Japan relationships will be critical determinants of the political realities of the Asia-Pacific. Over the longer term, Sino-Japanese relations will grow as a major factor in East Asian stability or the lack of it. In the interim, Sino-Japanese relations remain a dependent variable, with the United States the wildcard in the region.

## Notes

1. See Jim Mann, "China Assisted U.S. Efforts on N. Korea, Official Says," *Los Angeles Times*, June 29, 1994, p. A1, for documentation on Chinese pressure on North Korea prior to the visit to North Korea by former U.S. President Jimmy Carter. The author has also confirmed the People's Republic of China's (PRC's) role in influencing Pyongyang in discussions with U.S. officials.

2. See Desmond Ball, "Arms and Affluence," *International Security*, Winter 1993/1994, pp. 78–112, for a thorough analysis of Asian military spending and underlying rationales.

3. International Institute for Strategic Studies, *The Military Balance, 1999–2000* (London: Oxford University Press, 2000), p. 173.

## Suggested Readings

Ball, Desmond. "Arms and Affluence: Military Acquisitions in the Asia-Pacific Region." *International Security*, Winter 1993/1994, pp. 78–112.

Bellows, Michael D. (ed.). *Asia in the 21st Century: Evolving Strategic Priorities*. Washington, DC: National Defense University Press, 1994.

Bracken, Paul. *Fire in the East: The Rise of Asian Military Power in the Second Nuclear Age*. New York: HarperCollins, 1999.

Calder, Kent. *Asia's Deadly Triangle*. London: Nicholas Brealey, 1996.

Friedberg, Aaron. "Ripe For Rivalry." *International Security*, Winter 1993/1994, pp. 5–33.

Johnson, Chalmers, and E.B. Keehn. "The Pentagon's Ossified Strategy." *Foreign Affairs*, July/August 1995, pp. 103–14.

Mann, Jim. *About Face*. New York: Alfred A. Knopf, 1999.

Manning, Robert A., and Paula Stern. "The Myth of the Pacific Community." *Foreign Affairs*, November/December 1994, pp. 79–93.

———. "China's Syndrome: Ambiguity." *The Washington Post*, March 19, 1995, p. C1.

Manning, Robert A., and James J. Przystup. "Asia's Transition Diplomacy: Hedging Against Futureshock." *Survival*, Autumn 1999.

# 2

# Security in Southeast Asia

*James Clad*

### Fin de siècle

The twentieth century's passage has closed the door on more than just a turbulent hundred years in East and Southeast Asia. Unfortunately, the new century's gate has also closed on a more beneficial Asian feature—a thirty-year run by one of the most successful subregional groupings in contemporary international politics.

Although ultimately a passive beneficiary of global and East Asian trends, the now-passing Southeast Asian order brought a miscellany of states—powerful and weak, large and small, democratic and authoritarian, and industrial and agricultural—together into an often reified acronym known as ASEAN, the Association of Southeast Asian Nations. And though outsiders often mistook it for a cohesive alliance, ASEAN member states never had many illusions about the structure of their regional order. In particular, they have never permitted their grouping to assume even a pretense of supranationalism.

Instead, the recently expanded 10-nation grouping remained, even in the best years, "a device of minimal diplomatic utility." By that I mean a group maximizing a propitious historical moment, good leadership, and favorable external circumstances to leverage itself into a position to play minimal power-balancing games. This is an important point: Even in core issues—as when reacting cohesively to the 1979–91 Vietnamese occupation of Cambodia—ASEAN member states never became preeminent in the diplomacy. That fell to outside powers—the United States, Japan, China, Australia, and France.

These various brakes on the emergence of "true" intergovernmental regionalism never prevented using the "ASEAN" nametag to full effect abroad, when it suited the members. In consultative mechanisms at the UN and in major world capitals, "the ASEANs" play the game of regional integration as and when they find it useful to do so. For example, slogans such as "ASEAN—a 650 Million Strong Market" served as a force-equalizer in the days when "trading bloc" obsessions gripped economic and trade diplomacy prior to and during the Maastricht Treaty's ratification and the North American Free Trade Agreement (NAFTA) negotiations in the early 1990s.

Minimally, "ASEAN regional cooperation" became a fixture of ASEAN meetings. Numerous flights of fancy found a place in the ministerial communiqués, as in the 1970s creation of various "ASEAN joint investment projects," or "common effective tariff regimes," or an ASEAN "central bank policy clearinghouse," an ASEAN "investment corporation," and ASEAN "energy and environmental coordination exercises." Indeed, in the aftermath of the 1997 financial crisis, member states raced for confidence-bolstering reasons to reaffirm bogus commitments to patently unachievable free trade deadlines set out in "ASEAN Free Trade Area" (known as AFTA) common effective tariff program deadlines.

To be fair, all these initiatives held out the prospect of at least a nominally expanded market. But they have never resulted in anything more than an ersatz regionalism in which little underlying purpose or interest exists. To be sure, various regionally integrative forces *are* at work—notably ethnic Chinese financial flows, and market penetration efforts by outside companies (Ford, Matsushita, and the like) to achieve economies of scale to justify their capital investment in one or more ASEAN country. But government-led ASEAN initiatives have almost never departed from the least-common-denominator rule. As might be expected, Indonesia became the fiercest protector of infant industries while Singapore became the most committed free trader.

Driven by successive regional issues—e.g., the denial of Vietnamese-controlled Cambodia's UN seat, or trade-access diplomacy in Brussels or Washington—the ASEAN grouping built a passive construct. But their grouping, enabled by Suharto's rapprochement with Malaysia in the mid-1960s, still rests (as observers note nervously at century's end) on the unity and stability of the Indonesian archipelago.

Given this thin soil, the ersatz regionalism never had time to grow into something more substantive. Always a derivative of single issues and of second-order importance against broader shifts in Sino-Japanese-American relations, the putative regional order simply collapsed after truly daunting internal and external challenges became enmeshed with one another in the mid-1990s.

We must count the various political transitions—accelerated by the 1997 financial and bank crises—as the most pressing of these challenges. While attention focused on Indonesia's travails, fissures became apparent in some of Vietnam's restive northern provinces, in Thailand's recurrently restive southern Pattani area provinces, and in Malaysian federal/state relations—especially vis-à-vis oil and gas–rich Trengganu and the Borneo states. Quiescent after the early 1990s, the Philippines' rural insurgencies showed new signs of life by 1998.

In domestic politics, Malaysian prime minister Mahathir employed tired antiforeign campaign sentiment and passive reactive policies to Beijing. Meanwhile,

Singapore moved openly to anchor its security to the United States—by agreeing to widen dockyard facilities at Changi to enable U.S. aircraft carriers to berth. In domestic policies, therefore, there was a renewed attention to survival or to managing unwieldy coalitions. In security policy, a multilayered approach combining a "what-me-worry?" stance toward the emergence of China to private moves to cement interoperability and other needs to the U.S. (and sometimes Australian) military.

The mistimed enlargement of ASEAN to include Vietnam and (especially) Laos, Cambodia, and Burma/Myanmar also occurred at this time—as did increasingly clear signs of an emergent China little inclined to play the minimalist theater of "multilateral engagement."

ASEAN's reach always exceeded its arm—thanks to the enabling and permissive environment of American maritime hegemony (albeit for supply and access to areas of primary concern such as the Persian Gulf or Northeast Asia). But when even minimal regional cohesion could no longer be pretended, the unsteady edifice responded by offering a public rhetoric with new flights of fancy. The 1999 Manila ASEAN Summit signaled creation of working groups to strive for a common Asian Currency Area and an "Asia-First financial architecture," in one foreign minister's comment.

Yet the truth was that the modest recovery was achieved by deficit-deepening tax cuts and other stimuli domestically, and by merciful access for electronic production to the U.S. market. By century's end, the grouping's core financial problem—a banking system indifferent to due diligence and still unwilling, after two punishing years, to take responsibility or cash out debt. Instead, the time-tested system of favoritism providing credit lifelines to politically well-placed people and ethnic Chinese remained impervious to change.

Indonesia effectively opted to nationalize its commercial debt, equivalent to over 100 percent of GDP; one upshot is the virtual elimination of the national budget's "developmental spending" component. About half of all projected government revenue seemed destined to service just the interest payments on sovereign bonds floated to refinance the banks.

Meanwhile, Malaysian state-directed banking recapitalization favored the prime minister's party and business associates while draining the cash reserves of the state-owned oil monopoly Petronas and the Employees Provident Fund—with incalculable longer-term consequences. The Thais, characteristically, operated a more diffused response—some firms sought (temporary) recapitalization via minority buyouts by foreign firms. The large U.S. conglomerate General Electric in late 1999 bought a further US$1 billion equivalent of Thai domestic consumer debt on top of GE Fund's initial US$600 million investment.

Though reasonably well insulated from the worst banking irresponsibility by IMF tutelage since the collapse of the Marcos dictatorship in the mid-1980s, the Philippines squandered a chance emerging after the 1997 crisis. Though some firms transplanted to the region opted to shift their cheap labor production locales to the Philippines, President Joseph Estrada's administration succumbed early on to a type of crude cronyism not seen since Marcos's own fin de régime era.

In Vietnam, the protracted passage of Communist Party cadres in a type of slow-motion fin des aparats exacerbated the crisis-driven investment downturn, though some countervailing direct foreign investment in the Saigon area did occur —again, as in the Philippines, seeking nimble hands for assembly operations. Burma/Myanmar's dictatorship continued to operate a closed resource-extraction business favoring Sino-Thai business groups and, increasingly, mainland Chinese merchants moving down to Mandalay. Laos slumbered on, with growth projections forced down after the Thais canceled a major hydroelectric project; Cambodia attracted the worst of cheap labor investors and those operating polluting industries, though Hun Sen's strange regime consolidated beneath the country's ruined fin du roi.

The post-1997 crisis really energized only one ASEAN state—Singapore, vulnerable and worried by political transitions to its north and south. Policies making the city-state more attractive to top-scale foreign personnel, and encouraging a move from Hong Kong by the financial community, showed result by century's end. The People's Action Party's (PAP) grip tightened, with popular assent; the response to regional crisis vindicated the PAP's promise of good governance in return for a circumscribed civil society.

## Fin de régimes

Indeed, the region's response to the post-1997 financial and banking crises showed a breathtaking resilience of traditional adjustment strategies—whether by bankers, politicians, or opposition figures. Since the early 1990s, the impending domestic political transitions, especially in Indonesia, had thrown a long shadow over the durability of the regional order.

In particular, Suharto's sedulous work over thirty years resulted in a very atrophied political society that his government's neoliberal investment policies grafted to a growing export economy terribly vulnerable (as events proved) to demand or credit crises. The egregious nepotic greed evident from 1993 to 1996 exhibited classic fin de régime characteristics—near total removal from independent information, cryptic utterances passing for kingly pronouncements, and a house-of-cards solidity evident when abrupt economic distress punched through the society, putting all the shortcomings under a merciless spotlight.

By understanding what ASEAN could never become—a source of *independent* volition in regional economics or politics—one sees the shortcomings. By 1996, it had become clear that Indonesia's Suharto straightjacket[1]—and impending transitions in Malaysia, Vietnam, and elsewhere[2]—almost guaranteed a period of, at best, motionless survival or, at worst, increasing irrelevance. Briefly, the end of East Asia's *ad convenientum* tacit Cold War alliances left the grouping scrambling for devices to keep the United States involved (especially after Washington's quiet decision to let its naval and air bases revert to Philippine control—a decision formalized by the Philippine Senate's rejection of the renewed bases treaty in November 1991).

The ASEAN grouping's enlarged membership after 1995 and 1998–99 brought in far less developed societies with authoritarian mindsets and habits of being especially attuned to Beijing's concerns. The notion that ASEAN would evolve into a bigger proto-alliance tilting against China had always been absurd; Rangoon's, Vientiane's, Hanoi's, and Phnom Penh's voices ensured that little resolve could be mustered for any type of multilateral standoff—as had occurred following belated U.S. reaction, in May 1995, to Chinese seizure of the Mischief Reef atoll claimed by Manila.

Then, with its "core" membership of five still intact (six, when counting the compliant Brunei), the ASEAN states had used the U.S. posture, a mild but pointed briefing comment by the State Department spokesman that touched on freedom of navigation, to talk seriously to China in a multilateral meeting held in Hangchow. Contrast this net gain to the regional response to anxieties raised when China, at the height of the October 1998 monsoon period, added new structures and facilities on the same atoll. This work came on top of an agreed "code of conduct" signed between Beijing and Manila about their differences over South China Sea territorial disputes. Unilaterally raising the height of contested concrete structures scarcely fit the code's letter or spirit.

Yet the new Chinese move elicited echoing silence from the ASEAN Heads of Government Summit convening in Hanoi, in December 1998. American efforts to attract at least one ASEAN state to voice support for an American expression of concern met evasion by mid-1999 when senior "ASEAN-Plus" officials (ASEAN and its Nine Dialogue Partners) met. (This obviously did not include Manila, always keen to use Chinese intrusions as leverage for U.S. military concessionary sales).

None of this should be seen as adding credence to the "China-as-enemy" school, still agonizing about how directly challenging, and in what terms, the changing East Asian power equation has become for the United States.

The ASEAN states more realistically see China's pressure as a fact of regional life, with Beijing necessarily ready to apply steady pressure over issues of national sovereignty.

## Fin de l'ASEAN?

A game of diplomatic nudge-and-wink has existed in Southeast Asia for decades. The intersecting crises have simply brought the hypocrisy up to the surface. Woe betide any outsider decrying the emperor's lack of clothes; for a display of ASEAN unity watch the fierce criticism of crude Western myopia that is bound to erupt. To some extent, one sympathizes: In China's neighborhood and with long bouts of inattention from the Clinton administration, one's heart goes out to a region in bad economic trouble. For what had seemed the world's most successful developing country association, all the hobgoblins jumped out of the box at once, including:

- The bedrock of ASEAN cohesion, Indonesia, facing profound threats to its national unity;

- Difficult elite transitions to manage, in Burma/Myanmar, and in Vietnam;
- Overall bad ASEAN group dynamics between the old core group, and the new Indochinese and Burmese member states;
- As a subset of these problems, an emerging contrast between "speak-your-mind" democrats (in Thailand, Indonesia, and the Philippines) and authoritarian leaderships in Malaysia, Vietnam, Burma, and the smaller Indochina states;
- The exacerbating influence of economic distress on ASEAN's domestic internal cohesion;
- Reduced defense budgets as a consequence of public fiscal problems;
- Tremendous industrial overcapacity, especially in for-export manufacturing plants and oil refineries;
- Declining civility levels, even among "old" core ASEAN elites;
- Miserable local governance (as in Indonesia's vast forest fires in 1996–97);
- Insistent localism and demands for new ways to slice the patronage pie;
- China's broad and comprehensive emergence into the region, including unanswered South China Sea provocations, "look the other way" responses from Mekong River riparian states in response to China's construction of two hydroelectric dams near Kunming (dams disrupting water flow downstream into Cambodia, especially);
- The inability of ASEAN members to bury long-standing bilateral disputes (e.g., Malaysia/Philippine incidents in the South China Sea; exchanges of fire between Burmese and Thai border forces, and confrontational fisheries disputes between Malaysia and Thailand);
- Near-disappearance of Japanese political and strategic leadership and identification of Southeast Asia in Tokyo as a "problem area" where Japanese banks remain dangerously exposed;
- An invidious regional scorecard vis-à-vis China (and, potentially, India as well) in competition for direct foreign investment flows as well as in broader trends of regional export competitiveness vis-à-vis China;
- High-profile ASEAN diplomatic failures: to reverse premier Hun Sen's coup d'état against Prince Rannaridh in 1996; to sanitize the Burmese regime enough to avoid an EU "dis-invitation" of the Rangoon regime to attend an ASEM (Asia–Europe Meeting);
- A durable colonial era leftover, the Five Power Defence Arrangement (FPDA) grouping of Australia, Britain, Malaysia, New Zealand, and Singapore, declined after complex Malaysian-Singaporean disagreement halted joint exercises in 1998.
- Most of all, in the catalogue of multilateral failure, the ASEAN Regional Forum (ARF) has proved a disappointment. It has not generated serious momentum toward multilateral solutions—glaringly needed in East Timor after the August 30, 1999, plebiscite rejecting association with Indonesia. Instead, a UN transitional administration led by a Brazilian and a Japanese has stepped into the breach; so did a UN-sanctioned but Australian-led force that intervened in East Timor after September 8, 1999.

This laundry list of troubles should be placed in perspective. Southeast Asia has experienced periods of great turmoil, and memories run long and deep. Moreover, the skill set required to manage China comes more naturally to the Southeast Asians; speaking of Bangkok's propensity to try to please Beijing, Singapore Senior Minister Lee Kuan Yew once described the Thais as "bending even before the wind begins to blow." Indonesian president Abdurrahman Wahid's state visit to Beijing in December 1999 showed that the ASEAN state most ambivalent about a wide relationship with China may be making the necessary course adjustments. None in the region speaks of a crude Chinese hegemony, if that is what's in the making. Few Southeast Asian states exhibit any willingness to raise the alarm about China; even in the Philippines the foreign ministry, by the end of the decade, had moved to temper earlier shrill warnings about Chinese intentions.

Yet the longer-term prospects of accepting Southeast Asia as lying within China's backyard may not please the states now grouped in a weaker, disunited, and less cohesive ASEAN. Nor do they hold any appeal for Taiwan, Japan, Australia, or the United States. The passing of Southeast Asia's regional order, if it means a permanent diminution of regional cohesion and even minimal purposefulness, is going to make it a lot harder for any new U.S. administration trying to repair America's Asia policy during the 1990s.

## Notes

1. James Clad, "The End of Indonesia's New Order," *Wilson Quarterly* (Fall 1996).
2. James Clad, "Regionalism: A Bridge Too Far?" *Southeast Asia 1996* (Singapore: Institute of Southeast Asian Studies, 1997).

## Suggested Readings

Ellings, Richard J., and Sheldon W. Simon, eds. *Southeast Asian Security in the New Millennium.* Armonk, NY: M.E. Sharpe, 1996.

Henderson, Jeannie. *Reassessing ASEAN.* London: International Institute of Strategic Studies, May 1999, Adelphi Paper No. 328.

Schwarz, Adam. *A Nation in Waiting: Indonesia in the 1990s.* St. Leonards, Australia: Allen and Unwin, 1994.

# 3

# Security in South Asia

*Peter R. Lavoy*

How secure are the states of South Asia? After gaining independence from Britain in 1947, the largest countries of the region, India and Pakistan, have struggled for over fifty years to secure their borders, unify and protect their populations, and establish stable governments and economies. After engaging in three wars and innumerable crises, these quarrelsome neighbors have developed two of the world's most powerful militaries, recently equipped with nuclear weapons and ballistic missiles. Will these new weapons permit India and Pakistan to live in peace, or will they further undermine the security of the governments and people of South Asia?

In order to answer this question, this chapter describes the factors that create insecurity in South Asia. While the focus is on India and Pakistan, I also consider the security threats to the smaller states of the region: Afghanistan, Bangladesh, Bhutan, Nepal, and Sri Lanka. The chapter is organized around discussions of five sources of insecurity. First, I examine the contested borders and sovereignties that already have led to four wars and could produce violence again in the future. Second, I show how the multiple, contested identities of South Asians provide an inexhaustible fuel for ethnic and religious conflict and, more recently, terrorism. Third, I consider the issue of political instability, including the problems regional states have had in maintaining democratic governments and stable civil-military relationships. Fourth, I show how the deep-seated poverty found in and around the Indian subcontinent undermines the security of the region's population. And finally, I examine whether the advent of nuclear weapons and ballistic missiles will make South Asia safer or more dangerous in the future. I argue that while many sources of insecurity will persist for years to come, peace in the region depends largely on how well India and Pakistan manage their deadly nuclear competition.

## Contested Borders and Sovereignties

### Kashmir and the Three India–Pakistan Wars

Much of the violence in South Asia has deep roots going back to the Partition in August 1947, when India and Pakistan gained independence from Great Britain after decades of unrest and agitation. When the British prepared to depart United British India, communal rioting broke out on an unprecedented scale, first in the districts of Bengal and Bihar and then all across the subcontinent. Because the spreading violence threatened to engulf the region in civil war, London abandoned its plan to form a unified India and consented to Muslim demands to divide the colony along religious lines, a decision opposed by Hindu freedom fighters, such as Mahatma Gandhi and Jawaharlal Nehru. Ultimately, Mohammed Ali Jinnah, leader of the Muslim League, accepted a smaller Pakistan than the one he originally demanded (which included all of Punjab and Bengal). The Hindus became a majority in India, which Nehru's Congress Party would govern as a secular state. However, the Sikhs, the region's third largest religious group, failed to gain statehood and were forced to accept the division of Punjab and live as a religious minority in India.

Under the terms of Partition, contiguous Muslim-majority districts in Punjab and Bengal went to Pakistan, as did some of Assam and the entire Northwest Frontier Province. The princely states were left to join either India or Pakistan, and all but three of the more than five hundred of these states quickly acceded to Pakistan or India under the Partition guidelines. Hyderabad, a large princely state that was ruled by a Muslim but had a Hindu majority and was surrounded by territory that would go to India, and Junagadh, a small state with a Muslim ruler but a Hindu majority, both hesitated but eventually were absorbed into India. The accession of the third state, Jammu and Kashmir, could not be resolved peacefully.

Kashmir, a princely state headed by a Hindu Maharaja ruling over a largely Muslim population, probably would have gone to Pakistan, but when Pathan tribesmen invaded Kashmir in October 1947, the Maharaja sided with India as a condition for Indian military aid and his survival. Pakistan objected and full-scale fighting broke out between the two newly independent neighbors.[1] Despite early Indian military gains, the forces of Azad Kashmir ("Free Kashmir," as the part of Kashmir under Pakistani control is called) seized the initiative and drove the Indian troops from the border. In spring 1948, India mounted another offensive to retake lost ground, but New Delhi soon recognized that the war would not end unless Pakistan withdrew support for the Azad Kashmir forces. On the advice of Earl Mountbatten (Britain's last viceroy in India and governor general from 1947 to 1948), India invited the United Nations to mediate the conflict. As a condition for bringing the war to a close, India and Pakistan agreed to a UN Security Council resolution calling for Pakistani troops to depart Kashmir and for a referendum to allow the Kashmiris to choose between India and Pakistan. In the end, Pakistani troops did not budge, India refused to hold the referendum, and the high peaks and scenic valleys of the Himalayas have become a war zone.

War broke out again over Kashmir when Pakistani-sponsored guerrillas infiltrated into Indian Kashmir in August 1965. Indian forces scored early victories and fighting quickly intensified throughout Kashmir. In September 1965, Pakistan widened the conflict by counterattacking in Punjab, where Indian forces were caught unprepared and suffered heavy losses. The war had reached a point of stalemate when the UN Security Council once again brokered a cease-fire, which India and Pakistan accepted after suffering nearly 3,000 battlefield deaths apiece. The cease-fire line, or "Line of Control," now serves as a quasi-border in Kashmir.

India and Pakistan fought a third war in 1971 over the political status of East Pakistan, which is now Bangladesh. Pakistan's refusal to meet Bengali demands for autonomy led to secessionist action in 1971. Pakistan replied with a fierce campaign to suppress the resistance movement. Thousands of Bengalis died, and the Mukti Bahini (the guerrilla fighters) and nearly ten million refugees fled to sanctuary in India. Because it could not prevent India from giving arms, training, and sanctuary to the Mukti Bahini, Pakistan widened the war by attacking Indian airfields in the western sector. India retaliated and rapidly achieved air superiority. As Indian ground forces pounded Pakistani formations, the Indian air force destroyed the small air contingent in East Pakistan and disabled the Dhaka airfield. Meanwhile, the Indian navy blockaded East Pakistan. Dhaka fell to combined Indian and Mukti Bahini forces on December 16, and Bangladesh gained its independence.[2]

In the aftermath of the war, in which India and Pakistan each suffered over 10,000 casualties (including about 3,000 deaths), the two sides signed the 1972 Simla Agreement, in which they pledged to respect the territorial status quo and settle their differences peacefully. Despite this pact, the simmering dispute over Kashmir continues to cause tension and conflict. India accuses Pakistan of aiding infiltrators and backing the Kashmiri insurgency against Indian rule. Pakistan insists that it provides only moral and diplomatic support to the Kashmiri separatists.

### The Kargil Crisis: General War Narrowly Avoided

The most recent India–Pakistan conflict occurred in the spring of 1999 when Muslim mercenaries staged a series of well-planned ambushes and artillery barrages against Indian troops on the Indian side of the Line of Control. In all, over 600 well-armed militants from the Pakistani side infiltrated into two to three dozen well-fortified positions atop ridges in the Kargil, Drass, and Batalik sectors of Indian-held Kashmir. The area is particularly sensitive to India, as it overlooks the strategic highway that connects Kashmir's capital, Srinagar, to Leh, the largest city in the Ladakh region. Indian officials claimed that the mercenaries, believed to be Afghan and Kashmiri mujahadeen, were supported by the Pakistani military. The Pakistani government denied any involvement, but most observers believe that this large and well-organized operation could not have been mounted without Pakistani collusion.

India viewed the incursion as a Pakistani ploy to redraw the Line of Control, moving it deeper into the Indian side, in violation of the Simla Agreement. It thus came as no surprise when in May 1999 India launched a major offensive, combining ground operations and air strikes to oust the infiltrators. The Indian government placed strict limits on its military commanders by forbidding them to conduct land or air operations over the Pakistani side of the Line of Control. This policy brought important political benefits, but at the cost of greater losses among Indian troops.[3] Fighting around Kargil intensified when the Pakistani army stepped up its support to the insurgents. Informed observers openly speculated on the possible escalation to general war between the two nuclear-armed adversaries. On May 31, nuclear fears mounted when Pakistan's foreign minister declared: "We will not hesitate to use any weapon in our arsenal to defend our territorial integrity." Then, in early July 1999, Pakistani Prime Minister Nawaz Sharif made a surprise visit to Washington and pledged to U.S. President Bill Clinton that he would order his troops and the mujahadeen to withdraw immediately from Indian-held Kashmir. The fighting soon subsided, and India and Pakistan returned to their familiar cold war.

### The Sino-Indian Border War

South Asia's other major territorial dispute involves India and China. Beijing has two major claims on what India deems its own territory. One claim, in the western sector, is on Aksai Chin in the Ladakh district of Jammu and Kashmir. The other is in the eastern sector over a region included in the British-designated Northeast Frontier Agency, a portion of which India renamed Arunachal Pradesh and made into a state. Unable to reach political accommodation on these disputed areas along the 3,225-kilometer-long Himalayan border, the Chinese attacked India in October 1962. In four days of fighting, the well-trained and well-armed troops of the Chinese People's Liberation Army overpowered the ill-equipped Indian troops, who were not properly acclimatized to fight at high altitudes.[4] The Chinese halted their advance on November 21 and declared a unilateral cease-fire. The Chinese had accomplished their territorial aims, and under the worsening winter conditions any attempt to penetrate deeper into the plains of Assam would have overstretched their logistical capacity and their lines of communication. The war was over, but a new diplomatic struggle between India and China had taken its place.

After more than thirty years of border tension and stalemate, high-level bilateral talks were held in New Delhi beginning in February 1994 to foster "confidence-building measures" between the defense forces of India and China. After a brief period of improved ties between the two Asian giants, India sent the relationship into a tailspin when it attempted to justify its May 1998 nuclear tests as a necessary precaution to defend itself from future Chinese aggression.

### Contested Identities: Ethnic and Religious Conflict and Terrorism

While only India and Pakistan have fought over territorial disputes, every South Asian country has experienced severe ethnic or religious conflict. The region's bloodiest outbreaks of violence arise from the inability of governments to meet the political demands of various ethnic and sectarian groups. Extreme cases have included the Kashmir and Bangladesh wars, the Sri Lankan and Afghan civil wars, and recurring separatist struggles in Punjab and in the Northeast states of India and in Pakistan's Baluchistan and Sindh. Added to these ethnic and religious conflicts, the region is now torn by terrorist violence, some of which is inspired by the Saudi financier, Osama bin Laden, who conducts his terrorist operations in Afghanistan.

### India: Consolidation of the Nation-State

The Indian government has made much progress in building a nation and creating a stable political system in a land populated by dozens of groups insisting on some degree of political or social autonomy. Having fourteen official languages and twenty-four languages each spoken by more than a million people, India's top security concern is the disintegration of the state. Although India has successfully weathered several serious secession struggles—for example, by the Tamils in the south and by the Christian Naga, Mizo, and Gharo tribes in the northeast—national unity remains elusive. Violent autonomy movements by the Muslims of Kashmir, the Sikhs of Punjab, and the Assamese-speaking Hindus of Assam continue to threaten internal stability. New Delhi treats all separatist activities with the utmost concern because it fears that if any part of India, such as Kashmir or Punjab, were to win independence, then the entire state might unravel, as happened to the Soviet Union.

The Sikh movement is a case in point. In the early 1980s members of the Akali Dal, a moderate Sikh political party, launched a peaceful campaign to win religious concessions and greater political autonomy for the state of Punjab. Soon peaceful protests yielded to terrorist tactics to create an independent Sikh state called Khalistan. In June 1984, Prime Minister Indira Gandhi sent the army into the Golden Temple, the holiest Sikh shrine, to flush out a group of terrorists that had hidden there. This move resulted in considerable loss of life and intense Sikh resentment. In October 1984 two Sikh bodyguards assassinated Mrs. Gandhi, causing widespread Sikh–Hindu violence across northern India. Subsequently, peaceful political procedures have been restored in the Punjab and Indian security forces have managed to kill or capture senior Sikh militant leaders in scores of army, paramilitary, and police operations. As a result, Sikh terrorist attacks in the Punjab and elsewhere have abated considerably since the early 1990s.

Punjab is more stable, but internal security threats persist because of ongoing insurgencies in Kashmir and the northeast. In the 1990s alone, experts estimate that over 20,000 people have been killed in Kashmir.[5] Beginning in 1998, Kashmiri militant groups stepped up attacks against civilians and shifted their tactics from bombings to targeted killings, including massacres of Hindu villagers. Separatist violence in Kashmir climbed again after the fighting ended around Kargil, despite the presence of 700,000 Indian military and paramilitary forces in the area. The morale of the Kashmiri militants, estimated at two to three thousand by Indian officials, surged in December 1999 when unidentified hijackers held 155 hostages on board an Indian Airlines plane at an airport in Afghanistan. The kidnappers set the passengers free after the Indian government released three imprisoned militants. India accused Pakistan of masterminding the event. Charges and countercharges followed, while rebel violence in Kashmir increased to its worst level in a decade.

### Pakistan's Elusive Political Stability

Despite the loss of its east wing in 1971, Pakistan remains a varied and volatile mix of ethnic and sectarian groups. Although Islam is a unifying force, and most Pakistanis are Sunni Muslims, there is immense cultural diversity within and among the country's four provinces. Individual identification as Sindhis, Punjabis, Baluch, or Pakhtuns is strong, and provincialism and ethnic rivalries continue to impede national integration. Complicating the ethnic mix are over seven million mohajirs (refugees from India and their descendants) from various parts of India. Economic and political rivalries between the mohajirs and indigenous Pakistanis often turn violent, especially in Karachi. A further challenge to internal security stems from the 1.4 million Afghan refugees who came to Pakistan when the Soviets invaded their country and have not gone home due to continued violence there. Linguistic diversity is also a divisive force. Some twenty languages are spoken, and although Urdu is the official language, it is not native to the majority of Pakistanis.

Like India, Pakistan has seen a rise in internal violence in recent years. Sectarian and political violence surged in 1998 as Sunni and Shia extremists conducted attacks against each other, primarily in Pakistan's Punjab Province, and as rival wings of a mohajir party feuded in Karachi. According to press reports, one thousand people were killed in Karachi in 1998, the majority by acts of domestic terrorism. Ethnic and sectarian violence subsided after the army took power in October 1999, but few of the problems underlying these tensions have been resolved.

### Sri Lanka: Embroiled in Civil War

Sri Lanka is engulfed in its most serious conflict since independence in 1948. Although tensions have long existed between the country's largest ethnic group, the Sinhalese (who are Buddhists and form 74 percent of the island's population), and the next largest ethnic group, the Tamils (who are culturally and linguistically related to the Hindu Tamils of India), Sri Lanka plunged into civil war in 1983 when Tamil militants launched lethal attacks against government and civilian targets. The Colombo government could not combat the Tamil insurgency and in July 1987 asked Indian Prime Minister Rajiv Gandhi to help find a political solution to the conflict and enforce it with Indian peacekeeping troops. Fighting soon resumed, and Indian troops became active combatants to support the Sri Lankan government. By December, the Indian peacekeeping force had increased to 30,000 troops, and Sinhalese and Tamils alike expressed impatience at their extended presence. Indian soldiers finally left Sri Lanka in March 1990. After a few months of peace, the Tamil Tigers, as the militants are called, resumed lethal assaults against government facilities and officials, including suicide attacks against Sri Lankan President Ranasinghe Premadasa in 1993 and Prime Minister Rajiv Gandhi in 1991.

The Sri Lankan government now pursues a two-track policy of fighting the Tigers and building support for an ambitious package of political reforms aimed at addressing many of the Tamil minority's grievances. Recent military setbacks have pushed the government toward negotiations, but the Tamil Tigers have not agreed to talk. An end to the civil war seems as remote as ever. Government offensives in early 1999 resulted in territorial gains, but decisive military victory remains elusive.

### Afghanistan: From External War to Civil War

Afghanistan has experienced numerous bouts of violence and instability since its emergence as a state in 1747, but the civil war that began after the Soviets departed in 1989 has plunged the country into complete anarchy. Established as a buffer zone between British India and tsarist Russia, Afghanistan has never had any political, geographical, economic, or ethnic features to sustain its survival as a viable nation-state. When Soviet troops invaded Afghanistan following a communist coup in 1978, Afghanistan lost its buffer status and became a "frontline" state. Since then, external political influences have transformed the country's perpetual ethnic and tribal rivalries into the dividing lines of civil war. The emergence of a new group, the Taliban, has brought some order to the country, but Afghanistan remains, in one observer's words, "a legally undivided territory of fragmented power."

The Taliban began as a movement of zealous religious students, or talibs, under the direction of Mullah Omar. They now constitute a fierce military, political, and social force drawn mainly from illiterate mullahs and their followers. The Taliban's initial aim was to replace the corrupt and tribally divided mujahadeen with a purist Islamic regime in Afghanistan. The Taliban gradually gained control over most of the country and imposed a very strict interpretation of religious law (Sharia) on society, including the banning of photography and films, imposition of strict constraints on women and children, and capital punishment for beardless men.[6] United Nations efforts to negotiate a cease-fire in the Afghan civil war failed in 1999. Following these failures, the Taliban, which controls about 90 percent of Afghanistan, launched an offensive against the Northern Alliance led by Ahmad Shah Masood. Gains from the offensive were soon lost in counterattacks as Masood showed his determination to continue the fight. Then, in November 1998, the Taliban nearly went to war with Iran after several Iranian diplomats were murdered in the Afghan city of Mazar-i-Sharif. Iran amassed troops along its border with Afghanistan and held back its attack only when the Taliban agreed to stop the killings of the Shia minority population in northern Afghanistan.

Islamic extremists from around the world, including large cadres of Egyptians,

Algerians, Palestinians, and Saudis, use Afghanistan as a training ground and a base of operations for international terrorism. The Taliban facilitates the operation of training and indoctrination facilities for non-Afghans and provides logistical aid to members of various terrorist organizations. The Taliban provides refuge to Osama bin Ladin, who was indicted for the bombing of two U.S. embassies in East Africa in August 1998.[7] The United States and other governments have told the Taliban to stop harboring such terrorists. Despite the imposition of international sanctions in 1999, the Taliban has refused to expel bin Ladin so that he can be brought to justice.

## Political Instability and Strained Civil-Military Relations

No country in South Asia has an unblemished record of democratic governance. Even in India, where elections are held routinely and fairly, irregularities have occurred—most notably when Prime Minister Indira Gandhi declared a national emergency from June 1975 to March 1977 that allowed her to suspend the political rights and press freedoms of groups that opposed her rule.[8] Not counting Sri Lanka, which is still torn by civil war, and Afghanistan, where chaos reigns despite the Taliban's tightened grip over the country, the region's two most politically unstable states are Pakistan and Bangladesh. Below I discuss the political problems that have prevented these states from maintaining durable democracies and stable civil-military relations. I also consider the political circumstances of the Himalayan kingdoms of Bhutan and Nepal. The former has become quite stable under King Jigme Singye Wangchuk, while the latter remains rife with political infighting.

### Pakistan: Return to Military Rule

With Pakistan's emergence as an overt nuclear weapons state in 1998, the creeping deterioration of the country's political, legal, and social institutions is a source of considerable concern. Political instability is not new to Pakistan. Few of its leaders have survived full terms in office. Whether because of the enormous challenge of governing a country as diverse and poor as Pakistan, or because its leaders have been too corrupt and weak for the task, Pakistan has been plagued by ineffectual governments. As in many other developing countries, the military is an important force for social order and national integration. As the defenders of national security in a very troubled and volatile neighborhood, the army has played an unusually central role in the history of Pakistan. It has assumed political as well as security control of the entire country four times under proclamations of martial law. In fact, Pakistan has been under military control for nearly half of its existence.

The army's latest foray into politics occurred in October 1999, when the chief of army staff, General Pervez Musharraf, ousted Prime Minister Nawaz Sharif in a bloodless coup. Musharraf acted immediately after Sharif tried to dismiss him while he was abroad on army business. Because Sharif issued orders to withhold landing rights for the aircraft that carried Musharraf from Sri Lanka, the former prime minister was imprisoned on charges of treason, which is punishable by death. Deeper reasons for the coup include the army's dissatisfaction with Sharif's legendary corruption and poor handling of Pakistan's economic and internal security affairs. A further source of the army's reproach for Sharif stems from his decision to pull Pakistani armed forces out of Kargil and subsequent moves to blame the army for the whole Kargil crisis.[9] Whatever the causes, as a consequence of the coup, Musharraf now confronts the daunting task of reforming Pakistan's political, economic, and judicial system, restoring law and order in a nation plagued by ethnic and sectarian violence, and defending the country against a wealthier and stronger adversary, without any hope of significant external economic or military support.

## Bangladesh: Democracy under Siege?

Since gaining independence from Pakistan after the 1971 civil war, Bangladesh has not enjoyed a day of political stability. Every Bangladeshi ruler has either developed authoritarian tendencies while in power or been ousted in some bloody event, such as assassination or military coup. It thus is no surprise that scant progress has been made in the vital tasks of rehabilitating the nation following the hugely destructive war for independence, establishing a durable parliamentary democracy, and creating economic growth in what often is called the world's "largest-poorest" nation. In nearly three decades of statehood, Bangladesh has experienced four military coups, along with several soldier uprisings, assassination plots, and abortive rebellions. Like in Pakistan, military authorities have ruled Bangladesh, either directly or behind a nominally civilian government, for over half of the country's existence.

The army initially stepped into power when the nation's first prime minister, Sheikh Mujibur Rahman, was killed in a plot led by a group of officers who opposed his increasingly absolutist and "irresponsible" rule. Since then, the armed forces generally have distrusted civilian politicians and repeatedly have taken direct action to "safeguard" the nation's welfare and to prevent civilian "meddling" in military business, such as resource allocation, pay and benefits, and promotions. In recent years, however, the army has become more professional. Military officials continue to play a critical role in guiding the political process in Bangladesh, but the current prime minister, Sheikh Hasina, the daughter of Sheikh "Mujib," so far has been able to govern with less of the unconstitutional drama than was experienced in the past. With a deepening economic crisis (exacerbated by the devastating floods of 1998 and 1999), the persistence of factionalism in national politics, and increasing reports of terrorism and violence, it will be a major challenge for Sheikh Hasina to complete her term in office, much less bring political stability to Bangladesh.

## Bhutan: A Stable Himalayan Kingdom

The hereditary monarchy of Bhutan was established almost a century ago after 300 years of theocratic rule, and has been governed by four kings, beginning with Ugyen Wangchuck, who unified the nation in 1907, to Jigme Singye Wangchuck, who has ruled since 1972. Bhutan is a strategic buffer state wedged between India and China. Thus national security means internal political stability: An erosion of political control could create strong incentives for either of Bhutan's big neighbors to assert their influence, as occurred with neighboring Tibet. By regional standards, Bhutan is quite tranquil. In years past, it has experienced violent protests by Nepali refugees, who have been slow to assimilate into Bhutan's Buddhist society. But a series of political reforms introduced by the king in 1998 appear to have persuaded the Nepali Bhutanese to convey their demands in a peaceful political dialogue.[10]

The only other serious political problem Bhutan has experienced recently is an influx of dissident Assamese factions across the Indian border. These groups, the tribal National Democratic Front of Bodoland and the Assamese nationalist United Liberation Front of Assam, set up camps in southern Bhutan in order to evade Indian military forces. The Indian government, which is Bhutan's primary political and economic patron, has called on Bhutan to evict the rebels, and the Bhutanese have agreed to do so, but so far the rebels have not departed. The matter puts Bhutan in a tough predicament: either try to oust the rebels and risk invoking their wrath, or tolerate their presence and risk heightened political pressure and possibly military action by India. The security of the idyllic monarchy will depend largely on how well the king manages to resolve this dilemma.

### Nepal: National Stability in Spite of Political Instability

As with Bhutan, Nepal's precarious location between India and China colors the monarchy's national security policy and its domestic politics. In order to ensure the nation's survival, Nepalese leaders try to keep good relations with both neighbors and cultivate international recognition of Nepal's de jure status as an independent buffer state. This strategy proved difficult in 1989 when a protracted trade and transit dispute damaged Nepal's relations with New Delhi. Although the quarrel was resolved amicably in 1990, it reinforced the common Nepalese view of India as a hegemonic power prone to using coercive economic, political, and possibly military means to domineer its weak neighbors. While Nepalese leaders are cautious in their dealings with India, opposition figures generally make relations with the meddling Indian government the leading issue of political debate.

Nepal's present political system, a parliamentary democracy, is one decade old. In 1990 the king promulgated a new constitution granting legal and political rights to citizens, establishing a parliamentary government, and creating multiparty democracy based on universal suffrage.[11] An effective, competitive party system, however, has been slow to develop. Politics is still dominated by a few high-caste families, and their petty ambitions and rivalries, coupled with constant feuding among political parties, has created an atmosphere in which coalition governments remain unstable and quickly fall. Despite this tenuous political history, Nepal's only extraconstitutional challenge in recent years has been the "people's war" launched in 1996 by various Maoist groups in the kingdom's remote hill districts.

The leaders of this movement demand a "people's democracy" in place of Nepal's constitutional monarchy, but to date Nepali citizens have paid scant attention to this radical cause.

## Poverty and Insecurity

The ability of South Asian governments to deal with the enormous political, ethnic, sectarian, and military challenges to their security is complicated by the deep poverty and associated social woes that pervade the region. As shown in Table 3, every country in South Asia ranks in the bottom half of the world's population in the United Nations Development Program's Human Development Index. In fact, apart from Sri Lanka, each state ranks in the bottom quarter worldwide, while Afghanistan's human development status has become too bleak for measurement.[12]

Bangladesh is one of the world's poorest, most densely populated, and least developed countries. Nearly half of the population lives in poverty, malnutrition is high, and infant mortality is above average even for low-income nations. The economic conditions of Nepal and Bhutan are equally bad. They are two of the world's poorest and least developed nations, and half of their citizens live below the poverty line. Scant natural resources, rapid population growth, and environmental degradation present formidable development challenges. By contrast, Sri Lanka has made significant progress in evolving from a socialist, centralized economy to a more open, free market society. It has relatively good human and natural resources with comparatively impressive social indicators and improving economic growth. This progress notwithstanding, poverty persists, malnutrition is a problem, and the equitable distribution of the benefits of a growing market economy remains a concern, especially amid the nation's unresolved ethnic conflict. As Afghanistan enters its third decade of continuous warfare, the toll on human security has become tragic: education, health care, and economic growth have all but disappeared.

In spite of this poverty, South Asian defense spending grew by more than 5 percent in real terms to US$21 billion in 1998 from US$20 billion in 1997 (measured in 1997 U.S. dollars).[13] India accounts for over two-thirds of regional military spending, and India and Pakistan together account for nearly 90 percent. Can India and Pakistan afford this level of military expenditure?

Although they have relatively modern industrial sectors with expertise in nuclear energy, missile development, and armaments production, India and Pakistan have some of the world's worst poverty. Widespread unemployment, outdated infrastructure, rising food prices, and low living standards beset each society. According to one Indian estimate, a single Agni missile costs as much as the annual operation of 13,000 health care centers. More than 3,000 public housing units could be built for the price of one nuclear warhead. And nearly every Pakistani child could be educated and fed for the cost of the nuclear and missile arsenal that is being created for their "protection."[14]

Table 3

**Human Development Indicators for South Asia**

| Country | Life expectancy at birth (years) | Adult literacy rate | Real GDP per capita ($U.S.) | Human development index (HDI) value | HDI rank |
|---|---|---|---|---|---|
| Sri Lanka | 73.1 | 90.7 | 2,490 | 0.721 | 90 |
| India | 62.6 | 53.5 | 1,670 | 0.545 | 132 |
| Pakistan | 64.0 | 40.9 | 1,560 | 0.508 | 138 |
| Nepal | 57.3 | 38.1 | 59 | 0.463 | 144 |
| Bhutan | 60.7 | 44.2 | 1,467 | 0.459 | 145 |
| Bangladesh | 58.1 | 38.9 | 1,050 | 0.440 | 150 |
| Afghanistan | 47.3 | 31.5 | 800 | n.a. | n.a. |
| South Asia | 62.7 | 52.2 | 1,803 | 0.544 | — |
| World | 66.7 | 78.0 | 6,332 | 0.706 | 174 total |

*Source:* Adapted from UNDP, *Human Development Report 1999*; and Central Intelligence Agency, *The World Factbook 1999* (www.cia.gov/cia/publications/factbook/).

**Nuclear Weapons: A Source of Peace or Further Insecurity?**

Indian and Pakistani government officials insist that no expense should be spared to achieve national security. The development of nuclear weapons and missiles, they contend, is required to deter foreign hostility. This claim could be correct: Nuclear deterrence might foster peace and security in South Asia. But then again, it might fail. India and Pakistan could be drawn into a fourth conventional war— one that could go nuclear. Or, as the Soviet experience suggests, the cost of creating and maintaining a credible nuclear deterrent could bankrupt the government and society supporting the development of weapons of mass destruction. In short, India and Pakistan could be threatening their future prosperity, prestige, and security for questionable security gains.

Continued fighting over Kashmir suggests that nuclear deterrence has not yet taken hold in South Asia. With the Indian defense minister boasting, "We can beat Pakistan anytime anywhere," and Pakistani leaders matching this fulmination, the risk of another India–Pakistan war seems higher than ever. Added to this concern are new risks of inadvertent or accidental nuclear use because of unsophisticated nuclear command-and-control systems and poorly defined nuclear doctrines. And, even if India and Pakistan do manage to establish nuclear deterrence, the effect will be that every Indian and Pakistani will live under the fear of nuclear annihilation. As U.S. Deputy Secretary of State Strobe Talbott has stated, "India and Pakistan need security, deserve security, and have a right to determine what is necessary to attain security."[15] Are there ways for them to enhance their security without deploying nuclear weapons and missiles? Considering the dangerous and expensive record of the U.S.-Soviet arms race, the enormous political and economic costs of Indian and Pakistani deterrent programs, and the growing risk of nuclear war in South Asia, India and Pakistan should make every effort to pursue non-nuclear sources of security. In the meantime, they should pursue nuclear arms control and confidence-building measures. The fate of the entire region hangs in the balance.

### Conclusions: An Uncertain Future for South Asia

South Asia is one of the most insecure regions of the world. Many of the problems that fuel tension and violence today were created before or during the period of independence. Although most of the countries in the region have made progress in nation-building and national defense, internal and external security threats abound. Insecurity will abate when the states of South Asia increase economic development and reduce the poverty and illiteracy of their citizens, institute political reforms to blunt the extraconstitutional demands of disgruntled ethnic and religious groups, and develop stable democratic governments and balanced civil-military relations. Success in meeting these formidable challenges will come slowly. But there is one area in which South Asia has no margin for error or time to hesitate. The security of the entire region will depend on the ability of India and Pakistan to manage their nuclear deterrent relationship.

### Notes

The views expressed in this chapter are the author's alone; they do not represent those of the Department of Defense or any other agency of the United States government.

1. For background on the events leading up to the first Kashmir war, see Sumit Ganguly, *The Origins of War in South Asia: Indo-Pakistani Conflicts Since 1947* (Boulder, CO: Westview, 1986).

2. For background on the Bangladesh war, see Richard Sisson and Leo E. Rose, *War and Secession: Pakistan, India, and the Creation of Bangladesh* (Berkeley and Los Angeles: University of California Press, 1990).

3. Journalists report that each side lost more than one thousand lives in the fighting around Kargil. See Raj Chengappa, "Kargil: Holding the Heights," *India Today*, August 16, 1999; and Rahul Bedi, "The Real Cost of Victory," *Asiaweek*, August 13, 1999.

4. For background on the 1962 China–India war, see Steven A. Hoffmann, *India and the China Crisis* (Berkeley: University of California Press, 1990).

5. See Sten Widmalm, "The Rise and Fall of Democracy in Jammu and Kashmir," *Asian Survey* 37, no. 11 (November 1997), pp. 1005–30.

6. For background, see P. Stobdan, "The Afghan Conflict and Regional Security," *Strategic Analysis* (New Delhi) (August 1999).

7. Office of the U.S. Secretary of State, Office of the Coordinator for Counterterrorism, *Patterns of Global Terrorism: 1998*, April 1999.

8. See Robert L. Hargrave, *India: Government and Politics in a Developing Nation* (New York: Harcourt Brace Jovanovich, 1980).

9. See Bidanda M. Chengappa, "Pakistan's Fourth Military Takeover," *Strategic Analysis* (December 1999).

10. Leo E. Rose, "Nepal and Bhutan in 1998: Two Himalayan Kingdoms," *Asian Survey* 34, no. 1 (January/February 1999), pp. 155–62.

11. Craig Baxter et al., *Government and Politics in South Asia*, 3rd ed. (Boulder, CO: Westview Press, 1993), pp. 361–69.

12. United Nations Development Program (UNDP), *Human Development Report 1999* (New York and Oxford: Oxford University Press, 1999), pp. 134–37.

13. See the International Institute for Strategic Studies, *The Military Balance, 1999/ 2000* (Oxford: Oxford University Press, 1999).

14. Lt. General R.K. Jasbir Singh, "The Costs of Nuclear Weaponisation," in *Indian Defence Yearbook: 1999*, ed. R.K. Jasbir Singh (Dehra Dun: Natraj, 1999), pp. 128–36. See also Peter R. Lavoy, "The Costs of Nuclear Weapons in South Asia," in *U.S. Foreign Policy Agenda: Responding to the Challenge of Proliferation* 4, no. 2 (September 1999), pp. 31–34 (http://www.usia.gov/journals/itps/0999/ijpe/pj29lavo.htm).

15. Strobe Talbott, "U.S. Diplomacy in South Asia: A Progress Report," official press release, 12 November 1998, p. 2.

## Suggested Readings

Baxter, Craig, et al. *Government and Politics in South Asia*. 3rd ed. Boulder, CO: Westview Press, 1993.

Ganguly, Sumit. *The Origins of War in South Asia: Indo-Pakistani Conflicts Since 1947*. Boulder, CO: Westview Press, 1986.

Krepon, Michael, and Amit Sevak, eds. *Crisis Prevention, Confidence Building, and Reconciliation in South Asia*. New York: St. Martin's Press, 1995.

Shafqat, Saeed. *Civil-Military Relations in Pakistan*. Boulder, CO: Westview Press, 1997.

Thomas, Raju G.C. *Democracy, Security, and Development in India*. New York: St. Martin's Press, 1996.

# 4

# Security in the South Pacific Region

*Henry S. Albinski*

There is a necessary prologue to assessing security in the "South Pacific," a generic label that embraces some entities found *north* of the equator. The region's countries lie in an immense maritime environment. They are far removed from world centers of population and power. They are not astride the Pacific's principal lines of transport and communication. Individually, they comprise numerous and often scattered islands. The region at large houses three major ethnic groups—Melanesian, Polynesian, and Micronesian. Within their own boundaries, the countries are often culturally and racially diverse. Fiji, for instance, is almost equally divided between indigenous people of basically Melanesian extraction but with strong Polynesian traits, and Indians. New Caledonia is a mixture of indigenous Melanesians, other South Pacific and some Asian people, and a substantial European population. The South Pacific is a region of microstates, some with populations under or not much over 10,000. A number are in the 100,000 to 300,000 range. Fiji's 800,000 makes the country regionally very large. Papua New Guinea (PNG) is by far the most populous (4.5 million), and by far the largest territorially. It is also breathtakingly diverse—developmentally, ethnically, linguistically, and otherwise.

Most South Pacific countries are independent. A few function in special, voluntary association with metropolitan powers, such as Palau (United States) and the Cook Islands (New Zealand). The great majority of regional countries bear Anglophone colonial/administrative legacies. Vanuatu reflects its Anglo-French condominium inheritance. The region has three francophone entities. New Caledonia now enjoys considerable autonomy and in the coming years will be free to opt for unfettered independence. French Polynesia's self-management has increased, but independence is not foreshadowed. Only Wallis and Futuna are closely tied to French administration.

Regional country political structures largely reflect British or American features.

Strong strains of traditional forms of national authority persist in Polynesian culture countries, notably in the Kingdom of Tonga. Regional and local political/cultural attachments favoring personality politics are widespread in Melanesia. National political elites continue to be dominantly Western-educated and religiously and socially acculturated, and nonideological in disposition. Emergent elites are somewhat less culturally/conservatively bound than the immediate postcolonial leadership.

Discontinuities of scale, noticeable pockets of noncash economic practice, limited or unexploited natural resources, high population growth, and disproportionate and often inefficient and venal public sector employment are not uncommon. The South Pacific countries have been associated with low levels of cultural enterprise/entrepreneurial skills, and on a per capita basis constitute the world's most aid-dependent region. Remittances from overseas constitute a significant proportion of revenue for Samoa and the Cook Islands in particular.

## Security Issues and Vulnerabilities: External Dimensions

The region's extraregionally or intraregionally originated security dangers have been of a special order. Country remoteness, insularity, and a general lack of salience as objects of others' attention have generally been protective assets. The presence of the insurgent movement in Indonesia's Irian Jaya province, across its lengthy and porous border with PNG, has nevertheless been a sporadic source of friction between the two countries. PNG has strived to maintain amicable relations with its much stronger neighbor. PNG has variously expressed resentment over what it regarded as alleged countenancing by Solomon Islands of secessionist elements in Bougainville, which is more culturally akin to Solomon Islands than it is to PNG. Solomon Islands has on its part on occasion denounced alleged threats to its integrity posed by PNG Defense Force (PNGDF) personnel pursuing insurgents from Bougainville. Following the 1987 coups in Fiji, there were imputations of India's complicity in efforts to smuggle arms to the country's aggrieved Indians. Libya's attempts to establish a beachhead of influence in Vanuatu and to exploit political turmoil in New Caledonia proved transitory as well as unsuccessful.

During the Cold War, familiarity with and economic dependence upon former metropolitan powers such as Australia, New Zealand, and the United States contributed to a broadly pro-Western outlook in the region. There was little sense of being threatened by the Soviet Union or other communist nations. Major power Cold War rivalry, which incorporated the Western concept of strategic denial in the area, was for the most part perceived as the interplay of other nations' interests on South Pacific terrain. Some aversion to major power behavior lingers, especially as it relates to nuclear matters. The adoption of the South Pacific Nuclear Free Zone (SPNFZ) was, and remains, both a declaration of the region's intuitive antinuclearism and an appeal to external nuclear powers to practice restraint. That which is nuclear is often viewed as being dangerous, even threatening, in an ecosystemically fragile region that for years was the site of intensive testing, and again witnessed French tests in 1995–96. It also accounts for regional hostility to the transport or disposal of nuclear waste materials. Island country nuclear positions can, however, take curious twists, such as the periodically floated Marshall Islands' idea to turn uninhabited parts of its territory into revenue-earning nuclear waste disposal sites.

The South Pacific community has consistently construed "external" security threats as essentially nonmilitary, and scarcely linked to the strategic competition or regional defense presence of external powers. The island countries' frame of reference has been their viability as societies and polities; survival in the face of natural disasters; and in some instances in the face of imaginable, literal swamping by rising seas occasioned by global warming. In man-induced terms, regional countries have been preoccupied with protecting their precious offshore marine resources from poaching by distant nations' fishing fleets, and from unscrupulous foreign carpetbaggers. They have also become concerned with occasional landings of vessels carrying smuggled human cargo to other destinations.

### Security Issues/Vulnerabilities: Domestic Dimensions

Fueled by combinations of ethnic, political, and economic forces, domestically impelled problems within South Pacific countries have dominated their security circumstances. Domestic political violence is not endemic to the region as a whole, but has been disturbing, in Melanesia particularly. The affected nations have been the region's most populous, ethnically the most disparate, and susceptible to tugs-of-war over control of and benefits from economic resources.

In 1987, Fiji's military overthrew an elected, Indian population–supported government that was thought to imperil the economic standing and values of the indigenous populations. The two bloodless coups were carried out by a military mainly composed of indigenous personnel, with the blessing of traditional Fijian elders. Another coup, with similar inspiration, was carried out in 2000 mostly by armed civilians.

In the late 1980s, New Caledonia experienced sharp fighting between indigenous Kanaks and French security forces. The insurgents resented the privileged position of the sizable European community. They sought greater economic benefits, and a political system under their own authority. Creative thinking in Paris and accommodation by the country's major groups has now smoothed the path toward peaceful coexistence and likely future independence.

Vanuatu's independence was delayed after a 1980 secessionist movement on one of its islands was broken up by troops flown in from PNG. The causes of the secession included power jockeying between Vanuatans of anglophone and francophone background, territorial parochialism, and the influence of private American interests. Eight years later there was serious rioting in Port Vila. Precipitated by land and political issues, it was suppressed by local means, but with the prospect that foreign forces might again be called upon.

PNG has long endured fissiparous tendencies. The most serious has been the rebellion in Bougainville, occasioned by complaints that government revenues from the Pangua copper mine were not being shared equitably with the province. Bougainville's environment was claimed to be at risk, and there was resentment that the area was being overrun by mainland Papua New Guineans of different ethnic stock. The result has been a protracted, ugly, and deadly conflict between Bougainville militants and PNG security forces, with thousands of fatalities from starvation and disease as well as from the fighting.

Decades of ethnic tension on Solomon Islands erupted into violence. It was stoked by resentment that Malaitans who had settled on Guadalcanal were stealing jobs and taking land. Killings occurred, and thousands of Malaitans were driven away. By 2000, opposing militias fought openly, the prime minister having been forced to resign at gunpoint.

"Security" within South Pacific countries that have experienced such turbulence has been symptomatic of, and in instances has aggravated, weak political legitimacy, and therefore authority to govern. It has severely stressed national financial and manpower resources devoted to implementing counterinsurgency, and has led to controversial and arguably overreactive measures meant to ensure law and order countrywide.

If "security" for small, frail, underdeveloped countries equates with robust economic progress, then disruptive politics can be viewed as counterproductive. When the secessionists forced its shutdown, the Bougainville copper mine was providing 40 percent of PNG's annual export revenue. The conflict moreover emboldened indigenous landowners' claims, and encouraged episodic interruptions at other mining sites in the country. The military intervention in Fiji precipitated the flight of many educated and skilled Indians, whose services could not readily be provided by indigenous Fijians.

Overall, when national politics are seen to be in disarray, overseas investors turn cautious. Capital-deficient countries seeking to accelerate development become the losers.

Albeit on a case-by-case basis, it nevertheless is arguable that political turmoil—even outwardly crisis situations—could in the long run ironically prove to be therapeutic. It can force reconsideration of standing, wrongheaded policies, settlement if not reconciliation between rival parties to disputes, or a sense of public apprehension about the human and economic costs of festering conflict. The apparent political accommodation in New Caledonia is in this sense reassuring.

It is also necessary to point out that in the Polynesian states of Tonga and Samoa, populations are quite homogeneous, and cultural legacies favor less assertive modes than those characterizing Melanesia. Rising disaffection over the continuing grip of traditional authority there does not on balance presage political breakdown.

The success of South Pacific country developmental strategies—and therefore the nurturing of socioeconomically as well as politically grounded security—can be at risk for reasons quite separate from domestic disorder. The United States has pledged nearly half a billion dollars over fifteen years to the new, freely associated state of Palau, where 80 percent of the workforce in a population of about 15,000 is in the public sector, and the culture of enterprise is very low. Palau's ability to manage to live more or less within its means, and to enjoy a semblance of "security" when the largesse runs out, is unknown. Intensive logging has been profitable for the Solomon Islands, PNG, and Vanuatu. But these nations have been cheated through underpricing and underdeclarations of the timber harvest by foreign logging companies. They have lacked the ability, administrative probity, and indeed resolve to curb such practices. The logging has been indiscriminate; timber resources are in danger of being extinguished in a decade or two. Especially through Australian prodding, the Melanesian timber countries have finally determined to place the situation under control and move toward environmentally sustainable development.

## Managing Socioeconomic Security

The logging issue highlights a basic tenet of regional country socioeconomic security: These nations need to do more to help themselves, but usually cannot manage without the advice, prompting, or financial or technical support of outsiders.

Island country dependence on outsiders can lead to complacency, to unrealistic expectations about assistance from the ostensibly rich and powerful, and to hypersensitivity to what is often construed as gratuitous and lèse-majesté treatment. Gone are times when Western concerns over Soviet or Libyan insinuation into the region prompted political stroking and offers of aid programs, sometimes described as the purchase of influence. And although the South Pacific does not, by world standards, require the infusion of vast outside resources, the "aid fatigue" syndrome and a shift of overseas development assistance priorities have been worrisome to the regional community.

Foreseeable prospects for effective outside support for the region are not, however, bleak. The region's countries at times have been quite resourceful at supplementing their incomes, the schemes having included sale of passports and of broadcast transmission bands, and inviting flag of convenience arrangements. Kiribati's favorable location has enabled it to negotiate a place for American, Russian, Ukrainian, and Norwegian cooperation in commercial satellite launches, though to U.S. security chagrin it also struck a deal enabling China to set up a tracking facility. The United States retains a critical stake in its defense facilities on Kwajalein Atoll in the Marshall Islands, used for unarmed missile testing (including for a prospective theater defense missile [TMD] system) and other programs. Substantial American underwriting of the Marshallese economy expires in 2001. The Kwajalein contract as such can run for fifteen years beyond, regardless of any post-2001 economic settlement. The Marshall Islands feel the United States does not have much choice. If Washington is ungenerous, poisoned relations with the local workforce could foreshadow problems for the site's efficient operation.

The regional countries are increasingly being notified that aid programs are not open-ended; recipients must do more to put their own houses in order. Forms of assistance are shifting. Although the popular Peace Corps program is foreseeably safe, the United States has closed its small, conventional, bilateral South Pacific aid program, emphasizing instead what it regards as more fundamentally reforming trade and investment priority strategies. Under the South Pacific Regional Trade and Economic Cooperation Association (SPARTECA), New Zealand and Australia have liberalized terms on which they import goods from the region. Australia's massive support for PNG is being converted from outright budget subventions to focused, project-oriented aid.

Australia's Pacific patrol boat project, which has provided twenty-one boats for eleven regional countries, enables recipients to enhance their security by enforcing offshore fishing ground regulations and curtailing smuggling and trafficking. Australia's success in cajoling Melanesian countries to work toward a common code to which foreign logging interests would be held accountable, and to tighten their monitoring of exports, is supplemented by Australia's financial contributions.

For their own reasons, the end of the Cold War notwithstanding, various donor countries remain regionally active. The South Pacific countries are playing the new international climate for what it may be worth. Hence, although many of the island countries recognize Beijing diplomatically, they often openly deal with Taiwan, whose assistance is regarded as better value than that of the People's Republic of China.

Desperate for an infusion of fresh economic assistance, in 1999 a tottering PNG government decided to switch full diplomatic recognition from China to Taiwan. Already in a high state of tension with Taiwan, China was furious. Various Western as well as some regional capitals were nonplussed. Concerns were voiced that such seemingly localized, South Pacific nation maneuverings could carry destabilizing repercussions throughout Asia-Pacific.

Non-governmental organizations (NGOs) are regionally prominent. Often operating with foreign government as well as private funding, they tend to stress practical, self-help promoting projects, and frequently form close rapport with local authorities.

The prudence of island countries functioning together toward common, economically defined security objectives has long been recognized. The process is gaining incentives and opportunities. Such activity fosters habits of cooperation among widely scattered, disparate, and individually weak countries. It enables them to manage their own, interlocking regional concerns more economically and efficiently. When regional countries move in tandem, they are, moreover, better positioned to address and to impress outside actors. Interested outsiders have encouraged this trend by providing tangible diplomatic, financial, and technical support. The momentum of intraregional cooperation can be traced to several factors. The passage of Cold War considerations from outsiders' agendas has caused them to focus more on socioeconomic goals in regional and multilateral context. Relatedly, South Pacific countries have been persuaded to think more creatively and collectively about self-help strategies. As both cause and effect, this has more closely harmonized their foreign policy orientations and styles. China–Taiwan preferences have as seen been predicated on economic return rather than foreign policy calculation. There is now less prospect that the region might fragment into a coalition of larger and more assertive countries under the Melanesian Spearhead movement's auspices, and a countering body of smaller, more conservative, Polynesian countries.

The various countries' Pacific patrol boats now coordinate their activities, sharing information and responsibilities through a maritime surveillance communication network. Foreshadowed common codes and practices among the Melanesian logging nations should enable them better to withstand pressures from outside logging companies. The Forum Fisheries Agency's frequently united front tactics are designed to convince distant fishing nations to reach agreements with a collectivity that enjoys greater bargaining strength than do individual regional countries. The South Pacific Biodiversity Convention Program aims to integrate regional conservation and environmental objectives.

The South Pacific houses a variety of institutions. The premier body is the South Pacific Forum, which includes Australia and New Zealand. It has been seeking association with regional groupings that are evolving in Asia-Pacific, where economic growth was until 1997 exceptional and on which the industrial countries have been focusing. The Asian financial crisis underscored the South Pacific region's sense of being bystander to events in and repercussions flowing from elsewhere. Yet the South Pacific wishes to be taken into account, and as far as possible, to benefit from economic progress in its outlying neighborhood. Hence, while PNG has become a full member of the Asia-Pacific Economic Cooperation (APEC) organization, the Forum has acquired observer status at the United Nations, where smaller and less-developed countries carry special voice and weight, and can function in pragmatically formed coalitions. Because of their concerns with the impact of environmental degradation, the island countries have been especially eager to connect themselves with the Alliance of Small Island States (AOSIS), and to promote their interests through multilateral conclaves.

**Managing Internal Political Security**

The uniformed forces have not only been called upon to enforce order in what are for the most part weak and/or technically disputatious societies, but have been part of the problem.

Vanuatu's paramilitary forces were able to handle 1988 land protest disturbances, albeit with riot equipment borrowed from Australia. Eight years later, seeking redress over a pay dispute, they intimidated the civilian political authority including by abducting Vanuatu's president. The police force was sent in to arrest the mutinous paramilitaries. No one was actually hurt, the grievances were resolved, and the mutineers were pardoned. The paramilitary and police forces were subsequently merged, and training was explicitly shifted from military to internal security roles.

Fiji has an established military tradition and a notable record of overseas peace-keeping contributions, primarily in the Middle East. It was its army, overwhelmingly composed of native Fijians, that mounted the 1987 coup. As in Vanuatu a year later, soldiers carried weapons but violence was avoided. It was not party to the 2000 hostage-taking and coup, but broadly sympathized with its pro-indigenous ideals.

Fiji armed forces numbers rose dramatically after the coups, have since receded, and are likely to stabilize at about 4,000. Peacekeeping work matters in part because of revenues earned from United Nations and particular country sources, while civilian sector employment for retired soldiers is in short supply.

In Solomon Islands, allegations of ongoing, overzealous use of force by dominantly Malaitan security personnel contributed to the outbreak of violence by armed Guadalcanalians.

Five times as populous as Fiji, Papua New Guinea has armed forces about the size of Fiji's. Small PNGDF numbers and a shortage among the police force—widely disliked in the country—has severely stretched capabilities to deal with nationwide law and order as well as Bougainville-centered, anti-insurgency tasks. Such commitments have precluded overseas peacekeeping contributions or PNGDF civic action activity on any meaningful scale.

PNGDF members have suffered from budgetary neglect, logistical problems, and often thankless duty. Discipline has been affected, with instances of PNGDF members looting, rioting, committing arson, striking over nonpayment of wages, mutineering, engaging in human rights abuses, and refusing to undertake dangerous duty in Bougainville. Beginning in 1997, a confluence of events relating to Bougainville resulted in insubordination and grim warnings to the sitting government by the PNGDF commander, who opposed the deployment of hired mercenaries to help stamp out the Bougainville rebellion. Some troops mutinied in support of their commander. In the disorder that followed, his successor wound up under house arrest, precipitating another mutiny, accompanied by rioting and looting among the public.

These PNG disturbances highlighted the complexities of external assistance on behalf of regional country security. The mercenaries contracted for by the PNG government, from Sandline enterprises, were mostly Africans commanded by an ex-British army officer. Their arrival in PNG was met by a storm of protest. They left without entering Bougainville. Their heavy equipment was diverted to and impounded in Australia, which together with other countries was alarmed at the destabilizing prospect of outside interventions of such nature. Indeed, PNG's resort to mercenaries placed it at risk of forfeiting World Bank, International Monetary Fund, and various bilateral aid programs. Facing sequestration by Sandline of its nonofficial assets overseas for breach of contract, the PNG government was compelled to make a payout settlement from its scarce resources. Ironically, in the 1990s Solomon Islands was attempting to arm itself in defense against incursions by PNGDF personnel operating against Bougainville rebels.

South Pacific nations have become deeply reliant on external power security assistance, though only under some special circumstances has this represented any commitment to defend them. The miniature, freely associated Micronesian entities are contractually under ultimate American defense oversight. New Zealand maintains a responsibility for the defense of the Cooks and the Tokelaus, and carries a residual defense obligation toward Samoa. Through a series of written undertakings, most recently in 1997, Australia has promised to consult and, as it deems appropriate, to respond, should PNG face actual or threatened external attack. Such second-party links have little foreseeable bearing on the internal security of the island countries. Australia's nontreaty obligation toward PNG continues to be externally, not internally, directed, with Indonesia as the implied but hypothetical source of conflict.

External national defense assistance takes many forms. It ranges from coordinated, Australian, New Zealand, and French reconnaissance flights that monitor suspicious fishing craft and other movements at sea, to the training and arming of indigenous forces. Recipient countries are often assisted by more than one source, though Australia is preeminent in PNG, and New Zealand focuses on anglophone Polynesia. The United States has scattered defense assistance ties, and France maintains its formal defense hold over its dependent territories.

Some of the aid is de facto of a civil nature—for instance foreign and indigenous forces cooperating on engineering and sanitation projects. As seen, the more explicitly military features of defense cooperation have not been free of discomfort to both providers and recipients. After the 1987 Fiji coups, and again in 2000, Australia, New Zealand, and the United States suspended their defense assistance programs. After the 1987 events, Fiji began to turn to France; Australia and New Zealand reinstated their aid; the United States held out—but not on commercial arms sales and some informal projects. Australia in particular has worked to limit the nature and utilization of military equipment by both PNG and Solomon Islands. After the Sandline affair it blocked arms transshipments to PNG and imposed a lengthy ban of its own on arms transfers. It has been distressed by such behavior as PNG's deployment of Australian helicopters as gunships, and Solomon Islands' use of its maritime surveillance patrol boat during security operations.

Defense cooperation providers have on various occasions been the objects of South Pacific–source criticisms for intrusiveness, political partiality, and the like. Bougainville separatists have denounced Australia for siding with PNG national authorities to protect Australian investments. Some Solomon Islands sources have, for political effect, conjured up scenarios of Australian plans to destabilize their government through intimidating military displays.

Sensitive about their sovereignty, South Pacific elites are often suspicious of the motives of even normally friendly, yet by their standards very powerful, nations. Australia and New Zealand provided logistical support for PNG troops flown in to break up the 1980 secession in Vanuatu, and during the 1988 Vanuatu disturbances Australian troops were on alert at home. Australia has been prepared to use force, if necessary, to extricate its nationals during stages of the Bougainville crisis, and it and New Zealand were prepared to do likewise at the time of the first Fiji coup.

Australia and New Zealand were urged by various island country leaders not to consider any military intervention in Fiji. Mostly, but not exclusively, radical South Pacific sources have warned that external actors, especially the United States, would not hesitate to further their "imperial" interests through a swift strike against a helpless regional country. American interventions in Panama, Grenada, and even Haiti have been invoked to impute a perfidious or at least untrustworthy disposition.

Events in 1994 suggested still another approach to dealing with domestic turbulence in the region: a South Pacific peacekeeping force. After six years of conflict in Bougainville, a negotiated settlement seemed close. A force of about 400 military and paramilitary police forces from Fiji, Tonga, and Vanuatu was assembled. After some preparatory training in Australia, and with Australian and New Zealand transport and logistical assistance, the force was sent on a two-week deployment. It was to enforce an agreed-upon cease-fire, and to maintain order during negotiations aimed at settlement. The force arrived, deployed—and then departed. The Bougainville Revolutionary Army leadership refused to negotiate, damning the force as simply an Australian–New Zealand military exercise that was out of keeping with the Melanesian and Polynesian way of conflict resolution.

A variation on a peacekeeping arrangement for Bougainville was established in the aftermath of the Sandline episode. A creative, sensitively managed New Zealand initiative brought together contending parties, producing an agreed process aimed toward eventual, orderly, self-determination in the province. PNG is understandably uneasy about an independence outcome, inter alia fearing a precedent for other disaffected parts of the country. Various South Pacific countries, likewise unsettled about centrifugal trends in their midst, joined a mixed, uniformed, and civilian Peace Monitoring Group. It was originally dominated by New Zealanders, later Australians, and incorporated personnel from Fiji, Vanuatu, and a token from Tonga.

It is unclear whether the Bougainville experience, and a combined South Pacific force that might be deployed to control ethnic violence in a setting such as the Solomon Islands, might presage a more institutionalized, standby approach to regional peacekeeping. PNG and Vanuatu have in the past found the notion attractive—for timely intervention during security crises, or relief work following natural disasters. Australia and New Zealand, which would have the most to do with organizing, transporting, and supplying such deployments, have previously not been enthusiastic, and various island countries have been noncommittal. Misgivings about having their sovereign rights intruded upon have not been entirely dissipated—even under a multinational, South Pacific aegis, and especially if such a force were to feature PNG, the overshadowing regional power. New Zealand's brokerage of the Bougainville agreement could not have been led instead by Australia, whose links to PNG have held it suspect by many Bougainvillians.

Whatever the outcome, the debate about instituting an on-call multinational force discloses two things. One is that the region suffers from periodic domestic security traumas. The other is that such contingencies deserve to be treated as a matter of regional concern and helpful response. The experience of regionally evolved habits of cooperation has contributed to the discourse.

## Suggested Readings

Bergin, Anthony. *The Pacific Patrol Boat Project: A Case Study of Australian Defence Cooperation*. Canberra: Australian Defence Studies Centre, Australian Defence Force Academy, May 1994.

Claxton, Carl. *Bougainville 1988–98. Five Searches for Security in the North Solomons Province of Papua New Guinea*. Canberra: Strategic and Defence Studies Centre, Australian National University. Canberra Papers on Strategy and Defence, No. 130, 1998.

Colbert, Evelyn. *The Pacific Islands: Paths to the Present*. Boulder: Westview Press, 1997.

Dorney, Sean. *The Sandline Affair. Politics and Mercenaries: The Bougainville Crisis*. Sydney: ABC Books for the Australian Broadcasting Commission, 1998.

Fry, Greg. "Australia and the South Pacific: The Rationalist Ascendancy." In James Cotton and John Ravenhill, eds., *Seeking Asian Engagement. Australian in World Affairs 1991– 95*. Melbourne: Oxford University Press for the Australian Institute of International Affairs, 1997, pp. 291–308.

———. *South Pacific Security and Global Change: The New Agenda*. Canberra: Department of International Relations, Australian National University, Working Paper no. 1999/ 1, 1999.

Henderson, John. "Bougainville: The Uncertain Road to Peace." *New Zealand International Review*, May/June 1999, pp. 10–13.

Henningham, Stephen. *The Pacific Islands: Security and Sovereignty in the Post–Cold War World*. London: Macmillan Press, and New York: St. Martin's Press, 1995.

Herr, Richard. "Australia and the Pacific Islands." In F.A. Mediansky, ed., *Australian Foreign Policy. Into the New Millennium*. Melbourne: Macmillan Education Australia, 1997, pp. 231–50.

MacQueen, Norman. "Island South Pacific in a Changing World." *Pacific Review*, vol. 6, no. 2 (1993), pp. 145–54.

May, R.J. "The Role of the Papua New Guinea Defence Force in Building Papua New Guinea." In David Horner, ed., *Armies and Nation Building. Past Experience—Future Prospects*. Canberra: Strategic and Defence Studies Centre, Australian National University, 1995, pp. 183–99.

O'Callaghan, Mary-Louise. *Enemies Within. Papua New Guinea, Australia and the Sandline Crisis: The Inside Story*. Sydney: Doubleday Australia, 1999.

O'Connor, Michael. *Defending Papua New Guinea. A Study in National Maturity*. Canberra: Australian Defence Studies Centre, Australian Defence Force Academy, 1994.

Ross, Ken. *Regional Security in the South Pacific: The Quarter-Century 1970–95*. Canberra: Strategic and Defence Studies Centre, Australian National University, 1993.

Tara, Tarcisius. "Political Siege in Papua New Guinea and the Role of the Military in Melanesia." *Islands Business*, vol. 23, no. 5 (May 1997), pp. 54–56.

Young, Peter Lewis. "South Pacific Security: An Issue Half Forgotten." *Asian Defence Journal*, no. 8 (August 1994), pp. 44–48.

# Part II

## Multilateral Security Issues

# 5

# Nuclear and Missile Proliferation in Asia

*David G. Wiencek*

## Introduction

The proliferation of weapons of mass destruction (WMD), that is, nuclear, chemical, and biological weapons and the means to deliver them (which include ballistic
and cruise missiles), is one of the principal security concerns facing the international community today and for the early part of the twenty-first century. Official
U.S. sources estimate that over twenty countries worldwide currently possess or
may be developing WMD, while more than twenty-five countries have ballistic
missiles.[1] Meanwhile, some seventy-three countries worldwide possess cruise missiles, most of which are of the short-range, conventionally armed, anti-ship variety, a nonetheless valuable component in a nation's military arsenal. Of these,
eighteen countries—including five or six in Asia—have indigenous cruise missile
production capabilities and are working to obtain a range of different types of
systems, including land-attack cruise missiles (LACMs).

Nuclear and missile capabilities in particular are spreading throughout East and
South Asia, creating dangerous new instabilities and tensions in the conflict zones
between North and South Korea, China and Taiwan, and India and Pakistan. Countries are increasingly turning to these capabilities to enhance their international prestige, acquire the tools for long-range targeting, and obtain the ability to engage in
coercive diplomacy strategies. The new interest in nuclear and missile capabilities is
also driven by economic considerations: these capabilities can be acquired much
more cheaply than large, standing conventional forces. Nuclear and missile capabilities are also seen as important for engaging in "asymmetric" warfare strategies, that
is, having a weapon system that an opponent cannot readily defend against.

Specifically with regard to missiles, the United States faces emerging threats from long-range missiles from such sources as new Chinese intercontinental ballistic missiles (ICBMs) and submarine-launched ballistic missiles (SLBMs), from North Korea's Taepo Dong-2 ICBM, and even potentially from an Indian ICBM, a possibility that has been discussed by Indian strategists and that may be in the early stages of development. Europe also will increasingly face longer-range missile threats, primarily as a result of missiles and missile technologies imported from Asian and Russian sources by hostile Middle Eastern states, such as Iran, Libya, and, likely in the future, Saddam Hussein's Iraq.

Indeed, with the exception of the Middle East, no other region in the world today and for the foreseeable future holds greater potential for missile capabilities to influence the strategic environment and the military balance. Already, Asia has seen the impact of large-scale missile use during the civil war in Afghanistan, where some 2,000 short-range Scuds were launched over several years (mainly 1988–1991) against the mujahaddin rebels by the Afghan army, initially under the guidance of Soviet advisers.[2] In comparison, Saddam Hussein fired about eighty-eight Scuds during the six weeks of the Gulf War. But Asian missile capabilities are growing and improving, thus expanding the threat away from the extended battlefield, as in Afghanistan, to longer-range, strategic applications—for example, using missiles and nuclear threats to hold an adversary's key national assets and population centers at risk.

China's 1995–1996 actions opposite Taiwan show how its leaders have grasped the new realities of missiles as levers of strategic power in the post–Cold War era. Beijing's so-called "missile tests" (and associated large-scale military exercises) sent a clear and threatening message: Taiwan (and other regional states) is highly vulnerable to nuclear missile attacks in any major crisis with China. These tests were one of the most striking uses of ballistic missiles for the purposes of political intimidation ever seen.

In addition to the inherent regional threat, China and North Korea are aggressively marketing their missiles, with the effect of undermining international stability. For example, North Korea has transferred Scud variants to Iran, Syria, Libya, and Iraq. If North Korea were to transfer its Taepo Dong-2 ICBM to Iran, all of NATO Europe would be at risk, including major alliance population centers, such as London, Paris, and Berlin.

For its part, China too has been involved in highly publicized ballistic missile transfers to Saudi Arabia and Pakistan. It also has transferred anti-ship cruise missiles (ASCMs) to Iran, which are now deployed near the Strait of Hormuz, along vital commercial shipping routes. The United States has pressured China to adhere to the Missile Technology Control Regime (MTCR), the voluntary international agreement aimed at restraining missile exports. The United States imposed sanctions on China in 1993 for shipping M-11 ballistic missiles to Pakistan in contravention of the MTCR. These sanctions were lifted in late 1994, when China agreed to abide by MTCR guidelines. Fresh reports indicate the M-11s are in fact in Pakistan; other missile and nuclear assistance from Beijing to Islamabad is also occurring.

Nuclear and missile proliferation in Asia is clearly a key future security issue, and presents challenges to policymakers and defense planners in Asia and in the West. The balance of this chapter briefly reviews the nuclear and ballistic and cruise missile programs and capabilities in the region; U.S. and Russian (and former Soviet republics) systems are specifically excluded from this survey. The chapter concludes by assessing the implications for regional security.

## Nuclear Weapons

Outside of the superpowers and China's nuclear arsenal, nuclear weapons have not figured prominently in the defense strategies of Asian nations. In the last several years, however, the situation has changed dramatically. In May 1998, India and Pakistan, long believed to have latent nuclear weapons capabilities, broke self-imposed overt testing moratoriums and conducted a series of highly sensational nuclear tests. These tests were motivated in part by domestic politics, by prestige considerations, and in response to both countries' perception of the evolving military capabilities of its opponent. Such motivations obviously were very strong, given the instant international sanctions that were applied in the aftermath of the blasts. The tests also showed that both New Delhi and Islamabad were committed to developing nuclear warheads for their long-range missile forces (see below).

The nuclear tests of 1998 have paved the way for the future growth of nuclear arsenals in both countries. In 1999, India announced a nuclear doctrine that emphasizes the eventual development of a nuclear triad—land-, sea-, and air-delivered weapons. Pakistan will inevitably attempt to follow suit, as both countries place a high emphasis on the prestige aspects of possessing nuclear weapons and thus the need to match closely the capabilities of the other side. With small nuclear forces for the time being and weak command and control structures, the two sides will be vulnerable to pressures for preemptive attack in serious crisis situations, causing South Asia to remain a potential nuclear flashpoint for many years to come.

China is a declared nuclear weapons power of long standing, having exploded its first nuclear device in 1964. Western sources have maintained for some time that the Chinese possess a nuclear force consisting of about 400 weapons, although Taiwan's latest defense white paper puts the number at 1,000.[3] Whatever the exact figure, it will grow in the future, as China places increasing emphasis on its ballistic and cruise missile forces as key tools in its coercive diplomacy and war fighting strategies. In 1999, a U.S. investigation exposed wide-ranging Chinese espionage at U.S. nuclear laboratories. According to the report of the Select Committee on U.S. National Security and Military/Commercial Concerns with the People's Republic of China (also known as the Cox Committee), China stole nuclear weapons design information on America's most advanced thermonuclear weapons, including every deployed warhead in the U.S. ballistic missile arsenal.[4]

One of the main implications of this massive espionage effort is that it is assisting China in developing smaller warheads for its new longer-range missiles. Smaller warheads can be used on mobile missiles, which will increase the survivability and war fighting capability of China's nuclear force. But smaller warheads will also enable China to increase the size of its nuclear arsenal through the deployment of missiles with multiple warheads or multiple independently targetable reentry vehicles (MIRVs) in the future. Smaller nuclear weapons would allow the use of lighter and faster missile warheads, which will pose a challenge to any ballistic missile defense system the United States or its allies may deploy.

Thus Beijing will increase the size and quality of its nuclear forces in the years ahead, in effect leapfrogging years of technical effort. Chinese nuclear weapons are important tools in helping Beijing dominate regional rivals, such as Taiwan, Japan, India, and others. China's growing nuclear force also helps deter the United States and possibly limits U.S. options in serious crisis situations between the two countries.

Finally, in the nuclear area the case of North Korea stands out. This case illustrates how a rogue government with a small nuclear capability can gain blackmail leverage and influence against its adversaries. North Korea likely embarked on a covert nuclear program sometime in the 1980s. By 1993, there was substantial evidence that Pyongyang had extracted enough plutonium from its nuclear reactors to make a few nuclear bombs. In 1994, as the issue received widespread attention, the United States entered into the so-called Agreed Framework with North Korea, which sought to freeze Pyongyang's nuclear program in exchange for U.S. and international assistance, including the provision of two light water reactors, ostensibly for power generating purposes.[5] Even with this "freeze" in place, North Korea is believed to have enough material to fashion possibly four to six weapons. The latest official U.S. government assessment is that North Korea may have enough nuclear material for one or two weapons.[6]

One of the key questions is whether Pyongyang has developed the capability to deliver these weapons by long-range missile. If so, North Korea's ability to engage in blackmail will be dramatically enhanced. But even with one or two bombs in the basement North Korea will have the capability to terrorize its neighbors and the international community for some time. Nuclear blackmail will continue to help this rogue regime win concessions and international aid and improve its negotiating position despite its desperate domestic plight.

In short, the nuclear threat has grown in Asia in recent years and will continue to be a serious concern well into the twenty-first century. The nations who now possess nuclear capabilities see the many political/military advantages that can be obtained with these terror weapons. One of the key open questions facing the region is whether or not other nations, including the East Asian democracies of Japan, Taiwan, and South Korea, will feel compelled in the future to obtain their own nuclear capabilities. Certainly these three democracies have the technical wherewithal to do so. If they perceive their security situations to be seriously challenged, they too could opt to play the nuclear card as a self-defense measure. The twenty-first century could thus see a nuclear arms race emerge in Asia.

## Ballistic Missiles

Ballistic missiles are unmanned rockets powered during liftoff and the initial phase of flight. After their rockets burn out, the missile's payload (warhead) coasts on to the target on a "ballistic" (unguided) trajectory. Longer-range ballistic missiles fly outside the atmosphere before descending back to earth. Most ballistic missiles are ground-launched from either fixed or mobile (road or rail) launching platforms. The major powers (the United States, Russia, the United Kingdom, France, and China) also possess SLBMs, which can be fired from sea (or in port). Most ballistic missiles deliver conventional warheads to their targets. Advanced systems developed by the major powers employ nuclear warheads and it is possible to place a chemical or biological warhead on a ballistic missile.

Substantial offensive ballistic missile programs are under way in China, North Korea, India, and Pakistan, and these pose the greatest concerns in terms of regional stability. Taiwan, meanwhile, reportedly has a shorter-range system (Ching Feng, or Green Bee), in the form of a reverse-engineered version of the U.S. Lance short-range ballistic missile (SRBM), and may be developing a medium-range system (Tien Ma, or Sky Horse). South Korea has developed and deployed the NHK 1 SRBM (also known as the Paekkom, or Polar Bear), which is derived from the 1950s U.S. Nike-Hercules surface-to-air missile (SAM), but modified to operate in a surface-to-surface mode and with a conventional warhead instead of a nuclear warhead. A follow-on missile, variously referred to as the NHK 2 or the NHK-A (and also known as the Hyonmu, or Guardian Angel of the Northern Skies), has been deployed since 1987. Japan does not deploy ballistic missiles per se, but its extensive space launch vehicle (SLV) program provides an inherent capability for developing ballistic missiles. Japan's SLV program puts it in a position to create a missile force quickly if it chooses to do so. Indeed, all three East Asian democracies could well feel compelled to build up ballistic missile forces in the future in the face of unrestrained missile programs in China and North Korea.

Tables 4 and 5 summarize ballistic missile capabilities in Asia. Table 4 lists ballistic missiles by range categories, while Table 5 is a breakdown by country. Abbreviations and range classifications for both tables follow Table 5.[7]

## *China*

China has the world's third largest ballistic missile inventory (after the U.S. and Russia), and Beijing's missile force is the most advanced in Asia. It is a force that encompasses short-, medium-, and intercontinental-range missiles, as well as submarine-launched missiles. The size of the Chinese ballistic missile force remains shrouded in secrecy, and this lack of transparency inhibits accurate assessments. What is known is that China is engaged in an across-the-board missile buildup.

China is also a major missile exporter and has provided substantial technical assistance to Iran and Pakistan. In addition, China exported some thirty-six to sixty 2,800-km/1,736-mile-range CSS-2 intermediate-range ballistic missiles (IRBMs) to Saudi Arabia in 1988. China has accepted, in principle, some of the limits on its exports of ballistic and cruise missiles contained in the MTCR, but is not a full MTCR member. In practice, however, China has been willing to violate its MTCR commitments in order to export missiles and missile technology.

From a strategic perspective, Beijing clearly sees the value in improving its missile force in order to meet future security objectives. This was amply demonstrated with the 1995–1996 "missile tests" that China staged to intimidate Taiwan. China's high-visibility missile firings into the waters near Taiwan involved a total of ten launches—six in 1995 and four in 1996. In 1995, these firings had an initial adverse impact on Taiwan's economy—including a one-day 4.2 percent drop in the stock market—until calm was restored. Both sets of firings also affected air and sea traffic in and around Taiwan and generally raised regional tensions. The Taiwanese government stated in 1998 that it spent about US$23.7 billion to restore public confidence in the aftermath of the Chinese missile tests, including releasing large amounts of foreign exchange reserves in order to support its currency during the two crises.[8]

The missile firings opposite Taiwan highlight some future trends relative to Chinese missile modernization. For example, Chinese strategists have begun to outline war fighting doctrines that emphasize preemption and long-range attacks against adversaries. Ballistic missiles are generally well suited to help carry out such tasks. Moreover, there is increasing talk in Chinese military circles of the need for a more balanced mix of offensive and defensive forces, to include ballistic missile defenses, which help support a broader array of deterrence and war fighting postures. The Chinese also have emphasized the need to develop conventionally armed ballistic missiles, in addition to nuclear-armed missiles, which will help them fight regional conflicts without crossing the nuclear threshold. One long-range study by the U.S. Department of Defense postulated that by 2010 China could have as many as 2,000 conventionally armed ballistic missiles.[9]

China's current ballistic missile force is composed mainly of short- and medium-range systems, which would be used in local conflicts along the country's periphery and to attack targets in the Russian Far East and as far as Moscow, as well as the greater Pacific region. Of key importance is the missile buildup opposite Taiwan. In February 1999, the U.S. Department of Defense reportedly concluded that China has 150 to 200 DF-15 (M-9/CSS-6) SRBMs aimed at Taiwan, and that this number could grow to 650 by 2005. China will eventually supplement its DF-15 force in the near future with the DF-11 (M-11/CSS-7), a 300-km-range system that has been sold to Pakistan, but which is not yet in the inventory of the People's Liberation Army.

Beyond the threat to Taiwan, China is working to expand its ICBM and SLBM forces to support long-range targeting and help bolster its growing position as a global power. China currently has two new ICBMs under development—the DF-31 and the DF-41. Both of these ICBMs are solid-fueled, road mobile systems, which enhances their survivability. The DF-31 was flight tested in August 1999 and has a range of 8,000 km/4,960 miles. It is capable of targeting the U.S. states of Hawaii, Alaska, and Washington. Significantly, once the DF-31 is deployed, China will be only the second country in the world (after Russia) to operate mobile ICBMs. The DF-41, meanwhile, has an anticipated range of 12,000 km/7,440 miles and will probably come on line by 2010. The DF-41 is also likely to incorporate multiple warheads, or MIRVs. The Chinese move toward multiple warheads runs counter to other international trends and comes at a time when both the United States and Russia are scrapping such technology and deploying single-warhead ICBMs in an effort to improve strategic stability. Operating mobile ICBMs and ICBMs with multiple warheads highlights Beijing's intention to acquire the tools to engage in sophisticated nuclear war fighting strategies in the years ahead.

Additionally, the Cox Committee report noted above forecast that within fifteen years China could have 100 ICBMs with ten multiple warheads on each missile, for a total of 1,000 nuclear warheads. (China today is believed to deploy about twenty DF-5/5A ICBMs.) Coupled with its other missiles, China at that point would be a true missile superpower able to exert political and military influence on a global scale. This potential development has not received enough attention. Failure to address the issue of China's missile buildup will lead to adverse strategic consequences, particularly in light of the fact that the United States and Russia remain committed to strategic builddowns and could reach 1,500 warheads each under the proposed Strategic Arms Reduction Treaty (START) III.

China is also developing a new nuclear-powered submarine (SSBN), the Type 094, as well as a new SLBM, the JL-2 (a sea-based version of the DF-31 ICBM), also with an anticipated range of 8,000 km/4,960 miles. The Type 094 will be launched early in the next decade, and three boats may be operational by 2010. The JL-2 will enable China to "target portions of the United States for the first time from operating areas located near the Chinese coast."[10]

Broadly speaking, China is also exploiting qualitative advancements in its missile force. As noted, China is moving to solid-fueled, mobile systems, and to more sophisticated payloads incorporating multiple warheads, and perhaps such countermeasures as decoys and chaff. The Chinese are believed to employ another type of countermeasure, a separating warhead, on the DF-15 SRBM to increase its effectiveness in penetrating theater missile defense (TMD) systems. China also incorporates Global Positioning System (GPS) satellite updates in the DF-15's guidance, which helps make that missile a highly accurate system capable of precision targeting.

In sum, China is aggressively modernizing its missile force and exporting missiles and missile technologies to sensitive conflict zones in the Middle East and elsewhere. Beijing sees ballistic missiles as important components in its future security strategy and has shown a willingness to use missiles to obtain political-military advantages vis-à-vis Taiwan. These trends show no sign of abating and help contribute to missile threats and proliferation concerns in Asia and other regions of the world.

## North Korea

Despite severe economic hardship and recent widespread famine conditions, North Korea persists with its well-developed missile program. Pyongyang increasingly seeks an ability to hold targets in South Korea and Japan at risk, including U.S. forces deployed in those two countries. In the longer term, North Korea's Taepo Dong-2, which could be flight tested at any time, will enable Pyongyang to target portions of U.S. territory, such as the state of Alaska or the island of Guam in the Pacific Ocean. North Korean defectors have stated that reaching U.S. territory is the "ultimate goal" of Pyongyang's missile program, because it will allow North Korea to deliver a "fatal blow" to the United States in the event a major conflict breaks out on the Korean Peninsula.

North Korea currently produces two modified Scud SRBMs, the Scud B (300 km/186 miles) and the Scud C (500 km/310 miles). It is believed that North Korea possesses some 600 to 800 Scud Bs and Cs in its inventory. These missiles pose a major threat to South Korea. They can cover all significant targets in the South and would likely be used en masse at the start of any attack on South Korea to soften South Korean defenses and pave the way for a North Korean blitzkrieg.

In an effort to hold targets in Japan at risk, North Korea has developed the No Dong, a medium-range ballistic missile (MRBM) with a range of about 1,300 km/806 miles. It is a mobile missile that may incorporate a WMD warhead to compensate for what is believed to be generally poor accuracy. In June 1999, Japan's Foreign Minister confirmed that at least ten No Dongs are deployed in North Korea; additional No Dongs likely have been fielded since then.

Looking beyond the No Dong, North Korea is engaged in a long-range missile program called the Taepo Dong-2, which is assessed to have a range of 4,000–6,000 km/2,480–3,720 miles. The Taepo Dong-2 is believed to be a two-stage missile, with a new type of first stage, plus a No Dong second stage. If the payload is reduced, the Taepo Dong-2 could be used to attack the western portion of the United States. If a third stage were added, the Taepo Dong-2 could deliver a several-hundred-kilogram payload anywhere in the United States.[11]

In mid to late 1999, there was considerable evidence that a Taepo Dong-2 test was set to take place and that fuel, but not yet the missile, was in place at the suspected launch site on the northeastern coast in Musudan-ri, Hwandae County, North Hamgyong Province. The test was temporarily suspended as a result of negotiations with the United States in September 1999.

But in all likelihood, the test will eventually be carried out, either in North Korea or on the territory of one its missile customers, or under the guise of a "peaceful" space launch to put a satellite in orbit. Pyongyang is undeterred by U.S. and Western sanctions or threats. It has probably calculated that it has more to gain from a successful launch in terms of future missile sales to its established rogue nation customer base than it will immediately lose in international aid. In the end, North Korea realizes that the West is unprepared to enact serious reprisals against it, and its high-risk strategy will eventually pay off, both at the rogue missile cash register and in international aid from the West. International donors are likely to resume aid on the premise that engagement is the best strategy to employ with the Kim Jong Il regime, particularly in light of the 2000 summit meeting.

North Korea is one of the world's major missile exporters and is particularly active in supplying other rogue regimes, such as Iran, Syria, and Libya. North Korea exported the No Dong to both Pakistan (where it is called the Ghauri) and Iran (where it is called the Shahab 3). North Korea's missile sales are helping keep the Kim regime alive financially. Credible estimates indicate that North Korea has earned approximately US$1 billion over the last decade from missile exports, a fairly significant amount of money in the context of a GNP estimated at only US$21 billion. Thus, North Korea has much at stake and needs to test the Taepo Dong-2.

With this and its other missile systems, North Korea will be increasingly able to use missile threats to its advantage and against the security interests of South Korea, Japan, the United States, and others.

## India

India's missile force today is limited in size, but the country has a significant potential to expand its missile capabilities in the future due to its very strong science and technology base and its active SLV program. New Delhi clearly recognizes the importance of developing missile capabilities, as a tool to expand its strategic options in the broader Asian security environment and for conferring prestige on India's technical achievements, as well as an acknowledgment of its perceived status as a major power in Asia. One prominent Indian analyst, Brahma Chellaney, expressed well New Delhi's belief in the necessity for growing missile capabilities when he stated that:

> In the emerging security environment, a state could fall victim to punitive military action not for directly threatening a great power but for refusing to accept its "global" rules and standards. A bigger population or a larger standing army were traditionally seen as a security asset against a less-populated or less-militarised adversary. Now what matters is the sophistication of technology...[and] at the heart of [new] technologies...is missile prowess. Missiles...are the cutting edge of a modern military machine. They arm their possessors with the power to terrorise and blackmail and to inflict severe damage without bringing their forces into harm's way. [Similarly,] the only sure way to deter missile terror and blackmail is through a capability to strike back with missiles.[12]

This type of thinking appears to inform Indian defense policy, and could be the type of logic employed for developing longer-range missiles capable of deterring China, and ultimately, perhaps, the United States.

India currently produces the Prithvi 1 SRBM, a mobile, liquid-fueled system with a range of 150 km/93 miles. A Prithvi 2, with a range of 250 km/155 miles, is in production. Reportedly, some eighty Prithvi 1s and twenty-five Prithvi 2s were ordered in the initial production run, although few are believed to be deployed at this time. A 350-km/217-mile Prithvi 3 is in development; this is a naval missile (an SLBM) that has also been called the Dhanush, or Bow. While several types of conventional warheads are being developed for the Prithvi, it is expected that the system is nuclear-capable. The Prithvi provides India with the capability to target most of Pakistan, its main rival; it could also be used to target portions of China.

In the previous edition of this book, reference was made to the Sagarika (or Oceanic) system, which was initially identified as a sea-launched cruise missile. Recent reporting indicates that the Sagarika is in fact an SLBM, with a potential range of at least 290 km/180 miles and a target operational date of late in the next decade. The Sagarika program reportedly has benefited from Russian assistance dating back to 1995, although the Russians deny this.

Beyond these shorter-range missiles, India has developed the Agni IRBM, a two-stage, single-warhead system with a range estimated at 2,500 km/1,550 miles. The Agni could be used to target most of China, including Beijing, as well as all of Southeast Asia, Pakistan, Iran, central Asia, and parts of Russia. Three initial Agni tests were conducted up to 1994, but the program had essentially been on hold since then, largely due to outside political pressures. India's nuclear weapons tests in May 1998, however, signaled a clear intent to begin warhead development for ballistic missiles and hence a commitment to resume the Agni program.

The program then resumed in earnest in April 1999 with what is believed to be the system's final flight test from a rail launcher on Wheeler Island to an impact point in the Bay of Bengal. Reports at the time confirmed that the two-stage Agni 2 employed solid-fuel propulsion on both its stages, in contrast to the solid-liquid engine combination used on previous test models. A solid-fueled system ensures a high degree of mobility either by road or rail launcher. The Agni 2 is also believed to incorporate GPS updates to enhance targeting accuracy. Looking beyond this system, Indian commentators continue to raise the possibility of an even longer-range IRBM of approximately 3,500 km/2,170 miles. This system has been referred to as Agni 3.

Agni represents India's bid to have a capability to deter China in what is shaping up as a future competition between these two Asian giants. Indian thinking in this context has been reflected in the words of its Defense Minister George Fernandes, who stated in May 1998 that "China is potential threat No. 1."[13]

Finally, while little information is available on the Surya (Sun) ICBM program, it is believed to be in development and to draw on technologies associated with the country's very advanced SLV programs. One Indian commentator, Wilson John of the Defense Research Development Organization, has written that "Surya's targets will be Europe and the U.S."[14] This targeting suggestion is a rare public admission that India is looking to use its missile force to protect its strategic autonomy and project power and influence well beyond Asia as its indigenous technology base matures in the years ahead.

Table 4

**Ballistic Missiles in Asia** (By Range Categories)

| Name (alternates) | Range maximum (km) | Payload (kg) or N Config. | Country(ies) | Status |
|---|---|---|---|---|
| *Battlefield (to 150 km/93 miles) and Short Range (to 799 km/495 miles)* | | | | |
| Hatf 1 | 100 | 500 | Pakistan | In service |
| Green Bee (Ching Feng) | 130 | 400 | Taiwan | In service |
| Prithvi 1 (SS-150) | 150 | 1,000 | India | In service |
| NHK 1 (Paekkom) | 180 | 500 | South Korea | In service |
| Prithvi 2 (SS-250) | 250 | 500 | India | In service |
| NHK 2/NHK-A (Hyonmu) | 260–300 | nk | South Korea | In service |
| DF-11 (M-11) (CSS-7) | 300 | 800 | China, Pakistan | In service** |
| Hatf 2 | 300 | 500 | Pakistan | Terminated? |
| SS-1 Scud B | 300 | 985 | North Korea, Vietnam, Afghanistan | In service |
| Scud Mod B | 300 | 985 | North Korea | In service |
| Sky Halberd (Tien Chi) | 300 | nk | Taiwan | Development? |
| Scud Mod C | 500 | 500 | North Korea | In service |
| Unidentified | 500 | nk | South Korea | Development? |
| DF-15 (M-9) (CSS-6) | 600 | 950/1 RV | China | In service |
| Hatf 3 | 600 | 500 | Pakistan | Development |
| Shaheen 1 | 750 | nk | Pakistan | In service |
| *Medium Range (800 km–2,399 km/496–1,487 miles)* | | | | |
| Sky Horse (Tien Ma) | 950 | 500 | Taiwan | Development |
| No Dong | 1,300 | 1,000 | North Korea | In service |
| Ghauri | 1,300 | 1,000 | Pakistan | In service |
| DF-25 | 1,700 | 2,000 | China | Terminated? |
| DF-21/21A (CSS-5) | 1,800 | 600/1 RV | China | In service |
| Ghauri 2 | 2,000 | 1,000 | Pakistan | Tested |
| Taepo Dong-1 | 2,200 | 1,000 | North Korea | Tested |
| *Intermediate Range (2,400 km–5,499 km/1,488–3,409 miles)* | | | | |
| Shaheen 2 | 2,400 | nk | Pakistan | Development |
| Agni 2 | 2,500 | 1,000 | India | In service |
| DF-3/DF-3A (CSS-2) | 2,800 | 2,150/1 RV | China | In service |
| Agni 3 | 3,500 | nk | India | Development? |
| Ghauri 3 | 3,500 | nk | Pakistan | Development? |
| DF-4 (CSS-3) | 4,750 | 2,200/1 RV | China | In service |
| *Intercontinental (range) Ballistic Missiles (ICBMs) and Submarine-Launched Ballistic Missiles (SLBMs)* | | | | |
| Sagarika SLBM | 290+ | nk | India | Development |
| Prithvi 3 (SS-350) (Dhanush) | 350 | 500 | India | Development |
| CSS-N-3 (JL-1) SLBM | 1,700 | 600/1 RV | China | In service |
| Taepo Dong-2 | 6,000+ | 1,000 | North Korea | Development |
| JL-2 SLBM | 8,000 | 700/1 RV | China | Development |
| DF-31 ICBM | 8,000 | 700/MRV? | China | Tested |
| Surya | 12,000 | nk | India | Development |
| DF-41 ICBM | 12,000 | 2,000/MIRV? | China | Development |
| DF-5/5A (CSS-4) ICBM | 13,000 | 3,200/1 RV | China | In service |

*Note:* Notes for Tables 4 and 5 follow Table 5.

## Pakistan

In comparison with India, Pakistan has a smaller missile program, but has received substantial outside assistance, notably from China and, most recently, North Korea. Up to 1998, Pakistan's principal program was the Hatf (Deadly, or Vengeance) series of shorter-range missiles: Hatf 1/1A (80–100 km/50–62 miles); Hatf 2 (300 km/186 miles); and Hatf 3 (600–800 km/372–496 miles). The Hatf 1 is a solid-fueled, road mobile system and carries a single 500-kg/1,105-lb conventional warhead, although it is likely that these missiles are nuclear- (or chemical-) capable. The Hatf 1 would be limited to battlefield uses. In 1997, the U.S. Defense Department reported that the Hatf 2 program apparently had been discontinued.[15] The Indian capital New Delhi could be targeted with the Hatf 3, which was reportedly tested in 1997 and is believed to draw on technology associated with the Chinese DF-15/M-9 600-km/372-mile SRBM. China has also supplied Pakistan with some thirty to eighty-four M-11 300 km SRBMs, as well as an M-11 fabrication production capability and nuclear weapons design technology. Chinese nuclear and missile assistance to Pakistan has been substantial and continues despite American sanctions and warnings.

Pakistan's program received a major boost in April 1998 with the flight testing of the Ghauri MRBM. This missile has a range of about 1,300 km/806 miles, which is sufficient to enable Pakistan to reach key targets deep into Indian territory. The Ghauri is based on the North Korean No Dong. Another flight test of the Ghauri took place in April 1999. Pakistan referred to this system as the Ghauri 2 and stated that it had a range of 2,000 km/1,240 miles. Immediately following this launch, Pakistan also unveiled another new missile, the Shaheen (Eagle) 1 SRBM, which is a solid-fueled system with a range of 750 km/465 miles. A longer-range Shaheen missile is also reportedly under development and is referred to as the Shaheen 2. This is apparently an IRBM with a range of 2,400 km/1,488 miles.

Pakistani leaders have claimed since 1998 that they were working on a series of longer-range missiles. Given the range similarities, these programs suggest a link to the North Korean Taepo Dong missile. If true, this would be a very significant development. As noted above, the Taepo Dong-2 is a North Korean ICBM-range system under development. If Pakistan does gain access to Taepo Dong technology, it could provide a long-term basis for moving to an ICBM that would undermine stability in South Asia and the Middle East.

## Cruise Missiles

Cruise missiles are relatively small unmanned aircraft that can carry a warhead to a target with relative precision. They can be fired from fixed or mobile land launchers, from ships and submarines, or from aircraft. Like aircraft, most cruise missiles employ an air-breathing engine (e.g., turbofan or turbojet) and travel at aircraft-like speeds. Some, such as short-range ASCMs like the French Exocet, employ rocket motors and can achieve supersonic speeds, which reduce warning time for

Table 5

**Ballistic Missiles in Asia** (By Country)

| Country/<br>Name (Alternates) | Supplier | Type | Range<br>maximum<br>(km) | Payload<br>(kg) or<br>N Config. | Status |
|---|---|---|---|---|---|
| Afghanistan | | | | | |
| SS-1 Scud B | Russia | SRBM | 300 | 985 | In service |
| China | | | | | |
| DF-11 (M-11) (CSS-7) | Domestic | SRBM | 300 | 800 | In service** |
| DF-15 (M-9) (CSS-6) | Domestic | SRBM | 600 | 950/1 RV | In service |
| DF-25 | Domestic | MRBM | 1,700 | 2,000 | Terminated? |
| DF-21/21A (CSS-5) | Domestic | MRBM | 1,800 | 600/1 RV | In service |
| DF-3/DF-3A (CSS-2) | Domestic | IRBM | 2,800 | 2,150/1 RV | In service |
| DF-4 (CSS-3) | Domestic | IRBM | 4,750 | 2,200/1 RV | In service |
| CSS-N-3 (JL-1) | Domestic | SLBM | 1,700 | 600/1 RV | In service |
| JL-2 | Domestic | SLBM | 8,000 | 700/1 RV | Development |
| DF-31 | Domestic | ICBM | 8,000 | 700/MRV? | Tested |
| DF-41 | Domestic | ICBM | 12,000 | 2,000/MIRV? | Development |
| DF-5/5A (CSS-4) | Domestic | ICBM | 13,000 | 3,200/1 RV | In service |
| India | | | | | |
| Prithvi 1 (SS-150) | Domestic | SRBM | 150 | 1,000 | In service |
| Prithvi 2 (SS-250) | Domestic | SRBM | 250 | 500 | In service |
| Sagarika | Dom./Russia | SLBM | 290+ | nk | Development |
| Prithvi 3 (SS-350)<br>  (Dhanush) | Domestic | SLBM | 350 | 500 | Development |
| Agni 2 | Domestic | IRBM | 2,500 | 1,000 | In service |
| Agni 3 | Domestic | IRBM | 3,500 | nk | Development? |
| Surya | Domestic | ICBM | 12,000 | nk | Development |
| North Korea | | | | | |
| SS-1 Scud B | Domestic | SRBM | 300 | 985 | In service |
| Scud Mod B | Domestic | SRBM | 300 | 985 | In service |
| Scud Mod C | Domestic | SRBM | 500 | 500 | In service |
| No Dong | Domestic | MRBM | 1,300 | 1,000 | In service |
| Taepo Dong-1 | Domestic | MRBM | 2,200 | 1,000 | Tested |
| Taepo Dong-2 | Domestic | ICBM | 6,000+ | 1,000 | Development |
| Pakistan | | | | | |
| Hatf 1 | Domestic | BSRBM | 100 | 500 | In service |
| M-11 | China | SRBM | 300 | 800 | In service |
| Hatf 2 | Domestic | SRBM | 300 | 500 | Terminated? |
| Hatf 3 | Domestic | SRBM | 600 | 500 | Development |
| Shaheen 1 | Domestic? | SRBM | 750 | nk | In service |
| Ghauri | North Korea | MRBM | 1,300 | 1,000 | In service |
| Ghauri 2 | ? | MRBM | 2,000 | 1,000 | Tested |
| Shaheen 2 | ? | IRBM | 2,400 | nk | Development |
| Ghauri 3 | ? | IRBM | 3,500 | nk | Development? |

*(continued)*

Table 5 *(continued)*

| Country/<br>Name (Alternates) | Supplier | Type | Range<br>maximum<br>(km) | Payload<br>(kg) or<br>N Config. | Status |
|---|---|---|---|---|---|
| South Korea | | | | | |
| NHK 1 (Paekkom) | Domestic | SRBM | 180 | 500 | In service |
| NHK 2/NHK-A | | | | | |
| (Hyonmu) | Domestic | SRBM | 260–300 | nk | In service |
| Unidentified | Domestic | SRBM | 500 | nk | Development? |
| | | | | | |
| Taiwan | | | | | |
| Green Bee | | | | | |
| (Ching Feng) | Domestic | SRBM | 130 | 400 | In service |
| Sky Halberd (Tien Chi) | Domestic | SRBM | 300 | nk | Development? |
| Sky Horse (Tien Ma) | Domestic | MRBM | 950 | 500 | Development |
| | | | | | |
| Vietnam | | | | | |
| SS-1 Scud B | Russia | SRBM | 300 | 985 | In service |

** Not yet deployed in China.

*Abbreviations and Range Classifications:*

| | | | |
|---|---|---|---|
| BSRBM | Battlefield Short-Range Ballistic Missile | up to 150 km | up to 93 miles |
| SRBM | Short-Range Ballistic Missile | 150–799 km | 93–495 miles |
| MRBM | Medium-Range Ballistic Missile | 800–2,399 km | 496–1,487 miles |
| IRBM | Intermediate-Range Ballistic Missile | 2,400–5,499 km | 1,488–3,409 m |
| ICBM | Intercontinental-Range Ballistic Missile | 5,500 km and<br>above | 3,410 miles and<br>above |
| SLBM | Submarine-Launched Ballistic Missile | | |

*Other*

| | |
|---|---|
| nk | Not Known |
| N | Nuclear |
| RV | Reentry Vehicle |
| MRV | Multiple Reentry Vehicle |
| MIRV | Multiple Independently Targetable<br>Reentry Vehicle |

the defense and make them difficult to counter. The U.S. Tomahawk is perhaps the best known modern cruise missile. This category of weapons, like the ballistic missile, traces its history to the German "V" terror weapons of World War II. (Hitler's V-1 was the world's first operational cruise missile; the V-2 was the first theater ballistic missile.)

Cruise missiles are actually more widely proliferated than ballistic missiles. A prominent proliferation specialist, Dr. Kathleen C. Bailey, former Assistant Director of the U.S. Arms Control and Disarmament Agency, has stated that:

> Cruise missiles can pose as much, if not greater, danger as do ballistic missiles. For example, cruise missiles could be launched from sea platforms to reach the

continental United States, whereas few nations today possess ballistic missiles with adequate range to do so. And, the capabilities of cruise missiles to penetrate air defenses are enhanced by the increasingly wide availability of radar absorbing materials which make missiles more stealthy. . . . The technology to make cruise missiles has become less expensive and easier to acquire.[16]

Some seventy-three nations worldwide deploy some form of cruise missile today; most of these are short-range ASCMs, and most are conventionally armed. However, as U.S. analysts Dennis M. Gormley and K. Scott McMahon point out:

> . . . relatively low cost and technically straightforward modifications can convert antiship missiles for land-attack missions. Indeed, when antiship missiles are combined with cheap guidance, navigation maps developed from commercial satellite imagery, defense penetration measures, and improved propulsion systems, they present a stark reality: antiship cruise missiles transformed into precision land-attack models could emerge with little notice to threaten Western interests.[17]

So far, only the United States, Russia, and France are known to deploy nuclear-armed cruise missiles. In the future, however, there is concern that other nations could fit cruise missiles with WMD. Due to their relatively slow speeds, cruise missiles would be suitable delivery vehicles for chemical or biological aerosol weapons, which could be dispersed over a target. Similarly, outside of the United States, only France and Russia currently produce LACMs. However, the U.S. government projects that the number of LACM producers will expand to nine countries within the next decade.[18]

In Asia, fifteen nations have cruise missiles in their inventories and five (China, North Korea, India, Japan, and Taiwan) have confirmed indigenous production capabilities, with South Korea a possible sixth producer country believed to have capabilities under development. (Asian cruise missile holdings are shown by country in Table 6 below.) At present, China has the most diverse and extensive cruise missile capabilities in the region. China's program dates from the 1960s and was based initially on the Soviet Styx design. The Chinese modified the Styx into the HY-1 and HY-2 (Silkworm), a 95-km/59-mile-range, single-warhead, anti-ship coastal defense missile fired from a mobile launcher (air- and ship-launched versions also have been produced). The Silkworm has been sold to at least six countries, including North Korea, Iran, and Iraq, and total Chinese ASCM exports in recent years have been substantial. Iran has set up Silkworm batteries near the strategic Straits of Hormuz, posing a potential threat to Persian Gulf shipping traffic, and now possesses a Silkworm manufacturing capability of its own. China also has supplied Iran with land- and sea-based versions of the C-802 ASCM, a more advanced sea-skimming, turbojet system, with a 120-km/74-mile maximum range.

In the future, China, North Korea, and India will all be improving their cruise missile capabilities, as will others in Asia. China will have an improved, stealthy cruise missile between 2000 and 2010, which would enhance Beijing's naval capabilities and complicate Western defense planning. By then, China could also have nuclear, chemical, or biological warheads for its cruise missiles, as well as an LACM with advanced guidance. China could also have a strategic-range cruise missile during this period, capable of carrying out land-attack missions to distances similar to that of the U.S. Tomahawk cruise missile.

China is also receiving important technical assistance with new cruise missile programs from Israel, further evidence of the two countries' expanding defense ties. Such programs reportedly include the YJ-12A (a medium-range supersonic sea-skimming ASCM), the YJ-62 (a longer-range ASCM), and the YJ-91 (an air-launched anti-radiation missile). Israel is reportedly also developing for China a land-attack cruise missile based on technologies associated with the Delilah decoy and the Star-1 anti-radiation drone. This new cruise missile may have a range of 400 km, use GPS updates, and be fitted with a penetrating warhead for attacking hardened military targets.[19] This Israeli cruise missile assistance to China eventually may prove to be dangerous and shortsighted, as such systems could be used to threaten U.S. and other allied military forces in Asia.

China is also pursuing the direct technology transfer route. In 1997, China concluded an arms agreement with Russia that included the purchase of two Sovremenny-class destroyers equipped with SS-N-22 Sunburn/Moskit ASCMs. The 7,200-ton Sovremenny is designed principally for anti-surface warfare. Each destroyer carries two quad SS-N-22 launchers, providing eight missiles per boat. The SS-N-22 is a formidable Mach 2.5 ASCM with mid-course guidance, active radar homing, and a range in excess of 100 km/62 miles. It is reported that the SS-N-22 may actually be capable of a Mach 4.5 terminal dive speed toward its target that may render current U.S. and allied ship defenses ineffectual.[20] China took delivery of its first Sovremenny destroyer in  early 2000, with the second to be delivered in late 2000. Once fully deployed, the missiles aboard these ships will pose new threats to U.S. and allied naval forces in the Pacific.

North Korea's cruise missile activities also raise serious concerns. North Korea has its own Silkworm production capability dating from the 1970s. As part of a 1987 deal with Iran, North Korea shipped the Silkworm to Teheran. By 1994, North Korea was reported to be developing a longer-range (160 km/99 miles) Silkworm ASCM variant, and it is likely that, once developed, this will also be offered for sale abroad.

In response to missile and other military threats from North Korea, South Korea has apparently embarked on its own cruise missile development program. India, meanwhile, has started to produce its Lakshya, a turbojet-equipped pilotless target aircraft. While little public information is available on this system, it is expected to have a range of 500 km/310 miles and be usable in a land-attack mode. The Indians may make the Lakshya available for export.

Other Asian navies widely deploy ASCMs. U.S. friends and allies (Australia, Indonesia, Japan, Pakistan, South Korea, Singapore, and Thailand) deploy the U.S.-made Harpoon, with a range of 120 km/74 miles and a conventional, highly explosive (HE) warhead of 220 kg/486 lb. Several Asian navies deploy the French

Table 6

**Cruise Missiles in Asia** (By Country and System)

| Country/System | Supplier | Type | Launch method | Range maximum (km) | Payload (kg) | Status |
|---|---|---|---|---|---|---|
| Australia | | | | | | |
| AGM-84A Harpoon | USA | AS | A | 120 | 220 | In service |
| RGM-84A Harpoon | USA | AS | S | 120 | 220 | In service |
| | | | | | | |
| Bangladesh | | | | | | |
| FL-1 | China | AS | G/S | 40 | 513 | In service |
| HY-2 (Silkworm) | China | AS | G/S | 95 | 513 | In service |
| Brunei | | | | | | |
| Exocet MM-38 | France | AS | S | 42 | 165 | In service |
| | | | | | | |
| China* | | | | | | |
| SY-1/HY-1 | Domestic | AS | G/S | 50 | 513 | In service |
| HY-2 (Silkworm) | Domestic | AS | G/S | 95 | 513 | In service |
| HY-3/C-301 | Domestic | AS | A/G/S | 180 | 500 | In service |
| HY-4/C-201 | Domestic | AS | A/G/S | 200 | 500 | In service |
| FL-1 | Domestic | AS | G/S | 40 | 513 | In service |
| FL-2/SY-2 | Domestic | AS | G/S | 50 | 365 | In service |
| C-101 | Domestic | AS | A/G/S | 45 | 400 | In service |
| C-601 | Domestic | AS | A | 95 | 500 | In service |
| YJ-1/C-801 | Domestic | AS | A/G/S | 42 | 165 | In service |
| YJ-2/C-802 | Domestic | AS | A/G/S | 120 | 65 | In service |
| YJ-22/C-802 (Mod) | Domestic | AS/LA | A/G/S | 180+ | nk | Development |
| YJ-12A | Israel | AS | S | ? | ? | Development |
| YJ-62 | Israel | AS | S | ? | ? | Development |
| Delilah/Star-1 Mod. | Israel | LA | A/G | 400 | ? | Development |
| SS-N-22 (Sunburn) | Russia | AS | S | 110 | 500 | In service |
| Unidentified | Domestic | LA | A/G/S | 2,000 | ? | Development |
| | | | | | | |
| India* | | | | | | |
| Exocet AM-39 | France | AS | A | 50 | 165 | In service |
| SS-N-2c (Styx) | USSR | AS | S | 80 | 500 | In service |
| SS-N-2d (Styx) | USSR | AS | S | 100 | 500 | In service |
| SS-N-7 (Starbright) | USSR | AS | Sub | 65 | 500 | In service |
| Sea Eagle | UK | AS | A/S | 110 | 230 | In service |
| Lakshya | Domestic | LA | G/S | 500 | 200 | In service |
| Koral (SS-N-22) | Dom./ Russia | AS | S/Sub | 110 | 500 | Development |
| | | | | | | |
| Indonesia | | | | | | |
| Exocet MM-38 | France | AS | S | 42 | 165 | In service |
| RGM-84A Harpoon | USA | AS | S | 120 | 220 | In service |
| | | | | | | |
| Japan* | | | | | | |
| ASM-1 (Type 80) | Domestic | AS | A | 50 | 150 | In service |
| ASM-2 (Type 88) | Domestic | AS | A | 150 | 150 | Development |
| SSM-1 | Domestic | AS | G/S/Sub | 150 | 250 | In service |
| AGM-84A Harpoon | USA | AS | A | 120 | 220 | In service |
| RGM-84A Harpoon | USA | AS | S | 120 | 220 | In service |
| UGM-84A Harpoon | USA | AS | Sub | 120 | 220 | In service |

*(continued)*

Table 6 *(continued)*

| Country/System | Supplier | Type | Launch method | Range maximum (km) | Payload (kg) | Status |
|---|---|---|---|---|---|---|
| North Korea* | | | | | | |
| SS-N-2a (Styx) | Domestic | AS | S | 43 | 500 | In service |
| HY-1/-2 (Silkworm) | Domestic | AS | S | 95 | 513 | In service |
| Silkworm (Mod) | Domestic | AS | G/S | 160+ | nk | Development |
| South Korea* | | | | | | |
| Exocet MM-38 | France | AS | S | 42 | 165 | In service |
| AGM-84A Harpoon | USA | AS | A | 120 | 220 | In service |
| RGM-84A Harpoon | USA | AS | S | 120 | 220 | In service |
| Longer-range system | Domestic | LA | nk | 300? | nk | Development |
| Malaysia | | | | | | |
| Exocet MM-38 | France | AS | S | 42 | 165 | In service |
| Pakistan | | | | | | |
| FL-1 | China | AS | G/S | 40 | 513 | In service |
| HY-2 (Silkworm) | China | AS | G/S | 95 | 513 | In service |
| Exocet MM-40 | France | AS | S | 70 | 165 | In service |
| RGM-84A Harpoon | USA | AS | S | 120 | 220 | In service |
| Singapore | | | | | | |
| Exocet AM-39 | France | AS | A | 50 | 165 | In service |
| Gabriel II | Israel | AS | S | 36 | 100 | In service |
| RGM-84A Harpoon | USA | AS | S | 120 | 220 | In service |
| Taiwan* | | | | | | |
| Hsuing-Feng I | Israel/Dom. | AS | S | 36 | 100 | In service |
| Hsuing-Feng II | Domestic | AS/LA | A/G/S | 170 | 75 | In service |
| Thailand | | | | | | |
| Gabriel II | Israel | AS | S | 36 | 100 | In service |
| Exocet MM-38 | France | AS | S | 42 | 165 | In service |
| FL-1 | China | AS | G/S | 40 | 513 | In service |
| YJ-1/C-801 | China | AS | A/G/S | 40 | 165 | In service |
| AGM-84A Harpoon | USA | AS | A | 120 | 220 | In service |
| RGM-84A Harpoon | USA | AS | S | 120 | 220 | In service |
| Vietnam | | | | | | |
| SS-N-2b (Styx) | USSR | AS | S | 50 | 513 | In service |
| SS-N-22 (Sunburn) | Russia | AS | S | 110 | 500 | On order? |

*Notes:*
LA—Land attack
*—Cruise missile producer
nk—Not known
A—Air launched
S—Ship launched
AS—Anti-ship
Sub—Submarine launched
G—Ground launched
USSR—former Soviet Union

Exocet, including Brunei, India, Indonesia, Malaysia, Pakistan, South Korea, and Thailand. The Exocet is a highly capable air- and ship-launched ASCM that skims as low as two meters above the waves in the final approach to its target, making it very difficult to intercept; its maximum speed is Mach 0.9 and it has a range of 42, 50, or 70 km/26, 31, or 43 miles (depending on model) and a conventional HE warhead of 165 kg/365 lb. The Exocet was successfully used by Argentina during the 1982 Falklands war, where it sank the British destroyer HMS *Sheffield* and the container ship *Atlantic Conveyor* and damaged the destroyer HMS *Glamorgan*.

Bangladesh and Pakistan have the Silkworm and Thailand has the C-801, a Chinese-made air-launched ASCM based on the Exocet design. Vietnam deploys the SS-N-2 Styx and in 1994 entered an agreement with Russia for the acquisition of two Type 1241RA missile boats, based on the Tarantul class corvette, which can carry Styx or possibly even SS-N-22 Sunburn ASCMs. Japan produces two ASCMs, the ASM-1 and the SSM-1. Japan is also developing a turbojet ASM-2 with a range of 150 km/93 miles. Taiwan deploys two ASCMs, the Hsiung Feng I and II, the latter having a range of 170 km/105 miles. These Taiwanese ASCMs are based on foreign designs: the Hsiung Feng I on the Israeli Gabriel ASCM and the Hsiung Feng II on the U.S. Harpoon. The Hsiung Feng II will be deployed on two new classes of frigates (*Chengkung* and the French-built *Lafayette*), on patrol boats, in mobile land systems, and on attack jets.

**Implications and Conclusions**

Nuclear and missile threats are growing in East and South Asia. So far, the barrier to WMD use has held, but whether it will continue to do so in the years ahead remains an open question.

In South Asia, Indian and Pakistani capabilities are primarily aimed at each other, although New Delhi increasingly seeks to use its nuclear and missile forces to balance growing Chinese power. In East Asia, Chinese and North Korean missile activities are proceeding unconstrained, and may eventually force the hands of the three democracies of Japan, Taiwan, and South Korea, and push them toward new offensive missile programs of their own—perhaps even the nuclear option. In short, if existing trends continue, we could well see a nuclear missile race emerge in Asia over the next several years.

These issues are of considerable importance because any crisis involving the use of ballistic or cruise missiles holds the potential to inflict wide-scale damage and destruction and also raises the prospect of nuclear terror or response. Also, as we have seen, even the threatened use of missiles or small "test" firings can quickly undermine a country's economic security and investor confidence and contribute to wild, destabilizing stock market gyrations.

There is little chance that China, North Korea, India, or Pakistan will curtail their missile activities any time soon. All see these programs as enhancing their prestige, yielding important political-military benefits, and strengthening their coercive diplomacy strategies. Current and prospective capabilities provide more and better military targeting options, increase these countries' crisis bargaining leverage, and can be highly effective when used to intimidate an adversary. Given these motivations, diplomacy and arms control will have limited utility in containing these threats.

The United States and its friends and allies will require strong deterrence postures and defense programs to help minimize the risks posed by Asia's growing nuclear and missile threats. Advanced TMD capabilities should be introduced by the U.S. and Asian allies at the earliest possible time to help blunt these threats.

**Notes**

1. William S. Cohen, Secretary of Defense, *Annual Report to the President and the Congress 1999* (Washington, DC: U.S. Government Printing Office, 1999), Chapter 6.

2. The Afghan experience constitutes the largest missile campaign in the fifty years since Hitler's V-2 tactical ballistic missile attacks on London in World War II. In a 1989 offensive against Jalalabad, some 350 Scuds were fired in the space of a few weeks against the mujahaddin. Total ballistic missile–related casualties in Afghanistan are unknown. But in just one attack in April 1991, two to four Scuds were launched into the center of Asadabad, the capital of Kunar Province and a rebel staging area, located 180 km/112 miles from Kabul. This attack drew little notice in the West at the time, coming less than two months after the end of Operation Desert Storm. But contemporary press reports indicate that as many as 300–400 people were killed and 500–700 wounded during this single attack. By contrast, in the Gulf War total casualties from Saddam's Scuds were placed at approximately forty-two killed and 450 wounded, including twenty-eight U.S. soldiers killed and ninety-seven wounded in a single attack on a barracks in Dhahran, Saudi Arabia.

3. See, for example, Robert S. Norris, "Chinese Nuclear Forces, 1999," *Bulletin of the Atomic Scientist* (May/June 1999), pp. 79–80, and *1998 National Defense Report, Republic of China* (Taipei: Ministry of National Defense, April 1998), pp. 41–42.

4. Report of the Select Committee on U.S. National Security and Military/Commercial Concerns with the People's Republic of China (Washington, DC: U.S. Government Printing Office, May 25, 1999), Volume 1.

5. For background, see Chuck Downs, *Over the Line: North Korea's Negotiating Strategy* (Washington, DC: American Enterprise Institute Press, 1999), Chapter 9.

6. Statement by Dr. William Perry, Press Briefing on U.S. Relations with North Korea, as released by the Office of the Spokesman, U.S. Department of State, September 17, 1999, at Website http://secretary.state.gov/www/statements/1999/990917a.html.

7. Information in Tables 4–6 drawn from David G. Wiencek, *Dangerous Arsenals: Missile Threats in and from Asia* (Centre for Defence and International Security Studies, Lancaster University, UK, 1997).

8. Bear Li, "Taiwan: Impact of PRC Missile Exercises on Economy Assessed," Taiwan Central News Agency Website, 12 March 1998.

9. As reported in "Study Considers Impact of Large Chinese Ballistic Missile Force," *Inside Washington*, March 17, 1997, citing a 1996 study by the Office of Net Assessment, U.S. Department of Defense.

10. U.S. Office of Naval Intelligence, *Worldwide Submarine Challenges*, February 1997, p. 22.

11. National Intelligence Council, Central Intelligence Agency, "Foreign Missile Developments and the Ballistic Missile Threat to the United States Through 2015," September 1999, at website: www.odci.gov/cia/publications/nie/nie99msl.html.

12. Brahma Chelleney, "Enter Phase II of the Agni," *The Pioneer,* February 25, 1998, p. 10, in Foreign Broadcast Information Service (FBIS)-NES-98–056, February 25, 1998.

13. "India Claims Beijing placed nukes in Tibet," *Washington Times*, May 4, 1998, p. A1.

14. Wilson John, "India's Missile Might," *The Pioneer*, July 13, 1997, p. 1, in FBIS-TAC-97–195, July 14, 1997.

15. Office of the Secretary of Defense, *Proliferation: Threat and Response*, November 1997, p. 20.

16. See statement before the U.S. Senate Armed Services Committee, January 24, 1995, p. 3.

17. Dennis M. Gormley and K. Scott McMahon, "Counterforce: The Neglected Pillar of Theater Missile Defense," *International Defence Review* (May 1996).

18. National Air Intelligence Center, *Ballistic and Cruise Missile Threat*, Wright-Patterson Air Force Base, Ohio, April 1999, NAIC-1031–0985–99, p. 19.

19. Barbara Opall, "Congress to Press Israelis on Sales to China," *Defense News*, September 30–October 6, 1996, p. 3, and "Israel to Equip Chinese Cruise Missile with Penetrator Warhead," *Flight International*, 5–11 February 1997, p. 13.

20. Richard D. Fisher, "Dangerous Moves: Russia's Sale of Missile Destroyers to China," *Heritage Foundation Backgrounder,* February 20, 1997, p. 6.

## Suggested Readings

Commission to Assess the Ballistic Missile Threat to the United States (Rumsfeld Commission). "Executive Summary: Pursuant to Public Law 201, 104th Congress." Washington, DC: July 15, 1998.

Crum Ewing, Humphry, Robin Ranger, and David Bosdet. *Ballistic Missiles: The Approaching Threat*. United Kingdom: Centre for Defence and International Security Studies, Lancaster University, 1994.

Crum Ewing, Humphry, Robin Ranger, David Bosdet, and David Wiencek. *Cruise Missiles: Precision & Countermeasures*. United Kingdom: Centre for Defence and International Security Studies, Lancaster University, 1995.

Fisher, Richard D., Jr. *Missile Defenses Can Strengthen American Leadership in Asia*. Washington, DC: The Heritage Foundation, October 1995.

Institute for Foreign Policy Analysis. *Exploring U.S. Missile Defense Requirements in 2010: What Are the Policy and Technology Challenges?* Washington, DC: April 1997.

———. *A Prognosis for International Missile Developments: 2010*. Washington, DC: August 1997.

National Air Intelligence Center. *Ballistic and Cruise Missile Threat*. Wright-Patterson Air Force Base, Ohio, April 1999, NAIC-1031–0985–99.

National Intelligence Council, Central Intelligence Agency. "Foreign Missile Developments and the Ballistic Missile Threat to the United States Through 2015." At Website: www.odci.gov/cia/publications/nie/nie99msl.html, September 1999.

Office of the Secretary of Defense. *Proliferation: Threat and Response*. Washington, DC: November 1997.

Wiencek, David G. *Dangerous Arsenals: Missile Threats in and from Asia*. United Kingdom: Centre for Defence and International Security Studies, Lancaster University, 1997.

# 6

# Maritime Piracy in Asia

*William M. Carpenter and David G. Wiencek*

## Introduction

There have always been pirates. Today, we think of pirates as relics of the past, unlikely to be encountered on the high seas or in territorial waters. But they are back. The Cold War is gone but not the threat to ships at sea. Today's ships, with their valuable cargoes and small crews, are highly vulnerable to criminal predators in high-speed boats, armed with modern assault weapons and high-tech communications gear, and operating in sea-lanes that international carriers must traverse. Pirates are thus able to make surprise attacks on unarmed merchantmen and get away with money and loot.

The current form of piracy is more than a nuisance to commercial shipping. We assess it to be a strategic threat for several reasons: It affects maritime traffic in vital shipping lanes, particularly in Southeast Asia; attacks on oil supertankers hold the potential to ignite environmental disasters; attacks by pirate craft may invite military reprisals; and there has been a problem off the coast of China with what amounts to state-sponsored piracy by some official Chinese craft.

## Piracy Risks in Asia

Piracy is a security threat that is certainly well known in Asia, where pirates have been active throughout history along the coast of China and in the seas of Southeast Asia. Looking back,

> From individual fishing boats boarding small traders, there were pirate fleets operating from the Malay Peninsula, from Sarawak, from the Philippines and from China. In the early 19th Century it was estimated that there were "tens of thousands" of armed men making their living by pirating.[1]

Table 7

**Piracy in Asia, 1991–1999**

| Year | Total worldwide number of incidents | Number of incidents in Southeast Asia, South Asia, and Far East | Asian incidents as percentage of worldwide total |
|------|------|------|------|
| 1991 | 107 | 102 | 95.3% |
| 1992 | 106 | 75 | 70.7% |
| 1993 | 103 | 88 | 85.4% |
| 1994 | 90 | 73 | 81.1% |
| 1995 | 188 | 134 | 71.2% |
| 1996 | 228 | 165 | 72.3% |
| 1997 | 247 | 148 | 59.9% |
| 1998 | 202 | 121 | 59.9%** |
| 1999 | 300 | 209 | 69.7% |

*Source:* International Maritime Bureau (IMB), Regional Piracy Center (RPC), Kuala Lumpur, "Piracy and Armed Robbery Against Ships: Annual Report: 1st January–31st December 1998," January 1999, p. 3; and RPC, "Piracy and Armed Robbery Against Ships" Annual Report 1st January–31st December/January 2000."
*Note:* "Asia" as defined here does not include the Iran/Persian Gulf region.

More recently, in the late 1970s and early 1980s, international attention was drawn to pirates who preyed on the so-called "boat people," refugees escaping from Vietnam after the war. Since then, there has been an upsurge in worldwide piracy, with most incidents occurring in Asian waters.

It is true that so far among the thousands of ships plying the sea-lanes every day, only a small percentage of them are actually being attacked by pirates. Yet all available statistics indicate that the piracy threat is growing and that the true number of incidents is much higher than actually recorded in the statistics; for a variety of reasons, some attacks are not reported.[2] The trend has generally been upward and a majority of all international piracy incidents in the decade of the 1990s have taken place in Asia (see Table 7). The cost of piracy cannot be precisely known, but one reliable source estimates the worldwide total to be at least US$300–450 million per year.[3]

Today, the greatest number of attacks reported are in Southeast Asia, primarily in the waters off Indonesia, the Philippines, and Thailand, but pirates are active in other places as well, such as off the coasts of India and Sri Lanka, Africa, South America, and in the Caribbean. The main Asian danger area is Indonesia, with forty-seven incidents reported in 1997, sixty in 1998, and 113 in 1999. Many Indonesian pirate attacks have likely been driven by the economic and financial crisis that hit the country in recent years, weak law enforcement capabilities, and the natural cover afforded by the country's many islands. But pirate attacks can shift from place to place, as illustrated by the number of incidents in the so-called "Hong Kong–Luzon–Hainan triangle," a former piracy hot spot bounded by these three islands, which experienced twenty-seven incidents in 1993, twelve in 1994, but zero by 1998.[4]

Pirate booty ranges from a quick haul of cash and valuables readily available from the crew of the victimized ship, to the stealing of entire cargoes—and even the ship itself. The nationality of victim vessels varies widely; in 1993, for example, Russian ships suffered the most attacks altogether (twenty-eight), and of twenty incidents in the East China Sea that year, seventeen were targeted against Russian craft. With regard to vessel type, general cargo, bulk carriers, container carriers, and tankers are the most often attacked.

In addition to property, lives are lost in piracy incidents. Indeed, violence is being used with more frequency. In 1996, twenty-six crew members were killed, while in 1997 the number jumped to fifty-one. In 1998, sixty-seven sailors were killed and all but one of these deaths occurred in Asian waters. In one brutal case, all twenty-three Chinese crew members were shot and killed by pirates after the general cargo vessel *MV Cheung Son* was attacked on November 16, 1998, just outside Hong Kong. Local fishermen recovered seven of the bodies in their nets; the victims had been bound, gagged, and weighted down with iron ingots.

Maritime piracy occurs in some of the busiest shipping lanes in the world. The free flow of commerce through these sea-lanes is vital to the economies of East Asia. A substantial portion of the oil flowing to Japan and Korea is transported from the Middle East through the South China Sea. Piracy disrupts this commerce, and puts entire cargoes at risk. For example, in April 1991, a Japanese merchant vessel, the *Hai Hui*, was attacked by some twenty armed men within Vietnamese waters. The entire 400-ton cargo of the *Hai Hui*, which included 800 VCRs, other electronic gear, motorcycles, and beer was offloaded into another ship over four days, while the crew of the *Hai Hui* was handcuffed and secured in the chain locker.[5]

There is also the general risk in Asia that an attack by pirates of one nationality against another nation's vessel escalates to a level that may be out of proportion to the actual incident, particularly in disputed waters such as in the South China Sea. For example, in May 1992, a pirate vessel reportedly opened fire with small arms on a Russian warship off the Philippines. The Russian amphibious warfare vessel *Nickolai Vikov* fired several rounds of naval artillery at the pirate craft and caused it to withdraw.[6] This escalatory concern is underscored by the fact that pirate attacks in Asia have grown more violent in recent years; while some pirates still employ only swords or knives, others have turned to firebombs, pistols, automatic weapons, and rocket-propelled grenades.

Beyond strategic concerns, an environmental disaster as a result of a pirate attack on a mammoth oil tanker is a plausible scenario, particularly in the Malaccan Straits. Tankers have been frequent targets. From 1991 through 1998, some 195 tankers were reportedly attacked by pirates, representing approximately 15 percent of all worldwide pirate incidents, with most of the attacks occurring in the Malaccan Straits and the South China Sea.[7] In this regard, one International Maritime Bureau (IMB) official has offered the following warning of the consequences of a massive oil spill as a result of a piratical attack in the vicinity of the Malaccan Straits:

> Disastrous though the [1989] Exxon Valdez incident [involving a spill of 41.6 million liters of crude oil] was, in one respect, Alaska was probably the best place it could have happened, in that the area is sparsely populated. Transpose that incident to the Philip Channel and the resultant oil pollution would extend well into the Malaccan Straits, eastward to beyond the Horsburgh Lighthouse. Given the combination of wind and tide, the oil would completely surround Singapore and a multitude of Indonesian islands. Apart from the consequences of pollution, there is every possibility that the seaway would have to be closed to shipping and the fishing in the area would be ruined for years, if not permanently.[8]

In this regard, on January 16, 1999, a fully loaded Very Large Crude Carrier (VLCC) tanker vessel, *MT Chaumant,* was attacked by pirates while navigating in narrow waters of the Philip Channel, a busy 19.8-mile/32-km stretch of water between Singapore and Indonesia. The pirates threatened the chief officer with a machete on the back of his neck and tied his hands. After an alert crew member raised an alarm, the pirates panicked and escaped. In a report commenting on the incident, the IMB noted that "the serious consequences due to grounding or collision of a VLCC can not be overstated."[9]

The most spectacular recent incident was a collision on September 20, 1992, between the supertanker *Nagasaki Spirit* and the container ship *Ocean Blessing* at the northern end of the Malaccan Straits. The *Ocean Blessing,* which collided with the tanker, was apparently a "rogue ship," zigzagging across shipping lanes and possibly under the control of pirates. The collision and subsequent fire killed all the crew aboard the *Ocean Blessing* and all but two of the twenty-two crew members on the tanker. Some 13,000 tons of oil spilled, but most of it evaporated due to favorable weather conditions. The chance of a tanker having an accident is increased because several piracy incidents occurred in which the bridge watch was forcibly removed while the ship was still under way with the rest of the crew locked in a compartment, and while the pirates forced the master to open the safe in his cabin.

## Piracy and International Law

In today's terms, piracy could be called maritime terrorism, although terrorism and piracy stem from different motives. Terrorists try to make a political point, while pirates are almost solely motivated by greed. Strictly defined, under international law piracy is an act committed on the high seas. According to the 1982 United Nations Convention on the Law of the Sea (UNCLOS), piracy is "any illegal acts of violence, detention, or any act of depredation, committed for private ends...on the high seas against another ship or aircraft...outside the jurisdiction of any state."[10] Because there is a need today to bring together the problems of reporting, analyzing, and devising methods of response, the old definition of piracy should be broadened to include incidents in territorial seas or in port.

According to international maritime boundary expert Daniel J. Dzurek:

> Perhaps the most disturbing aspect of modern piracy is the negative effect of recent developments in the Law of the Sea, which put piratical incidents and lairs beyond the reach of international law. This is because the very definition of piracy under international law is area-specific; the piracy must occur on the high seas and be for private ends. By this definition, most of the seaborne violence in Southeast Asia is not piracy under international law, since the attacks occur in jurisdictional waters of coastal states, which may or may not define such activities as piracy.
>
> A more commonsense view is that piracy is an act of violence against persons or goods committed on the sea by a private vessel against another vessel, or by mutinous crew or passengers against their own vessel. In Southeast Asia, most piratical incidents occur within newly expanded internal waters, territorial seas, and recently recognized archipelagic waters of the coastal states. Most of these developing countries lack the resources to police their vast maritime areas effectively.[11]

The London-based IMB has begun to use the following definition: "Piracy is the act of boarding any vessel with the intent to commit theft or any other crime and with the capability to use force in the furtherance of the act."[12] Times change and definitions and concepts necessarily change. Because the international law definition is too narrow, the IMB's definition seems eminently practical for today's needs and is broad enough to cover the widening variety of types of attacks being seen today.

### Types of Piracy

Incidents of piracy in port are not something entirely new, but rather a modern version of the old practice of robbing ships while docked. Some pilferage at dockside has long been a hazard while ships are loading or unloading. The difference today is the existence of well-organized criminal gangs, who plan their attacks carefully, often to seize specific kinds of cargo, and who are prepared to kill or maim to accomplish their aims.

A ship at anchor, often awaiting a dockside berth, is in similar danger from organized piracy gangs, who usually board during darkness. They are even less likely to be deterred or apprehended by police than those committing dockside thievery and mayhem.

More akin to pirates of old are those who attack a ship at sea. Here, again, they come prepared to act with force. Boarding is usually from astern from a fast boat, or alongside, where ships such as tankers have a low freeboard. There are three general types of attack: a quick boarding and rapid departure, taking money and other easily portable valuables; a temporary seizure, to take the ship to some prearranged port for offloading the cargo being stolen, then releasing the ship and its crew; and third, a long-term seizure involving illegally re-registering of the ship under a succession of fake names, engaging in one after another scheme of enticing a shipper to entrust his cargo to their ship, which claims to be in normal business—cargo the shipper will never see again.

It is from this latter type of piracy that the crew of the victim ship is in greatest danger: in some way the crew must be "disposed of" by the pirates. The pirates will then operate the ship themselves. This kind of operation requires a thorough knowledge of shipping practices, of places where registry is not carefully administered, or where there are temporary registers, and of ports where valuable cargo can be obtained. It is difficult for authorities to trace this kind of piracy because in the re-registering process a ship seems to "disappear."

One recent example of this problem involved the bulk carrier *MV Anna Sierra*, which was hijacked in September 1995 in the Gulf of Thailand by thirty masked pirates armed with machine guns, pistols, and knives. The ship's US$4 million cargo of sugar was found to have been presold to a Chinese trader, who had paid about US$1 million in advance to the pirates. Once on board, the pirates repainted the hatch covers, masthouses, and other parts of the ship, and then changed her name to *Arctic Sea*. During the incident, the crew were handcuffed and locked up for two days. They were then split into two groups, and cast adrift in the open sea, one group on a makeshift pontoon, and the other in a life raft. The pirates opened fire on the crew, but none was injured; they were eventually rescued unharmed.

The pirates sailed the vessel to Beihei, in southern China, where it remains four years after the incident. As of mid-1999, Chinese workers reportedly had begun breaking the ship apart. According to IMB authorities, the pirates were repatriated to their homelands, while Chinese authorities had demanded US$400,000 for the release of the vessel to its owners.[13]

**International Developments**

In the international arena, much has been written in recent years about "state-sponsored terrorism," but so far there has been no mention of "state-sponsored piracy." Incidents off the coast of East Asia raise the possibility of the latter. Beginning in the early 1990s, ships sailing near the coast of China were either fired upon, stopped, or seized by patrol-type craft manned by seamen speaking Chinese, carrying Chinese weapons, and wearing Chinese military uniforms. In some cases, these crews declared themselves to be members of China's Public Security Bureau (PSB), which performs customs functions. The reason usually given for stopping these ships is to prevent smuggling into China. Large fines are often imposed before the ships are allowed to proceed. More significantly, there has been a trend in these cases of hijacking a vessel's cargo or even the entire ship.

One incident involving suspected official Chinese craft is particularly troubling. In June 1995, the 1,000-ton, Panamanian-registered bulk container *Hye Mieko*, carrying a US$2 million cargo, was hijacked at gunpoint off Cambodia while en route from Singapore by a boat resembling a Chinese customs launch and forced to sail over 1,000 miles to Shanwei in China's Guangdong province. Despite its Southeast Asian location, Chinese authorities charged the vessel with attempting to smuggle its cargo of cigarettes into the country and therefore were required to seize her. The *Hye Mieko* was subsequently released, minus her cargo.[14]

This activity has also apparently led to internal clashes among competing Chinese agencies. For example, on July 26, 1998, a violent clash occurred between elements of the Chinese navy and the marine police of the PSB, which resulted in eighty-seven casualties, including thirteen deaths. The incident took place off the coast of Shandong in the Yellow Sea. Reports indicate that the navy had arranged to send four tankers carrying smuggled oil to Yantai military harbor. When the tankers entered Chinese waters, they were met by an escort group consisting of four gunships, two submarines, and one transport ship. Learning of the smuggling operation, the PSB appealed to the military to forego the operation. When it did not, the PSB mobilized twelve anti-smuggling gunboats to stop the naval group. The navy vessels then began a live fire "exercise." After a brief stalemate, two navy ships rammed PSB ships. Gunfire ensued, and the entire skirmish lasted over fifty minutes. Eventually, the tankers made port, where the oil was offloaded onto military trains and shipped for sale in Hebei and Henan provinces, ultimately netting a high profit.[15] In response to this activity, Chinese authorities have begun to cooperate in some piracy cases with the IMB and reportedly have cracked down on this type of corruption within their own official agencies.

In 1993, the Russian freighter *Valery Volkov* was carrying metal from Vladivostok to China when Chinese patrol boats shot at and then boarded the freighter while it was passing through Korean waters. Nothing was taken and the ship was allowed to proceed, but because of this and other incidents against Russian ships, the Russian Pacific Fleet deployed a flotilla to the East China Sea to protect Russian merchantmen. In the flotilla were the *Kara*-class cruiser *Petropovlosk* and the training ship *Borodino*, plus replenishment ships. The Republic of Korea (ROK) also acted in 1993 to suppress pirate attacks on Korean shipping by sending ROK navy units and maritime police to patrol the East and South China Seas. An even firmer response was taken by North Korea, which felt no hesitation in issuing a diplomatic note to Beijing regarding a July 1993 incident in which a strong Chinese boarding party was ejected by the crew of a North Korean merchant ship.[16]

On the industry side, owners and operators recognize the growing piracy problem, and some of them have taken specific action. For example, a major oil company operating in Asia reports substantial success from on-board measures taken by its tankers. Deck patrols, increased lighting on deck and around the rail, full pressure on the fire hoses, and careful scheduling of sailing to avoid passing through danger areas (such as the Philip Channel) at night have lessened the incidence of pirate attacks.

## The U.S. Response

Piracy, however defined, has not yet received much public attention in the United States. Pirate attacks on U.S. ships have been few—partly, no doubt, because the U.S. merchant marine is comparatively small. However, there have been attacks on U.S. merchant ships, and the substantial fleet of American-owned, foreign-registered ships does provide many more targets for pirates. For example, the U.S.-flagged tanker *Ranger* was attacked by pirates, who escaped with US$23,000, while the ship was transiting the Philip Channel off Singapore on September 11, 1991. As long ago as January 1984, the *Falcon Countess* (chartered to the U.S. Navy) was boarded in the Malaccan Straits by six pirates armed with knives, who tied up the master and made off with US$19,000 from the ship's safe.

There have been other attacks on U.S. ships, and there seems little reason to believe that there will not be more.

In 1999, the U.S. Navy indicated it was working with Southeast Asian navies on counter-piracy training. A Navy spokesman also stated that the United States was providing health and other forms of assistance in local communities in the region as a means of preventing individuals from turning to piracy.[17]

## International Responses

A number of steps have been taken in the last few years to improve collection and dissemination of intelligence information on the piracy threat. The London-based IMB, in particular, has been at the forefront of these efforts, working closely with law enforcement and private industry. In 1992, the IMB established the Regional Piracy Center in Kuala Lumpur, Malaysia. The Center's main responsibilities are to broadcast warning messages to vessels; receive warnings concerning suspicious craft movements; collate information; liaise with law enforcement agencies; and provide post-incident support services. The Center is funded by industry and all services are provided free of charge. Its activities and initiatives have proven to be a success in raising awareness about international piracy, conducting investigations, developing countermeasures, and helping recover losses where possible.

But more and better intelligence sharing among governments and between governments and industry is required, particularly with respect to the role of organized crime in piracy. Like drug runners and terrorists, pirates are also successfully exploiting jurisdictional gaps between law enforcement and military agencies. As Vice Admiral (Retired) Ko Tun-hwa of the Republic of China observes, pirate attacks frequently occur in maritime "vacuum spots," such as at the border of territorial waters shared by neighboring nations, which raises further questions about jurisdictional responsibilities.[18]

Sharing responsibilities may be one of the best ways to overcome such difficulties. Joint patrols among regional navies, for example, can help pool resources to combat piracy. Singapore and Indonesia, Thailand and Vietnam, and Thailand and Malaysia have conducted recent patrols, but more could and should be done in this regard.

There is a growing consensus that the greatest opportunities for defeating pirates lie in measures that can be taken on board ships that may be targets for pirates. Lights along the rail illuminating the hull between the deck edge and the waterline, provided they do not violate international rules of the sea, will disclose any pirate craft coming close aboard. A crew member with ready access to a searchlight can shine the beam at the pirate craft, effectively blinding and confusing the pirate crew. Boarding can be made more difficult by installing barriers along the rail, such as concertina wire. Fire hoses fully charged and available near the rail can be used to deter a boarder who is attempting to scale the ship's side and come over the rail. This tactic can be effective even if more than one boarder is coming at once. These are but some of the measures that can be employed by shippers to counter modern pirates, whether at sea, at anchor, or in port.

The IMB has also recently embraced a satellite tracking system called SHIPLOC, which is capable of providing the positional location of a vessel at sea or in port using Global Positioning System (GPS) satellite updates. SHIPLOC uses a small transmitter concealed on board a ship that transmits positional updates. The service is available to shippers for a reasonable monthly fee and can be used to track the location of a pirated ship.

Beyond these measures, private sector companies have begun to offer rapid armed crisis response services to deal with piracy incidents. But these services appear to be employed cautiously and on a limited basis, as shippers remain concerned with the implications of introducing firearms on board their vessels.

Without doubt, naval escorts or regular naval patrols are a major step up from the very practical on-board measures individual ships can take or even the cooperative efforts of law enforcement and other agencies to share intelligence or engage in maritime surveillance. In the future, if the threat grows, coordinated multinational patrols and escorts could be an avenue to explore, perhaps under the auspices of the Association of Southeast Asian Nations (ASEAN) or the United Nations.

### Conclusions

If piracy is a renewed and serious threat to safety at sea, as the mounting evidence shows it to be, the question is what to do about it. Piracy itself is not new, but the present form is new. Traditionally, pirates have been resisted by whatever force could be mustered. Naval forces at sea were authorized to pursue and attack pirate ships. In the post–Cold War world, the nations who have observed the new menace of piracy—with a few exceptions noted above—do not seem inclined to send naval forces either to escort threatened merchant ships or to establish regular anti-piracy patrols in areas of frequent incidents.

Diplomatic means can and should be employed—for example, to press China to curb what appear to be continuing problems amounting to piracy by Chinese uniformed personnel serving in Chinese official craft. The United Nations and the International Chamber of Commerce, through its IMB, have taken action to collect and disseminate information on pirate attacks and to give out practical advice on shipboard protection against pirate attacks. However, the main burden of countering piracy appears to fall upon the ship vulnerable to attack.

Ships that have taken defensive measures have in some cases thwarted what might otherwise have been successful attacks. The situation on each ship is peculiar to that ship; variations in preparatory measures must accord with the characteristics of the ship, with crew size, and with the level of training and competency of the crew. The key appears to be, when in areas where pirates may lurk, to "think pirates." Pirates seem to avoid a ship that appears alert and ready to defend itself; they go on to seek an easier target.

The present reality is that most ship owners have been reluctant to spend money to improve on-board preventive capabilities. Insurance companies, meanwhile, seem willing to pay out small claims rather than pressing ship owners to take defensive measures. The situation is unlikely to improve until the courts make a major compensation award for injury or death.

The reactions of ship masters to the recommendations they are receiving to deal with piracy are mixed, but most go along with the prohibition on the use of firearms. The frustration of masters with the inaction toward the piracy problem and their perception that not enough is being done to help them is revealed in the comments of one master, who wrote to the industry paper *Lloyd's List* in 1993: "We are so used to having bodies issuing recommendations just to leave us with the real problems, that one more useless paper does not really matter. We are denied the right of self defence and we are denied a legal system and special compensation in the case of injury or death."[19] Many masters may sympathize with this frustration, but at the same time they recognize that in the real world of today theirs is the burden and they must do the best they can. In the end, a combination of measures undertaken by the masters, the shipping industry, and governments will be required to safeguard merchant fleets, defeat piracy, and help ensure the continued free flow of commerce through vital waterways. It seems a safe conclusion that we have not heard the last of the new piracy.

## Notes

1. Brian Parritt, "The Problem of Piracy: An Old Problem, A New Solution?" *Intersec* (The Journal of International Security), April 1999, p. 118.

2. International Maritime Bureau (IMB) Deputy Director Captain Jayant Abhyankar stated in early 1999 that: "We used to think we got to hear about one out of every three attacks, but now I think it could be one in eight." Quoted in *The Straits Times*, February 6, 1999, p. 46. A 1999 survey of eighty-seven Japanese shipowners, meanwhile, revealed that sixty-six Japanese ships had been attacked by pirates in Southeast Asia and Africa since 1994; IMB data indicate only seven attacks on Japanese ships during that same period. See "Japanese Shipowners, Govt. Discuss Piracy in S.E. Asia," *Business Times* (Singapore), July 6, 1999, p. 1, and IMB Regional Piracy Center, Kuala Lumpur, "Piracy and Armed Robbery Against Ships: Annual Report: 1st January–31st December 1998," January 1999, p. 8.

3. Geoffrey Till, "Coastal Focus for Maritime Security," *Jane's Navy International* 1, no. 4 (May 1996), p. 10. A figure of US$16 billion in annual piracy losses has recently been attributed to the IMB, as cited in Kevin Sullivan and Mary Jordan, "High-Tech Pirates Ravage Asian Seas," *Washington Post*, July 5, 1999, p. A18.

4. IMB Regional Piracy Center (RPC), "Piracy and Armed Robbery Against Ships: Annual Report: 1st January–31st December 1998," p. 3.

5. IMB, *Special Report: Piracy* (London: IMB, June 1992); and Allan Farnham, "Pirates!" *Fortune*, July 5, 1991, p. 112.

6. IMB, *Special Report: Piracy*.

7. U.S. Department of Energy, Office of Threat Assessment, "Piracy: The Threat to Tanker Traffic," no. 2 (March 1993), and IMB data.

8. Comments by IMB Deputy Director Captain Jayant Abhyankar as quoted in Dominic Nathan, "Pirates Kill and Plunder, But No Stopping Them," *The Straits Times*, April 26, 1999, pp. 2–3.

9. RPC, "Piracy and Armed Robbery Against Ships: Report for the Period: 1st January–30th June 1999," 15 July 1999, p. 11.

10. UNCLOS incorporated the piracy definition contained in the 1958 Geneva Convention on the High Seas. See John E. Noyes, "An Introduction to the International Law of Piracy," *California Western International Law Journal* 21 (1990): 106–7.

11. Daniel J. Dzurek, "Piracy in Southeast Asia," *Oceanus* 32, no. 4 (Winter 1989–90): 66–68.

12. IMB, *Special Report: Piracy*.

13. For background, see RPC, "Piracy: Annual Report: 1st January–31st December 1995," January 1996, pp. 4–5; RPC, "Piracy and Armed Robbery Against Ships: Annual Report: 1st January–31st December 1998," p. 18; Abby Tan, "In Asian Waters, Sea Pirates Eschew Eye Patches, Steal Ships Via the Internet," *Christian Science Monitor*, June 13, 1996, p. 7; and, Dorinda Elliott, "Where Pirates Still Sail," *Newsweek*, July 5, 1999, p. 46.

14. "Captain Says His Freighter Hijacked by Chinese," Reuters, July 24, 1995.

15. *Inside Mainland China*, November 1998; "Army's Zhang Wannian Reportedly to Be Made to Resign Over Army Smuggling," Hong Kong *Ping Kuo Jih Pao*, September 24, 1998, p. A24, as cited in British Broadcasting Corporation, FE/D3342/G, September 26, 1998; and Jonathan Manthorpe, "Seaborne Crime Huge Business: The Pirates Know Exactly What Ship They Want and What Cargo It Has," *Vancouver Sun*, January 15, 1999, p. F3.

16. *South China Morning Post*, July 16, 1993, p. 3.

17. "U.S. Navy Helps Asian Counterparts Combat Piracy," Associated Press, April 6, 1999.

18. Tun-hwa Ko, "Piracy and Anti-Piracy," in Tun-hwa Ko and Phillip M. Chen, eds., *Sea Lane Security Studies: Some Vital Issues* (Taipei: Asia and World Institute, July 1986), p. 16.

19. Quoted in Brigadier (Ret.) B.A.H. Parritt, CBE, "An Attack at Sea: What If It Happens?" *Intersec*, November–December 1993, p. 222.

## Suggested Readings

Ellen, Eric. ed., *Piracy at Sea*. Paris: ICC Publishing, 1989.

Elliott, Dorinda, "Where Pirates Still Sail." *Newsweek*, July 5, 1999, p. 46.

International Shipping Federation. *Pirates and Armed Robbers: A Master's Guide*. London: International Shipping Federation, 1992. Second Edition (revised).

Parritt, Brigadier (Ret.), B.A.H. CBE. *Security at Sea: Terrorism, Piracy and Drugs: A Practical Guide*. London: The Nautical Institute, 1998.

# 7

# Illegal Narcotics in Southeast Asia

*William. J. Olson*

The countries of Southeast Asia present a very mixed picture. Three countries in the region—Thailand, Malaysia, and Singapore—have vibrant market economies and functioning democratic processes, although in the latter two cases the record is mixed. One country, Burma, is ruled by a military oligarchy and exists more as geographic terminology comprising numerous competing groups rather than a unitary state. Cambodia is a muddle of conflicting tendencies and is recovering, poorly, from years of civil war and near national suicide. The remaining states, Laos and Vietnam, are recovering Marxist-Leninist polities with tremendous economic and social deficits. Despite this very mixed bag, all the states in the region share one thing in common. All are involved in illegal drug production or transit.

Southeast Asia is a major producer, marketer, and consumer of illegal drugs, principally opiates and increasingly methamphetamine. The indications are that these activities will continue and grow worse in the foreseeable future. The production, transportation, and use of illegal drugs—which, along with the laundering of illegal drug proceeds, constitute the "drug cycle"—are the source of deep-seated social problems, broad-based corruption, and continuing violence in all the countries of the Golden Triangle region (Burma, Thailand, and Laos). Drugs are the largest source of income for ongoing criminal enterprises, with increasingly internationalized connections, which make the problems of the Golden Triangle a matter of international concern. The growth of market economies and links to the international financial community have only facilitated the drug cycle and have spurred its expansion.

The true extent of the drug business—its size, reach, and consequences—is difficult to measure. In the case of the major illegal drug, opium—an agricultural crop at its source—measurement of cultivation is an inexact science at best. Imagery and ground-source information produce rough estimates of cultivation on the order of some 140,000 to 150,000 hectares of poppy per year—mostly in Burma—depending on weather, local conditions, and marginal eradication efforts. This cultivation potentially yields some 2,000 metric tons of opium gum, which, based on a further, inexact formula, could produce as much as 200 metric tons of heroin per year.[1]

Since this production is in the hands of criminal gangs or secretive organizations, the precise monetary return from this production is equally obscure. Criminal gangs do not file financial disclosure forms. Estimating annual income is further complicated by the fact that much of the opium/heroin produced in the region is locally consumed at or near the source at fluctuating prices difficult to assess. Conservative calculations, however, indicate that the criminal organizations engaged in the international heroin trade could earn as much as US$10 billion annually from heroin alone—more than the combined gross domestic product (GDP) of Vietnam, Laos, and Cambodia.[2] In addition, criminal gangs also produce and market marijuana and are increasingly manufacturing methamphetamine and methylenedioxymethamphetamine (MDMA, or Ecstasy) for local and international sale. Quantities produced and income earned are equally mysterious.

### It's Business: The Link Between Drugs and the Marketplace

The use of opium in the Golden Triangle is not recent. It has been used for generations as a medicine in mostly poor and agricultural areas, which still predominate in the region. Early on, however, the "recreational" potential of opiates, as opposed to the medicinal use, was realized and became common, if limited. In the nineteenth century, it was the British who realized the economic potential of large-scale opium cultivation for non-medical uses and encouraged a rapid expansion of production, aided by two successful wars with China that legitimized the trade regionally. In the late nineteenth century, two further developments, linked to scientific inquiry, made for dramatic changes to occur later.

The first was the discovery of morphine—a refined opiate derivative that concentrated the analgesic qualities long noticed in opium. The second was the discovery of heroin by scientists with the German giant Bayer chemical and pharmaceutical company. At first it was thought that heroin was a safe substitute for morphine and a possible cure for morphine addiction, which was an all too common side effect of the medicinal use of morphine. It became clear fairly quickly, however, that heroin not only did not have any medical utility but was also powerfully attractive as a recreational drug and equally powerfully addictive. The scientific process had improved and concentrated the inherent narcotic qualities of opium—a process that would also "improve" and concentrate the psychotropic qualities of another agriculturally derived drug—cocaine. All of this would have been a mere curiosity but for an important connection—the link between drugs and the marketplace.

The pure, white powder Heroin-4 used by addicts in Europe, Asia, and America begins as a rather attractive flowering plant growing on mountainsides in largely inaccessible, back-of-beyond areas in Southeast and Southwest Asia. How the gummy residue from this flowering plant in rural Asia becomes a highly concentrated, highly addictive drug of abuse in cities all over the world is no accident. It is big, if illegal, business. In most cases in Southeast Asia, it is a business connected to the Chinese diaspora, a link that may have its origins in the opium wars of the early nineteenth century, which created a vast local market for non-medicinal opiates and the internationalization of Chinese criminal gangs— often one of several Triad groups—that followed the movement of emigrating Chinese all over the world. It is a remarkable, dynamic process involving the integration of cultivation, agricultural extension services, product collection, chemical processing, transportation, marketing, cash management, and investment worldwide, while protecting the whole enterprise from official intervention, disruption, or sanction at every step in the process—from fields in Asia to streetcorners in London or Chicago and back again as money flows from sales.

For the drug traffickers, money is everything. The product is only a means to make money, and lots of it. That those involved in this process know that drug use is dangerous and wrong is shown by the fact that most growers and producers do not use the drugs themselves or permit their own family members to use them. But profit from the folly of others is their bread and butter. This is bad enough, but it is not the end of the tale.

There is no one-size-fits-all formula for describing or understanding the drug cycle, in Asia or elsewhere. To some extent, drug traffickers exploit the natural advantages of local states to determine their role in the drug cycle. Burma, for example, is a largely rural country with limited government presence but it lacks extensive financial facilities. It is not surprising, therefore, that it or Laos, similarly a largely rural, undeveloped society, are major growing areas but not major money laundering centers. The beginning of the process, cultivation itself, is variegated. Not all countries in the region are major growers, although virtually all of them could be. Burma is by far the largest grower, with Laos a distant second. Thailand, once the third largest grower, has largely eliminated the crop but has become a major transit country, a money laundering center, and a base of operations for drug traffickers. Heroin moves from Thailand in various ways, but it quite often finds its way to U.S. markets in New York and Chicago through couriers controlled by Nigerian trafficking organizations. Thailand may also become a center for methamphetamine production. Vietnam is becoming a major transit point for heroin and there are signs of some local opium cultivation as well. Like Thailand, Malaysia is also a transit point and the Gulf of Thailand is a major conduit for heroin moving by coastal craft to rendezvous with oceangoing ships moving to Europe, Australia, and the United States. Singapore, despite tough drug laws, is also a transit point, but its major role in the drug cycle is as a money laundering center, either through formal financial markets or through an extensive informal banking network managed by the Chinese overseas community. Drug traffickers have also included south China in their distribution network, moving heroin through southern China to Hong Kong and directly from there or through Taiwan to the Pacific Northwest of the United States and Canada.[3]

The money generated by this flow is then moved back to the Golden Triangle through a host of formal and informal financial mechanisms to fund other illegal operations or is invested in legitimate financial instruments, real estate, front companies, and banks around the globe. A percentage of this money is also put to work to protect the enterprise or to fund the activities of putative liberation groups, principally in Burma.

Opium growing, heroin production, and drug trafficking are illegal in all the countries of the region. Money laundering, although sheltered in the shade of bank secrecy environments in a number of countries, is also illegal. Thus, the whole drug cycle is an illegal activity, both in terms of local laws and in international law, to which the countries of the region subscribe.[4] Despite this, drugs continue to be produced and transited, in large part because of local corruption and official collusion. Drug money, as noted, also supports other, ongoing criminal enterprises and is the major source of funding for many of the ethnic-based, so-called national liberation fronts, such as the United Wa State Army, the Shan United Revolutionary Army, and several others in Burma.

In the case of the ethnic-based opposition movements in Burma, it is no longer clear, if it ever was, whether these groups are drug trafficking organizations that use a cover of nationalism to give their activities a patina of legitimacy or whether they are national liberation movements that turned to drug trafficking as a means to raise money. It may be that it is a distinction without a difference and in terms of international effects it most certainly is. Regardless of the underlying motive, the consequences for individual users and their collective societies is the same.

### Double Trouble: Social Costs

The drug trade may generate income for a small group of farmers and enrich an even smaller group of major traffickers, but the harm caused by this process is considerable. The direct harm is caused to users, their families, and ultimately to the social service systems that must intervene to deal with the consequences of drug use. For societies with limited incomes, the medical and social service costs place considerable strains on already overburdened systems with only limited capabilities. Treatment for addicts, where it exists, is long-term, costly, and of qualified utility. It must be repeated many times over a user's lifetime and even then it may not lead to abstinence. These sustained health care costs place significant burdens on overtaxed systems already inadequate for local health needs arising from non-drug-related ailments. But use has further collateral effects.

It contributes to crime and violence by addicts—either in search of money to support a habit or as a result of individual pharmacological changes that promote aggression. This raises the social costs. In addition, as heroin use has spread so has intravenous drug use. With this has come the spread of HIV and AIDS. The number of HIV/AIDS sufferers in countries in the region is difficult to assess, but indications are that it is a growing and significant population. Even for relatively wealthy countries in the region, such as Thailand or Malaysia, this adds yet more burdens to the costs of social and medical services. Thailand has one of the highest HIV infection rates in Asia, with total health care costs running at about 12 percent of total government expenditures.[5] For poorer countries, the costs can be prohibitive. Although heroin remains the main drug of choice—spurred by its availability, low local costs, and poor enforcement—designer drugs, such as methamphetamine, are starting to make their appearance. Their ease of production and the fact that most of these drugs are stimulants could well mean a growing problem.[6]

In addition to these direct and indirect costs, drugs levy a further penalty on the region in the form of corruption and organized crime.[7] No major illicit activity on the scale of opium and opiate production in the region can escape official notice. To some degree, the fact that widespread cultivation continues despite its illegality is a function of the limited law enforcement capabilities of countries such as Burma and Laos to police their own territories. This would be the case even if Burmese authorities did not have to contend with the military organizations that protect much of the drug trade in Burma. Nevertheless, large-scale production, transit, sale, and the laundering of the resulting proceeds continue because of the ability of the traffickers to corrupt government officials at all levels. Chinese and Vietnamese authorities tacitly admit that many local police and government officials are on the payrolls of drug traffickers. In both Burma and Vietnam, local development efforts may also be funded by drug money as a means to launder funds. Military officials in Thailand and elsewhere have also been implicated in receiving payments to not interfere with, and in some cases to facilitate, the movement of drugs or precursor chemicals used in their manufacture. This corruption in relation to drug smuggling then involves these officials in other aspects of ongoing criminal activities, spreading the effects and undermining legitimate authority. By prejudicing the enforcement of laws and actions of officials on behalf of criminal gangs, corruption robs governments of credibility and the basic decency and honesty necessary for political development. Moreover, this facilitation undermines legitimate economic activity.

In some minds, the enormous incomes generated by drug production create the impression that despite the negative effects of drug use, trafficking benefits local economies by funneling large sums of money into the system. While it is difficult to assess, a growing body of analysis indicates that this benefit is illusory and that significant damage is actually done to local economies. This can come in several forms, from the so-called "Dutch Disease," which distorts market development, to the diversion of labor and tax income from legitimate enterprise.[8] Bad money drives out good money. In addition, most of the money generated from illicit sales does not find its way back into the local incomes but instead flows to major capital markets and investment opportunities. What money remains locally, then, distorts the economy—in some cases of countries already suffering severe economic problems—and fuels further illegality, corruption, and violence.

## The International Connection

Long before major banks discovered the joys of banking without borders, major criminal gangs developed and exploited an internationalized informal banking system to help them launder the money they use to finance their activities.[9] As major, legal banks have begun to explore the possibilities of more liberalized financial markets and Internet access, so too have criminal gangs, who continue to exploit the advantages of longstanding informal banking networks and increasingly the opportunities of offshore banking, bank secrecy havens, and the sheer complexity and volume of international financial transactions to facilitate their business activities. In addition, criminal organizations formerly confined to their own geographic regions have begun to develop links to similar organizations in different parts of the world, forming strategic alliances to help facilitate criminal activities and further insulate them from law enforcement.[10]

This cross-pollenization has helped to expand the reach of various criminal groups, allowed them to share information on business opportunities and how to avoid law enforcement, and improved money laundering possibilities. The consequence is that no localized law enforcement organization—no matter its size or sophistication—is able to tackle the full range of the drug cycle or the other activities of major criminal gangs. As noted above, few such omni-competent law enforcement organizations exist in the Golden Triangle, and rampant corruption at all levels of government vitiates much of the limited capabilities that do exist. Although the United States, the European Community, the United Nations, the G-7, the World Bank, the International Monetary Fund (IMF), and many other organizations and states are providing assistance to combat the drug cycle in the region and working to improve local capabilities, the prospects for improvement in the near term are slim. The reach of criminal gangs in the Golden Triangle is likely to extend its grasp in the near future, and expanding drug markets make that grasp a considerable one.

## Notes

1. The best source for cultivation numbers is the annual *International Narcotics Control Strategy Report (INCSR)* from the U.S. Department of State. This report contains estimates of poppy cultivation in all major poppy-producing countries based on imagery. The size of cultivation is derived from a statistically based extrapolation. All estimates are approximations at best.

2. This number is an extrapolation of potential income based on marketing one hundred metric tons of heroin internationally. The calculation is based on an international average price for a kilogram of heroin of US$100,000—the retail average price ranges from US$80,000 in Europe to as much as US$200,000 in the United States. See *World Drug Report* (UN: Oxford University Press, 1997), p. 126, for a rough estimate of heroin prices.

Wide variations in price between Asian, European, and U.S. markets, plus significant fluctuations within these markets based on local availability, makes arriving at numbers pure guesswork. A generally accepted number for the income from all international drug sales is around US$500 billion annually.

3. For information on growing patterns and money laundering in the region see U.S. Department of State, *INCSR*, 1999.

4. The principal international instrument for controlling the drug cycle is the 1988 UN Convention on Psychotropic and Narcotic Drugs. For copies of international law governing the drug cycle, see *International Narcotics Control and United States Foreign Policy: A Compilation of Laws, Treaties, Executive Documents and Related Materials*, a report prepared for the Senate Caucus on International Narcotics Control and the Committee on International Relations, U.S. House of Representatives, 105th Congress, Congressional Research Service of the Library of Congress, September 1997.

5. *World Drug Report*, p. 304.

6. Drug users tend to polidrug use rather than concentrating on only one drug. Heroin is a depressant. For drug users, adding a stimulant to the mix can increase or prolong the high associated with use. Methamphetamine and other designer drugs produced at low cost in "kitchen" labs may not replace opiate use but could easily become a major source of further problems. As in the United States, meth and Ecstasy use tend to appeal, at this point, to blue collar workers, especially those in transportation-related jobs.

7. The World Bank and the IMF have taken an increased interest in the consequences for development of widespread corruption. This marks a change in policy focus. See, for example, James Wolfensohn's 1996 president's address to the World Bank group, October, 1996, "Annual Meetings Speech." For a general overview of the effects of corruption see the summaries on the high costs of corruption in *Trends in Organized Crime*, vol. 2, no. 4, (Summer 1997).

8. See *World Drug Report*, pp. 142 ff. For a lengthy discussion of the economics of the drug trade, although in a different context, see Patrick Clawson and Rensselaer Lee, *The Andean Cocaine Industry* (NY: St. Martin's Press, 1996).

9. It is only recently that the literature on international organized crime has begun to catch up with these developments. Governments and academics have only slowly come to the idea that there is such a thing as organized crime at all, much less an emerging web of relationships among groups across international frontiers. For access to this emerging literature, see *Trends in Organized Crime*, an international journal, and *Transnational Organized Crime*, also a relatively new peer-reviewed journal. The United Nations has also undertaken a number of major international conferences on the threat of organized crime, the proceedings and research papers for which are valuable sources of information and can be accessed through the UN's website. Also see Roy Godson and William J. Olson, *International Organized Crime: Emerging Threat to U.S. Security* (Washington, DC: National Strategy Information Center, 1993).

10. See Jack Blum et al. "Financial Havens, Banking Secrecy and Money Laundering," UN Drug Control Program, Issue 8, Technical Series of the *Crime Prevention and Criminal Justice Newsletter*, 1998. On the development of strategic links between criminal organizations see Phil Williams, "Transnational Criminal Organizations: Strategic Alliances," *The Washington Quarterly*, vol. 18, (Winter 1995).

## Suggested Readings

Leader, Stephan H., and David G. Wiencek. "International Terrorism: The Drug Connection." *Jane's Intelligence Review*, February 2000.

United States Department of State. *International Narcotics Control Strategy Report*. (Annual).

# 8

## Conflict Potential of the South China Sea Disputes

*John C. Baker*

The South China Sea's importance for national security, economic development, and even environmental well-being has fueled numerous disputes among the littoral countries resulting from conflicting maritime claims. Among these longstanding disputes, the Spratly Islands and their surrounding waters have gained international notoriety because China and several Association of Southeast Asian Nations (ASEAN) countries claim all or some of the Spratlys and their surrounding waters.[1] Several countries have constructed military outposts on the desolate islands and reefs of the Spratlys to buttress their claims. Although these disputes mostly are confined to a war of words and diplomatic protests, some incidents have involved the use of force and even the loss of life. Thus, the unresolved disputes over the Spratlys present a continuing flashpoint for conflict in the South China Sea that could upset regional stability if the maritime incidents escalate into armed conflict.

### The Spratly Islands Disputes

Situated in the southern reaches of the South China Sea, the Spratly Islands consist of some 170 low-lying features, including about three dozen small islands along with various reefs and submerged banks and shoals.[2] The total land area of the tiny islands is no more than two to three square kilometers in an ocean area covering over 200,000 square kilometers. Yet this maritime region's importance arises from its wealth of natural resources and its strategic location astride one of the world's main crossroads for maritime commerce and naval movements.

China, Malaysia, the Philippines, Taiwan, and Vietnam all claim at least some

Table 8

**Occupation Forces in the Spratly Islands**

| Country | Number of islands occupied and some key features | Estimated number of troops |
|---|---|---|
| PRC | seven islands and reefs; several helicopter pads | 260 |
| Philippines | eight islands; one with a 1,300-meter runway | 480 |
| Vietnam | twenty-seven islands and reefs; one with 600-meter runway | 600 |
| Malaysia | three islands; one with 600-meter runway | 70 |
| Taiwan | one island with helicopter pads; plans for runway | 100 |

*Source:* Cheng-yi Lin, "Security Implications of Conflict in the South China Sea: A Taiwanese Perspective," in Carolina G. Hernandez and Ralph Cossa, eds., *Security Implications of Conflict in the South China Sea: Perspectives from Asia-Pacific* (Quezon City, the Philippines: Institute for Strategic and Development Studies, 1997), p. 104; and Bradford L. Thomas and Daniel J. Dzurek, "The Spratly Islands Dispute," *Geopolitics and International Boundaries*, 1 (Winter 1996), pp. 302–306.

portion of the Spratly Islands and the surrounding waters.[3] Each country has established a continuous human presence on the small islands and larger reefs in Spratly Islands using military outposts and other facilities to demonstrate the seriousness of its sovereignty claims.[4] One estimate is that about 1,500 troops are deployed on some forty-six islands and reefs in the Spratly Islands and sustained by the various claimant countries (Table 8). However, even this estimate could be outdated, particularly given recent events that include new occupations by Vietnam and Malaysia, and China's major expansion of the living facilities at Mischief Reef.[5]

Each country offers particular historical or legal rationales to support its jurisdictional and territorial claims to the disputed Spratly Islands.[6] But four reasons largely explain why these countries expend their limited resources to show their flags in these remote locations: sovereignty, fishing resources, hydrocarbon potential, and security concerns.

*Sovereignty.* The sovereignty issue alone offers a powerful impetus for various countries to engage in this territorial dispute in the South China Sea. The longstanding diplomatic dispute between Argentina and the United Kingdom that unexpectedly escalated into the Falklands War in mid-1982 suggests that countries are willing to use force when they believe that their sovereignty is being unacceptably violated. In the case of the South China Sea disputes, growing nationalism among many Asia-Pacific nations in the post–Cold War era only increases the domestic political obstacles for national leaders in exhibiting diplomatic flexibility on the Spratly Islands disputes. Even if competition for natural resources were not a salient issue, as it is in the South China Sea case, sovereignty is often a sufficient condition for countries to assume intractable positions and to take actions that increase the risk of armed conflict.

*Fishing resources*. Another prominent factor underlying the Spratly Islands disputes is the growing competition for maritime resources, particularly fishing resources.[7] The rich fishing grounds of the South China Sea offer an indispensable source of food and protein for many Asian nations, as well as providing an important source of employment and substantial foreign exchange earnings.[8] But the long-term productivity of the South China Sea is declining under the combined pressures of overfishing, coral reef damage, and growing coastal pollution. Hence the competing national governments are particularly sensitive to incursions by foreign vessels into the rich fishing grounds that they claim for their own use and that they perceive as a limited resource. The scramble for such potentially valuable maritime resources is exacerbated by how some countries interpret the United Nations Convention on the Law of the Sea (UNCLOS) to support their national claims for an Exclusive Economic Zone (EEZ) extending out to 200 nautical miles based on continuously occupying key locations among the Spratly Islands.[9]

*Hydrocarbon potential*. The South China Sea has been touted for years as potentially rich in both oil and natural gas resources. Although the suspected deposits are mostly located outside the Spratlys area, the competition over access to these hydrocarbon regions has spilled over to the Spratly Islands. Despite years of active exploration for oil deposits and limited offshore drilling operations, the extent of the oil reserve, particularly oil that is economically recoverable, remains highly uncertain. In fact, a 2000 assessment by the U.S. Energy Information Administration notes that despite the continuing speculation that the South China Sea region contains extensive oil resources, there are no proven oil reserve estimates for the Spratly or Paracel Islands because of the absence of exploratory drilling.[10]

In comparison, natural gas could be the more abundant hydrocarbon resource in the South China Sea, and could be more economical to recover. China and Malaysia are already developing their offshore fields for natural gas production, and Indonesia has begun developing the large Natuna gas field located in the southern region of the South China Sea.[11] Although great uncertainty surrounds the extent and accessibility of hydrocarbon resources in the South China Sea, and particularly in the vicinity of the Spratly Islands, the claimant states are nevertheless quick to view energy exploration and recovery operations by other states as provocative challenges to their sovereignty claims.

*Security concerns*. Another important consideration for several of the countries is national security. China's expansive claims to the South China Sea appear partially rooted in its naval strategy, which extends its power projection capabilities well beyond its coastal regions. In comparison, the Philippines, Vietnam, and Indonesia have viewed Chinese claims to South China Sea waters relatively closer to their countries as an unacceptable challenge to their national security. Such littoral states see the control of some portion of the Spratly Islands as integral to their national security.

And even countries besides the territorial disputants—other East Asian countries, such as Japan and Thailand—have strong concerns over the vulnerability of

Table 9

**Spratly Islands Occupations by Various Countries**

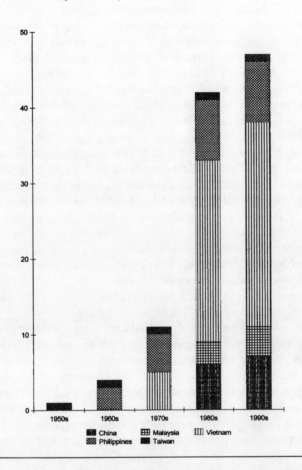

the vital sea-lines of communication (SLOC) being disrupted by deliberate military action or inadvertent conflict arising over the Spratly Islands. Such countries heavily depend on the flow of energy, mineral resources, and food supplies that routinely transit through the South China Sea.[12] The sea-lanes also provide passage for both merchant and naval ships of many other nations, including the United States, which has made it clear to the claimants to the Spratly Islands that they must be careful to respect freedom of navigation in the South China Sea. Hence a military clash among the claimants for the Spratly Islands and the surrounding waters could escalate the local conflict by driving other countries to take steps to protect the sea-lanes from being disrupted.

## Nature of the Conflict

The drive to stake out sovereignty claims has encouraged the various claimant countries to establish outposts—mostly manned by military personnel—throughout the Spratly Islands. The number of permanently occupied locations has sporadically grown over the past five decades (Table 9) as one country and then another staked out its territorial and maritime claims to the Spratly Islands. The initial postwar occupation began in the mid-1950s, but the pace did not actually accelerate until the 1970s, when several countries began creating outposts among the Spratlys.[13] The number of occupied locations more than tripled during the 1980s as Vietnam, China, Malaysia, and the Philippines all expanded their holdings on the Spratly Islands. Even though the pace of occupations largely declined in the 1990s, Chinese activities at Mischief Reef have attracted international attention.

Recurring incidents highlight the potential conflict risk associated with coercive diplomacy and even military conflict among the various claimants to the Spratly Islands. Experts have identified some of the potential triggers that could fuel conflicts among various countries over the Spratly Islands.[14] They include:

- *Creeping Occupation*. Each claimant has pursued a policy of "effective occupation" of key islands and reefs among the Spratly Islands to reinforce their sovereignty claims. In some cases this has entailed constructing outposts, such as the Chinese facilities at Mischief Reef, upon maritime features because land was unavailable.
- *Exploration or Exploitation Activity*. Unilateral steps to explore or exploit the hydrocarbon resources of the South China Sea can also be a major catalyst for conflict because such actions directly raise the sovereignty issue. China has been quite sensitive to the efforts of other claimants, such as Vietnam and the Philippines, to grant oil and natural gas concessions to commercial firms.
- *Aggressive Patrolling*. A more routine source of incidents in the South China Sea involves aggressive maritime patrols using naval ships and military aircraft, which increase the risk that an incident at sea will escalate into an armed clash between territorial claimants.[15] These incidents usually involve one claimant seizing another country's fishing boats and detaining the crews to demonstrate a willingness to enforce its maritime claims.
- *Armed Displacement*. The claimants could resort to military force to press their territorial claims even though the likelihood of armed conflict is normally not very high given the serious diplomatic consequences of fighting and the limited capabilities of claimants to project their military power. However, some instances of military intimidation have already occurred in the South China Sea. The most serious military clash took place in early 1988 when China displaced Vietnam from Fiery Cross Reef. Chinese warships attacked and sank three of Vietnam's vessels, with the loss of some seventy Vietnamese lives. Chinese forces now occupy this location.[16]

## The 1995 Mischief Reef Incident

The potential risk of conflict is best illustrated by the continuing dispute between China and the Philippines over Mischief Reef, an aptly named reef less than 200 nautical miles from the Philippine coastline that falls within the EEZ claimed by Manila. The conflict potential between the Philippines and China substantially increased in early 1995, when Chinese ships arrived with construction personnel and built several octagonal structures on stilts at various locations on the reef. Beijing declared these shelters were for Chinese fishing boats operating in the area. However, Manila viewed the alleged "fishermen structures" as Beijing's effort to advance its territorial and maritime claims to the Spratly Islands, and made strong verbal protests against China's bold action. Beijing appears to have been somewhat surprised that its actions at Mischief Reef galvanized its smaller neighbors in ASEAN to take an united stand vis-à-vis China as the most appropriate strategy to finding a diplomatic solution to the Spratly Islands problem. Along with bringing the Spratly Islands dispute to world attention, ASEAN reaffirmed its 1992 Declaration on the South China Sea, which endorsed a peaceful resolution of all sovereignty and jurisdictional disputes.

At the same time, American officials declared in May 1995 that the United States had "an abiding interest in the maintenance of peace and stability in the South China Sea," and declared that maintaining "freedom of navigation is a fundamental interest of the United States." In addition to urging the claimants to the Spratlys to exercise restraint and to avoid destabilizing actions, the U.S. policy statement also declared:

> The U.S. takes no position on the legal merits of the competing claims to sovereignty over the various islands, reefs, atolls, and cays in the South China Sea. The United States would, however, view with serious concern any maritime claim, or restriction on maritime activity in the South China Sea that was not consistent with international law including the 1982 United Nations Convention on the Law of the Sea.[17]

Thus the United States has carefully avoided taking any sides in the Spratly Islands claims to date. Beyond reaffirming the U.S. unwillingness to abide by any restrictions on the principle of freedom of navigation on the seas, and calling for a peaceful resolution of the competing claims, Washington has traditionally opted for a low-profile position on the South China Sea disputes to avoid becoming directly involved in these complicated, multinational disagreements.[18]

## Mischief Reef II Incident, 1998–1999

After several years of relative calm, the risk of conflict over the disputed Spratly Islands significantly increased again in late 1998. In what could be called the Mischief Reef II incident, the Philippines and China have engaged in a major diplomatic dispute over a sudden move by Beijing in late 1998 involving a major expansion of its facilities at Mischief Reef.

This potentially serious incident occurred in November 1998 when a group of seven Chinese naval and support ships arrived at Mischief Reef with a large construction crew, which proceeded with a substantial upgrade of the earlier modest octagonal "fishermen structures" into much larger concrete buildings. Chinese officials declared that this renovation is needed to sustain the deteriorating structures against weather damage. However, Manila has charged China with undertaking a creeping invasion of its sovereign territory. Philippine officials charge that Beijing is pursuing a "talk and take" strategy aimed at consolidating its political and military position in the South China Sea. Tensions between the two countries were fueled through early 1999 by a series of developments, including heated rhetoric, increasingly close aerial overflights of the Chinese construction activities undertaken by the Philippines, and two separate incidents at sea where the Philippine navy chased down and sank Chinese fishing boats that Manila claimed were illegally operating in the waters of its EEZ.[19]

At the same time, efforts to defuse the Spratly dispute between Manila and Beijing through talks have been inconclusive, as China reasserted its indisputable sovereignty over the Spratly Islands, which it calls the Nansha Islands. The Philippines have repeatedly rejected Beijing's offers for joint use by fishermen of the Mischief Reef facilities because of Manila's concern that any such agreement would be a tacit admission of the legitimacy of China's claims to the Spratlys. Similarly, Manila has unsuccessfully attempted to increase its diplomatic leverage over China by internationalizing the dispute by seeking support from the United Nations, ASEAN, and even the Asia-Europe Meeting (ASEM) talks. Beijing has adamantly opposed any effort to address its disputes with the various ASEAN countries at any multilateral forum. It prefers bilateral discussions, where it enjoys relatively greater leverage compared with any ASEAN country.

In comparison, Manila has been somewhat more successful in gaining bilateral support for its position from certain countries, such as Thailand, which is concerned about the risk of conflict in the South China Sea. Manila also made major progress in rejuvenating its security relationship with the United States by finally receiving legislative approval of the Visiting Forces Agreement (VFA) with the United States in May 1999. Washington had made passage of the VFA a precondition for reinstitution of a strong military-to-military relationship with the Philippines, which includes joint military training and exercises. Manila is also looking for help from Washington in substantially modernizing its outdated and weak military forces.[20] But U.S. officials made clear that the U.S.–Philippines security relationship does not extend to Manila's claims on the Spratlys.

Nonetheless, there is some indication at the time of this writing that the volatile developments in the South China Sea are beginning to attract greater diplomatic attention among the ASEAN countries in the wake of the Mischief Reef II incident and as the worst of the Asian financial crisis appears to be over. For example, at the

ASEAN Regional Forum (ARF) session in Singapore in late July 1999, U.S. Secretary of State Madeleine Albright took advantage of the opportunity to call on all members of this forum to help break the cycle of growing regional tensions over the South China Sea rather than to sit on the sidelines. Against the protests of the Chinese representative, the ARF proceeded to discuss the growing tensions in the South China Sea.

## Means for Encouraging Conflict Avoidance

Both formal institutions and informal or "track two" dialogues have been central to regional efforts to manage the South China Sea disputes.[21] China's growing power creates a complex challenge for the various members of ASEAN. These smaller countries are concerned with avoiding conflict over the Spratly Islands disputes even though claimants, such as Vietnam, Malaysia, and the Philippines, are unwilling to accept China's expansive claims to the South China Sea.

The ASEAN countries look to multinational venues for dealing with China on the contentious Spratly Islands issue. In particular, many count on the ARF, a large multilateral forum for consultations among countries with interests in Asia-Pacific security issues, to engage China on ways to defuse tensions over the Spratly Islands and to explore possible confidence-building measures. The potential leverage offered by the ASEAN countries standing together in dealing with China on South China Sea issues was highlighted in the August 1995 meeting of the ARF, which occurred in the wake of the Mischief Reef I showdown between China and the Philippines. The meeting was successful in that Chinese officials offered pledges to respect the right of safe passage and freedom of navigation through the South China Sea.[22] Several proposals for joint exploitation of the maritime resources associated with the Spratly Islands have been offered, but progress is usually stymied by the underlying sovereignty issues at stake.[23] Until recently, however, the focus of the ASEAN and ARF meetings has been on more pressing regional issues, including the security implications of the Asian financial crisis, security developments on the Korean Peninsula, and nuclear proliferation in South Asia.

A "track two" process that sustains a dialogue on difficult security issues, including Spratly Islands issues, has been operating in parallel with the more formal governmental discussions for some time now. A key venue for this dialogue has been the "Workshops on Managing Potential Conflict in the South China Sea," which were initiated in 1990 by Indonesia and actively supported by Canada.[24] This process has produced a series of technical working groups that focus on issues of common concern to the states bordering the South China Sea, such as "Marine Scientific Research," and "Resource Assessment."[25] Another important forum for "track two" discussions among regional experts is the Council for Security Cooperation in the Asia Pacific (CSCAP), which fosters an exchange of views among experts concerned with regional security issues problems, including the South China Sea disputes.

Nonetheless, little direct progress has occurred in resolving the territorial disputes in the South China Sea, despite continual official and nongovernmental efforts. This situation suggests that new alternatives need to be considered. One possibility is to make greater use of improving information technologies, including commercial observation satellites, to enhance regional transparency as an interim measure for mitigating the risk of armed conflict in the South China Sea arising over miscalculations by the countries with competing claims to the Spratlys.

A new generation of commercial observation satellites is beginning to become operational that features major improvements over the earlier civilian observation satellites, such as Landsat and SPOT. These satellites offer improved resolution and greater timeliness in collecting satellite images and disseminating the imagery data to users. They create new opportunities for all countries and even nongovernmental organizations to obtain nonmilitary satellite imagery with sufficient resolution to observe politically significant activities among the disputed Spratly Islands.[26] This advance will facilitate the development of a cooperative monitoring regime that could enhance regional stability and transparency in the South China Sea by giving the littoral countries a less provocative means for monitoring developments in the Spratly Islands that can provide a basis for data sharing and discussion.

**Implications for U.S. Policy**

Even a limited military conflict in the South China Sea could have detrimental consequences not only for the disputants, but also for other Asian countries, such as Japan and Singapore. As noted earlier, a regional conflict arising over the Spratly Islands could disrupt the critical sea-lanes of communication that pass through the South China Sea. Furthermore, a serious confrontation involving China might create a political stumbling block for regional economic cooperation at a time when Beijing is making an important contribution to sustaining the financial stability of East Asia.

A military confrontation between China and one or more of the ASEAN nations, such as the Philippines, would place the United States in a problematical position. Official U.S. policy can be described as one of "active neutrality," because while avoiding any position on the legal merits of the various sovereignty claims in the South China Sea, Washington consistently urges the countries involved to find peaceful means for resolving their disagreements. But outside of encouraging the work of the ARF and the Indonesian-sponsored "track two" workshops, American officials are particularly circumspect in discussing what diplomatic or military role the United States might assume in a regional conflict sparked by the Spratly Islands disputes.

Nonetheless, a serious military clash involving China and an ASEAN nation, such as the Philippines, could pose a policymaking dilemma for U.S. officials. On the one hand, if the United States exhibits no show of military force, then it might appear to be acquiescing in China's use of military force to resolve the territorial disputes surrounding the Spratly Islands. On the other hand, U.S. military deployments or active support for an ASEAN country would likely have major spillover effects on U.S. diplomatic and trade relations with China. Hence, to avoid this policy dilemma Washington has a strong interest in supporting efforts that seek to avoid or contain potential regional conflicts arising from the Spratly Islands disputes.

The resurgent risk of armed conflict over the Spratly Islands is all the more dangerous because its routine nature conceals an underlying unpredictability. For the most part, this territorial dispute is characterized by diplomatic exchanges, as well as by occasional provocative actions, such as fishing ship incursions or oil explorations in the disputed areas by one claimant that stimulate another one to make a strong diplomatic response or even a show of force. However, some events in the Spratly Islands have escalated into more serious showdowns, including the use of deadly force, such as the 1988 clash between China and Vietnam.

Hence, the cyclical pattern of conflict in the South China Sea dispute is manifested in continuing low-level incidents punctuated by sporadic flare-ups among the disputants that occasionally involve the use of force. The possibility of a regional conflict arising from military miscalculations by one or more sides in a territorial dispute, such as occurred in the Falklands war between Argentina and the United Kingdom, cannot be completely ruled out given the continuing diplomatic deadlock to resolve the South China Sea disagreements. The United States and other countries concerned with the risks of a military conflict erupting over the disputed Spratly Islands therefore need to be proactively involved in pressing the claimant countries to explore ways to mitigate the risk of armed conflict while pursuing long-term ways of addressing the underlying diplomatic and economic sources of the Spratly Islands disputes.

## Notes

1. Although there exists a continuing risk of armed conflict over the Spratly Islands, it is worth noting that other regions of the South China Sea have been flashpoints for conflict at different times. Perhaps the most well known is the Paracels, a small group of islands in the northern region of the South China Sea, which received international attention when Chinese troops occupied them in early 1974 after forcibly ousting their South Vietnamese garrisons. The clash over the Paracels appears to offer certain similarities to the Spratly Islands disputes in terms of conflicting territorial claims, energy interests at stake, and the potential for military confrontation. For background, see Marwyn S. Samuels, *Contest for the South China Sea* (New York: Methuen, 1982), pp. 98–103.

2. Daniel J. Dzurek, *The Spratly Islands Dispute: Who's On First?* Maritime Briefing, vol. 2 (Durham, UK: University of Durham, International Boundaries Research Unit, Department of Geography, 1996), pp. 1–3. Identifying particular locations can be a problem because each of the territorial claimants has its own names for many of the key features among the Spratlys. For example, China and Taiwan call this area the Nansha Islands or Archipelago, while Manila calls the portion of the Spratly Islands that it claims Kalayaan or "Freedomland." For purposes of convenience, this chapter uses the traditional English names. For a comparison of names used by different claimants for the same disputed locations, see the table contained in Dzurek, *The Spratly Islands Dispute*, pp. 56–57.

3. Brunei has made a maritime claim that extends into the Spratly Islands area. However, its position is somewhat ambiguous and Brunei does not have troops or personnel occupying any of the Spratly Islands features as of this writing. Bradford L. Thomas and Daniel J. Dzurek, "The Spratly Islands Dispute," *Geopolitics and International Boundaries*, 1 (Winter 1996), p. 306.

4. Scott Snyder, *The South China Sea Disputes: Prospects for Preventive Diplomacy, A Special Report of the United States Institute of Peace* (Washington, DC: United States Institute of Peace, August 1996), p. 5.

5. Vietnam reportedly sent troops to seize two additional submerged reefs in the Spratly Islands (probably Orleana Shoal and Kingston Shoal on Rifleman Bank) in September 1998 and Malaysia constructed new facilities at Investigator Shoal in June 1999. These actions could increase the number of occupied locations in the Spratly Islands in Table 8 to about forty-eight.

6. For detailed assessments of the conflicting claims to the Spratly Islands and the waters surrounding them, see Bob Catley and Makmur Keliat, *Spratlys: The Dispute in the South China Sea* (Aldershot, UK: Ashgate, 1997), pp. 24–110; Thomas and Dzurek, "The Spratly Islands Dispute," pp. 302–310; and Christopher C. Joyner, "The Spratly Islands Dispute in the South China Sea: Problems, Policies, and Prospects for Diplomatic Accommodation," in Ranjeet K. Singh, ed., *Investigating Confidence-Building Measures in the Asia-Pacific Region* (Washington, D.C.: The Henry L. Stimson Center, May 14, 1999).

7. See Mark J. Valencia, *China and the South China Sea Disputes*, Adelphi Paper 298 (London: International Institute for Strategic Studies (IISS), 1995), pp. 8–11 ; and Catley and Keliat, *Spratlys: The Dispute in the South China Sea*, pp. 44–65.

8. Alan Dupont, *The Environment and Security in Pacific Asia* (London: IISS, June 1998), Adelphi Paper 319, pp. 50–54.

9. For discussions on how the Law of the Sea Convention has influenced the competing claims for the Spratly Islands, see Thomas and Dzurek, "The Spratly Islands Dispute," pp. 307–310; and Lee G. Cordner, "The Spratly Islands Dispute and the Law of the Sea," *Ocean Development and International Law* 25 (January–March 1994), pp. 61–74.

10. See the website of the United States Energy Information Administration, "South China Sea Region," January 2000 (at http://www.eia.doe.gov/emeu/cabs/schina.html); and also see Erik Kreil, Paul F. Hueper, John H. Noer, and David Gregory, "Energy in the South China Sea," *Geopolitics of Energy* (Washington, DC, July 1997), pp. 2–6.

11. Ibid.

12. John H. Noer with David Gregory, *Chokepoints: Maritime Economic Concerns in Southeast Asia* (Washington, DC: National Defense University Press, 1996), pp. 7–22.

13. Several islands were initially occupied by South Vietnamese forces in the early 1970s and then displaced by troops sent by Hanoi. Dzurek, *The Spratly Islands Dispute: Who's On First?* pp. 20–21.

14. This listing is mainly drawn from Ralph A. Cossa, "Summary and Recommendations," in Carolina G. Hernandez and Ralph Cossa, eds., *Security Implications of Conflict in the South China Sea: Perspectives from Asia-Pacific* (Quezon City, Philippines: Institute for Strategic Development Studies, Inc., and Pacific Forum/CSIS, 1997), pp. 221–222; and Scott Snyder, "Preventing Escalation of Disputes in the South China Sea: An American Perspective," draft paper prepared for "Promoting Trust and Confidence in Southeast Asia: Cooperation and Conflict Avoidance," co-sponsored by the Institute of Strategic and Development Studies, University of the Philippines, and CSIS/Pacific Forum, Manila (October 16–18, 1997).

15. A good example of this aggressive patrolling occurred in May 1997 when a boatload of amateur radio hobbyists from various nations, which sailed out of a Chinese port to Scarborough Shoal, landed on some small volcanic rocks located in the Philippine's declared EEZ in the northern portion of the South China Sea to conduct some broadcasts. They were overflown by military reconnaissance aircraft and later challenged by four Phil-

ippine naval gunboats because of Manila's concern that their activities gave credence to China's territorial claims. Shortly afterward, a boatload of Philippine legislators traveled to Scarborough Shoal to make a show of planting the Philippine flag, and subsequently the Philippine navy detained some Chinese fishermen who were operating near the shoal. Andrew Sherry and Rigoberto Tiglao, "Law of the Seize," *Far Eastern Economic Review*, June 12, 1997, pp. 17, 20–21.

16. Valencia, *China and the South China Sea Disputes*, pp. 8–13.

17. This U.S. policy statement is reprinted in Carolina G. Hernandez and Ralph Cossa, eds., *Security Implications of Conflict in the South China Sea: Perspectives from Asia-Pacific* (Quezon City, Philippines: Institute for Strategic and Development Studies, 1997), pp. 252–253.

18. An example of this cautious policy approach is the almost complete lack of discussion of U.S. concerns over developments in the South China Sea in the most recent Department of Defense (DOD) strategy report on the Asia-Pacific region. See *The United States Security Strategy for the East Asia–Pacific Region* (Washington, DC: Department of Defense, 1998).

19. "China, Philippines: A Clash at Sea," *New York Times*, May 26, 1999.

20. Ian Storey, "Manila Looks to USA for Help over Spratlys," *Jane's Intelligence Review*, 11 (August 1999), pp. 46–50.

21. Joyner, "The Spratly Islands Dispute in the South China Sea: Problems, Policies, and Prospects for Diplomatic Accommodation."

22. Snyder, *The South China Sea Disputes: Prospects for Preventive Diplomacy*, p. 14.

23. Valencia, *China and the South China Sea Disputes*.

24. Snyder, *The South China Sea Disputes: Prospects for Preventive Diplomacy*, p. 9.

25. Catley and Keliat, *Spratlys: The Dispute in the South China Sea*, pp. 152–153.

26. John C. Baker and David G. Wiencek, "Sat-Images Could Be Spratlys' Salvation," *Jane's Intelligence Review* 11 (February 1999), pp. 50–54.

## Suggested Readings

Baker, John C., and David G. Wiencek, eds. *Cooperative Monitoring for the South China Sea: Using Satellite Imagery to Mitigate the Spratly Islands Dispute*. Praeger Publishers, 2001 forthcoming.

Cossa, Ralph A. *Security Implications of Conflict in the South China Sea: Exploring Potential Triggers of Conflict*. Honolulu: Pacific Forum Special Report, March 1998.

Djalal, Hasjim and Ian Townsend-Gault. "Managing Potential Conflicts in the South China Sea: Informal Diplomacy for Conflict Prevention," in Chester A. Crocker, et al., eds., *Herding Cats: Multiparty Mediation in a Complex World*. Washington, DC: USIP, 1999: 107–33.

Dzurek, Daniel J. *The Spratly Islands Dispute: Who's on First?* Durham, UK: University of Durham, International Boundaries Research Unit, Department of Geography, 1996, Maritime Briefing. Vol. 2.

Snyder, Scott. *The South China Sea Disputes: Prospects for Preventive Diplomacy, A Special Report of the United States Institute of Peace*. Washington, DC: United States Institute of Peace (USIP), August 1996.

Thomas, Bradford L., and Daniel J. Dzurek, "The Spratly Islands Dispute." *Geopolitics and International Boundaries* 1 (Winter 1996): 300–26.

Valencia, Mark J. *China and the South China Sea Disputes*. London: International Institute for Strategic Studies, 1995. Adelphi Paper 298.

# Part III

## Security-Oriented Country Profiles

# 9

# Australia

*Bruce Vaughn and Sean M. McDonald*

## Introduction

This chapter focuses on Australia's evolving strategic posture in the Asia-Pacific region, primarily since March 1996 when the Liberal Howard government assumed power after thirteen years of Labor Party rule under Prime Ministers Hawke and Keating. Specifically, the chapter seeks to address the following three key questions:

1. In what direction has the Howard government taken Australian defense policy?
2. Is the Howard government's defense policy well suited to address Australia's security needs in the rapidly changing geopolitical environment of the Asia-Pacific region?
3. Do the Howard government's policy initiatives represent continuity or departure for Australian defense policy?

To address the first question, four specific points from the Howard government's first term are examined. First, the Sydney Declaration of July 1996 was issued at the conclusion of the 1996 Australia–United States Ministerial (AUSMIN) talks, at which the Howard government sought to reinvigorate the U.S. alliance (a campaign pledge) and to place this important alliance more firmly within an Asia-Pacific regional context. Second, the 1997 Defence Efficiency Review and the Defence Reform Program sought to streamline defense to free significant resources for other defense-related purposes. Third, the August 1997 publication of the first Department of Foreign Affairs and Trade (DFAT) White Paper on Australia's foreign and trade policy entitled *In the National Interest* affirmed (yet again) that

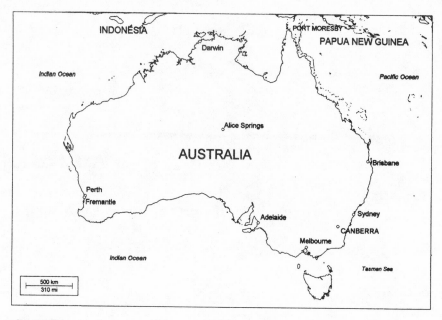

## Australia

Australia need not choose between its history and geography. This not only recognized the economic importance to Australia of the United States and its Asian trading partners but, for the first time, explicitly linked trade policy with defense and national security. Fourth, the December 1997 publication of *Australia's Strategic Policy* outlined the Liberal government's defense policy on forward cooperation. While the previous Labor government had emphasized continental defense through protection of the northern sea/air gap approaches to Australia, the new strategic review returned to a modified policy of forward defense, now called forward cooperation.

The second point of inquiry asks the question of whether or not the Howard government's defense policy is well suited to address Australia's security needs in the rapidly changing geopolitical environment of the Asia-Pacific region. Australia has been adjusting its strategic relationships to better structure its defense posture to the evolving post–Cold War correlates of power in the Asia Pacific. The 1997 strategic review emphasizes the centrality of the Asia-Pacific region as a whole to Australia's security. The importance of new power relations between China, Japan, and the United States are similarly emphasized. The "unique place" that Indonesia occupies in shaping Australia's strategic environment is also recognized. Regional stability will be increasingly important to Australia's economy as well as to national defense policies.[1] The results of these recent adjustments include a proper focus on the defense of Australia that is coupled with constructive engagement with Australia's neighbors, as well as renewed emphasis on the American alliance.[2] The full extent to which the recent financial and economic crisis in Southeast and East Asia will result in increased political instability and potential security concerns remains to be seen. The ongoing crisis in Indonesia has the potential to affect Australia directly should the economic and political situation deteriorate further. Australia's security interests could be affected should internal destabilization in Indonesia produce an outflow of refugees or inhibit Indonesia's ability to protect its interests in the South China Sea. *Australia's Strategic Policy* defines Australia's basic strategic interests and objectives as follows:

1. Help avoid destabilizing strategic competition between the region's major powers.
2. Help prevent the emergence in the Asia-Pacific region of a security environment dominated by any power(s) whose strategic interests would likely be inimical to those of Australia.
3. Help maintain a benign security environment in Southeast Asia, especially in maritime Southeast Asia, which safeguards the territorial integrity of all countries in the region.
4. Help prevent the positioning in neighboring states by any foreign power of military forces that might be used to attack Australia.
5. Help prevent the proliferation of weapons of mass destruction in the region.

This strategic review will be examined to determine whether it clearly and accurately identifies the current threats to Australia and addresses them in an appropriate fashion.

The third and final question addressed is whether or not these policy initiatives, including the strategic review, represent continuity or departure for Australian defense policy. We conclude that the Howard government's defense policy initiatives are not a radical departure but a logical continuation of previous policies taking into account the new regional and global realities.

### Strengthening Australia's American Connections

The U.S. alliance remains Australia's "most important strategic relationship." Further, Australia perceives "America's continued defense presence in the Asia Pacific as fundamental to regional stability." These Australian defense policy statements have had a significant impact on the relationship.[3] It is also Australian policy to encourage "other countries to support the United States presence."[4]

In March 1997, 21,500 American and 5,700 Australian troops along with 43 ships and 252 aircraft participated in Operation Tandem Thrust 1997 in Australia.[5] This exercise, Australia's largest joint military operation with a foreign force in recent times, was the most visible manifestation of the importance placed on the relationship by the Howard government. The need for increased emphasis on the bilateral relationship with the United States was articulated by the Liberal/

National Party Coalition during the 1996 election campaign, when it made improved relations with the United States a plank in its party platform. Joint exercises with the United States continue to be a regular feature of the bilateral relationship. In addition to other regular exercises with the United States,[6] Australia was also one of the first to support the United States during the 1998 buildup of tensions with Iraq. Australia deployed RAAF 707 refueling aircraft, support crews, and special Air Service Regiment personnel on February 17, 1998.[7]

The Howard government began to implement its campaign promise in July 1996 at the AUSMIN meeting. This meeting marked the first time since the end of the Cold War that leading American defense and foreign policy officials had traveled to Australia. This meeting served to formalize Australian initiatives to strengthen what was already a robust Australia–United States defense relationship. U.S. Secretary of State Christopher, Secretary of Defense Perry, Chairman of the Joint Chiefs of Staff General Shalikashvili, and Commander of the Pacific Fleet Admiral Prueher met with Australian Prime Minister Howard, Defence Minister McLachlan, and Foreign Minister Downer on July 26–27, 1996, to hold the annual AUSMIN talks. What resulted was a reaffirmation of a very close defense and intelligence relationship. Further, at the time of the AUSMIN talks, it was anticipated that President Clinton would travel to Australia to give his personal seal of approval to the strengthened relationship between the two countries.

President Clinton's visit was the fourth U.S. presidential trip to Australia and was a major milestone in the bilateral relationship.[8] He had been preceded by President Lyndon Johnson's two visits, which had inspired Australian Prime Minister Harold Holt to state that he was "all the way with LBJ," and one by President George Bush to Prime Minister Bob Hawke. The atmosphere surrounding these visits demonstrates a maturing of the relationship. While Holt has been described as "sycophantic"[9] for his remarks and Prime Minister Hawke's almost automatic commitment of Australian forces to the Gulf War was questioned, on this most recent occasion it was the Australian-led initiative that raised Australia's position in the eyes of Washington at a time of growing geostrategic uncertainty in the region. This coincides with popular perception in America. With a 77 percent approval rate, the average American views Australia as America's third best ally after Canada and Great Britain.[10]

In a rare speech to a joint sitting of both houses of Parliament, President Clinton emphasized the importance of the relationship by using the visit to make the first key foreign policy speech of his second term, in which he stressed "stronger alliances, deeper engagement with China, and a larger community of democracies."[11] Within this rubric he reemphasized America's commitment to "about 100,000 troops across the Pacific." He went so far as to describe the Australia–New Zealand–United States (ANZUS) alliance as one "not just for this time, but for all time."

The 1996 AUSMIN, President Clinton's visit and Tandem Thrust 97 all clearly demonstrated the Howard government's commitment to improving Australia's strategic partnership with the United States. The renewal of this relationship did not happen within a geopolitical vacuum. Various constituencies in Asia and Australia were left wondering how a renewed relationship with the United States would modify previous policy positions. Asian states wondered how this squared with the previous Keating government's emphasis on Australia's place in Asia, while Australian defense academics began to question how the policy would be reconciled with Australia's defense policy of self-reliance. Most ominously, China took umbrage at the idea and viewed it as further evidence that the United States was positioning itself to "contain" Beijing. From the Chinese perspective, Australia and Japan were the two key pincers of an American strategy aimed at containing China.

The Howard government continued to improve its bilateral relationship with America at the October 1997 AUSMIN meeting in Washington, DC. The new American team, Secretary of State Albright and Secretary of Defense Cohen, met with Australian Defence Minister McLachlan and Foreign Minister Downer on October 9, 1997—a meeting that produced an agreement outlined in a 10-page joint communiqué.[12] The United States renewed its commitment to maintain 100,000 troops in the Asia-Pacific region and agreed to help Australia with the development of its high-tech military operations, which are in line with the new "revolution in military affairs" being pursued in both countries.[13] This will enable U.S. and Australian troops to work in close cooperation in the future. Additionally, the United States eased Australian fears by stressing the importance of maintaining a sound relationship with Indonesia.[14]

The 1998 AUSMIN talks built on the progress made during the previous two AUSMINs. AUSMIN 98 covered regional security issues such as the Asian financial crisis, developments in Indonesia, the nuclear weapons tests by India and Pakistan, and Iraq's compliance with UN Security Council resolutions. AUSMIN 98 also included agreement to further develop the interoperability of U.S. and Australian forces. As the United States increasingly integrates revolutionary technologies into its armed forces there is an increasing fear that it will be unable to operate with less technologically advanced allies. While this is a potential problem area, Australia is focusing on it more than many other states. Within this context an understanding was reached on technology sharing (in areas such as submarines, airborne early warning and control, and combat aircraft) that will improve the defense forces capacity to contribute to coalition operations.[15]

### Defense and Security Framework

These recent developments need to be understood within the historical context of Australian defense policy. Self-reliance was never meant to be self-sufficiency. From its inception self-reliance embodied a relative emphasis rather than an absolute ideal. While Australian self-sufficiency in defense industry expenditures has increased over the past decade, thus bringing Australia closer to the ideal of self-sufficiency, it was always considered unlikely that Australia would ever become totally independent of the world's arms bazaar, in which America is Australia's primary supplier.

Table 10

**Australian Defence Force's Capital Equipment Expenditure
in Australia and Overseas**

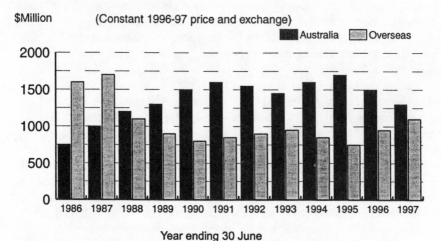

$Million        (Constant 1996-97 price and exchange)

■ Australia    ▨ Overseas

**Year ending 30 June**
*Updated by IPD Domestic Capital Equipment and US IPD/GNP and exchange

*Source: Defense Annual Report 1996/1997* (Canberra: Australian Government Publishing Service, 1997), p. 291

Table 10 lists the Australian Defence Force's (ADF's) capital equipment expenditure in Australia and overseas.[16] The 1998–99 Defense Budget of almost A$11 billion is approximately 2 percent of Australia's gross domestic product (GDP). Also of note is that 85 percent of logistics and 50 percent of capital equipment expenditures in the 1998–99 Defense Budget is sourced in Australia.[17] The total size of the regular defense force will be 50,000, with 65 percent of this number in combat and related positions.[18]

The use of Australia for U.S. military training, and for the prepositioning of military equipment, is potentially a controversial area of defense cooperation. An element of the Australian populace takes the position that with the end of the Cold War there is less reason to become entangled in America's affairs. To this segment of the population, any notion of creating new bases, at a time when they see less of a rationale for such, would likely stir up controversy in the press.[19] Australian Defence Minister Ian McLachlan stated that "The [U.S.] Marines have felt, since they lost their bases in the Philippines, that they haven't got the range of training facilities as they would like and they see the north of Australia as giving them a greater variety of training arrangements, and we agree."[20]

The role that the alliance with the United States plays in Australian defense has received greater attention as a result of the change from Labor to Liberal government in 1996. Australian initiatives, settled on at the AUSMIN talks in July 1996, are seeking to strengthen Australia's defense ties with the United States by emphasizing "robust defence forces capable of a high degree of interoperability."[21] Joint military exercises are an integral part of developing interoperability. In its focus on interoperability Australia is more farsighted than many of America's friends and allies. Future viable coalition warfare will depend on nations' abilities to operate in an interoperable fashion. General Charles Krulak, U.S. Marine Corp Commandant, had proposed using an Australian port for the prepositioning of U.S. military equipment. This proposal followed the unsuccessful attempt in 1994 to gain approval for prepositioning from Thailand.[22] The media also reported that the United States approached the Philippines and Vietnam.

In the near future the United States "plans to significantly boost the amount of equipment it has prepositioned in areas of potential conflict, particularly the Persian Gulf region and South Korea. . . . [T]he Army plans to more than double the square footage of cargo it prepositions afloat by the end of the decade."[23] To implement this the Navy is buying eight large medium-speed roll-on/roll-off vessels. While the United States has made the decision to preposition more equipment afloat it also recognizes the difficulties associated with finding anchorage for the ships.

One problem with augmenting U.S. prepositioning ships is the limited number of places where the Department of Defense (DOD) can put them. Much of today's current and planned fleet would be based at Diego Garcia, in the Indian Ocean. The number of unused anchorages there is dwindling, however, especially since ships that contain ammunition cannot be placed as closely together as other ships.[24]

For some time the United States has had three squadrons of prepositioned ships, including five ships at Diego Garcia, four at Guam in the Pacific, and four in the Mediterranean. In late 1996 a fourth prepositioning squadron of five ships was established in the Arabian Gulf.[25] Each squadron can provide all the equipment and supplies necessary to support a Marine Corps Air Ground Task Force of about 17,300 troops for thirty days. The United States had expressed interest in placing further stores between Diego Garcia and Guam but publicly rejected the Australian offer because it believes that Australia would be too far removed.[26]

The prepositioning issue is another example of the desire of the Howard government to put substance into its rhetoric on reinvigorating the alliance. Indeed, the prepositioning proposal had been part of the Coalition's election platform. The Howard government's initiative on prepositioning was viewed by the Australian press as a means to "lock in" a continued American presence in the Asia-Pacific region.[27] Further, prepositioning is part of Washington's "places not bases" concept, which seeks to minimize the political liabilities of basing large numbers of American troops abroad.

The Australian training grounds are a welcome addition for the United States at a time when it has had to reduce its operating room in Japan. In reaffirming their security alliance on April 17, 1996, the United States agreed to return 20 percent of the space used by the 47,000 American troops currently stationed in Japan and to restrict live fire artillery drills.[28] These reductions were initiated in the wake of public outcry over the rape of a Japanese schoolgirl by U.S. armed service personnel. Similar concerns about the conduct of U.S. personnel have been raised in Australia. Labor Senator Margaret Reynolds called for the inclusion of a special code of conduct agreement to cover U.S. military personnel while training in Australia and stated that, "Unfortunately U.S. troops have a record of violations against women."[29] Australian public opinion toward American military operations in Australia could deteriorate should American access to facilities in Australia come to be viewed as tantamount to Australia becoming an American "base."

**Joint Defense Facilities**

The Joint Defence Facilities at Pine Gap, Nurrungar, and North West Cape have been key components of the U.S.-Australian defense and intelligence relationship. Their relevance continues even as technology and priorities change. The shift from Cold War priorities to those more closely associated with regional contingencies and rogue states has maintained the importance of the facilities. The facilities have adapted to these new realities while remaining important to both the United States and Australia.

The Joint Defence Space Research Facility at Pine Gap, near Alice Springs in the Northern Territory, opened in 1969. Australia developed, with U.S. assistance, the Jindalee Over the Horizon Radar (OHR) located at Alice Springs, which can detect over-the-horizon targets out to 3,000 kilometers.[30] After falling three years behind, Telstra pulled out of the project in February 1997. Day-to-day management of Jindalee was taken over by Transfield and Lockheed Martin corporations at that time.[31] Project DUNDEE (Down Under Early-Warning Experiment) utilizes Jindalee as part of a joint U.S.-Australian experiment to detect ballistic missile launches.[32] A ten-year extension of the Pine Gap Treaty was signed in June 1998.[33]

The Harold Holt Naval Communications Station at North West Cape, opened in 1967, was an integral component for communications with the U.S. undersea nuclear submarine fleet. The station has a Very Low Frequency (VLF) transmitter, which enables it to communicate with submarines.[34] Technological innovation has reduced its value to the United States. The station will allow communications with Australia's *Collins* class submarines. In 1974 it became a joint U.S.-Australian facility. In 1991 arrangements were made for its transfer to Australian control by 1999.

The Joint Defence Space Communications Station at Nurrungar, near Woomera in South Australia, was opened in 1971 and has played a key role in ballistic missile early warning as part of the Defense Support Program (DSP). Australia's value as an alliance partner was demonstrated during Operation Desert Shield/Desert Storm when Patriot missile batteries relied on the Nurrungar facility for DSP cueing data to engage Iraqi Scud ballistic missile launches.[35] It was also reported that Washington was considering using Woomera as a weapons testing and training ground. Australian

Minister for Industry Olsen stated that, "Given the U.S. defence force is no longer welcome in the Philippines and difficulties are appearing in Japan, we would argue that Australia and Woomera are logical bases."[36] Following the July 1996 AUSMIN, it was announced that the facilities at Nurrungar will be closed by 2000 after a new relay ground station is co-located at the Joint Defence Facility at Pine Gap. This new facility will accommodate the Space Based Infra-Red System (SBIRS), which is the follow-on system to DSP.[37] The new Pine Gap facility will continue to handle DSP ground relay as the new SBIRS program comes on line.

Given current U.S. budgetary constraints, and growing concern with ballistic missile defense, it is likely that this new relay facility will be of importance to the United States for some years to come. The Gulf War and the continued proliferation and development of ballistic missiles by rogue states have led the United States to be increasingly concerned with both Theater Missile Defense (TMD) and National Missile Defense (NMD). This places continued emphasis on early warning systems, which are crucial to both TMD and NMD systems. The proliferation of Chinese and North Korean ballistic missiles could rapidly expand regional capabilities should regional states come to have a desire to possess such missiles.

Proposals for ballistic missile defenses in Asia have kept pace with the mounting threat, and Australia's role in the Defense Support Program continues to give it a role in the early warning aspect of such defenses. A month after the North Koreans test fired a No Dong missile into the Sea of Japan, the United States and Japan began considering developing a TMD system for Japan. As part of this, the Pentagon agreed to supply Japan with early warning data from "Defence Support Program Satellites that detect infrared radiation at the time of the launch."[38] The Defence Science Technology Office is also engaged in the above-mentioned DUNDEE cooperative relationship with the U.S. Ballistic Missile Defense Organization (BMDO). Under the project, missile tests will be conducted to test the ability of the Alice Springs–based Jindalee Over the Horizon Radar Network's ability to detect ballistic missiles in the boost phase, the period immediately after launch.[39] While Australia is not presently threatened by ballistic missiles, the Defence Minister has stated that, "It is prudent that we acquire an understanding of ballistic missile technologies."[40]

Speaking at the Center for Strategic and International Studies in Washington on May 9, 1996, U.S. presidential candidate Bob Dole, in his first major foreign policy speech of the campaign, spoke of the need for a "Pacific Democracy Defense Program" that would defend "people and territory from Aleutians to Australia."[41] In the lead-up to the 1996 AUSMIN talks Defence Minister McLachlan acknowledged speaking to Republicans about presidential candidate Dole's East Asian missile defense proposal.[42] While the possibility of a ballistic missile attack against Australia is at present low, ballistic missile proliferation could lead to the emergence of such a threat in a relatively short period of time. For this reason a degree of familiarity with ballistic missile defense is a prudent precautionary measure despite the lack of a present threat specifically to Australia.

Another arena of increased U.S.-Australian cooperation is in the private sector. The United States and Australia's private defense firms, Lockheed Martin and Transfield, have formed a joint venture to bid for defense contracts in Australia and Southeast Asia.[43] This further facilitates important acquisition linkages between the United States and Australia.

The efforts of the Howard government have had a positive impact in Washington. Admiral Prueher, Commander in Chief United States Pacific Command, described Australia as "a critical ally and a traditional friend that shares our values, interests, and world view. Australia's participation in combined exercises, operation of joint defense facilities, and granting of access to U.S. ships and aircraft is absolutely essential to our forward presence."[44] House International Relations Asia-Pacific Affairs subcommittee Chairman Doug Bereuter has similarly remarked that, "The previous Australian government was very friendly and very cooperative in every way. But they [the Coalition government] have gone out of their way to suggest [they] are looking for a more enhanced relationship, which we can only welcome."[45]

The Coalition government's initiatives have done much to dispel several misconceptions that have clouded American perceptions of Australia. Former Prime Minister Keating's efforts to forge closer relations with Asia muddled American perceptions of Australia. Many in the United States viewed this as an effort to move away from the United States and the West. Further, many in the United States failed to make a distinction between New Zealand's nuclear policy and that of Australia. While domestic support for defense ties with the United States is declining in Japan and Korea, it has recently received a boost in Australia.[46] In 1996, 88 percent of Australians believed that ANZUS was important to Australia's security. In 1993 only 77 percent agreed.[47]

## U.S.-Australian Relations' Effect on Sino-Australian Relations

The decision to reemphasize the U.S. security connection was not well received by China. China took the view that enhancement of the relationship was further evidence that the United States was seeking to "contain," or encircle, rather than "engage" China. As a result, the Chinese press attacked Australia after the July announcement of the joint U.S. and Australian exercise Tandem Thrust 97. This attack was part of an orchestrated attempt by the Chinese to undermine the U.S. position in the Asia-Pacific region. This Chinese maneuver may eventually place Australia in a difficult predicament, as it could be caught between a rising Asian power and its North American ally. To reduce the chance of this happening Australia has sought to enhance its relationship with China, as demonstrated by the Australian and Chinese defense ministers' talks in Canberra on February 18, 1998.[48] Recent Sino-U.S. summitry has also lessened tensions, which should help alleviate Chinese concerns over Australian-U.S. ties.[49]

One can understand how the Chinese could view Tandem Thrust 97 as a threat. The types of maneuvers practiced during Tandem Thrust 97 included amphibious landing and airborne assault in the Shoalwater Bay area of Queensland in the North of Australia. Such power projection exercises, while intended to practice counteroffensive measures, could be threatening to the Chinese. Conversely, they may have been used by the Chinese as a pretext for criticizing a continued American presence in the region.

While Defence Minister McLachlan has described China as an "assertive" power, he has also stated, at the time of President Clinton's 1997 visit to Australia, that he was "strongly committed to building links with China."[50] This view of China, which perceives the necessity of seeking a working relationship while also being concerned about the consequences should that effort fail, is consistent with evolving discourse on China in the United States. Defence Minister McLachlan held talks with China's Minister for National Defense General Chi Haotian in Canberra on February 18, 1998. They agreed to further meetings at the defense minister level and to enhance dialogue on strategic developments.[51]

## The Indonesian Agreement

For Australia, the Australia–Indonesia Agreement on Maintaining Security, signed in December 1995, is second in importance only to the ANZUS Treaty. The agreement formalizes and institutionalizes relations with Australia's most significant neighbor. Indonesia is the world's fourth most populated nation (with a population of 202 million, as compared to Australia's 18 million), which until the crisis of 1997 had enjoyed annual economic growth rates of 7 percent. Despite recent economic problems, Indonesia is the significant strategic player in Southeast Asia and Australia's closest neighbor.

The signing of the agreement marked a major achievement given the history of relations between the two countries. Australian forces, as part of the British Commonwealth Far East Strategic Reserve, fought against Indonesian forces on Borneo during Indonesia's Konfrontasi (confrontation policy) with the Federation of Malaysia between 1962 and 1966. In 1964 the Menzies government pledged Canberra bombers and Saber fighters to Operation Addington, which would have conducted extensive bombing raids over Indonesia had Indonesia escalated the conflict,[52] in which Indonesian President Sukarno had sought to "destabilize and ultimately destroy" Malaysia. The conflict ended with the signing of a peace treaty between Indonesia and Malaysia in Bangkok in 1966.[53]

As a result of this initial confrontation, Australia alternately viewed Indonesia as a relatively benign neighbor and as a potential threat until the mid-1980s. Following the initial Konfrontasi period, the Gorton government took the position, in 1969, that Australia faced no immediate or obvious threat. By 1971, the Strategic Basis Paper sought to articulate a "uniquely Australian Strategic perspective," which viewed threats to Australia as either emanating from or transiting through the Indonesian archipelago.[54] By the mid-1970s the perceived imperative for positive security relations with Indonesia tempered Australia's response to the East Timor crisis of 1975. By 1976, the Strategic Assessment Paper stated that, "A major threat would be beyond Indonesia's own capability. . . ." The lingering perception that Indonesia could be the source of a threat to Australia can be seen in the 1983 Strategic Basis Paper, which asserted that Australia's enduring strategic interest was to "avoid significant Indonesian attack against, or foreign occupation of Papua New Guinea," which was implicitly tantamount to a threat against Australia itself.[55] It was not until Paul Dibb's *Review of Australia's Defence Capabilities* in 1986 that Indonesia itself was no longer identified as a potential threat to Australia. This perspective was later codified in the 1987 document *The Defence of Australia,* where Indonesia was viewed as "a protective barrier to Australia's northern approaches. . . ."[56] This relatively benign view of Indonesia's strategic posture continues.

The 1995 Australia–Indonesia Agreement on Maintaining Security is a significant departure from the past. Now Indonesia is viewed by Australia more, if not entirely, as an ally than as a potential adversary. The agreement contains three key clauses. They are as follows:

1. regular ministerial consultations about matters affecting mutual security;
2. consultations in the face of adverse challenges to either country;
3. promotion of cooperative activities in the security field.[57]

The "adverse challenges" language is ambiguous and has led to some speculation as to its meaning. The vagueness of the phrase indicates the representation of a more holistic view of security that is not limited to traditional security concerns. The Australia–Indonesia Agreement on Maintaining Security has dramatically changed the tone of the relationship between these two countries, as well as Australia's relationship with the region as a whole. Defense ties have acted as a key link between Australia and Indonesia that has led to a well-rounded and robust relationship.[58]

While both Australia and Indonesia have avoided mentioning China as a factor behind the December 1995 agreement, many security analysts feel that the specter of an emergent China was a major impetus for the agreement. The agreement also demonstrates that both Australia and Indonesia have "accepted a holistic definition of security where external military attack is but one of a number of possible security challenges on which Australia and Indonesia would consult."[59] Indonesia's concern over China's actions in the South China Sea has led Jakarta to send a significant message to China through its military exercises near Indonesia's natural gas fields, where over 40 percent of Indonesia's natural gas reserves are to be found.[60]

Critically, Australia's initiative to seek an agreement with Indonesia demonstrates that Australia was, within the context of self-reliance during the Keating government, looking to secure its interests within its immediate region of security through bilateral agreements and cooperative understandings. In doing so, Australia refined its rhetoric about being a member of the region while also maintaining its ability to continue, and indeed strengthen, its ties to the United States and the

West. Further, Australia's role in acting as "the southern anchor"[61] for continued American presence in the region is appreciated by other regional states who, for domestic political reasons, are not in a position to be outspoken in their support for continued American presence in the Asia-Pacific region. The possible exception to this is Singapore.[62]

By securing the agreement, Australia has initiated an institutional framework that should help insulate Australian-Indonesian relations from the vagaries of political transition. Recent events have highlighted the foresight of achieving such an agreement; however, these events have the potential to pose serious problems for Australia and the entire region. The potential destabilization of this strategically vital country has serious potential ramifications for Australia's strategic policy.

## Relations with Asia

Australia does not view the development of its relations with Asia in zero sum terms. Relations with both Asia and America can be strengthened at the same time and the Howard government has sought to do just that. Prime Minister Howard stated that "We do not have to choose between Asia and the U.S.; we do not have to choose between our history and geography." That said, the dramatic increase in Australian trade with the region has made Australia more cognizant of Asia. In 1995 more than 60 percent of Australian exports went to Asia, while 11 percent went to the European Union and only 7 percent went to the United States.[63] It would not be out of place to ask if, in the eyes of others, increased relations with the United States were not incompatible with regional engagement. Based on public rhetoric, China, and to some extent Malaysia, would like to make Australia rethink its ties with the United States.

## Impact of Domestic Politics

The strategic debate is wedded to shifts in Australian identity. The former Keating government's call for making Australia a republic by 2000 (to coincide with the opening of the Olympic Games) did much (too much in the eyes of the current government) to push the notion that Australia was an independent nation and a part of Asia. Less than 5 percent of Australia's eighteen million people are of Asian descent. This debate has been focused on whether or not to abolish Australia's monarchical ties to Britain. At present the English Crown at least nominally appoints the Australian head of state. The nation is split roughly evenly on the issue.[64] Should the Republicans win out over the monarchists it would do much in the eyes of Australia's neighbors to further establish Australia's independent credentials and in turn its ability to come closer to its Southeast Asian neighbors.

The race/identity debate sparked by MP Pauline Hanson, who questions the level of Asian immigration into Australia, put forward the old Australian fear of being "swamped" by Asians.[65] While the Hanson debate began as a race and immigration debate it broadened to ask whether Australia's destiny is with the rising nations of Asia or whether it remains with Australia's traditional ties to Europe and America. The Liberal Party's reemphasis on Australia's American security connection, as juxtaposed with the former Keating government's emphasis on Australia's economic and geographic ties with Asia, further complicates the issue in the eyes of Australia's Asian neighbors.[66] This has been compounded by the Howard government's early reluctance to denounce Hanson and her policies. It had been thought that Hanson and her One Nation Party were waning in popularity until One Nation received 23 percent of the vote in the Queensland regional elections of June 1998. At that time One Nation's popularity was estimated at 13 percent. Despite the strong showing in Queensland, One Nation failed to win a seat in the October 1998 national elections.[67]

Immigration is a key issue both for defining Australian identity and for its impact with Australia's neighbors. Australia's immigration has declined in recent decades from 1.1 million per year during the 1980s to 0.39 million per year during the period 1990–1996. Of that total, 39.9 percent of immigrants in 1995–1996 were of Asian origin. A November 1996 poll asked Australians, "Should the proportion of Asian immigrants be reduced?" Some 53 percent responded "Yes," while 62 percent said that they supported a short-term freeze on immigration.[68]

## Other External Linkages

With the Indonesian Agreement, Australia has roughly completed a complex web of alliances, agreements, and bilateral defense relations with the states of its region of strategic importance. Australia continues to maintain security linkages with Malaysia and Singapore through the Five-Power Defence Arrangement (FPDA) of 1971, with Papua New Guinea (PNG) through the 1987 Joint Declaration of Principle, and with the ASEAN states through the ASEAN Regional Forum (ARF) and through the Council for Security Cooperation in the Asia Pacific (CSCAP). A high level of bilateral and multilateral exercises has Australian Armed Forces train or exercise with Southeast Asian forces once every ten days.[69]

In 1971, Australia entered into the FPDA with Malaysia, Singapore, the United Kingdom, and New Zealand. This loose framework's original intent was to provide a basis for the immediate consultation on a course of action should either Malaysia or Singapore be threatened with attack. Until 1988 Australia had based two squadrons of Mirage aircraft at Butterworth Airbase in Malaysia. Australia also has a defense agreement with PNG, which has come under scrutiny as a result of PNG's conflict with secessionists in Bougainville.[70] In 1998, Australian troops served alongside New Zealand, Fijian, and Vanuatu counterparts as part of the multinational Truce Monitoring Group in Bougainville.[71] In a December 2, 1997, statement, Minister for Defence McLachlan went further when he identified "working with neighbours to strengthen their security, thereby preventing the intrusion of foreign military forces which might attack Australia" as a strategic policy fundamental for Australia.[72]

Australia continues to maintain a close relationship with New Zealand, with which it shares close cultural and historical ties. The lingering tensions between New Zealand and the United States based on New Zealand's decision to bar U.S. nuclear warships from New Zealand's ports have complicated relations within ANZUS. Australia's partnership with New Zealand is founded on the Australia–New Zealand Agreement (ANZAC) spirit and finds its formal expression in the Canberra Pact and the ANZUS Treaty. The current relationship is further enhanced by the guiding principles that are part of the Closer Defence Relations (CDR) Accord, which affirms Australia's and New Zealand's defense and security partnership for the long term.[73] Despite such statements, Australia remains troubled by the low level of New Zealand's defense spending.

Australia and New Zealand are gradually increasing the number of joint defense acquisitions, though Australia still argues that New Zealand should commit more financial resources to defense. Joint procurement and development projects are covered by the 1991 CDR Accord. The two countries are presently procuring Steyr F-88 rifles, L-118 105-mm light guns, and the *ANZAC* class frigates. Discussions for the joint procurement of *ANZAC* maritime helicopters and new C-130J Hercules transports are also under way.[74] The joint procurement program increases interoperability between the two nations' armed forces, and promotes cost savings through economies of scale.

Australia's traditional role in the Southwest Pacific has focused on aid, nuclear policy, and resource management. Australia continues to maintain[75] and develop a "partnership with Pacific Island countries which promotes regional stability through economic development and the encouragement of shared perception of strategic and security interest."[76] With A$450 million in annual aid Australia is the Pacific's largest aid donor.

Among the recent initiatives, which continue to maintain Australia's partnership with the region, is Australia's Patrol Boat Program. Australia has provided twenty patrol boats to eleven different Pacific states to assist them in enforcing offshore fishing regulations. The effectiveness of the program has been enhanced through the sharing of information between states through a maritime surveillance communication network.

Australian economic and security interests in Northeast Asia, when coupled with its more traditional interests in Southeast Asia, have led Australia to focus more attention to the north and to view the Asia-Pacific region as a single strategic system. This perspective on the Asia-Pacific region differs somewhat from the American academic and policy perspective, which views Asia more often through the separate sub-regions of East Asia, Southeast Asia, South Asia, and Australasia or Oceania. The notable exception to this is Commander-in-Chief, Pacific (CINCPAC); this American command covers the entire Asia-Pacific region.

Australia's increased emphasis on Northeast Asia is demonstrated by its recent overtures to Japan and China. In a September 9, 1997, speech at the National Defense Academy in Yokosuka, Australian Defence Minister McLachlan spoke on

Australian and Japanese efforts to broaden dialogue in the security area. After pointing out that both states share close security linkages with the United States, Defence Minister McLachlan highlighted that they both have the common objectives of promoting cooperative relations with China and promoting peace and stability in the region. Defence Minister McLachlan also discussed the August 1997 Australia–Japan Ministerial Committee's "Partnership Agenda," which recognized the importance of expanding bilateral security and defence dialogue between the two states. As part of the "Partnership Agenda," Japan and Australia agreed to more frequent contacts at both the ministerial and senior official level and to develop closer contact in the peacekeeping and intelligence areas.[77]

Since coming to office the Howard government has initiated annual security talks with Japan and South Korea.[78] These are to strengthen the relationship and supplement Australia's other regional security talks with states in its more immediate sphere of strategic interest. In this way the security relationship with Japan and Korea is following the increased economic importance of these two countries to Australia. The Republic of Korea is second only to Japan as a destination for Australian exports and the two combined account for 40 percent of Australian exports.[79] On the military side of the equation, technological developments such as new North Korean long-range ballistic missiles add to Australia's interest in the security dynamics of Northeast Asia.[80] Further, Australia realizes that the dynamics of the United States' relationship with Japan are of the utmost importance for maintaining a robust American presence in the region. Should that relationship diminish, the future of America's military presence in the Asia-Pacific as a whole would be tenuous.

A reduction in American commitment would have broad geopolitical implications for Australia and the region. Indeed, the mere debate has had the effect of influencing states' perceptions, and hence planning, for future contingencies. Australia and other regional states increasingly feel they must be individually or collectively self-reliant to be prepared for a future security environment where a robust American presence may be less than assured. Australia needs to watch events carefully, both within the domestic political milieu of the United States and within the Asia-Pacific region, so that it will not be caught unprepared by a reduction of American forces from the region even if such an eventuality is unlikely in the foreseeable future. It is also in Australia's interest to keep America engaged in Asia. An American withdrawal from Asia, when coupled with a rising China, would likely lead to the remilitarization of Japan and an increasingly destabilized security environment.

## Commitment to Multilateral Forums

Australia is firmly committed to supporting various multilateral forums as it seeks to secure its foreign trade and security interests. The ARF, while still in its evolutionary phase, has promise as an emerging regional security forum for consideration and discussion of regional security concerns. The ARF facilitates security discussion and confidence building among its members. Should a threat to the region emerge, it could also act as a starting point for joint discussion of how to deal with the threat. Further, its basis in the region gives it increased legitimacy for its member states. The inability of the regional multilateral forums to address problems stemming from the Asian financial crisis is a cause for concern and demonstrates their still-limited abilities.

Peacekeeping offers training and development benefits for the ADF, while allowing Australia to contribute to the United Nations and other multinational peacekeeping efforts. Financial constraints limit the resources available for peacekeeping. That said, peacekeeping provides Australia with an opportunity to be a good international citizen. Peacekeeping also allows Australia to make a positive contribution to peace and stability in its region, as demonstrated by its participation in peacekeeping activities in Cambodia, Bougainville, and, most recently, in East Timor. (However, the full ramifications of how the 1999 East Timor deployment will affect Australia's engagement with the region are, at the time of this writing, unclear.) Given its limited resources and geographic location, Australia would be well advised to focus its peacekeeping efforts within the Asia-Pacific region where its greater knowledge and experience will provide maximum effect.

## Rearticulation of Australia's Strategic Posture

The Howard government's emphasis on improving the American alliance is in part a shift away from the policy of self-reliance, as articulated in the 1987 Defence White Paper, which followed on the Dibb Report of 1986. Further, the Howard government's shift in policy emphasis did raise questions that warranted review of the 1994 Defence White Paper. The emphasis on self-reliance remained in place at the time of the writing of the 1994 Defence White Paper.[81] As mentioned above, the Howard government's new strategic policy is one of forward cooperation.[82] While self-reliance will remain an integral part of Australia's defense posture, it will be adapted to operate in tandem with renewed emphasis on forward cooperation, coalition warfare, and the need for interoperability with American forces.[83] The need to focus on interoperability with the United States will be driven by the revolution in military affairs, which will make effective coalition warfare dependent on extensive prior joint training. The American Alliance, which has been central to Australian security since the signing of the ANZUS Security Treaty in 1952, will remain critical to Australia's defensive strategies.

The Howard government's strategic review of Australia's defense posture was commissioned to provide a strategic architecture to guide Australian defense planning. Rear Admiral Don Chalmers led the review. While the previous Labor government had emphasized continental defense through protection of the northern sea/air gap approaches to Australia, the new strategic review returned to a modified policy of forward defense, now called forward cooperation. According to Chalmers, the area of future Australian military operation is "further to the north than the sea air gap." The review has been described as a "Northeast Asian centric" report[84] and differs from previous reviews in four ways:

1. The review describes a maritime strategy for defending Australia.
2. It moves beyond low-level contingencies to focus on the capacity to defend Australia in a wide range of circumstances.
3. It links Australian territorial defense with wider regional security.
4. It details vigorous priorities for force development and equipment acquisition.[85]

Such a reorientation of Australian defense policy will have an impact on Australia's procurement decisions. For example, Australia may seek to augment its F-111 strike capability by acquiring cruise missiles for its *Collins* class submarines, and extensive multi-billion-dollar upgrades for the seventy-one FA-18 fighters and the surface fleet.[86]

At the same time that the strategy and efficiency reviews were examining the direction and functioning of the Department of Defence, the Howard government undertook the task of writing Australia's first Foreign Affairs white paper. Evidently the draft of the white paper produced in February of 1997 by a 16-member panel did not satisfy Foreign Affairs Minister Downer. He apparently viewed the document as displaying too much of the previous Labor government's penchant for internationalist foreign policy and not enough hard realism. In Mr. Downer's words, "The dominant reality continues to be the state. And the paradigm upon which conflict is most generally founded is State versus State. National interests continue to be the basis for regional affairs...."[87] The final version of the white paper on Australia's Foreign and Trade Policy, *In the National Interest*, emphasizes the primary importance of the United States, Japan, China, and Indonesia, as well as the emerging importance to Australia of India and South Korea. This is consistent with Australia's increasing focus on the Asia-Pacific region and the Indian Ocean in terms of both defense and trade.[88]

The downturn in the Asian-Pacific economies as a result of the Asian financial crisis and the decision by India and Pakistan to become declared nuclear states has changed the geopolitical and geoeconomic landscape significantly in the short months since the DFAT white paper was published. While there is general agreement that the current Asian financial/economic crisis has the potential to develop politico-security dimensions, to what extent is currently unclear. As a result, the implications for Australia's security are uncertain. Some of the most likely security scenarios that could affect Australia include:

1. The Indonesian economy collapses and/or further persecution of the Chinese Indonesians leads to a significant refugee problem.

2. Weakened regional economies lead to significantly reduced arms purchases by regional states. This could have a dampening affect on any potential interstate conflict in the region. It would also allow Australia to continue its qualitative military advantage within the region. (During the 1980s Australia's defense budget equaled defense spending of all of the ASEAN states. Prior to the financial crisis it was thought that more than one Southeast Asian state could spend more on defense than Australia.)[89]
3. Weakened regional states find themselves unable to counter pressure from China in the South China Sea. (With a 40 percent reduction in its currency, the Philippines has had to postpone its defense modernization plans, which were in part a response to China's actions on Mischief Reef.)[90]
4. Regimes threatened by the financial crisis resort to nationalistic rhetoric and the demonization of outside forces to focus popular frustration away from their regime. This could lead to increased tension between regional states.

Defence Minister McLachlan noted that "a militarily capable Southeast Asia is a strategic asset for us because if our neighbours can defend themselves they deter external or internal trouble-makers." Defence Minister McLachlan also observed that "improved military capabilities within the region—especially in the event of a deterioration of stability—make for a more demanding operating environment for the ADF."[91]

### Military Structure

These efforts to strengthen Australia's external relations have been matched by a strong commitment to maintain a solid defense posture at home. Australia has maintained its commitment to defense even in an atmosphere of budget restraint. As part of his plan to revamp the army, Defence Minister McLachlan has proposed the acquisition of new attack and troop lift helicopters, new armored troop carriers, and enhanced command and control units. The Royal Australian Navy's *Collins* class subs and ANZAC class frigates mark Australia's commitment to maintaining and updating its naval capabilities. The Royal Australian Air Force is also looking to acquire airborne early warning aircraft. Additionally, Australia has signaled its willingness to consider joining the U.S.-led Joint Strike Fighter (JSF) development program and may sign up for official observer status by the end of 1998.[92] Currently the Macchi 339, the Hawk 100, and the McDonnell-Douglas T-44 are under consideration in the lead in fighter competition.

The maturing of Australia's defense relationships should be welcomed by both its neighbors and by the United States. The Indonesian agreement, and the augmentation of the American alliance, represent a further maturation of Australia's evolving security policy. Australia is increasingly an independent actor that is shaking the perception—still held by some Asians—that it is in some way a stalking horse for American interests in the region. The Indonesian agreement adds substance to Australia's claim that it is firmly grounded in the Asia-Pacific region. This will give Australia more credibility with its Asian neighbors, who may find Australian defense relations to be beneficial for training and other purposes in the years ahead. The strengthening of the American alliance will reinforce a critical strategic relationship for Australia while providing the United States with a welcome staunch ally in a region of strategic importance and increasing instability. An improved Australian-American relationship further ties the United States to the region at a time when many Southeast Asian states, while concerned with a growing China, feel unable to do more to keep the United States engaged in the region.

While placing renewed emphasis on Australia's ties with the United States at this time is a prudent policy for Australia, such emphasis needs to be done in a subtle and finessed manner. Indeed, there are indications that the U.S. Navy was concerned about the possibility of negative fallout prior to the initiation of Tandem Thrust 97. The U.S. Navy was initially concerned that the decision to exclude regional states from the exercise would strain relations with Malaysia and Indonesia. Further, it was pointed out in the media at the time that "neither the Australian nor the American governments have been able to mount a cogent argument about just what *Tandem Thrust* is supposed to achieve."[93] The lack of clearly articulated objectives, when combined with a decision to restrict transparency, after calling on the states of the region to increase theirs, and the use of the exercise to practice force projection type amphibious and airborne assault exercises opens the way for regional states to speculate about where Australia is headed in national security terms. Such ambiguities, when coupled with rising anti-Asian sentiment, as demonstrated by the increasing popularity of the One Nation Party, open the way for the possible deterioration of Australia's relations with its Asian neighbors. Without decisive leadership to allay Asian states' concerns, Australia's achievements in defense and foreign policy could be undermined.

## Conclusions

These recent defense and foreign policy initiatives have implications for the conceptual orientation of Australia's security posture. While the strengthening of the American alliance is not a return to the old policy of forward defense, it does have ramifications for Australia's defense policy of self-reliance. The Howard government's defense policy initiatives, specifically "forward cooperation," are a key component of Australia's new strategic posture.[94] Forward cooperation should provide Australia with the ability to defend its territory, protect its eastern and northern approaches, and be able to serve throughout the globe as part of a larger coalition.[95]

Forward cooperation is best understood as an extension of Australia's previous defense posture. It builds on the significant economic and defense linkages that Australia has developed with regional states during the previous Keating and Hawke governments, while also reinvigorating the bilateral relationship with the United

Table 11

**Australia's Defense Posture**

| Strategy | Force orientation |
|---|---|
| I.   Forward Defense/External Guarantee <br>     Great Britain <br>     The United States | Deploy out of area within allied structure <br>Boer War, WWI, WWII, Malaya, <br>Korea, Vietnam |
| II.   Self-Reliance/Defense in Depth <br>     Continental defense <br>     Multilateral participation <br>     Regional engagement <br>     Continuation of Alliance relationships | Increased independent operability <br>Northern repositioning of forces <br>Peacekeeping: Cambodia etc. <br>Defense training, ARF <br>Gulf War, intelligence sharing |
| III.   Forward Cooperation <br>     Self-defense <br>     Regional engagement <br>     Reemphasis on American alliance | Enhanced Alliance Participation <br>Force structure development <br>Regional defense relations, ARF <br>Develop interoperability to forward <br>deploy, intelligence sharing, increased <br>joint training, coalition with Southeast <br>Asia |

States. The Howard government's defense policy initiatives are not a radical departure but a logical continuation of previous policies, taking into account the new regional and global realities.

To sum up, Table 11 places Australia's current strategy of forward cooperation within the historical context of the evolution of Australia's strategic posture. The three key phases identified in the table mark Australia's progression from dependent colonial ally through its search for self-reliance to the present more balanced policy, which emphasizes regional security linkages and the American alliance, as well as territorial defense.

By simultaneously seeking to strengthen regional security linkages, the American alliance, and Australia's own defense capabilities, Australia should be better prepared to meet the uncertain challenges stemming from the changing correlates of power and the financial crisis in Asia.

### Notes

The authors would like to thank Pat Carroll, Counsellor for Defence Policy, The Embassy of Australia, Washington, DC, for his many insights, helpful criticisms, and suggestions. The views expressed in this chapter are those of the authors alone and do not necessarily reflect official policy.

1. Department of Defence, *Australia's Strategic Policy* (Canberra: Defence Publishing, 1997).

2. Department of Foreign Affairs and Trade (DFAT), *In the National Interest: Australia's Foreign and Trade Policy* (Canberra: National Capital Printing, 1997).

3. Office of the Minister for Defence, "Australia's Strategic Policy," ACDSS, Canberra, ACT, February 18, 1998.

4. The Hon. Ian McLachlan, Minister for Defence, "Defence Challenges and Australia's Changing Security Outlook," Parliament House, Canberra, ACT, June 18, 1998.

5. Chuck Downs, "Strategic Alliance for All Times," *Washington Times*, October 7, 1997.

6. Office of the Minister for Defence, "Australian Forces Join Pacific Rim Exercises off Hawaii," Parliament House, Canberra, ACT, June 21, 1998.

7. Office of the Minister for Defence, "Australian Defence Force Personnel to Be Withdrawn Soon," Parliament House, Canberra, ACT, June 2, 1998.

8. Wallace Brown, "Clinton Visit to Seal Pact," *Courier Mail*, August 2, 1996.

9. Lindsay Murdoch, "Mr. Howard, This Is America Calling," *The Age*, November 23, 1996.

10. Hans van Leeuwen, "Australia Ranked Third as U.S. Ally," *Financial Review*, November 28, 1996.

11. President Clinton, "Address of the President of the United States of America," *Hansard*, November 20, 1996.

12. Don Greenless, "Downer Delights as U.S. Backs Indonesian Ties," *The Australian*, October 10, 1997.

13. "Australia–United States Ministerial Consultations (AUSMIN): Joint Communiqué," Washington DC, October 10, 1997.

14. Greg Truman, "Australia and U.S. Link Arms for Future Wars," *The Age*, October 10, 1997.

15. Office of the Minister for Defence, "AUSMIN 98 Enhances Defence Cooperation." Parliament House, Canberra, ACT, July 31, 1998.

16. Resources and Financial Programs Division, *Defence Budget Brief 1995–1996* (Canberra: Australian Government Press, 1995).

17. The Hon. Ian McLachlan, Minister for Defence, "Defence and Australian Industry." Canberra, ACT, June 2, 1998.

18. Office of the Minister for Defence, "Combat Force Grows," Parliament House, Canberra, ACT, December 9, 1997.

19. M. Denbourough, "Time We Got Rid of U.S. Bases," *The Canberra Times*, February 16, 1997.

20. Graham Armstrong, "Pact to Strengthen Security Ties to U.S.," *The West Australian*, July 25, 1996.

21. "Australia–United States Ministerial Consultations (AUSMIN): Joint Communiqué," Canberra, July 27, 1996.

22. Barbara Opall, "Krulak Pursues Base Alternative," *Defense News*, June 10, 1996.

23. Congressional Budget Office, *Moving U.S. Forces: Options for Strategic Mobility* (Washington: U.S. Government Printing Office [GPO], 1997) pp. 33, 39.

24. Ibid., p. 39.

25. Military Sealift Command, "Afloat Prepositioning Force Fact Sheet," February 1997.

26. Michael Stutchbury, "Howard Pushes for Closer Security Ties," *Financial Review*, June 7, 1996.

27. Peter Wilson, "Marines Prepare to Storm Our Beaches," *The Australian*, June 27, 1996.

28. Warren Strobel, "U.S., Japan Reaffirm Their Security Pact," *The Washington Times*, April 17, 1996. Teresa Watanabe, "U.S., Japan Plan Return of Land to Okinawans," *Los Angeles Times*, April 15, 1996.

29. Ian McPhedran, "Senator Seeks Tight Rein on U.S. Military," *The Canberra Times*, July 19, 1996.

30. Craig Skenan, "Telstra Pulls Out of $800 in Defence Watch Project," *The Sydney Morning Herald*, February 13, 1997.

31. Sean Smith, "Jindalee 'Flawed,'" *Herald Sun*, August 30, 1997.

32. Minister for Defence, The Hon. Ian McLachlan MP, "Australia and the United States Cooperate in Missile Detection," Media Release, August 8, 1997.

33. Office of the Minister for Defence, "Ten Year Extension to Pine Gap Treaty," Parliament House, Canberra, ACT, June 4, 1998.

34. "North West Cape," Australian Government Document, 1992.

35. Senator Robert Ray, Minister for Defence, "News Release: The Role of the Joint Defence Facility Nurrungar in the Gulf War," November 5, 1991.

36. "U.S. Military Base Plan for Woomera," *Sunday Mail* (South Australia), August 11, 1996.

37. Office of the Minister of Defence, "Australian Cooperation with U.S. Early Missile Warning Program to Continue," Parliament House, Canberra ACT, July 6, 1996.

38. Naoaki Usui, "Pentagon to Supply Early-Warning Data to JDA," *Defense News*, June 10, 1996.

39. Ian McPhedran, "Four U.S. Rockets to Test Sensors," *The Canberra Times*, September 4, 1996.

40. Office of the Minister of Defence, "Australia and United States Cooperate in Missile Detection," Parliament House, Canberra ACT, August 8, 1997.

41. Senate Majority Leader Bob Dole, "America and Asia: Restoring U.S. Leadership in the Pacific," remarks prepared for delivery, Center for Strategic and International Studies Statesman's Forum, May 9, 1996. Nigel Holloway, "Asian Star Wars: Debate Heats Up Over East Asian Missile Defence," *Far Eastern Economic Review*, June 6, 1996, p. 20.

42. Armstrong, "Pact to Strengthen Security Ties to U.S.," *The West Australian*, July 25, 1996.

43. "Transfield, Lockheed to Form Joint Venture Firm," *The Canberra Times*, August 7, 1996.

44. Statement of Admiral Prueher, CINCPAC, before the United States Senate Armed Services Committee Posture Hearing, March 28, 1996.

45. Don Greenlees, "Howard Pushes for Stronger U.S. Ties," *The Australian*, June 7, 1996.

46. Only 7 percent of Japanese polled in 1995 wanted the American bases maintained as they are. Karlyn Bowman, *America and Japan: How We See Each Other and Ourselves* (Washington: American Enterprise Institute, 1996).

47. Malcohn Farr, "U.S. Spy Satellite Links to Expand," *The Daily Telegraph*, July 27, 1996.

48. Office of the Minister for Defence. "Australia–China Defence Ministers' Talks," Parliament House, Canberra ACT, February 19, 1998.

49. "Clinton and Jiang: Who Won?" *The Economist*, July 10, 1998.

50. Scott Emerson, "Enhanced U.S. Ties No Threat," *The Weekend Australian*, November 23, 1997.

51. Office of the Minister of Defence, "Australia-China Defence Ministers' Talks," Parliament House, Canberra ACT, February 19, 1998.

52. Michael Dynes, "Britain, Australia Were Ready to Bomb Indonesia in '64," *The Times of London*, February 10, 1995.

53. Peter Dennis et al. *The Oxford Companion to Australian Military History* (Melbourne: Oxford University Press Australia, 1995) pp. 171–73.

54. Allen Dupont, *Australia's Threat Perceptions: A Search for Security* (Canberra: Australian National University Press, 1991), pp. 67–68.

55. Ibid., pp. 84–85.

56. Kim Beazley, *The Defence of Australia* (Canberra: Australian Government Publishing Service, 1987).

57. Allen Dupont, "The Australia–Indonesia Security Agreement," *The Australian Quarterly*, Vol. 68, No. 2, 1996.

58. *In the National Interest: Australia's Foreign and Trade Policy* (Canberra, ACT: DFAT, 1997. p. 61.)

59. Allen Dupont, "The Australia–Indonesia Security Agreement."

60. Allen Dupont, "Why Beijing's Muscle-Flexing Frightens the Neighbours," *The Australian*, September 10, 1996.

61. These are the words used by U.S. Secretary of Defense Perry to describe Australia. Jaqueline Rees and Nigel Holloway, "Cold Comfort: New Australia–U.S. Security Pact Causes Waves," *The Far Eastern Economic Review*, August 8, 1996.

62. Foreign Minister Jayakumar, speech before the Asian Studies Program at Georgetown University.

63. "Australia's Engagement Rings," *The Economist*, June 22, 1996. See also Lotte Chow, "Queen or Country," *Far Eastern Economic Review*, February 20, 1997.

64. Fifty-five percent of Australians favor the Republic. "A National Identity Crisis," *The Economist*, December 14, 1997.

65. The 23 percent of the vote by Hanson's newly formed political party (One Nation) in the June 1998 Queensland election has refocused national and international attention on this debate.

66. These debates and the Howard government's views are examined by: Meg Gurry, "Whose History? The Struggle Over Authorship of Australia's Asia Policies," *Australian Journal of International Affairs*, Vol. 52, No. 1, 1998.

67. See Ross Peake's review of Paul Sheehan's *Among the Barbarians: The Dividing of Australia* (Sydney: Random House Press, 1998) in *Foreign Policy*, Summer 1999, pp. 125–28.

68. Kevin Sullivan, "Scare Crusade Pulls in Votes in Australia," *The Washington Post*, July 6, 1998.

69. "Australia's Engagement Rings," *The Economist*, June 22, 1996.

70. Henry Albinski, "Security in the South Pacific Region," in William M. Carpenter and David G. Wiencek, eds., *Asian Security Handbook: An Assessment of Political-Security Issues in the Asia Pacific Region* (Armonk, NY: M.E. Sharpe, 1996), p. 59.

71. Office of the Minister of Defence, "Aussie Truce Monitoring Troops Back from Bougainville," Parliament House, Canberra ACT, February 16, 1998.

72. The Hon. Ian McLachlan, "Australia's Strategic Policy," House of Representatives speech, Parliament House, Canberra ACT, December 2, 1997.

73. Office of the Minister of Defence, "Joint Statement on Future Directions in Closer Defence Relations (CDR)," Parliament House, Canberra ACT, March 27, 1998.

74. Gregor Furguson, "Australia, New Zealand Bolster Cooperative Acquisition Efforts," *Defence News*, July 15, 1996.

75. Lindsay Murdoch, "Win to Howard at Pacific Forum," *The Age*, September 5, 1996.

76. Senator Gareth Evans and Bruce Grant, *Australia's Foreign Relations in the World of the 1990s* (Melbourne; Melbourne University Press, 1991).

77. The Hon. Ian McLachlan, "Shared Interests: The Australian-Japanese Security Dialogue," address before the National Defense Academy, Yokosuka, Japan, September 9, 1998.

78. Robert Karinol, "Australia, USA Reinforce Ties With Joint Exercises," *Jane's Defence Weekly*, August 14, 1996.

79. Greg Sheridan, "Canberra Seeks Bigger Share of Action in North-East Asia," *The Australian*, August 15, 1996.

80. Eighteen thousand Australian soldiers fought in the Korean War of 1950–53.

81. Robert Ray, Minister for Defence, *Defending Australia*, Defence White Paper 1994, (Canberra: Australian Government Printing Service, 1994).

82. *Australia's Strategic Policy*, Australian Department of Defence, 1997.

83. *The Courier Mail* (Brisbane), "New Power in the U.S. Relationship," July 30, 1996.

84. Ian McPhedran, "Defence Thrust into North Asia," *The Canberra Times*, December 4, 1996.

85. The Hon. Ian McLachlan, Minister for Defence "Australia's Strategic Policy," ACDSS, Canberra, ACT, February 18, 1998.

86. Don Greenlees, "Defence Plans Big Boost in Firepower," *The Australian*, December 1, 1997.

87. Mr. Downer as quoted in G. Barker, "Downer Demands Policy of Realism," *Financial Review*, February 18, 1997.

88. *In the National Interest*, White Paper on Australia's Foreign and Trade Policy, 1997.

89. The Hon. Ian McLachlan, Minister for Defence, "Australia's Strategic Objectives," Australian Defence Studies Centre, Canberra, ACT, November 11, 1997.

90. Steven Watkins, "Philippines Will Freeze Modernization Program," *Defense News*, July 21, 1998.

91. The Hon. Ian McLachlan, Minister for Defence, "Australia's Strategic Objectives," Australian Defence Studies Centre, Canberra, ACT, November 11, 1997.

92. Gregor Ferguson, "Australia Weighs Observer Position in JSF Program," *Defense News*, June 15–21, 1998.

93. Ian McPhedran, "U.S. Bid to Avoid Forces Joining," *The Canberra Times*, March 10, 1997.

94. The Hon. Ian McLachlan, Minister for Defence, "Opening Address to the Australian Defence Studies Centre 10th Anniversary Conference," Canberra, ACT, 11 November 1997.

95. Ian McPhedran, "Downer's Sights on Regional Stability," *The Canberra Times*, December 2, 1997.

## Suggested Readings

Denis, Peter et al., eds. *The Oxford Companion to Australian Military History*. Melbourne: Oxford University Press, 1995.

Department of Defence. *Australia's Strategic Policy*. Canberra: Commonwealth of Australia, 1997.

Department of Foreign Affairs and Trade. *In the National Interest: Australia's Foreign and Trade Policy White Paper*. Canberra: Commonwealth of Australia, 1997.

Malik, J. Mohan. *Australia's Security in the 21st Century*. Sydney: Allen and Unwin Publishers, 1999.

# 10

# Burma

## Maureen Aung-Thwin

A military regime still rules Burma, also known as Myanmar, more than a decade after the army crushed a popular uprising for democracy. A political stalemate between tenacious soldiers and the civilian National League for Democracy (NLD), the opposition party that won a landslide election in 1990, continues to paralyze Burma. This stalemate frustrates the international community, which has tried both constructive engagement and isolation to pressure the military regime into dialogue with Burma's democrats. The Asian financial crisis that began in mid-1997 made matters even worse. The regime's "opening" of its controlled economy to foreign investment and free markets, for the first time since the army took over in 1962, was in name only. The bankrupt economy today is kept afloat largely by imported Chinese arms and consumer goods, coerced labor for infrastructure development, and investment capital from the nominally illegal narcotics industry. Basic freedoms are still denied the populace. Universities, perceived hotbeds of political dissidence, have been closed for most of a decade. Inflation and massive unemployment have driven over a million Burmese abroad in search of subsistence jobs. At home Burma confronts a growing population of drug addicts and an alarmingly high growth rate of citizens infected by the HIV-AIDS virus.

The insistence of the generals to maintain both economic and political control at apparently all costs makes Burma one of the most unpredictable and volatile nations in the region. A few generals may have begun to concur: moderate elements in the military power structure appear ready for some sort of compromise with the opposition—provided that it does not divide the unity of the armed forces or diminish their control.

The United States and other Western nations sharply criticize the Burmese regime. But there is a limit to how much diplomatic, economic, and other pressure can be exerted on a recalcitrant nation located halfway around the world from the

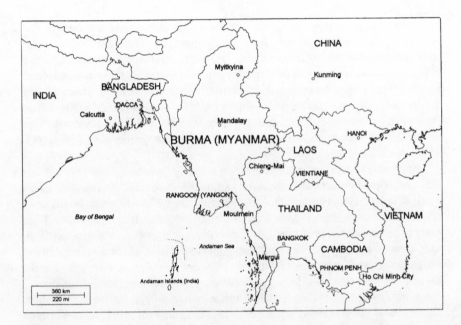

## Burma

critics. Lasting change in Burma will instead depend on her immediate neighbors and biggest trading partners, namely her colleagues in the Association of Southeast Asian Nations (ASEAN), and the region's richest country, Japan. These neighbors will have to help enlightened elements of the Burmese army negotiate a way to return Burma to the fold of rational nations.

### Political Framework

The regime has kept an iron grip on the country while professing to be searching for an ideal called "disciplined democracy." In practice, the current junta has devoted the years since it took over power in 1988 as the State Law and Order Restoration Council, or SLORC, to consolidating control of Burmese society, methodically eliminating all challenges to its authority.

Nominally at least, the regime has reached its first goal. There is almost no political, economic, or social space in Burma today that does not have an imprint of the military authorities or their close associates. On the surface the democratic opposition appears weakened, but eliminated it is not. Millions of Burmese (including members of the military) in the summer of 1988 joined the nationwide demonstrations to end the dictatorship. All these people have not changed their minds just because they have been silent.

With no free press and an intimidated populace, the pulse of the nation is difficult to take. Burma's many ailments preclude an easy prognosis for the health of its future. But history is clearly on the side of the democracy movement. The political transformations in such former authoritarian nations as Indonesia—the erstwhile model of the Burmese regime—no doubt serve as a cautionary tale. But Indonesia should really serve as a transition model, for the Burmese generals have borrowed much from their Jakarta counterparts on how to hang on to power; it is now time to learn how to let go—with a minimum of disruption. Ordinary Burmese citizens, after decades of isolation from the rest of the world and with very limited access to international media, finally feel that they are a part of the worldwide trend toward democracy.

The regime's main challenger, the NLD, is led by Daw Aung Suu Kyi, who has been part of the international community since she was a child. As daughter of the father of independent Burma, General Aung San, Daw Suu first went abroad when her widowed mother was made Burma's ambassador to India. Her subsequent years in other international cities, though condemned by the junta as a contaminant, have given her a deep understanding and experience of the meaning of freedom in a universal, national, and individual sense. The decade-long struggle she has led since her return to Burma in 1988 has slowly captured the imagination—and sympathy—of the silent Burmese majority and a large international public. The regime's campaign to disparage Daw Suu in official propaganda has only served to enhance her status: cobra, sexual pervert, and Western pawn are some of their tamer sobriquets for her.

The NLD has shown a remarkable ability not only to stay alive, but also to keep the legal and moral high ground under trying conditions. The military regime conjures up the most convenient weapons available to forward its agenda—be it threat of jail, force of arms, or manipulation of the legal system. For example, the generals conjure up a wide range of laws—from colonial British days to regulations created on the spot—to harass opponents and keep the people cowed. Somehow the NLD has managed to challenge authority overtly in Burma and survive, proving time and again that they are astute politicians as well as idealists. In 1998— still not allowed to convene as a parliament and tired of waiting—251 MPs from the NLD and other parties that won seats in the 1990 elections created a ten-member group, the Committee Representing the People's Parliament, or CRPP, to represent their interests. This move, more than any other display of defiance by the NLD, has clearly rattled the regime. The generals, even under their own peculiar interpretation of the law, are unable to figure out how to denounce the CRPP as illegal, so instead they have demanded its dissolution as a condition for dialogue.

There has been no shortage of volunteers, including representatives of the United Nations Secretary General, offering to broker dialogue and negotiations between the opposing parties in Burma. The generals say they prefer an indigenous solution to the deadlock. But they themselves do not always speak with one voice; the military is not as monolithic as it appears. For example, Burmese Foreign Minister U Win Aung, one of the regime's more articulate and sophisticated spokesmen, was asked at a private meeting in New York last year why his government's newspaper, the *New Light of Myanmar,* used such ludicrously crude and ultimately ineffective language to attack its enemies. He nodded, slightly embarrassed: "I know, I know, but we have no control over what *they* put in the press." U Win Aung, at the same meeting, sounded similar to the opposition, using words like "power sharing," stressing the need to "heal the nation's wounds," and he seemed sincerely concerned that certain ethnic states in Burma would "try to secede if not given genuine autonomy." These are powerful words, but difficult to gauge if such visionary thoughts are part of a performance to lure potential American investors or a demonstration that the Burmese military regime may be seeking a permanent solution for Burma's long nightmare.

Whenever change comes to Burma, it will be largely because those in the regime pragmatic enough to compromise are confident it won't spell the end of power for the Tatmadaw, or defense forces. No change in Burma will last, however, if the serious concerns finally acknowledged by the foreign minister are not addressed.

## Military Structure

Historically, the Burmese army has reason to glory in the special place it commands in the collective national consciousness. In Burma the armed forces have been looked up to as saviors of the country from almost a century of colonial British domination and a short Japanese occupation during the Second World War. Even the military coup in 1962 ending independent Burma's first civilian government and policies that reduced the country to a "least developed nation" status in the United Nations did not totally tarnish the nationalist reputation of the Tatmadaw. However, the brutality displayed against its own citizens during the 1988 uprising and the subsequent abuse of power has created a deep resentment and anger against anyone in uniform.

Economic mismanagement by the generals has made that resentment even stronger. After enduring twenty-six years of the "Burmese Way to Socialism" promoted by the original coup leader, General Ne Win, the ordinary Burmese became used to "shared poverty," as economists have described the pitiable state of affairs. Today corruption is endemic, and the country's resources are squandered by a poorly educated military elite at the top end of an enormous income gap that never before existed in Burma.

Maintaining a military dictatorship at the turn of the millennium is also an expensive, labor intensive, and thankless venture. Just attempting to censor information to 46 million disgruntled countrymen who have some degree of access to telephones, short-wave radios, the Internet, and satellite TV—in addition to over a thousand miles of porous land and maritime borders with neighboring open societies—is a futile task.

The Tatmadaw will remain an important institution in Burma, but not necessarily *the* indispensable force. After all, in recent years the country has rejected military rule not once but twice: vociferously in 1988 and officially two years later in the 1990 elections. The regime has since searched for ways to regain the favor of the Burmese people and legitimize its rule.

Just in case the generals fail to restore the trust of the people, though, they have infiltrated every sector of society. On a basic everyday level, the military already controls all aspects of daily life—from what one is allowed to publish and read, to when and where (and if) one can meet, travel, where one can live, if sick be treated, if dead, be buried. (Life for the rich and connected is less constricted because money and influence overcome most regulations.)

Over the years the generals have tightened their already considerable hold on Burma's economic, social, cultural, and religious life. The junta that came to power in 1988 as the SLORC purportedly abandoned the socialist economics of General Ne Win, and promised to open the economy, privatize the state sector, and embrace the free market. In reality the military controls most means for creating and maintaining wealth. The country's single largest conglomerate, for example, is the Union of Myanmar Economic Holdings (UMEH), which is owned in part by a Department of the Defense ministry and the rest by military personnel and veterans, though it is called a "private enterprise." Its chairman is an army officer who also serves as a judge attached to the Defense Ministry.

A proliferation of GONGOs—or "government-controlled non-governmental organizations"—dealing with social services and community development has extended the military's reach down to the most basic levels of society. Buddhism, the nation's primary faith, has been a primary target. Burmese Buddhist monks, known as the *sangha,* have throughout history expressed support or disdain of unworthy rulers through symbolic acts, such as denying merit-making possibilities. Monks played a significant part in the 1988 uprising, and some brave ones continue to show sympathy for the democracy cause.

The regime tries both cajoling and threats to keep the *sangha* in line. It has forcibly registered the *sangha,* showered favors on compliant abbots, and defrocked those deemed subversive. The generals have also built and restored dozens of pagodas and buildings of religious significance, in order to burnish their image as protectors of the state religion.

The ruling military junta at the end of 1997 changed its name from the sinister-sounding SLORC, to the SPDC, which stands for the State Peace and Development Council. It then went on to purge its ranks of some corrupt officials and increased the official power circle to nineteen officers. Many are younger field commanders brought in for the first time to serve from the capital, Rangoon. Whether this infusion from another generation of relative youth implies a more enlightened and conciliatory army is debatable. Some Burma observers feel that power never shifted, and is still in the hands of the top few generals, who themselves constantly jockey for power. The rotation of commanders, one theory goes, brings field officers to serve in Rangoon—where they are easier to control—and allows others a chance at serving upcountry in the heart of the heroin industry, where the opportunity to make money is unparalleled.

The ad hoc decisionmaking by the junta seems deliberate—or at least unavoidable. There is no apparent grand plan for transition. After 1988 the regime found itself faced with too many domestic challenges to its authority. It made it a priority to negotiate ceasefires with the more than dozen ethnic insurgencies. The ethnic forces were permitted to keep their arms and engage in any economic activity, including the growing of opium poppies, in exchange for not fighting government troops. Given the accommodation with drug lords, the moribund economy, and the political stalemate, Burma's economic dependence on drug revenues can only increase. The widespread description of the regime as a "narco-dictatorship" is sadly coming true.

**Risk Assessment**

Burma remains unstable as long as present economic and political conditions persist, and will probably remain so for some years into a transition. Many Burma analysts assume that the Burmese generals who have stayed in control for almost forty years think rationally—in the conventional understanding of the term. For over a decade various means of persuasion have been tried to move the regime: sanctions, boycotts, constructive engagement, along with an assortment of carrots, sticks, roadmaps, and benchmarks to point the way toward rejoining the world community. The regime frequently acts even against its own interests, which only adds to its mystique.

The potential for reviving ethnic insurgencies or violent dissent exists. A daring takeover in October 1999 of the Burmese Embassy in Bangkok by exiled former students demonstrated that even the best-equipped military in Burma's history would always be challenged by frustrated disenfranchised youth. The Burmese junta's decision to preempt potential dissident student activity by keeping most universities closed for over a decade could be considered a form of cultural genocide. Thousands of students who led, then fled, the turmoil of 1988 to neighboring Thailand, India, and points beyond are Burma's future human resources, as the generals well know—but fear.

An impressive 2,000 or more former students of this "lost generation" are still living near the borders of Burma, continuing their political struggle while learning new skills or finishing their education under very difficult circumstances. Some who have completed their education in the United States and other Western countries often return to the border to keep in touch with their "revolutionary" roots.

The youths, who occasionally get out of hand, are but a symptom of the larger security problems posed by an arrogant military regime ruling against the mandate of its own people. Even if the impasse between the military and its opposition should be broken tomorrow, three main issues still will concern Burma's neighbors as well as the international community:

1. *Drugs*: Burma, one of the world's top heroin-producing nations, is now the

major source of *yaaba*, or methamphetamine, that has overrun neighboring Thailand, which only fairly recently managed to contain its own heroin industry. The Burmese generals today depend on the investment capital of supposedly rehabilitated drug kings such as Khun Sa and Lo Hsing Han, while field commanders thrive on direct payoffs from the traffickers in their territories. Income from drug-related ventures is estimated to account for at least half of Burma's economy, and drug money very likely props up the value of the local currency, the kyat. The drug trade has contributed to trafficking of women through the region, an increase in domestic addicts, and high growth of HIV-AIDS infection (mostly through shared needles), now estimated at 1.8 million among the population.

2. *Refugees*: Burma's generals have amply demonstrated that they do not know how to manage or share the nation's great wealth with its citizens. The cumulative effects of such practices as forced labor, widespread abuses of human rights, and lack of civil liberties have resulted in an internally displaced and refugee population of a couple of million people that surely threatens the domestic politics and economics of neighboring countries. In recent years the population shifts to Thailand have not been political exiles and dissidents, but civilian families in search of food and work.

3. *Arms*: Burma sustains a growing small arms manufacturing industry and imports more sophisticated weapons and equipment from all over the world. Burma today has one of Southeast Asia's largest and best-equipped armies. In addition to the regime's coziness with and dependence on China, the regional superpower, the increased military capability of the Burmese armed forces—where there is no external threat—is itself a threat to regional stability.

## Conclusions

In the last decade many former authoritarian states have made peaceful transitions to civilian rule. Whether Burma soon will have a government that is legitimate and enjoys popular support is not unthinkable. But whether any such transition will endure in Burma in the long term will depend on the collective goodwill of all the various interests that represent the complex entity that is Burma today.

The Burmese regime may look invincible at the moment, but it is vulnerable for reasons beyond its control. There is almost universal disdain for the armed forces today. Moreover, a decade of being maligned at home and shunned as a pariah abroad in an increasingly democratic-looking world has demoralized and embarrassed the once proud Tatmadaw. The generals' obsession to rule by force goes against a global trend toward smaller and increasingly multitasked armies.

In a post–Cold War globe sprouting with democracies, Burma's generals are discovering that throughout the world governments are being held accountable for past misdeeds. Calls for investigations of official abuses and establishment of justice tribunals have added urgency to the generals' plight. In just the past few years, the Burmese regime unexpectedly lost its model and mentor, former Indonesian president General Suharto; observed the extradition woes of another strongman, former Chilean president General Pinochet; and heard East Timor's once-imprisoned new leader, Xanana Gusmão, pledge support for the cause of Burmese democracy.

Asia's own emerging democracies will play the most vital role in ensuring Burma's future. In October 1999, when young Burmese dissidents laid siege to the Burmese Embassy in Bangkok, Thai officials helped negotiate a peaceful end and release of both hostages and captors. This plunged bilateral relations with Burma's important neighbor to an all-time low—but it also highlighted the huge gulf between Burma and more democratic members of ASEAN.

Japan played an important role in Burma's past, and will also in the country's future. Japanese governmental and private business interests have been angling for years to find a way to resume substantial aid and trade with one of Asia's most resource rich—and underdeveloped—countries without risking the wrath of the international community. If Japan and the countries of ASEAN are sincerely interested in participating economically in a stable Burma, then they must find ways to help Burma's de facto rulers reconcile with their fellow countrymen rather than helping the Tatmadaw consolidate their dictatorship into another wasteful decade.

## Suggested Readings

All Burma Students' Democratic Forum (ABSDF). *To Stand and Be Counted: The Suppression of Burma's Members of Parliament*. Bangkok: 1998. Contact: lurie@mozart.inet.co.th.

Alternative ASEAN Network on Burma (ALTSEAN). *Burma Special Report: The Committee Representing the People's Parliament (CRPP)*. September 1999. Contact: altsean@ksc.th.com.

Ball, Desmond. *Burma's Military Secrets: Signals Intelligence (SIGINT) from the Second World War to Civil War to Cyber Warfare*. White Lotus Press, 1998.

*Burma: Acts of Oppression*. Article 19, 1999. Contact: article19@gn.apc.org.

Burma Lawyer's Council. *Burma: The Military and its Constitution. An Introduction to the Military Controlled Constitution Drafting Process and the Military's Constitutional Principles*. Bangkok: 1999. Contact: blcsan@ksc.th.com.

Fink, Christina. *Living Silence: Burma under Military Rule*. London: Zed Books, 2001, forthcoming.

Ghosh, Parimal. *Brave Men of the Hills: Resistance and Rebellion in Burma, 1825–1932*. London: C. Hurst, 1999.

Gravers, Mikael. *Nationalism as Political Paranoia in Burma: An Essay on the Historical Practice of Power*. Richmond: Curzon, 1998. NIAS reports, no. 11.

Houtman, Gustaaf. "Mental Culture in Burmese Crisis Politics: Aung San Suu Kyi and the National League for Democracy." Tokyo University: Institute for the Study of Languages and Cultures of Asia and Africa, monograph series #33. 1999

Lintner, Bertil. *Burma in Revolt: Opium and Insurgency Since 1948*. Chiang Mai, Thailand: Silkworm Books, 1999.

Maung Mya. *The Burma Road to Capitalism: Economic Growth Versus Democracy*. Westport, CT: Praeger, 1998.

*Myanmar, Cambodia and the Asian Crisis: Challenges of ASEAN Membership*. Tokyo, Japan: Research Institute for Peace and Security, 1999.

Rotberg, Robert I., ed. *Burma: Prospects for a Democratic Future.* World Peace Foundation; Brookings Institute, 1998.

Smith, Martin J. *Burma: Insurgency and the Politics of Ethnicity* (revised and updated). London: Zed Books, 1999.

Taylor, R.H. "Elections in Burma/Myanmar: For Whom and Why?" in R.H. Taylor, ed., *The Politics of Elections in Southeast Asia* (Cambridge: Woodrow Wilson Center Press, 1996), pp. 164–83.

U.S. Department of State. *International Narcotics Control Strategy Report 1998.* Washington, DC, 1998. Released by the Bureau for International Narcotics and Law Enforcement Affairs, February 1999.

U.S. Embassy, Rangoon, Burma. *Foreign Economic Trends Report: Burma 1997.* 1997.

# 11
# Cambodia

*Paul C. Grove*

## Culture of Violence

Political instability has been the hallmark of Cambodia since 1955, when Prince Norodom Sihanouk formed his own political party and Cambodian communists began organizing in the countryside. In 1967, the Khmer Rouge (as the communists were dubbed by Sihanouk) took up armed struggle against the government, setting a violent tone that has been present in every regime since 1970. The country has been a near continuous battlefield throughout its own civil war, the Vietnam conflict, and Vietnam's occupation in the 1980s. This propensity for confrontation and chaos—which reached its apex during the genocidal rule of Pol Pot and the Khmer Rouge from 1975 to 1979—has created a culture of violence that will take decades to reverse.

Violence and political instability have exacted a heavy price from the Cambodian people. In 1999, the first census in Cambodia in over thirty years revealed a population of 11.4 million, with some 45 percent of the populace under the age of 15 years. Life expectancy in Cambodia is less than 50 years. According to the United Nations, in 1997 the country had 6 million land mines, or nearly one for each Cambodian boy and girl aged 14 years and younger. In 1998, the UN World Food Program assisted 1.7 million people and estimated that one-fifth of Cambodians younger than 5 years were acutely malnourished from lack of food and nearly half had stunted growth from prolonged malnourishment.[1] According to the United Nations Development Program, the country has the highest rate of increase of HIV-AIDS in all of Asia (which could cost the country's economy US$2.8 billion by 2006) and Cambodia is ranked 140 out of 174 nations listed in its 1998 Human Development Index. Finally, the country received the lowest score possible in the 1997 Freedom House Index for political rights.

## Cambodia

### Recent Political History

The 1991 Paris Agreements and the United Nations–sponsored national elections in May 1993 were catalysts for the return of former armed resistance groups and over 360,000 refugees from Thai border areas to Phnom Penh. With the exception of the Khmer Rouge—who boycotted attempts at reconciliation—the royalist United Front for an Independent, Neutral, and Peaceful Cambodia (FUNCINPEC) party, the Buddhist Liberal Democratic Party (BLDP), the Vietnamese-backed Cambodian People's Party (CPP), and sixteen other registered political parties participated in elections conducted and supervised by the United Nations at a cost of US$2 billion. Registration exceeded 90 percent of eligible voters.

Although marred by pre-election violence, the 1993 elections brought the Cambodian people their first real political choice in decades. While FUNCINPEC received 45.47 percent of votes (58 of the 120 seats in parliament), a coalition with the ruling CPP party was brokered by King Norodom Sihanouk under threats of CPP upheaval. CPP won 38.22 percent of votes (51 seats), BLDP received 3.81 percent (10 seats), and the small Molinaka party won 1.37 percent (1 seat). Power sharing was lopsided, as the CPP maintained control of provincial governments and key ministries in Phnom Penh. Despite the designation of Norodom Ranariddh as FUNCINPEC First Prime Minister and Hun Sen as CPP Second Prime Minister, the coalition existed in name only and lacked a unifying platform beyond the vague concept of "national reconciliation."

A series of tense political incidents from 1994 to 1997—including the ouster of Finance Minister Sam Rainsy for his efforts to investigate official corruption and the sham trial and exile of reformist former foreign minister and FUNCINPEC General Secretary Norodom Sirivudh for allegedly plotting to assassinate Second Prime Minister Hun Sen—led many to question the success of the UN polls. Grenade attacks against a BLDP party congress in September 1995 and a Khmer Nation Party rally in March 1997 were further destabilizing events.[2] Tensions came to a head in July 1997 when Hun Sen staged a coup d'état and sacked his political opponents. Under the pretext of preventing the return of the Khmer Rouge through the FUNCINPEC party, CPP soldiers assassinated over one hundred royalist supporters, while countless others fled to the Thai border. Purged opposition leaders rallied in Bangkok and formed the Union of Cambodian Democrats (UCD) as a united front against CPP. Opposition party property, files, and organizations were decimated during the coup.

International condemnation of the coup was swift and decisive. Many foreign donors, including the United States and Germany, suspended or curtailed official assistance to the Cambodian government. The Association of Southeast Asian Nations (ASEAN) voted to postpone the admission of Cambodia until elections were held, and the United Nations left Cambodia's seat vacant. The United States convened a "Friends of Cambodia" working group and the ASEAN "Troika" (Indonesia, Thailand, and the Philippines) engaged in shuttle diplomacy to help resolve the crisis. The combination of these factors—and King Sihanouk's open snub of the CPP when he established his residence in Seam Reap following the coup d'état—pressured the ruling party into moving forward with election preparations. With the opposition in exile, Cambodia's legislature passed the Ministry of Interior's party and election laws.

From November 1997 to March 1998, members of the UCD returned to Phnom Penh to reclaim their seats in parliament and begin the arduous task of rebuilding their parties and preparing for elections. Prime Minster Norodom Ranariddh's return proved difficult as CPP-controlled courts had charged him with weapons smuggling and collusion with the Khmer Rouge. Hun Sen insisted that the First Prime Minister stand trial, but Ranariddh refused to return to a certain guilty verdict and imprisonment. A proposal by the Japanese broke the impasse: Ranariddh was tried in absentia, and pardoned by King Sihanouk.

The July 26, 1998, elections proved extremely controversial. The destruction of opposition party offices and organizations during the coup gave CPP a distinct advantage at the polls. Pre-election violence and intimidation instigated by the ruling party further created an unfavorable electoral environment. CPP's control of the media stifled attempts by the opposition to transmit their messages and platforms. Election institutions—including the National Election Commission (NEC) and the Constitutional Council (charged with adjudicating election-related disputes)—were stacked heavily in favor of CPP and failed to operate in an impartial manner. Following the elections, the NEC and the Council failed to consider any complaints filed by the opposition. Controversy over the formula for the allocation of seats would further fuel tensions between competing parties. While election day was relatively orderly and peaceful, the post-election period was marked by demonstrations, a violent crackdown by CPP, and an unconstitutional ban on foreign travel for members of the opposition.

Lieutenant General John Sanderson (Force Commander of UN soldiers during the May 1993 elections) and Michael Maley (Senior Deputy Chief Electoral Officer for the UN in Cambodia) concluded that the elections were not free or fair because of "conscious political acts by the ruling group [CPP], reflecting a lack of genuine commitment to the process, and to the rights of individual Cambodians."[3] The U.S. International Republican Institute and the National Democratic Institute, which jointly sponsored an election observation delegation for the July polls, reached a similar conclusion.

A more positive view of the elections was offered by the United Nations Joint International Observer Group (JIOG), which stated in a July 27 press release that election day and the counting process "was free and fair to an extent that enables it to reflect, in a credible way, the will of the Cambodian people." This finding would be echoed by many in the international community, including ASEAN neighbors, who were eager to break the post-election deadlock. UCD members challenged the JIOG finding as premature and reflective of "Cambodia fatigue" by the international community. In a September 1998 Joint Statement by FUNCINPEC and the Sam Rainsy Party, the premature endorsement of the elections by the JIOG, ASEAN, and Japan was characterized as damaging to "the prospects for Cambodia's long-term political stability."

The outcome of the elections was not an endorsement of CPP's monopoly on power. CPP received 41 percent of the votes (64 seats in parliament), FUNCINPEC won 33 percent (43 seats), and the Sam Rainsy Party (so renamed because the Ministry of the Interior prohibited the Khmer Nation Party from registering) received 14 percent (15 seats). Despite protesting the outcome and the failure of the NEC and the Council to resolve their disputes, a coalition government between FUNCINPEC and CPP was formed in November 1998 under pressure from King Norodom Sihanouk and the international community. The 1998 Human Rights Watch World Report characterized donor responses to the elections as "weariness with Cambodia's seemingly never-ending problems, eagerness to sign off on a flawed electoral process, and acquiescence in Hun Sen's consolidation of power." A bicameral legislature was created to maintain a balance of power within CPP and to provide a respectable haven for unsuccessful FUNCINPEC and BLDP candidates.

Today, Hun Sen is the sole Prime Minister of Cambodia, Ranariddh is the President of the National Assembly, and Chea Sim (CPP faction leader) is President of the Senate. Sam Rainsy's party is, in his words, "a token, virtually powerless opposition allowed to exist only to give the country a most false appearance of pluralism and democracy."[4] King Norodom Sihanouk—affectionately called the of Nation" (Samdech Oeuv) by the Cambodian people—is no longer directly active in the country's politics, but continues to be a moral authority to the country (on such issues as a genocide tribunal) and a peacemaker between the competing political parties.

## Security Issues

*Foreign Policy*: There are three major alignments in Cambodia's foreign policy: the People's Republic of China, "other donors" (including Japan), and ASEAN.

Since 1997, Cambodia and China have moved closer in terms of political, economic, cultural, and military ties. Indications of this trend are: (1) the elevation of China as the single largest bilateral donor in Cambodia in 1999, with a US$220 million package of interest-free, unconditional, and commercial loans and grants for infrastructure and industrial development;[5] (2) a 1999 government decree banning the participation of government and military officials in any activities held by Taiwanese nationals; (3) a 1999 pledge by China for US$1.5 million in military assistance to Cambodia; (4) the 1999 signing of agreements on Sino-Cambodian economic and technological cooperation, an extradition treaty, cultural cooperation, and cooperation facilitating tourism between the countries; (5) a US$1.25 million agreement to restore the Chau Say Tevoda temple in Siem Reap (China's first temple restoration project outside its borders); (6) the termination of an agreement with Taiwan's EVA Airways to open a route between Phnom Penh and Taipei in July 1997, and (7) the closing of the Republic of Taiwan's representative office in July 1997.

While China has enjoyed a close association with King Norodom Sihanouk (particularly after he was ousted in a 1970 coup d'état), its relations vis-à-vis the ruling CPP party have been mostly defined on the battlefield. For over a decade, China supported the Khmer Rouge, who fought against Hun Sen's Vietnamese-installed government. The ascendancy of China as Cambodia's number one bilateral donor and the signing of multiple agreements in 1999 are signs of a normalization of Sino-Cambodian relations, Chinese interests in securing a toehold in Southeast Asia, and Chinese efforts to contain its historical enemy, Vietnam.

Cambodia's interaction with "other donors" (including the United States, France, Australia, and Japan) is contentious and subject to scrutiny of the country's domestic political situation. Accountability, transparency, and respect for human and legal rights have been central themes in international criticisms of the Cambodian government. The conditioning of assistance and perceived foreign intrusion in Cambodian affairs has been an annoyance to the CPP ruling party, and in December 1995, then Second Prime Minister Hun Sen lashed out at America and France:

> I wish to warn foreigners that they should look out for demonstrators who may storm their embassies. Look! This matter [the arrest and trial of Norodom Sirivudh] is an internal affair of Cambodia. . . . Now I want these words conveyed to the U.S. Senate: If you want to help, then help. If you do not want to help, it is fine, but you must compensate the Cambodians for overthrowing their king and creating

war in Cambodia.... How much? Only about [US]$20 billion. Moreover, the Americans should also be tried in the international court like Pol Pot.... Never again act as a superpower and bank on sending your planes. You were defeated once; do you want to be beaten again?[6]

Foreign assistance has been consistently used as leverage to bring about reform. Following the July 1997 coup, the United States immediately suspended all non-humanitarian assistance to the country, Australia suspended its military aid program (but continued with humanitarian assistance), and Japan briefly halted its programs out of concern for the safety of its staff in Cambodia. In February 1999, Cambodia received a pledge for US$470 million in loans and grants from the international community, with Japan pledging the largest share—US$100 million. The funds are conditioned on the successful implementation of reforms promised by the Cambodian government, with a donor review occurring quarterly. As of late 1999, the United States was continuing its suspension of nonhumanitarian assistance to Cambodia.

Cambodia's role within ASEAN is in the process of being defined, and it is unclear how the country's record for political instability may effect intra-ASEAN relationships. ASEAN members delayed the entry of Cambodia into the Association following the July 1997 coup, and disagreements on when Cambodia should become a member pitted Singapore, Thailand, and the Philippines (who advocated delaying entry until the new coalition government proves its viability) against Vietnam, Burma, Laos, Indonesia, and Malaysia. Border disputes with Thailand (in Banteay Meanchey and Pursat provinces) and Vietnam (in Prey Veng and Takeo provinces) may be sources of tension within the Association, and an October 1999 informal meeting between Cambodia, Laos, and Vietnam in Vientiane has raised suspicion of the development of an "Indochina" faction within ASEAN. Also unclear is how Cambodia's growing relationship with China may affect competing interests in the South China Sea. China may exact a quid pro quo from Cambodia on recognition of its territorial claims.

*Royal Cambodian Armed Forces (RCAF)*: RCAF poses no immediate military threat to Thailand, Laos, or Vietnam. A largely unprofessional and undisciplined military (army, navy, reserves, and air force) under CPP command totals 140,500 soldiers.[7] While the Cambodian government has stated that 55,000 soldiers will be demobilized, the process and funding source for downsizing is unclear. One proposal was to pay each soldier US$1,200 before discharge (nearly was twice the per capita GDP), but this was reduced to US$240 due to international criticism. The extent of nonexistent troops is not known, although an adviser to Prime Minister Hun Sen estimated that 20,000 soldiers do not exist and that senior officials are pocketing these "ghost soldiers'" pay.[8]

Challenging demobilization efforts is a bloated officer corps and the integration of ex–Khmer Rouge soldiers. RCAF has more generals than the Chinese People's Liberation Army and reportedly a ratio of two officers per single soldier. Ranks are being swelled by the integration of former Khmer Rouge guerillas, and major discrepancies exist between RCAF and ex-guerilla leaders on exactly how many soldiers will join government forces. RCAF officials are known to be involved in illegal logging and land confiscation, and are suspected of involvement in narcotics and human trafficking.

*Khmer Rouge*: Speaking before the fifty-fourth session of the United Nations General Assembly in 1999, Prime Minister Hun Sen stated: "Cambodia is now a fully integrated country without rebels or separatists and without internal strife, or conflict for the first time in many decades." While undoubtedly trying to put the best face on a turbulent past, earlier warnings by Hun Sen, Ieng Sary (former senior Khmer Rouge cadre), and Y Chhien (former Khmer Rouge military commander) allude to continued civil conflict should an international genocide tribunal be established. Military authorities in Phnom Penh acknowledge that the former guerillas continue to be armed and that command and control structures are in place. While estimates vary widely on the strength of the ex–Khmer Rouge, renewed conflict will be politically, socially, and economically destabilizing—particularly in the countryside.

Equally destabilizing may be the popular backlash from an orchestrated genocide tribunal in Cambodia's notoriously corrupt legal system. The United Nations has been negotiating with government authorities to allow the participation of the international community in the formation and workings of the tribunal. Hun Sen's objections to direct international involvement are rooted in issues of national sovereignty. King Sihanouk, viewed by many Khmer as the father of modern Cambodia, supports international participation in the tribunal as a means to ensure justice. Spontaneous protests similar to those that followed the controversial July 1998 elections may occur if Cambodians feel justice is being denied.

*Narcotics Trafficking:* The U.S. Department of State's International Narcotics Strategy Reports for 1996–1999 highlight the use of Cambodia as a transshipment point for heroin from the Golden Triangle to the United States and Europe. The 1996 National Narcotics Intelligence Consumers Committee (NNICC) Report identified the country as the "most prominent" producer of cannabis in Southeast Asia, and the country is suspected of possible small-scale opiate, amphetamine, and heroin production.[9] Money laundering has been identified as a problem, although the U.S. Department of State reports provide few details on the extent of this illegal activity. In 1995, a confidential Ministry of the Interior report implicated 19 of the country's 29 banks as involved in money laundering.[10] Chinese heroin trafficking networks and West African groups in Phnom Penh are thought to be responsible for the transshipment of narcotics through Cambodia. In July 2000, the *Bangkok Post* stated that Cambodia ws set "to rival and surpass Burma" in the Narcotics trade.

*Human Trafficking*: Cambodia has become a hub for trafficking in Chinese nationals, many of whom are destined for the United States and Europe. An accurate estimate of the extent of illegal migrant transit through Cambodia is unknown, although national police estimated that in 1997 some 10,000 Chinese nationals were illegally residing in Phnom Penh awaiting transit to a third country.[11] Senior government and police officials are suspected of involvement in human trafficking and have been implicated in obstructing investigations into this transnational problem.

*The Rule of Law*: The single greatest obstacle to the political, economic, and social development of Cambodia is the absence of the rule of law. The U.S. Department of State's 1998 Cambodia Country Report on Human Rights Practices is critical of the Cambodian government's lack of political will and weak judiciary as obstacles in pursuing human rights violators. A more frank assessment of Cambodia's legal system was conducted by the U.S. Agency for International Development's (AID) Office of Transition Initiatives (OTI). A 1999 internal report recognized the "complete failure" of Cambodia's justice system, in which "[P]ower counts. Fairness doesn't." The OTI report recommended "retiring all judges in Cambodia and replacing them with international judges for a period of 10 years, with training a new cadre starting in year six." In April 1999, Amnesty International stated, "[I]mpunity remains Cambodia's most serious human rights problem."[12]

Official corruption is an accepted practice in Cambodia and is seemingly endorsed by the government. Special Advisor on Investment to the Council of Ministers Ted Ngoy stated: "Investors have to go along with a country's tradition [whether] in Indonesia, Vietnam, or China. We have to do things like [bribery] to do business. It's not a bad thing."[13] Revenue lost to corruption is enormous. In 1997, US$12.4 million in forestry revenue went into government coffers; US$225 million lined the pockets of corrupt government and military officials.[14] The 1998 Heritage Foundation Index of Economic Freedom scored Cambodia among the least free countries in the world.

### Conclusions

Cambodia has endured a uniquely violent past that will impede political, legal, economic, and social development for decades. Regional conflict, civil war, and occupation by Vietnamese forces have taken their toll on the Cambodian people and the country's infrastructure. Ranked among the poorest of the world's nations and heavily dependent upon foreign assistance, the country will remain underdeveloped for the foreseeable future.

While not an immediate military threat to its neighbors, Cambodia's political instability may continue to be an irritant to Thailand and Vietnam. The country's role within ASEAN is being defined, and any Cambodian alliance with Burma, Laos, and Vietnam may prove divisive to more moderate members, especially Thailand and the Philippines. Cambodia's growing relationship with China is also a cause for concern, and increases in bilateral assistance may decrease the ability of the "other donor" community to effect positive political and economic changes.

Cambodia's lawlessness will continue to perpetuate cycles of corruption and gross human rights abuses. A partial judiciary will deny Cambodians fair representation and will continue to erode investor confidence. Without genuine political will to institute political, legal, economic, and social reforms, peace and stability will continue to elude the Cambodian people.

## Notes

1. Chris Fontaine, "Rural Cambodians Battle Hunger," The Associated Press, December 28, 1998.

2. The Khmer Nation Party was founded by Sam Rainsy following his expulsion from the FUNCINPEC party. No serious Cambodian investigations or arrests have been made in either grenade attack.

3. John M. Sanderson and Michael Maley, "Elections and Liberal Democracy in Cambodia," Australian Institute for International Affairs, 1998, p. 241.

4. Sam Rainsy interview with author, October 21, 1999.

5. Phelim Kyne, "From China With Cash," *Phnom Penh Post*, April 30–May 13, 1999.

6. MacAlister Brown and Joseph Zasloff, *Cambodia Confounds the Peacemakers 1979–1998* (New York: Cornell University Press, 1989), p. 247.

7. John Dori and Richard D. Fisher, Jr., *U.S. and Asia Statistical Handbook 1998–1999* (Washington DC: The Heritage Foundation), p. 41.

8. *Phnom Penh Post*, "The Delicate Challenge of Downsizing RCAF," April 13–29, 1999.

9. *1996 National Narcotics Intelligence Consumers Committee (NNICC) Report*, p. 68.

10. Nate Thayer, "Medellin on the Mekong," *Far Eastern Economic Review*, November 23, 1995, p. 25.

11. Bruce Gilley, "No Questions Asked," *Far Eastern Economic Review*, May 14, 1999, p. 34.

12. Amnesty International, "Cambodia: No Solution to Impunity," April 22, 1999.

13. Phelim Kyne, "Cambodia's Kingdom of Corruption: The High Cost of Doing Business," *Phnom Penh Post*, June 25–July 8, 1999.

14. Ibid.

## Suggested Readings

Becker, Elizabeth. *When the War Was Over*. New York: Simon and Schuster, 1986.

Brown, MacAlister, and Zasloff, Joseph. *Cambodia Confounds the Peacemakers: 1979–1999*. New York: Cornell University Press, 1998.

Chandler, David. *The Tragedy of Cambodian History*. New York: Vail-Ballou Press, 1991.

Doran, James. *A Report on the March 30, 1997 Grenade Attack in Cambodia*. U.S. Senate Foreign Relations Committee, September 1999.

Findlay, Trevor. *Cambodia: The Legacy and Lessons of UNTAC*. New York: Oxford University Press, 1995.

Gilley, Bruce. "Dancing with the Dragon." *Far Eastern Economic Review*, December 11, 1997.

International Republican Institute. *Observation Report: Kingdom of Cambodia Parliamentary Elections, July 26, 1998*. February, 1999.

Kamm, Henry. *Cambodia: Report From a Stricken Land*. New York: Arcade Publishing, 1998.

Thayer, Nate. "Medellin on the Mekong." *Far Eastern Economic Review*, November 23, 1995.

# 12

# China

*Robert Sutter*

### The Political-Security Environment

Post-Mao leaders have achieved considerable success in efforts since the late 1970s to pursue military modernization. The goal of senior leader Deng Xiaoping and his associates was establishing a professional military force equipped with modern weapons and doctrine. In keeping with Deng's mandate, the People's Liberation Army (PLA), which includes the strategic nuclear forces, army, navy, and air force, demobilized over three million personnel since 1978 and introduced modern methods in such areas as recruitment and manpower, strategy, and education and training. The overall size of China's armed forces is approximately three million. Beijing appears committed to further troop cuts over the next few years, during which it will continue to upgrade equipment and training, especially for the air force and navy.

Following the June 1989 Tiananmen crackdown, when PLA troops were used to restore control and stability, ideological correctness temporarily revived as the dominant theme in Chinese military affairs. More recently, reform and modernization appear to have resumed their position as the PLA's priority objectives, although the armed forces' political loyalty to the ruling Communist Party of China (CCP) remains a leading concern.

Outside analysts have been able to discern core goals in Chinese security policy, notably involving support for the security of the Chinese state and its Communist Party leadership; development of China's wealth and power; and China's strong desire to stand strong and independent in world affairs. Nevertheless, the frequent shifts in priorities and tactics sometimes caught Chinese leaders unaware or unresponsive, leading to leadership confusion and conflict. Domestic politics would

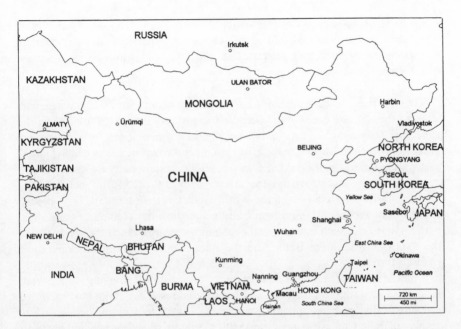

## China

on occasion spill over into Chinese foreign and international security policy, leading to sometimes serious leadership foreign policy debates. Perhaps the most graphic example of the latter occurred in the mid to late 1960s, during the most violent phase of the Cultural Revolution. This period saw a collapse of Chinese foreign and international security policy, amid a broader collapse of Chinese government and party institutions, reflecting the life-and-death struggle for power then under way among the senior leaders in China.

In contrast, post-Mao leaders have generally adhered to a logic underlying the pragmatic trend in Chinese international security and foreign policies since the late 1970s:

- Post-Mao Chinese communist leaders need to foster a better economic life for the people of China in order to legitimize and justify their continued monopoly of political power. These leaders cannot rely as Mao did on enormous personal prestige as a successful revolutionary, or on the appeal of communist ideology: they have little of Mao's prestige, and the appeal of communist ideology is largely a thing of the past.
- China depends critically on foreign trade, and related foreign investment and assistance, for its economic development.
- China depends particularly heavily on its neighbors for aid, investment, and trade benefits, and on the United States to absorb its exports.

- Therefore, to buttress their survival politically, post-Mao leaders emphasize their concern with maintaining a "peaceful" international environment that assures continued trade, investment, and assistance flows so important to Chinese economic well-being.

Thus, Chinese leaders put aside past ideas of autarchy and self-reliance and allowed the Chinese economy to become increasingly integrated into the world economy. They sought to avoid dependence on any one power by encouraging broad competition. Beijing made efforts to meet the requirements of the United States and others regarding market access, intellectual property rights, and other economic issues, and strove to become a member of the GATT (General Agreement on Tariffs and Trade) and the World Trade Organization (WTO). Chinese leaders duly accepted commitments and responsibilities stemming from their participation with such international economic organizations as the World Bank, the Asian Development Bank, and the Asia-Pacific Economic Cooperation (APEC) forum.

Chinese leaders remained sensitive on issues of national sovereignty and were less accommodating on international security issues. They did adjust to world pressure when resistance appeared detrimental to broader Chinese concerns. Examples include Chinese cooperation with the international peace settlement in Cambodia in 1991; Beijing's willingness to join the Non-Proliferation Treaty and to halt nuclear tests by the end of 1996 under an international agreement banning nuclear tests; China's willingness to abide by terms of the Missile Technology Control Regime (MTCR) and the Chinese leaders' reportedly helpful efforts to assist the United States in reaching an agreement with North Korea in October 1994 over the latter's nuclear weapons program. Beijing also endeavored to meet international expectations on other transnational issues, like policing drug traffic, curbing international terrorism, and working to avoid further degradation of the world's environment.

It is easy to exaggerate the degree of Chinese accommodation to international concerns. Beijing's continued hard line against outside criticism of Chinese political authoritarianism and poor human rights record graphically illustrate the limits of Chinese accommodation. Chinese firmness on this issue is said to reflect a deeply felt concern on the part of senior Chinese military and other leaders about the need to maintain political control and "stability" during a period of rapid economic and social change and a time when the prestige of communism in China and abroad has seriously fallen. Continued Chinese transfer of sensitive military technology or dual-use equipment to Pakistan, Iran, and other potential flashpoints is widely criticized in the United States and elsewhere. The Chinese political and military leaders are not reluctant to use rhetorical threats or demonstrations of military force in order to intimidate and deter those in sensitive areas—like Taiwan, the South China Sea, and Hong Kong—who are seen by Beijing as challenging its traditional territorial or nationalistic claims.

In short, Beijing has been widely seen as accommodating pragmatically to many international norms, but not because such accommodation is seen as inherently in China's interest. Rather, Beijing is said to view each issue on a case-by-case basis, calculating the costs and benefits of adherence to international norms in each case. Thus, for example, Beijing saw by 1991 that maintaining its past support for the Khmer Rouge in Cambodia would be counterproductive regarding China's broader interests in achieving a favorable peace settlement in Cambodia and solidifying closer relations with the Association of Southeast Asian Nations (ASEAN) countries, Japan, and the West—all of whom saw continued Chinese aid as a serious obstacle to peace. By the same token, the U.S.-led international moratorium on nuclear testing had reached a point in 1994 that Beijing had to announce its decision to stop nuclear testing by the end of 1996, and join a comprehensive nuclear test ban, or risk major friction in its relations with the United States, Japan, Western Europe, and Russia.

Underlying the case-by-case approach is a rising sense of nationalism among Chinese leaders. Viewing the world as a highly competitive state-centered system, Chinese leaders remain deeply suspicious of multilateralism and interdependence. Rather, they tend to see the world in more traditional balance-of-power terms, and therefore argue that the current world trend is more multipolar (i.e., a number of competing nation states) than multilateral (a system where nation-states sacrifice their independence and freedom of maneuver for the sake of an interdependent international order).[1]

At bottom, Chinese suspicions of many multilateral efforts center on the role of the United States and the other developed countries. These nations are "setting the agenda" of most such multilateral regimes. They are accused of doing so to serve their own particular national interests and to give short shrift to the interests and concerns of newly emerging powers like China. As a result, many leaders in China see U.S. and other efforts to encourage or press China to conform to multilateral standards on international security, human rights, and economic policies and practices as motivated at bottom by the foreign powers' fear of China's rising power, their unwillingness to fairly share power with China, and their desire to "hold down" China—to keep it weak for as long as possible.

**Assessment and Prospects**

The above analysis of the international behavior of the People's Republic of China (PRC) in recent years suggests several key themes:

1.  Chinese leaders now see the security environment around China's periphery as less likely to be disrupted by a major international power than at any time in the past. Of course, the reduced big power military threat does not preclude danger posed by possible conflicts between China and its neighbors over territorial disputes or other issues that China itself might provoke. Nor does it automatically translate into growing Chinese influ-

ence in Asia or sanguine Chinese leadership attitudes regarding the evolving balance in Asia. Regional economic and military powers (e.g., Japan and India) are among leaders asserting their influence as East–West and Sino-Soviet tensions have ended.

2. Regional security trends are generally compatible with China's primary concern with internal economic modernization and political stability. So long as the regional power balance remains stable and broadly favorable to Chinese interests, it will not intrude on Beijing's recent effort to give pragmatic development of advantageous economic contacts top priority in its foreign affairs. At least some leaders in Beijing appear prepared to embark on a more assertive Chinese stance in the region, presumably after China has achieved solid progress in its economic modernization program.

3. Ideological and leadership disputes have less importance for Chinese foreign policy than in the past. Although Chinese leaders could be divided between more conservative officials and those who are more reformist, the differences within the leadership over foreign affairs have appeared markedly less than they were during the Maoist period.

4. Reflecting the more narrow range of foreign policy choices present among Chinese leaders, Beijing's foreign policy has become more economically dependent on other countries—especially the Western-aligned, developed countries—than in the past. Particularly as a result of the openness to foreign economic contacts and the putting aside of Maoist policies of economic self-reliance, Beijing has come to see its well-being as more closely tied to continued good relations with important developed countries, notably Japan and the United States. They provide the assistance, technology, investment, and markets China has needed to modernize effectively.

5. China's overall pragmatic adjustments in world affairs are not dependent on just one or two leaders in China. Although Deng Xiaoping picked up senior foreign policymaking duties from Mao Zedong and Zhou Enlai, the policies followed have represented, in broad terms, an outline agreed upon among senior Chinese leaders who are advised and influenced by a wide range of experts and interest groups in China. Many of these groups have a strong interest in dealing pragmatically with world affairs. This has included particularly strong economic, technological, and other interconnections between Chinese enterprises and interest groups and counterparts outside China. As a result, they are loathe to pursue autarchic, confrontational, or provocative policies that could jeopardize their particular concerns as well as China's economic progress in an increasingly interactive world. However, a substantial segment of the Chinese leadership does remain suspicious of U.S. pressure and very sensitive regarding issues of national sovereignty.

The outlook for Chinese foreign and international security policy over the next five to ten years remains uncertain. Optimists in the West tend to extrapolate from the pragmatic trends seen in Chinese foreign policy behavior since the death of Mao and the rise of pragmatic nation building policies initiated by the late Deng Xiaoping. They argue that the logic of post-Mao foreign policy will continue to drive Chinese leaders in directions of greater cooperation, accommodation, and interdependence with the outside world, and especially China's neighbors and the advanced developed countries, led by the United States. According to this view, as China becomes economically more advanced, it will undergo social and eventually political transformation that will result in a more pluralistic political decisionmaking process in Beijing that will act to check assertive or aggressive Chinese foreign actions or tendencies. Moreover, as Beijing becomes more economically interdependent on those around China and the advanced developing countries, it will presumably be less inclined to take aggressive or disruptive actions against them.[2]

Pessimists in the United States and elsewhere in the West are more inclined to focus on the strong nationalistic ambitions and intentions of the Chinese leaders. They are often struck by the strong nationalistic views of at least a segment of PRC leaders in recent years who voice deep suspicion of U.S. pressures directed against China. These Chinese leaders see these U.S. pressures and other U.S. policies, such as support for Taiwan, as fundamental challenges to China that must be confronted and resisted.

In the past, Chinese nationalistic ambitions ran up against and were held in check by U.S.-backed military containment or Soviet-backed military containment. Later, Beijing's need for advantageous foreign economic interchange to support economic development at home, and thereby legitimate continued communist rule in China, caused it to curb assertive, nationalistic behavior abroad. But the pessimists believe that Beijing has now reached, or will soon reach, a point of economic development where it will no longer need to cater so much to outside concerns. For example, the government in Beijing may have reinforced its political legitimacy by its record of material progress in recent years. China's economy has become such a magnet for foreign attention that the Sino-foreign tables could be reversed—that is, foreign countries now will feel an increasing need to accommodate China or risk being closed out of the booming China market, rather than China's feeling a need to accommodate foreign interests.[3] China is now widely acknowledged as a world-class economic power and possibly a nascent superpower. None of this is unrecognized by China's leadership.

Whether China will follow the path of the optimists or pessimists, or some other future course, will depend heavily on two sets of factors:

1. Internal—political stability and the course of economic and political performance.
2. External—the interaction of Chinese relations with key states around its periphery and Chinese adjustment to international trends in the so-called "new world order."

There remains the distinct possibility that outside forces (e.g., the United States, Russia, and Taiwan) may adopt policies that challenge fundamental Chinese interests and prompt assertive Chinese responses. Thus, for example, Beijing has threatened repeatedly that it would resort to force to halt movement in Taiwan to declare the island an independent country. However, most of Beijing's recent security concerns that are not focused on domestic security are centered on the United States.

## Role of the United States and U.S. Policy Choices

Although the United States does not border on China, Beijing recognizes that the United States still exerts predominant strategic influence in East Asia and the Western Pacific; is a leading economic power in the region, surpassed locally only by Japan; and is one of only two world powers capable of exerting sufficient power around China's periphery to pose a tangible danger to Chinese security and development. As the world's only superpower, the United States also exerts strong influence in international financial and political institutions (e.g., the World Bank and the United Nations) that are very important to Beijing, and its role in particular areas sensitive to Beijing—notably policy regarding Taiwan and international human rights—is second to none.

The pattern of international interchange with China's growing strength in recent years appears to underline the importance of the U.S. role. Few of China's neighbors are willing to challenge or express strongly different views than the PRC on major issues. They privately support a significant U.S. military presence in the region, partly because it serves as an implicit counterweight to China's military power. They and more distant developed countries also privately support firm U.S. efforts to open China's markets, end unfair commercial practices, and protect the integrity of the world trading system. They appreciate the U.S. efforts to press China to end nuclear testing and proliferation of equipment and technology for weapons of mass destruction. Notably, however, this support is usually not expressed openly.

Beijing too sees the United States as the key link in the international balance of power affecting Chinese interests. This judgment goes far toward explaining why Chinese leaders so avidly sought a visit to China by President Clinton. The June 1998 visit signaled to all at home and abroad that the United States has muffled its opposition to and endorses cooperation with the Beijing government. Of course, as noted above, some Chinese leaders remain deeply suspicious of U.S. motives. They believe the U.S. government is conspiring to weaken and undermine the Chinese leadership and "hold back" China from a more prominent position in world affairs.[4]

There is general agreement in the United States that Washington should use its influence in order to have Beijing conform to international norms and over time to foster changes in China's political, economic, and security systems to make them compatible with American interests. At the same time, there is little agreement in

Washington on how the United States should achieve these objectives. In general, there are three general approaches influencing current U.S. China policy and little indication as to which approach will ultimately succeed.

On one side is an approach favored by some in the Clinton administration, the Congress, and elsewhere, who argue in favor of a moderate, less confrontational and "engaged" posture toward China. Some in this camp are concerned with perceived fundamental weaknesses in China and urge a moderate U.S. policy approach out of fear that to do otherwise could promote divisions in and a possible breakup of China, with potentially disastrous consequences for U.S. interests in Asian stability and prosperity. Others are more impressed with China's growing economic and national strength and the opportunities this provides for the United States. They promote close U.S. engagement with China as the most appropriate way to guide the newly emerging power into channels of international activity compatible with American interests.

Sometimes underlying this moderate approach is a belief that trends in China are moving inexorably in the "right" direction. That is, China is becoming increasingly interdependent economically with its neighbors and the developed countries of the West, and is seen as increasingly unlikely to take disruptive action that would upset these advantageous international economic relationships. In addition, greater wealth in China is seen pushing Chinese society in directions that seem certain to develop a materially better off, more educated, and cosmopolitan populace that will over time press its government for greater representation, political pluralism, and eventually democracy. Therefore, U.S. policy should seek to work ever more closely with China in order to encourage these positive long-term trends.

A second, tougher approach is that of some U.S. advocates inside and out of the U.S. government who have doubts about the interdependence argument. These U.S. policymakers and opinion leaders stress that Beijing officials still view the world as a state-centered competitive environment where interdependence counts for little and compromises sovereign strength. China's leaders are seen as determined to use whatever means at their disposal to increase China's wealth and power. At present, Beijing is seen biding its time and conforming to many international norms as it builds economic strength. Once it succeeds with economic modernization, the argument goes, Beijing will be disinclined to curb its narrow nationalistic or other ambitions out of a need for international interdependence or other concerns for world community. When strong enough, China, like other large powers in the past, will possess great capabilities and will attract few friends or allies.

Under these circumstances, this approach encourages U.S. leaders to be more firm than moderate in dealing with China. Rather than trying to persuade Beijing of the advantages of international cooperation, the United States is advised to keep military forces as a counterweight to rising Chinese power in Asia; to remain firm in dealing with economic, arms proliferation, and other disputes with China; and to work closely with traditional U.S. allies and friends along China's periphery in order to deal with any suspected assertiveness or disruption from Beijing.

A third approach is favored by some U.S. officials and others who believe that the political system in China needs to be changed first before the United States has any real hope of reaching a constructive relationship with China. Beijing's communist leaders are seen as inherently incapable of long-term positive ties with the United States. U.S. policy should focus on mechanisms to change China from within while maintaining a vigilant posture to deal with disruptive Chinese foreign policy actions in Asian and world affairs. They believe the development of an authoritarian superpower more economically competent than the former USSR is not to be aided. The Chairman of the Senate Foreign Relations Committee, Senator Jesse Helms of North Carolina, has been associated with this view.

## Notes

1. See, among others, *Trends of Future Sino-U.S. Relations and Policy Proposals*, Institute for International Studies of Beijing Academy of Social Sciences, et al., September 1994, and *Sino-U.S. Relations: Status and Outlook—Views from Beijing*, Congressional Research Service memorandum, August 15, 1994.

2. Discussed, among others, in Zhang, Ming, "China and the Major Power Relations," *The Journal of Contemporary China*, Fall 1994.

3. Discussed, among others, in Chong-Pin Lin, "Chinese Military Modernization: Perceptions, Progress and Prospects," *Security Studies*, Summer 1994.

4. See, among others, *Sino-U.S. Relations: Status and Outlook—Views from Beijing*, Congressional Research Service memorandum, August 15, 1994.

## Suggested Readings

Bernstein, Richard, and Ross Munro. *The Coming Conflict with China*. New York: Knopf, 1996.

Economy, Elizabeth, and Michel Oksenberg. *China Joins the World*. New York: Council on Foreign Relations, 1999.

Kim, Samuel, ed. *China and the World*. Boulder, CO: Westview Press, 1998.

Lilley, James R., and David Shambaugh, eds. *China's Military Faces the Future*. Armonk, NY: M.E. Sharpe, Inc., and Washington, DC: American Enterprise Institute, 1999.

Nathan, Andrew, and Robert Ross. *The Great Wall and Empty Fortress*. New York: Norton, 1997.

$$\text{\textemdash\textemdash\textemdash 13}$$

# India

## Satu P. Limaye

### Introduction

Some fifty years after achieving independence, India is reshaping itself internally and redefining itself abroad. The so-called *Nehruvian consensus*[1] (named after the country's first and long-serving prime minister, Jawaharlal Nehru) on secularism, socialism, and nonalignment has frayed, but not torn. The rise to power of the Bharatiya Janata Party (BJP), with its conservative, nationalist agenda and links to fundamentalist Hindu groups, poses no immediate threat to the official policy of secularism. However, the party's rise does highlight the current struggle over India's identity being waged between those who would define it religiously and culturally as Hindu and those who would define it in more secular, modern terms.

India's commitment to a Fabian socialist economy is eroding, though fitfully.[2] The country's debt crisis in 1991 telescoped economic reforms that were only being tinkered with a half decade earlier under the modernizing Prime Minister Rajiv Gandhi. India's economic growth rates since the reforms, though well below those of China or the "Asian Tigers," have hovered close to 6 percent, nearly doubling the anemic growth rates of 3 percent during the preceding four decades. India's economic reforms, which have made possible the higher rates of growth, are politically viable because they are limited and cautious. Reforms and the resulting faster growth rates, when combined with a rate of population growth that is still burdensome but manageable, could lead to real improvements in the lives of India's people during the years ahead. Still, India remains reticent about full liberalization of the economy, and India's role in an increasingly internationalized economy is marginal. With nearly 18 percent of the world's population, India accounts for only 0.5 percent of world trade and attracts but a fraction of foreign direct investment.

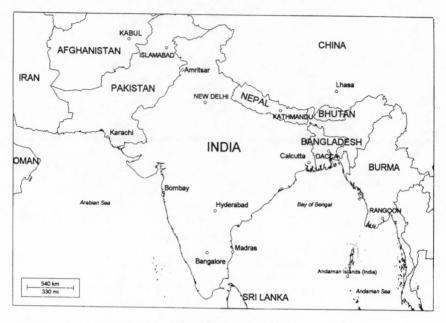

## India

With the collapse of the Soviet Union, India's main political, economic, and military partner of the last fifty years has disappeared. And with the end of the bipolar international order, nonalignment, the guiding principle of India's post-independence foreign policy, is essentially meaningless. India worries that a unipolar world constrains its margin for maneuver. These two major international developments have had the effect of increasing pressure on India to achieve its long-cherished goal of strategic autonomy.

Despite these rather profound changes, one thing has not altered—India's commitment to democracy, though it is certainly a different kind of democracy than during Nehru's time. India's democracy today is deeper and more inclusive than in the past. The power of the elite has ebbed with the rise of lower caste involvement in politics at the national, state, and local levels, not only as voters, but also as officials at the highest levels. India's governance is being indigenized. All of this means more political turbulence in the form of short-lived governments, rougher politics, and the hurly-burly of coalition machinations. But India is edging toward a new political order in its own lumbering, seemingly anarchical way. That these processes of social transformation, economic reform, and foreign policy adjustment are being undertaken within a democratic framework is a testament to India's underlying strengths.[3]

India also has begun to make serious changes in its defense and national security attitudes and policies. Prime Minister Nehru's "strategic culture," which did not dwell on either the armed forces or threats to India's national security, is being demolished. The most dramatic sign of the repudiation of Nehru's approach to national security was India's decision to conduct five nuclear tests in May 1998 and declare itself a nuclear weapons state (NWS). India has begun to rethink its defense policymaking structure with the establishment of a National Security Council (NSC). Indeed, it was an NSC Advisory Group that issued India's draft nuclear doctrine. However, the long-awaited National Security Review (NSR) by the NSC itself has not yet materialized. Consideration is also being given to forming a Defense Intelligence Agency and creating a Chairman of the Chiefs of Staffs Committee. Military requirements and capabilities, defense doctrines, and decision-making structures are also under review. One thing, however, is unlikely to change—civilian control of the military. As the May–June 1999 military conflict in Kargil demonstrated, India's military remains firmly under civilian control.

The evolution of India's military forces is far from certain. But certain observations can be made. First, perhaps at no time since the defeat in the Sino-Indian border war of 1962 has there been a more serious reappraisal of India's military, including its roles and capabilities. Second, service chiefs are likely to have greater say in defense policymaking and national security in the future, and they are certainly clamoring for it. However, developments on this front will be slow and arduous. Third, all the services appear to be intent on modernizing their forces through the development or acquisition of new arms and the introduction of the latest computer and information technology. However, serious problems confront force modernization. Some of these trends have been visible for years, but India's declaration that it is a nuclear weapons power is likely to buttress them.

**Political Framework**

India's democracy has defied the odds. Despite the country's dizzying diversity, poverty, and high level of illiteracy—all factors that conventional wisdom predicts make democracy unlikely—India's vibrant democracy persists. The media, both in English and the vernacular languages, is boisterous and free. Civil society in the form of associations and nongovernmental organizations is rich and varied. The judiciary is cumbersome but respected and increasingly activist in ensuring citizens' rights. The National Human Rights Commission and the National Election Commission have gained considerable credit for their fairness and effectiveness. More power is devolving to the states, and village councils are empowering millions who have had no direct political voice. The proliferation of political parties and the rising involvement of lower castes in electoral politics suggest that India is moving away from the one party–preeminent, elitist, dynastic democracy. Indian democracy is not without serious deficiencies. These include excessive use of "President's Rule" to dismiss elected state governments, corruption, unstable governing coalitions, inadequate decentralization, outbreaks of communal violence and terrorism, and the politicization of the bureaucracy.

India is a parliamentary democracy comprising the House of the People (Lok Sabha) and the House of the States (Rajya Sabha). The Prime Minister is the head of government though the President is the head of state and the Supreme Commander of Indian Armed Forces. Defense policymaking in the post-independence period has gone through a number of organizational changes.[4] Today, national security policy formulation and decisionmaking are concentrated in the office of the Prime Minister and key members of his cabinet. This Defense Committee of the Cabinet has as its chair the Prime Minister and the ministers of Home Affairs, Finance, Transport, Communications, and others as the need arises. The ultimate authority for national security policy thus rests with elected officials. Below this level, the civilian bureaucracy exerts an important influence, especially through the Defense Minister's Committee of the cabinet, which includes key civilian personnel, such as the Minister of State for Defense Production and the Secretary of Defense as well as the three service chiefs. The third level of policymaking is the service Chiefs of Staff Committee. Other relevant parts of the Indian bureaucracy, such as intelligence organizations, scientific and technical advisory bodies, and defense production, as well as research and development groups, support the work of these higher-level committees. At the present time, it is not known how the newly established NSC will relate to this in-place defense policy apparatus.

In addition to the three military services—army, navy, and air force—there are a number of paramilitary and reserve forces, all of which have grown immensely with the increase in internal threats from the 1960s through the present. As local police forces proved unable to maintain law and order, and as India's armed services in the early 1990s began to be increasingly hesitant to play domestic roles, the paramilitary and reserve forces were expanded. Today they number close to 700,000 personnel.[5] In some cases, the police forces have been given wide latitude to counter internal security challenges. For example, the police chief in Punjab, K.P.S. Gill, used very harsh methods to quell the insurgency movement in that state.

### Risk Assessment

#### Internal Security

Internal problems pose the most immediate challenges for Indian national security. Insurgencies, in varying degrees of severity, persist in Jammu and Kashmir, northeast India (i.e., mainly Assam and Arunachal Pradesh), and even Punjab, though this last conflict is at present under control. In addition to these insurgencies and secessionist movements, there is religious strife between Hindus and Muslims, and more recently between Hindus and Christians. Many observers blame Hindu nationalists for the increase in ethnic and religious conflict, but the evidence suggests that such conflict has been on the increase for over two decades.[6] Caste conflict persists, particularly in the countryside, from which regular reports of intercaste slaughter are received. These internal problems tie down India's security forces and cost the country millions of dollars. The strategies used by India to respond to internal security threats have differed by case, but usually have involved both carrots and sticks.

The use of the armed forces for maintaining internal order has become very controversial and at times has had very negative effects on the military. A case in point was the use of the army to storm the Sikh religion's holiest temple in 1984. Operation Bluestar resulted in mutinies by Sikh soldiers. The armed forces have argued that their growing use in internal security management has undermined morale, politicized their forces, and exhausted their very limited resources and personnel.

### External Security

There is considerable divergence between the views of the Indian masses and Indian defense intellectuals regarding the main external threats to the country. For the majority of Indians, the enemy is Pakistan. The Kargil conflict during the summer of 1999, India's first televised war, has intensified the identification of Pakistan in the Indian psyche as India's most pressing enemy. Many Indians feel a deep sense of betrayal by what they regard as Pakistan's direct support for armed intrusion into Kargil. That this intrusion came in the wake of a heady attempt at rapprochement by Indian Prime Minister Vajpayee and his Pakistani counterpart—the now-deposed Nawaz Sharif—during their famous meeting in Lahore in February 1999 has made skeptics of even some Indians who wish to move their country beyond a persistently conflictual relationship with Pakistan. The December 1999 hijacking of an Indian airliner brought India–Pakistan relations to a new low, with India accusing Pakistan of having supported the hijackers and Pakistan suggesting that India's intelligence agencies were responsible for the event. Given the historical legacy of India–Pakistan tensions, the asymmetries of power, the rivalry's use in respective domestic politics, and the competing nationalisms that the two states represent, there is little prospect for an end to their conflict.

However, for most of India's defense elite, the main, long-term concern is China. For example, both before and after India's nuclear tests in May 1998 the country's defense minister, George Fernandes, issued harsh condemnations of China, calling it India's number one potential enemy. Given China's size, population, and potential economic and military might, Indians consider China to be their country's out-year rival. In the Indian perspective, the "China threat" takes many forms. The first is a contested border in the northeast (over which India fought and lost a brief border with China in 1962) and Chinese occupation of Indian territory in the northwest (Aksai Chin). A second Indian concern is Beijing's support of its rival Pakistan through the supply of military equipment, including nuclear and missile technology. India's foreign minister Jaswant Singh specifically cited this issue in justifying his country's recent nuclear tests.[7] Finally, historically, India and China have competed for influence in the wider region, and may do so again. Despite the immediate post-nuclear test freeze in

Sino–Indian relations, both countries have moved to repair relations during 1999–2000. However, Indian defense planners continue to make decisions about doctrines and acquisitions with at least an eye toward China.

The United States and India have been described as "unfriendly friends" or "estranged democracies" and their bilateral relations as a "cold peace." Despite the commonality of democracy and the end of the Cold War, little warmth or substantive cooperation has developed between the two countries. India's May 1998 nuclear tests created much acrimony in bilateral relations, including the imposition of sanctions on India, but ironically led to the most sustained and high-level dialogue ever between the two countries. These talks, between Deputy Secretary of State Strobe Talbott and India's Foreign Minister Jaswant Singh have led to little progress on core issues emanating from disagreement about India's nuclear weapons program. On the other hand, during the Kargil crisis, Washington was seen as supportive by most Indians but later there was disappointment at U.S. reticence to censure Pakistan for what India believes was its complicity in the hijacking of an Indian airliner in December 1999. Given the underlying differences of national interests, the "roller-coaster" nature of U.S.–India relations is not likely to end soon.

Though India's armed forces have little in the way of force projection capabilities, they have been used beyond pure defensive purposes. Two such examples are their deployment in Sri Lanka to fight the Liberation Tigers of Tamil Eelam (LTTE) and their use to put down a coup in the Maldives off the coast of India. Indian forces also are active in international peacekeeping activities.

## Military Structure

India's army has been the dominant service, receiving most of the budget allotted to the armed services. However, the relative importance of the different services may shift following the issuance of the much-awaited NSR and decisions regarding nuclear doctrine, development, and deployment. India's fiscal year 2000–01 defense budget increased by 28.2 percent, the largest single increase ever. The army budget showed the largest increase, from US$4.8 billion to US$6 billion while the navy's allotment rose only slightly to US$1 billion. However, the navy budget has almost doubled over the past three years. Total defense spending, at US$14 billion, is about 2.5 percent of gross domestic product (GDP). This increase in defense spending reflects such factors as the Kargil campaign, but also emerging adjustments in military doctrine and greater foreign policy activism following the 1998 nuclear tests.

At present, all indications are that the Indian armed forces' plans to modernize and expand their capabilities will be constrained by budgetary, bureaucratic, personnel, and technology impediments. Despite a vast defense production network, the outputs have been unsatisfactory in the view of the military. The Defense Research and Development Organization (DRDO)—the state-run entity responsible for providing India with military hardware—has come under criticism for its work by the Parliamentary Standing Committee as well as by the military. A number of key projects are well behind schedule, including the Arjun Main Battle Tank (MBT), the Light Combat Aircraft (LCA), the Advanced Light Helicoptor (ALH) and the Advanced Technology Vessel (ATV) nuclear-powered submarine.[8] India has made better progress in the area of missile development and the development and deployment of several navy craft as well as small arms. There is growing debate about how much to privatize the defense sector, primarily as a result of the collapse of the Soviet Union, India's main defense supplier. However, little headway has been made because of resistance from the Ministry of Defense's civilian bureaucracy, which is seen as wanting to protect employment in the overstaffed state industries. The loss of the Soviet connection as an arms supplier was a major blow to India. However, in recent years, India and Russia have worked out new modes of cooperation that transcend earlier barter deals and straight-out purchases to ones that involve greater technology transfers, personnel exchanges, and joint development of weapons systems. Finally, some thought has been given to exporting arms to make up for budget shortfalls. But as yet, little concrete work has been done in this area, and India's arms exports are likely to remain minimal.[9]

## Conclusions

India is undergoing considerable change at home and abroad. The very foundations of India's domestic order are beginning to shift. However, these changes are likely to be managed in a democratic framework. India will likely remain officially secular, but with a more conservative, nationalist, and Hindu outlook. India's economy will become less regulated at home and more open abroad in terms of investment and trade, but within limits. Economic growth rates will be higher than in the past. India's search for strategic autonomy will lead it to much greater pragmatism in international affairs. Unlike in the past, India is giving serious attention to military capabilities and doctrines, but progress in achieving objectives will be slow. The military will increase its role in defense decisionmaking as India restructures her policymaking system, but this will not happen soon or without controversy.

## Notes

The views expressed in this chapter are the author's alone; they do not represent those of the Department of Defense or any other agency of the United States government.

1. The preamble of India's constitution commits the country to socialism, secularism, and democracy.

2. A good overview of India's economic reforms is Francine R. Frankel (ed.), *A Decade of Economic Reforms: Political Discord and the Second Stage*, Special Issue of *Doing Business in India*, Fall 1999, available at website www.sas.upenn.edu/casi.

3. See the three articles on India's democracy in *Journal of Democracy*, July 1998.

4. A good source of information on India's armed forces is their official website at www.bharat-rakshak.com.

5. See James Heitzman and Robert L. Worden (eds.), *India: A Country Study* (Washington, DC: Library of Congress, 1996).

6. For a short analysis of ethnic and religious strife in India see Ashutosh Varshney, "Governance, Pluralism, and Ethnic Conflict in India," in Satu Limaye and Ahmed Mukarram (eds.), *India, Southeast Asia and the United States: Governance Issues* (New York: The Asia Society, 1998).

7. See Jaswant Singh, "Against Nuclear Apartheid," *Foreign Affairs*, September/October 1998.

8. A good review of Indian efforts at military modernization is Rahul Bedi, "Mixed Fortunes for India's Defense Industrial Revolution," *Jane's International Defense Review*, May 1999.

9. See Amit Gupta, "Determining India's Force Structure and Military Doctrine," *Asian Survey* 35, No. 5, May 1995.

## Suggested Readings

Bajpai, Kanti, and Varun Sahni. *Secure and Solvent: Thinking About an Affordable Defence for India*. New Delhi: Rajiv Gandhi Institute for Contemporary Studies, 1994.

Gupta, Shekhar. *India Redefines Its Role*. London: International Institute of Strategic Studies, 1995, Adelphi Paper No. 293.

Heitzman, James, and Robert L. Worden, eds. *India: A Country Study*. Washington, DC: Library of Congress, 1996.

Smith, Chris. *India's Ad Hoc Arsenal: Direction or Drift in Defence Policy*. New York: Oxford University Press, 1994.

Tanham, George. *Indian Strategic Thought: An Interpretative Essay*. Santa Monica, CA: Rand Corporation, 1991.

# 14

# Indonesia

*John B. Haseman*

Indonesia's people have discovered that becoming the world's third largest democracy will not be an easy process. After more than thirty years of autocratic rule under President Soeharto (Suharto), repressed desires for a more open political system burst violently into reality in May 1998. Two years after Soeharto's resignation, Indonesia's social, political, and security challenges are more difficult than before. The country has a new president and vice president, a democratically elected parliament has been seated, and now reality has set in. The hard work to overcome those challenges has just begun.

The reasons for Indonesia's difficult challenges are many. They are intertwined with the country's complex society and recent history, regional economic factors, and its uniquely disparate geography. A momentous political transformation is under way as Indonesia changes from the autocratic rule of the Soeharto era to the more open political environment of the new century. It will be a slow and sometimes difficult process. In addition to the difficulties inherent in major political change, the country must simultaneously cope with economic reform and repair a badly torn social fabric. One of these challenges is difficult; Indonesia must cope with three at the same time.

## Emerging Political Framework

The key to solving these challenges is a secure and stable environment within which to practice social, economic, and political reforms. There has been little development of the tools and mechanisms of democracy. Thus it can be expected that there will be considerable experimentation as the new political leadership attempts to find the right formula that will combine a reasonably open political system with the time needed to educate and train a new leadership infrastructure.

## Indonesia

Governance during the Soeharto era employed a simple formula: The government undertook to provide economic development and gradually improve prosperity for all. In return it imposed tight political controls and tolerated little criticism or political opposition. The formula worked well for many years. Soeharto led Indonesia away from the economic disaster of Sukarno's final years and restored social and political harmony—at the cost of freedom of political expression.

Political historians will debate for years the efficacy of the formula, and to determine the point when perhaps a more prudent ruler would have adjusted the parameters of the formula to gradually open the political arena for greater popular participation. For now, however, the legacy is clear: Soeharto kept the political lid on Indonesian society for too long.

### Internal Security Environment

The Indonesian military leadership has always identified internal instability as the country's greatest security problem. Indonesia is an inherently centrifugal country. With its fragmented geography of more than 17,000 islands, more than 300 separate ethnic and linguistic groups, religious diversity, and glaring imbalances in economic distribution and social levels, the nation needs a strong central government to keep its volatile population at peace with itself. Even in the best of times during the late 1980s and early 1990s, when its economy experienced annual growth rates of 7 to 8 percent, flareups of ethnic or social-based violence illustrated how close to the surface friction lay.

More serious for Indonesia's economic and political reform process are the continual outbreaks of violence between ethnic and religious groups all over the country. Clashes between Ambonese Muslims and Christians, between Dayaks and Madurese, between Sumatran Bataks and Flores Catholics, are just the most recent in a continuous series of violence that has wracked Indonesia for more than two years.

This type of violence is known by the Indonesian acronym "SARA," which stands for ethnic groups, social groups, and religion. During the Soeharto era SARA conflicts were invariably dealt with quickly and ruthlessly. It was an item of faith that such violence was never to be tolerated and certainly not to be allowed to spread.

Ironically, that very tight security response to ethnic and religious violence may be responsible for the ongoing outbreak of clashes among ethnic and religious groups today. The combination of strong pressure against political development under Soeharto, as well as instant repression of religious and ethnic violence, kept a tight lid on the natural pressures that exist throughout Indonesian society between its many ethnic and religious groups.

For many years it has been difficult for ethnic leaders to gain a following because they were often assumed by the government to be preparing for political leadership competition with the ruling party and government authorities, or against another ethnic group. Traditional ethnic leaders were stripped of their powers to control their own peoples. Those responsibilities became part of the duties of government-appointed political leaders at the regency and village level. Their management of interethnic relations often consisted of calling out the army or police to repress real or imagined confrontations.

In August 1999, clashes on the previously peaceful island of Batam illustrated the complexity of the problems facing security forces. Batam is an artificially wealthy island only a few miles across the Singapore Strait from that booming island nation. Agreements between Singapore and Indonesia allowed major industrial development on Batam in schemes that used the economic advantages of both countries—Singapore's investment capital and Indonesia's cheap land and manpower.

Recreational development of Batam and adjacent Bintan Island brought beach resorts and golf courses, as well as other recreational attractions that the more straight-laced Singapore government does not tolerate gladly. The result is a booming economy, a huge weekend exodus of wealthy Singaporeans to the islands, and the inevitable migration of Indonesians from all over the country attracted to better job possibilities.

The Batam clashes were interethnic and interreligious, but they had their base cause in economic conflict over business and territorial rights. The object was the transportation business, both trucking and taxicabs. The opposing parties were the Bataks of North Sumatra, largely Protestant and Islamic, and natives of the island of Flores, almost entirely Catholic. The fighting was over "turf"—who had the right to run the transport system—and initially had no bearing on the religion or ethnicity of the opposing parties. But because of the inability of security authorities and intelligence agencies to recognize the depth of competition, the violence was entirely unanticipated.

Indonesia's clashes are almost always sparked by a single act of violence or a personal clash which, because those involved were of different ethnicity or religion, quickly takes on the larger character of ethnic or religious warfare. In fact, few were started by members of an ethnic or religious group who deliberately determined to begin a violent clash with another, "different," group. This is what has made diagnosing and predicting violence so difficult.

In short, many of Indonesia's current problems were caused by three decades of tight political autocracy, during which it was impossible for any type of alternative leadership to emerge, practice leadership, or gain a following. The resulting leadership vacuum at the head of newly emerging political, ethnic, and social groups has encouraged demagoguery and violence.

Easier to analyze is what has made ending the violence so difficult. Simply put, the Indonesian police and armed forces are so damaged by revelations of prior, routine, violent abuse of human rights throughout the country's trouble spots that they have little credibility in the eyes of the population, and can arguably be said to be engaged in a crisis of confidence on their own part.

The police and armed forces are further hampered in their domestic security responsibilities by a lack of training in, and equipment for, nonlethal crowd and riot control. Selected military and police units in some urban areas have received this kind of training and equipment, and have used that experience to ameliorate the number of casualties that are inevitable in such situations. But when violent incidents occur frequently, in cities and towns throughout the country, trained units and equipment do not stretch nearly far enough. It is unrealistic to expect the army continuously to fly its well-trained quick-reaction troops from Jakarta to all the far-flung islands of the country in reaction to violence that erupts, often spontaneously, due to unforeseen causes.

The alternatives when persuasion fails in such cases are very stark: defuse a real or potential riot with deadly force, or allow part or all of a city to be destroyed by rampaging crowds. The unfortunate result is that civilian casualties will rise as outmanned and underequipped troops are deployed against an unruly populace. This in turn can only worsen relations between the armed forces and the population, raise criticism from concerned outside countries, and adversely affect plans for political reform and economic recovery.

Indonesia is the world's most populous Muslim nation, and also its most moderate. There are significant numbers of members of most of the world's other major religions, and throughout its history the official tolerance of religious freedom was a keystone to domestic harmony. Yet in places like Ambon—where the balance between Christians and Muslims is approaching equality—there remain deep gaps between official tolerance and local acceptance of ethnic and religious differences.

Indonesia's major internal security problems have involved separatist groups in three areas of the country: East Timor, Aceh, and Irian Jaya. It is important to

stress the differences between secessionist guerrilla groups, whose goal is to secede from the country and gain formal independence for their region, and
nonsecessionists, whose grievances center around economic and social exploitation by the central government but who do not advocate formal independence.

East Timor was the most difficult security problem for Indonesia for many years.
Indonesia's Foreign Minister Ali Alatas once described East Timor as "a pebble in
Indonesia's shoe." That pebble caused a major stone bruise for the country, se-
verely damaged its international image, and cost uncounted billions of rupiah and
thousands of lives. Like many of Indonesia's problems, previous intransigence on
East Timor by Soeharto allowed the problem to fester to an unmanageable level.

Shortly after taking office in 1998 President B.J. Habibie unveiled a major autonomy package for East Timor that would allow the province to control virtually
every aspect of life except defense, foreign affairs, and monetary issues. Ironically, a similar proposal was floated back in 1995 by then-colonel Prabowo Subianto,
whose name has since been linked with extensive human rights violations in East
Timor, Jakarta, and perhaps elsewhere. But his 1995 proposal was summarily rejected by Soeharto.

Indonesia gained the agreement of both Portugal and the United Nations for the
autonomy package and for a ballot by the East Timorese on whether to accept or
reject the proposal. President Habibie further complicated the East Timor issue
when he announced that rejection of the autonomy package would cause Indonesia to grant independence to East Timor. An extensive United Nations operation
called UNAMET—United Nations Mission in East Timor—was formed to over-
see preparation for the vote and the balloting process itself.

Indonesia was, unfortunately, unable to preserve a peaceful environment in the
months leading up to the vote. Opposition to potential independence by hard line
elements of the military, which was not allowed a voice in President Habibie's
decision, was based on two major worries. One was that allowing East Timor to
split away from Indonesia would make national unity far more difficult to preserve, particularly in the restive provinces of Aceh and Irian Jaya. The second was
an emotional tie to East Timor, which refused to consign pro-Indonesian authorities and peoples to "revenge" by pro-independence elements.

The result was the poorly hidden formation and arming of civilian militia groups
whose purpose was to "encourage" a pro-Indonesia vote in the UN-sponsored
ballot. Many contend that East Timorese may well have voted for continued integration with Indonesia had the election been held shortly after agreement was
reached on the balloting process. But the vicious terrorist activities of pro-Indonesian
militia groups rebounded against Indonesia.

An astounding 98.5 percent of registered East Timorese voted in the August
1999 referendum, and by a margin of almost 78 percent they voted against the
Habibie autonomy package and thus for independence. The wave of violence after
the results of the vote were announced so angered the outside world that Indonesia
was forced to accept an international peacekeeping force to restore order and se-

curity. After the newly elected parliament chose Mr. Abdurrachman Wahid and Mrs. Megawati Soekarnoputri as president and vice president, respectively, the legislature also ratified the results of the August referendum. East Timor was separated from Indonesian sovereignty shortly thereafter.

The effect of East Timor's experience has already given encouragement to separatists in Indonesia's northwesternmost province of Aceh. A hotbed of anti-center sentiments for hundreds of years, the Acehnese have historically opposed rule from Jakarta, whether by the Dutch colonialist government or the independent government of Indonesia. Since the fall of Soeharto and the removal of many of the army troops that had controlled an uneasy security situation there, violence in Aceh has escalated dramatically.

The rise in violence has its roots in many causes. The historical opposition to outside rule is one. Another is the legacy of violence by the Indonesian security forces during the Soeharto era and since. The army's propensity to treat all civilians as actual or potential guerrilla supporters, which contributed to the lack of success in East Timor, has also harmed government pacification efforts in Aceh. A record of egregious human rights violations on the parts of both the army and the separatist Aceh Merdeka (Free Aceh) guerrillas has inflamed passions on both sides.

Unlike East Timor, which became a part of Indonesia only in 1976, Aceh has always been a part of Indonesia. And while problems in East Timor were of minor interest to the Indonesian population over the years, they are keenly interested in the situation in Aceh and adamantly oppose allowing the province to split away from the country.

A third major cause of unrest in Aceh is the diversion of the province's natural wealth to the center. Acehnese resent the fact that only a tiny percentage of the monies derived from its huge natural resources is returned to the province. This grievance can be addressed by enlightened policies from Jakarta. Already tabled in Parliament are a number of proposals to devolve considerable political powers to the provinces. More significantly, the proposals will increase dramatically the percentage of income from local resources that will remain in the provinces.

But before meaningful results of the devolvement of power and money to the provinces can be discerned in Aceh, a halt to the escalating violence is urgently needed. To date the military has been unable to find the right balance between force to preserve security on the one hand and allowances for local guerrillas to retain some degree of influence on the other. Until a ceasefire arrangement can be found to halt the violence, the political changes promised by the Habibie and Wahid governments cannot be implemented. Aceh is thus likely to become the single most important security concern of the government for the next several years.

President Wahid has taken some steps to address the challenge. He appointed a native Acehnese as the country's first Minister of State for Human Rights. The Deputy Commander-in-Chief of the Armed Forces is an Acehnese officer. Several government investigations of military violence are under way and the government has hinted that prosecution will be handled by the civilian court system, not the military tribunals that have had jurisdiction in the past. Whether or not these measures will help to reduce tension, however, remains to be seen.

Irian Jaya remains a security concern as well. Small and uncoordinated separatist groups have conducted anti-government operations for years. Now, with the change in government in Jakarta, those groups have begun to coordinate and communicate among each other and the threat for potential separation is greater now than in the past. However, it remains to be seen how strongly the collectively named Free Papua Movement feels about separation. Like elsewhere in Indonesia, its grievances include the low return to the province of its huge natural resources, as well as strong resentment of the government and military attitude toward the local tribal population.

Given the huge natural resources in both Aceh and Irian Jaya it is highly unlikely that Indonesia will allow the provinces to separate. Thus the key to security in both regions is a reduction in tensions between government and populace, agreement on devolvement of political power and budget to the province and regency levels, and a revised formula for the local and national security apparatus to carry out legitimate police and defense missions. The central government has already proposed the split of huge Irian Jaya into three provinces, a step with the potential to increase local political powers and to impose a greater sharing of income from immense petroleum and mineral resources.

## External Security Environment

The primary responsibility of the Indonesian armed forces, like all nations' armed forces, is to counter any threat to the country's security, whether foreign or domestic. Indonesia is fortunate in that it does not confront a significant external threat. The most serious external problems involve overlapping claims of sovereignty in the South China Sea of its partners in the Association of Southeast Asian Nations (ASEAN) and those of China. Indonesia has no overlapping sovereignty claims with its ASEAN partners in the South China Sea. An increasingly assertive China looms as the region's most worrisome future threat.

But even this relatively benign international environment has worrisome changes coming. Economic downturns throughout the South China Sea region increase the value of potentially important undersea resources such as petroleum, natural gas, and minerals. Thus the potential for clashes over rights to develop such resources may be increasing.

The political harmony of the formerly six-nation ASEAN has begun to fray at the edges with the admission to membership of the economically less developed and politically more repressive countries of Burma, Cambodia, Laos, and Vietnam. The long-hallowed principle of noninterference in fellow ASEAN members' domestic affairs is being challenged by the free democracies, who now criticize the human rights abuses of other members.

Powerful regional neighbors such as China and new nuclear power India will undoubtedly seek greater influence in the region. Thus Indonesia's armed forces must be mindful of the probable change of the heretofore benevolent regional security situation. For example, Indonesia has a large territorial claim around the Natuna Islands, which until comparatively recently was included in China's broad claims to virtually all of the South China Sea. China figures large in Indonesia's concerns over possible future outside threats to its economic interests and sovereignty. It was no coincidence that the scenario for the military's last major multiservice training exercise focused on Natuna Island. The exercise tested planned operations to regain the island from "an outside invading force."

## Military Structure

The political future of the Indonesian armed forces is no longer clear. Challenged as an institution, its reputation badly damaged by revelations of brutality on a general scale, and its dominant political role under intense debate, the military must now repair cracks in its structure, reassert its unity and integrity, and find an accepted place for itself in Indonesia's angry society.

While many will look at emerging political leaders and economic policies for solutions, the key to political and economic change and recovery lies, as it always has, with the country's armed forces and their ability to support significant reform and simultaneously to enforce a reasonable degree of domestic security.

Indonesia's armed forces are in vastly different circumstances than anyone might have imagined just a short time ago. The military establishment is essential for national survival, but its effectiveness in assuring law and order and domestic security is in question. Under attack for decades of abuses during the era of Soeharto's rule, its reputation has sunken to a low ebb in the esteem of the population.

Now, in addition to the normal challenges facing any armed force, the armed forces must meet the challenge of regaining the respect of its people. The military's reputation has been deeply damaged by a wave of national revulsion over revelations of major and systematic human rights violations in the past. Only after the military regains the respect of its population can it most effectively assist the country to restore a tattered economy and implement political reform.

### Role of the Military

The military's reputation has been badly damaged by years of use as a political tool by the Soeharto government. The military has pledged to avoid such a political role in the future. Its commitment to this pledge may well become the key to future acceptance by the Indonesian people.

The armed forces are now known by a new name—Tentara Nasional Indonesia (TNI). Although the English translation "Indonesian Armed Forces" is the same as the old term ABRI (Angkatan Bersenjata Republik Indonesia), the switch to TNI, which was the accepted terminology before the Soeharto era, reflects the devolvement of the national police from the armed forces structure as well as a symbolic change in the military's role and charter within Indonesian society.

It may well turn out that the bellwether time of change for TNI was the June 1999 national election. In one of the largest democratic elections ever, Indonesians went to the polls on June 7, 1999, to elect members of parliament. More than 110 million Indonesians voted—90 percent of the eligible electorate—in the first free elections to be held in Indonesia for forty years.

The election campaign and voting were virtually free of security problems, to the surprise of many, given the violent disturbances throughout Indonesia during the past two years. But perhaps the most significant departure from the staged elections of the Soeharto era was the role of the armed forces. For the first time in thirty years the military took virtually no part in the campaign and election process.

The anticipated depoliticization of the Indonesian military is of considerable importance to the evolvement of more participatory democracy in Indonesia. The military has already initiated some reforms. One was the separation of the national police from the armed forces establishment; another was the taking of a new name. The military kept its pledge to remain neutral in the election process. Military officers serving in civil government postings now must retire from the armed forces to keep their jobs. A navy officer is Commander-in-Chief of the Armed Forces, the first time in history an army officer has not held the post. A civilian serves as Minister of Defense for the first time since the early years of the Sukarno government forty years ago. But internal reforms and changes in military security policies are likely to be taken slowly, at a pace that may not be acceptable to the country's newly enfranchised population.

The military still remains the single most powerful segment of Indonesian society. Though small in numbers, its influence is significant and widespread. The Armed Forces Commander-in-Chief, Admiral Widodo, appears determined to implement reforms, although he is criticized by reformers for moving too slowly on some needed changes, and by opponents of reform—many of them senior military officers—for moving too quickly on others.

Most Indonesians acknowledge the importance of a disciplined and capable military establishment for the country's stability and unity. Indonesia is a centrifugal country. Its multi-ethnic, multi-religious society and its geographical fragmentation require a strong central government and a police and military apparatus capable of maintaining domestic stability. As noted, there are more than 300 separate ethnic and linguistic groups in Indonesia. On some islands, peoples in adjacent valleys speak mutually unintelligible languages and view their neighbors with considerable suspicion.

**Defense Requirements**

The only major change in the TNI in recent years was the 1999 separation of the national police from the armed forces structure. Strength of the remaining military force has changed little over the past fifteen years, and remains one of the lowest per capita military forces in the world. Despite its loss of stature because of human rights violations, the force remains well trained and disciplined overall. Like many Asian forces, its primary weaknesses lie in the fields of maintenance and logistical support.

Because of its traditional low priority in budgetary allocations under the Soeharto government, the TNI has had few modern systems acquisitions in recent years. The most significant addition of the past five years or so was the purchase of most of the East German navy, a policy decision urged by B.J. Habibie back when he was Minister for Science and Technology. That decision is still highly controversial because of the costs to modernize and refit those ships. President Wahid's announcement that protection of maritime resources will be a high priority of his government, and the appointment of a naval officer as military commander, indicate that the navy and air force may now assume a higher priority.

The air force has upgraded its strength with Hawk fighters purchased from the United Kingdom. But neither the "new" navy nor the "new" air force acquisitions are first-rank equipment. The force needs upgraded strategic mobility—both ships and transport aircraft—to defend its huge and fragmented territory and to improve movement of ground forces around the country. The shortcoming was particularly noticeable over the past two years when reserve battalions were repeatedly, and often slowly, moved around the country in response to major outbreaks of domestic violence.

Despite the separation of the national police, and the primary mission for internal security that went with them, the army has announced plans to expand its territorial structure in response to the spate of violence across the country. In many cases this will involve re-forming regional commands closed during an important restructuring in 1983, when the major territorial commands were drastically reduced in number. The army needs to upgrade its armor and transportation capabilities but is unlikely to see major funding for those acquisitions for the next decade.

### TNI and the New Indonesia

Overarching all armed forces priorities is the need to regain public respect. The well-publicized series of revelations of atrocities allegedly committed by soldiers in the past has stunned the rank and file of the armed forces just as it has outraged the public at large. National credibility is at stake as well, as foreign governments watch closely to see how the post-Soeharto military polices itself.

The military leadership is in a quandary. They know it is essential to investigate crimes against civilians in Aceh and elsewhere. There is less unanimity inside the armed forces, however, that those investigations must be transparent, though they agree that any scrutiny of past events be perceived to be fair and complete. There are major difficulties involved in this aspect of military reform. Military and civilian leaders who have distinguished themselves in the post-Soeharto government have been implicated in alleged wrongdoing in the past. It is neither fair nor appropriate to judge the actions of units and individuals operating under the imposed rules of the past by the new rules in effect today. But excesses against civilians that violated orders and procedures in effect at the time of those human rights abuses are grounds for punishment. Therefore it is essential to the restoration of TNI's reputation and prestige that those investigations move forward.

The armed forces played the key role in the constitutional process that removed Soeharto from the presidency. At that time General Wiranto was widely praised for his insistence on constitutional change. When the moment of crisis came in May 1998 the Indonesian armed forces supported the will of the people and the dictates of the constitution rather than the will of the man who was president and who had controlled ABRI for thirty-two years. Military leaders effected the constitutional removal of the world's second longest serving strongman without taking up arms against the people.

The armed forces establishment remains the single most influential and powerful element of Indonesian society. Most Indonesians realize that a strong and effective military force is essential to a smooth transition to a more democratic system and to guarantee the nation's security, particularly during the turbulent times certain to stretch into the future.

The TNI's senior officers believe they can regain the people's trust, but that it will require hard work. They are confident that there is a reservoir of goodwill for the armed forces among the population, and a realization among the populace that a strong military is essential for continued national recovery and progress. But that goodwill could quickly be lost if the TNI loses its momentum toward internal cleansing and reform. Investigation of reported misdeeds, and prosecution of officers found guilty of misbehavior, will assist in restoring that prestige.

Now it is acceptable and expected that senior military officers speak out on matters of political, economic, and social reform. They will be among the most listened to voices of the new Indonesia.

## Suggested Readings

Haseman, John B. "Jakarta's Democratic Dalliance Turns Sour." *Jane's Intelligence Review*, October 1999, pp. 40–45.
———. "National Security." Chapter V in *Indonesia: A Country Study*. Washington, DC: U.S. Government Printing Office, 1994.
Masters, Edward. *Indonesia's 1999 Elections: A Second Chance for Democracy*. New York: Asia Society, May 1999.
Schwarz, Adam. *A Nation in Waiting: Indonesia in the 1990s*. St. Leonards, Australia: Allen and Unwin, 1994.
The United States–Indonesia Society (USINDO). *Parliamentary Elections in Indonesia: Consensus, Coalitions, or Confusion?* Washington, DC: USINDO, June 22, 1999.

# 15

# Japan

## William M. Carpenter

### Introduction

Japan is an anomaly. In spite of the late-nineties recession that sharply slowed Japan's gross national product (GNP) growth rate, it is still the second-ranking economic power in the world and the first in Asia. It has a population of 126 million, and is strategically located off the northeast coast of Asia, yet it is not a superpower. Japan has a modest military force of about 236,000 men and women, but because of the restrictions of its constitution and its self-imposed policies limiting the size and deployment of its armed forces, Japan's strategic role in the global power equation remains a minor one. Nuclear weapons are proscribed under present policy, although many years ago Japan's Supreme Court ruled that the restrictions of Article 9 of the Constitution do not prohibit the possession or use of defensive nuclear weapons. The Japanese government has for many years pursued a policy of limiting defense expenditures to less than 1 percent of gross national product (GNP), and no party in power has had sufficient political strength or courage to break that ceiling. This puts a clear limit on the total strength of the national defense, although, as a consequence of Japan's high-tech industrial base, it is a high-tech armed force. Economic power without commensurate military power limits Japan's political power; thus Japan has only one strong element of the three usual attributes of strategic power (political, economic, and military).

Nevertheless, although Japan is not a strategic power, the longstanding U.S.–Japan alliance gives Japan a key regional role in Asia, and, as the millennium ends, Japan's role in its own defense and in its contribution to the alliance may increase. Japan is the forward base of U.S. forces in the western Pacific Rim. It can be said that since World War II Japan has been a protectorate of the United States, enjoying assured protection against external aggression and possessing the opportunity to

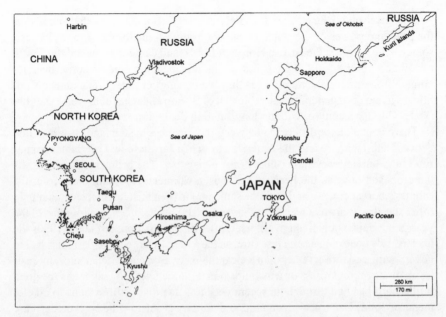

## Japan

turn all its energies toward rapid economic growth. As a consequence of its economic growth, Japan has built up a positive trade balance with nearly every country in the world, a situation that is both economically beneficial to Japan and somewhat embarrassing politically for most of its trade partners. On the downside for Japan, it has been among the nations hardest hit in the Asian financial crisis of the late 1990s.

The United States is Japan's largest debtor nation, and after more than twenty years of talking about the problem without success in solving it, the United States came to the point of taking action to curb the trade deficit. During all the years of the buildup of the trade surplus with the United States, economic and military negotiations with Japan pursued separate tracks. Now these have come together, resulting in a more realistic approach to the issue of preservation of the strategic framework long in place in Northeast Asia.

### Political Framework

Japan is a constitutional democracy with a two-house parliamentary system; the prime minister is the chief executive. The emperor, the "symbol of the state," has no real power; he accepts the "will of the people," and thus it is the legislature (Diet) and the cabinet ministers who govern. At the urging of the American occupying authorities after World War II, Japan denied the divinity of the Emperor—by a statement from the Emperor himself. The Diet was already functioning before World War II, although the militarists had preempted power in the 1920s, pursuing an exaggerated nationalist policy that eventually led the nation into a disastrous war.

The lower body, the House of Representatives, is popularly elected and wields the principal power of the state. The upper body, originally the House of Peers, somewhat resembles the British House of Lords, and came to be called the House of Councillors in the 1947 Constitution. Its members are elected rather than appointed from among the nobility (as they were in earlier times). Thus Japan's political system does generally resemble that of Britain and it has achieved a stability remarkable for a country with no longstanding democratic roots.

There is one major difference between the Japanese system and Britain's (and between the Japanese and the American system): Japanese law originates primarily in the bureaucracy rather than in the legislature. The prime minister submits the proposed laws as the head of his chosen cabinet—receiving them from the cabinet's bureaucracy—and with the same majority in the Diet that elected him to office, he almost always sees them duly enacted. This has been true for most of the years since Japan began to govern itself after the occupation, but in the 1990s the leadership's control has been less sure, as the Liberal Democratic Party has had to govern with a coalition rather than a clear majority. Even the bureaucracy, more or less permanent regardless of who holds power in the Diet, no longer has the great influence it has had throughout recent decades. Its power still extends to all elements of policy—political, economic, and military—but now the bureaucrats more often yield to the politically elected or appointed officials. The foreign minister, or the trade minister, when negotiating, has in the past closely followed the guidelines set by the bureaucrats. This has in the past been frustrating for foreign diplomats who may have tried in vain to change a Japanese negotiating position at what in most international meetings is the bargaining table—the minister was reluctant to change the position the bureaucrats had taken. However, as Japan tries to find its place in the international community at the close of the century, there are already changes in the way political and economic systems work in Japan. A half-century of success resulting from the generally smooth operation of its closely related political and economic systems appears to be giving way to a greater opening to the outside world, which necessarily will affect how the systems work in the nation and in the interfaces with the outside.

The business sector in Japan is leading the way; political leaders are reluctant to approve of breaking away from lifetime employment, but business leaders are laying off unnecessary workers and adopting innovations better to meet world competition. In the 1980s, many Americans thought of emulating "Japan, Inc." but now the astute Japanese CEOs are looking to the United States for the entrepreneurial methods that are sustaining America's strong economy. This will be a sea change of life in Japan.

### Risk Assessment

Japan does not face a serious military threat, except possibly from the rogue state of North Korea. When the Soviet Union was intact, there was the latent possibility that Soviet forces might attack Japan, perhaps even make an airborne or amphibious assault on Hokkaido or northern Honshu, but that threat has disappeared. One Cold War legacy that has been carried forward and continues to be a concern in Japan's relations with the newly independent Russia is the unresolved territorial dispute over the Northern Territories, although this too is no longer the threat it used to be, and eventually, over the long term, should give way via a negotiated settlement that links a future resolution to Japanese aid to Russia. The only threat that Japan sees would be from the Korean Peninsula. The threat is twofold: present and future. The present threat is alarm over longer-range missiles in North Korea, heightened by the possibility that the missiles might have nuclear warheads—in spite of U.S. efforts to prevent it. The longer-range threat is the possibility of Korean unification. Even though the prospect is slight that Korea would be unified under the domination of North Korea—the U.S. guarantee of South Korean security plus the strength of the South Korean forces will continue to deter the North—Japan harbors a latent fear of any kind of unified Korea because of the legacy of resentment in Korea for the thirty-five years of Japanese occupation of the peninsula. Even a democratically unified Korea may be seen as a "dagger pointed at the heart of Japan." The U.S. military presence in both Japan and Korea prevents any likelihood of military conflict between the two neighbors, and thus both Japan and Korea are reluctant to see the Americans depart. It does appear that in the near future the United States will maintain a strong presence in Northeast Asia, not just to protect Japan and Korea but to preserve enduring U.S. interests in East Asia and the western Pacific.

## Military Strength

Japan's military forces are modest in size, but the substantial Korean ground force plus respectable sea and air forces, plus the U.S. forces in both countries, will deter any likely regional aggressor. Japan's ground force is the largest element of the Self Defense Force (SDF); its strength of about 148,000 is organized into five regional commands. The Ground Self Defense Force (GSDF) has one armored division, twelve infantry divisions, and several specialized brigades, including at least five attack helicopter units. Equipment includes over 1,000 modern tanks, plus artillery, mortars, and air defense weapons. Mobility is provided by transport aircraft and helicopters. Deployment is concentrated in northern Japan, where threats have seemed greatest from the Russian-occupied islands near Hokkaido.

The Maritime Self Defense Force (MSDF) has a strength of about 43,000, including 12,000 in the maritime air arm. The fleet includes some one hundred ships of destroyer or frigate type, seventeen defensive submarines, forty minecraft, six amphibious ships, and twenty support ships. The MSDF air arm has about one hundred anti-submarine surveillance aircraft, one hundred anti-submarine helicopters, and thirty search and rescue aircraft.

The Air Self Defense Force (ASDF) has about 44,000 personnel, with seventy attack aircraft, 225 fighters, ten airborne early warning aircraft, fifty transports, and ten heavy-lift helicopters. There are sixty additional aircraft for search and rescue missions. Air-to-surface and air-to-air missiles are carried by the ASDF; there are six air defense missile groups armed with 120 surface-to-air missiles.

In addition to the branches of the SDF, Japan has a Maritime Safety Agency (MSA) or Coast Guard; its 12,000 personnel man forty-eight offshore patrol ships, thirty-six coastal craft, and about 250 inshore patrol craft. The offshore ships carry search and rescue helicopters. The MSA also has about twenty land-based search aircraft and some forty search helicopters.

U.S. forces in Japan: 44,800 total, 1,900 Army, 7,300 Navy, 20,000 U.S. Marines (Okinawa), and 15,600 U.S. Air Force personnel. The U.S. Seventh Fleet has a carrier battle group based at the Yokosuka Naval Base.

## Military Strategy

Japan's military strategy since World War II has stressed a defensive posture. Immediately after the war, there was no military strategy. In the brief period between the end of the war and the Korean War, Japan had no military forces except some very small remnants from the war, such as a few minesweepers that were used in cooperation with the American occupying authorities in clearing the mines in and around the Japanese islands. Of necessity, when the United States and its UN allies were confronted with the North Korean aggression in 1950, Japan assisted by creating a police force, which subsequently became the SDF, so named in deference to Article 9 of the Japanese constitution, which says that "land, sea, and air forces, as well as other war potential, will never be maintained." It was the original intent of the occupying forces that Japan should be completely demilitarized and hence without any forces at all, but the Korean War and early stirrings of the Cold War put aside the earlier impulse of the victors to see Japan impotent. Reality demanded that so strategically important a nation as Japan should have at least a modest defensive capability, to assist in the security of the free world.

The end of the Cold War brought no immediate change in Japan's strategy or force structure, but as the millennium ends, new and more realistic thinking is appearing in the Japanese leadership. As the threat from the former Soviet Union melted away, Japan began to watch with concern the unpredictable and truculent regime in nearby North Korea. While the United States—and South Korea and Japan—began applying a carrot-and-stick strategy to prevent North Korea from making its own nuclear weapons, Japan saw a dangerous defiance in the holdout communist regime in Pyongyang. In August 1998, North Korea fired a missile over Japan, claiming that it was an attempt to launch a satellite, but it was the consensus of most observers that it had been a test of the Taepo Dong ballistic missile. For Japan, the lesson was obvious: The range of the missile was sufficient to reach Japan, and it could carry a nuclear warhead. In the following months, Japanese newspapers began to report statements by senior lawmakers and political analysts saying that Japanese opinion was changing dramatically—for the first time both public and government people were speaking openly about the need for Japan to defend itself.

Japan and the United States had been talking since the early 1990s about a greater defense effort by Japan. In early 1995, a Japanese defense advisory group recommended that Japan should seek closer cooperation with the United States in developing a theater missile defense (TMD) system against nuclear attack. By the late 1990s, this concept began to take shape in serious talks about action; one result was the Japanese announcement in 1999 that it would engage in joint research with the United States on a missile defense system—despite objections from China. The two nations agreed on a plan to spend up to a half billion U.S. dollars over some five years on a joint ballistic missile defense program, and if Japan's economy continues its slow but apparently steady recovery, this plan will probably be carried out.

Not only was there a greater focus on defense between Japan and the United States, but between Japan and South Korea as well. South Korea's memory of the Japanese occupation from 1910 to 1945 has up to now inhibited any willingness on Korea's part to engage in bilateral defense talks with Japan. Such talks as did take place were usually with the United States at the table with Japan and South Korea. North Korea has changed the situation, on both sides of the Korea Strait. Tomahisa Sakanaka, president of the Research Institute for Peace and Security in Tokyo, said in 1999 that North Korea's adventures have encouraged Japan and South Korea to cooperate on regional security. One result: In August 1999, Japan and South Korea carried out their first joint naval exercise, a search and rescue exercise that involved escort ships, surveillance ships, and maritime helicopters.

On the U.S.–Japan axis, going beyond talks on missile defense, Japan and the United States agreed in 1997 to a significant change in Japan's role in support of the bilateral alliance. Japan agreed to upgrade its scope of cooperation with U.S. military forces, if future conflict situations arise. Under the new Defense Guidelines, gradually coming into effect on the Japanese side as the result of new legislative changes, there will be greater logistic support of U.S. forces (although excluding the provision of war munitions), sea and air reconnaissance (aided by the launching of Japan's own spy satellite into orbit), minesweeping, and search and rescue. Another Japanese role intended for inclusion in the Guidelines called for assistance by Japan in enforcing a blockade—this would involve stopping foreign ships at sea. As this can be construed by Japan as a "combat role," it is not likely that this kind of support will be a part of the Guidelines.

Even as it embarks on an upgrade of its security role, Japanese strategy will continue to rely heavily on the U.S.–Japan Security Treaty, which dates from 1951, to guarantee Japan's survival. The U.S. nuclear umbrella is the beginning of the strategy, followed by a cooperative arrangement by which Japan will make the initial defense against any aggressive assault, holding off the enemy until U.S. forces can come to Japan's aid.

Japan has a modernized air defense and warning system and a defensive fighter force for resisting attack by aircraft. Japan takes responsibility for defending its sea-lanes out to 1,000 miles from Tokyo Bay, for which it has a force of anti-submarine warfare (ASW) surface ships and submarines, and land-based ASW air-craft. For full effectiveness in this mission, Japan should have at least one ASW aircraft carrier.

Another recommendation of the 1995 defense panel was that Japan should take part in UN peacekeeping missions, including the sending of forces armed with combat weapons. Up to now, Japan has sent forces solely in non-combat roles, for example, in Cambodia in 1993.

In sum, Japan holds to an overall defensive military strategy, placing great reliance on the protection provided by the United States. But some leaders in Japan now show interest in a regional defense alliance such as the North Atlantic Treaty Organization (NATO). Japan's strategy may gradually change, as the Defense Guidelines are implemented. Nevertheless, even as they are adopted, the changes now in prospect will not alter Japan's basic military orientation. They should, however, make the present strategy more effective in Northeast Asian security. But there is one disturbing factor in all that is taking place for future regional security, a subject now more openly expressed in Japan. It is the occasional stated lack of confidence in the hitherto widespread belief in the commitment of the United States to defend Japan. For some Japanese policy planners, this is a more cogent reason for upgrading defense than the fear of North Korean missiles.

## Armaments Industry

As a major industrial power Japan is fully capable of providing high-technology military equipment in quantity. It has been national policy over many years for Japan to produce its own ships, aircraft, tanks, radars, and other kinds of armaments, even though it often would have been cheaper to buy the equipment from foreign sources. This practice is sometimes modified, as in the case of U.S.-Japanese cooperation in joint production agreements. The FS-X joint project for producing a new defensive fighter aircraft came about as a compromise between the U.S. desire to produce and sell an advanced fighter to Japan and Japan's desire to go it alone. It turned out to be mutually advantageous to exchange technology so that the best from each side might go into the aircraft.

In the early days of rebuilding Japan's industrial economy the United States transferred much high technology to the Japanese side, mostly a one-way operation at that time. As Japan's technical expertise increased, an agreement was reached to transfer Japanese technology, including military applications, to the United States. In the case of the FS-X project, there are disagreements as to which side benefited the most, but overall it has been a practical arrangement.

Japan sells some non-lethal military equipment to other countries, and has received requests to sell all kinds of military hardware. Present policy limits sales to such equipment as radar, small naval patrol craft, and military vehicles. Japan produces a highly effective tank, but so far declines to sell it abroad. Were Japan to relax its restrictions on sales of combat equipment, American and European producers of military hardware would feel the competition, just as the automobile companies have experienced Japanese competition since the 1970s. For the present, it does appear that Japan will confine its production of combat equipment to the supplying of its own forces.

## Conclusions

Japan is likely to be an anomaly in the international community for some time. The island nation is groping for its proper role, torn between the desire—spoken by some of Japan's leaders in the early years after World War II—to be the first major nation whose position in the world was based on economic strength rather than military power, and the traditional norm of a nation's gaining recognition by having a strong industrial economy and formidable military strength. It could be said that for four decades after its defeat in war Japan did appear to come close to accomplishing the aim of being recognized as economically strong but without being strong militarily. The world recognizes the economic, technological, and management prowess of a people who rose from military defeat and by a combination of self-denial and hard work—aided by highly protective laws favoring rapid domestic economic growth—made Japan a by-word for success. Japanese export products can be found in the most remote corners of the world, from radios and televisions to four-wheel-drive vehicles. Japan has acquired a modest military establishment, and will continue to increase its quality if not its quantity, but so far, has not frightened its neighbors; economic penetration is more feared than military invasion. The Japanese dream of the 1930s of creating a Greater East Asia Co-Prosperity Sphere failed as a military venture but came to be an accepted reality after World War II through the exercise of Japan's economic and technological prowess.

All this took place during the Cold War. As the Cold War ended, Japan was forced to reassess its global role. No longer is there a clearly defined security threat that was manageable within the limits of the Japanese-American alliance. The new world environment is far more complex. Conflict can arise in many places, in forms that defy the simpler logic of Cold War confrontations. Ancient hatreds among peoples came to the fore after long suppression, in places where previously the superpowers deterred each other with their huge military arsenals and their suppression of latent indigenous conflict. Peacekeeping is a major challenge in today's world and Japan is wrestling with how to respond. The nation did make a breakthrough by the Diet's passing of a law allowing Japan to participate, but only in non-combat roles. The size and shape of Japan's armed forces are under new scrutiny. The total force may be smaller, and less oriented toward the previous heavy strength of ground forces, but with greater emphasis on mobility and more efficient command and control. It has modernized defenses against missiles and the ability to protect the sea-lanes, and with a new emphasis on coping with domestic crises, such as earthquakes, or the threats of terrorists.

Relations with the United States will remain a high-priority issue. Specific initiatives are under way from both Washington and Tokyo to preserve what is best from the longstanding alliance and to prevent the U.S. concern over economic and trade issues from damaging what has been a mutually beneficial relationship. Probably the most serious threat to the stability of U.S.–Japan security relations came as a consequence of an incident in Okinawa in 1995, when three American servicemen raped a twelve-year-old Japanese girl. The heavy news coverage of the incident and the trial in a Japanese court aroused strong emotions in the Japanese public, and especially on Okinawa, where the U.S. military presence is much more visible than anywhere else in Japan. There were many protests from Okinawa residents, demanding that all U.S. forces be removed. The three men were convicted and sentenced in March 1996 (two for seven years in prison, and one for six and one-half years) but the Japanese people regarded these terms as too short, while the reaction of the American relatives of the convicted men was that they were too long. Senior officials on both sides tried to put the incident behind them and get on with the needs and benefits of the alliance. In early 1996, the United States agreed, as the two nations reviewed their security relationship, to return part of the land used for U.S. bases in Okinawa to the local owners. The strength of U.S. forces based in Okinawa will remain about the same, but they will use less land. On the Japanese side of the adjustment, the prime minister agreed that Japan could give logistic support to U.S. forces if they are used in war.

Parallel to the question of adjusting to current and projected needs of the U.S.–Japan relationship is Japan's problem of working out its relationships with its Asian neighbors. The 50th anniversary of the end of World War II has brought this question to the fore. Japan will probably remain something of an anomaly in Asia as well as worldwide, but it will be necessary for all concerned that Japan seek and find its proper place in the global environment.

### Suggested Readings

Blank, Stephen J. "East Asia in Crisis: The Security Implications of the Collapse of Economic Institutions." Strategic Studies Institute, U.S. Army War College, February 1999.

Cossa, Ralph. *The Japan–U.S. Alliance and Security Regimes in East Asia*. A Workshop Report prepared by The Institute for International Policy Studies (Tokyo) and the Center for Naval Analyses (Alexandria, VA), January 1995.

———. "U.S.–Japan Bilateral Dynamics: Pre-Crisis/Crisis Management." In Frances Omori and Mary A. Sommerville, eds., *Strength Through Cooperation: Military Forces in the Asia-Pacific Region*. Washington, DC: National Defense University Press, 1999, pp. 213–32.

Imai, Ryukichi. "Japan's Nuclear Diplomacy." Tokyo: Institute for International Policy Studies, June 1999.

Japanese Defense Agency. *Defense of Japan 1996* (translated into English by Japan Times, Ltd.), July 1996.

Kim, Andrew H.N. "Japan and Peacekeeping Operations." *Military Review*, April 1994, pp. 22–33.

Morimoto, Satoshi. "The Japanese Self-Defense Force: Its Role and Missions in the Post–Cold War Period." In Michael D. Bellows, ed., *Asia in the 21st Century: Evolving Strategic Priorities*. Washington, DC: National Defense University Press, 1994, pp. 171–88.

Struck, Doug. "Japan Reluctantly Sharpening Its Sword." *Washington Post*, August 2, 1999.

# 16

# Laos

## William M. Carpenter

### Introduction

Although in the early 1990s there were trends within Laos suggesting a shift away from a communist-style political and economic structure, elections in the late 1990s reversed the trend. Old party members replaced the younger technocrats, who had been trying to liberalize the Lao economy—this small landlocked nation is still a communist state.

Virtually defenseless on its own behalf, Laos has for centuries been at the mercy of its neighbors, most of whom have had malign intentions. Illustrative of the vulnerability of Laos to foreign intervention is its geography—it has sixteen provinces, and each borders a foreign country.

### Political Framework

The present system of government was imposed upon Laos during and after the Vietnam War years, mainly by the former Soviet Union, but also by China and by North Vietnam (under Soviet domination). While these outside influences and forces have in the main departed, the nation is still struggling to find the right formula for its political and economic structure. An economic downturn in the late 1990s, and alarm in the minds of old hard-liners about the influx of corruption, gambling, prostitution, and drug abuse prompted a return to stronger party control. During such a period, national security policy and foreign relations are in an evolving state.

### Risk Assessment

It appears that Laos is not now seriously threatened militarily—a fortunate situation, because the nation is not well prepared to defend itself. Courting friendship

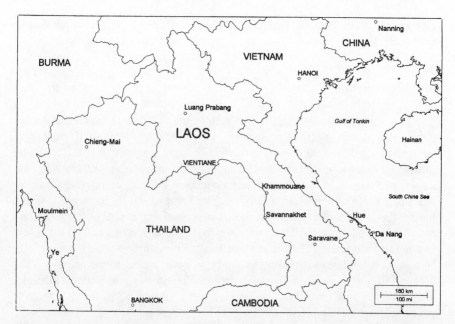

## Laos

with its neighbors is both necessary and wise; Laos must buy time to stabilize its internal situation and get on with economic growth, so that in time a respectable national defense may be feasible and affordable.

The geography of Laos makes it a transit route between its neighbors: east and west between Vietnam and Thailand, and north and south between China and Thailand (and Cambodia, Malaysia, and Singapore). The route between Singapore and China is most direct through Laos, and highways are being built there to accommodate the increasing traffic flow. The new Mitraphap (Friendship) Bridge over the Mekong River near Vientiane carries a steady and growing flow of trucks and autos between Thailand and Laos. The new Highway 13 makes it possible to drive on a paved road from Singapore up the Malay Peninsula into Laos and on into China, and eventually as far as Beijing. In 1994 an agreement was reached between Laos and its neighbors to the north and west to build a 250-kilometer highway from the city of Ban Houay Sai on the Mekong River (across from north Thailand) to the Chinese city of Boten—an all-weather road linking Thailand and China, with Laos as the willing link.

This situation creates both potential benefits and dangers to Laos. The benefit is hoped to be economic: gaining profit from the trade route by providing services along the Laotian portion of the highway and by facilitating imports and exports over the truck routes. The negative side is being seen in the influx of foreign influences, bringing pollution, deforestation, corrupt practices, and the threat of infection from AIDS and other diseases; this has caused an early negative reaction to foreign influences. National defense is likewise made difficult; it is not possible to defend all the routes into Laos at one time with the comparatively small Laotian armed forces.

## Military Structure

The Lao army was barely half its strength in the mid-1960s, when army manpower peaked at 58,000 (of a total armed forces strength of 60,000). Current army strength is about 33,000, deployed in four Military Regions; it consists of five infantry divisions, seven independent infantry regiments, five artillery and nine air-defense battalions, and sixty-five independent infantry companies. There is one small flight of army liaison aircraft. The force has thirty main battle tanks, twenty-five light tanks, seventy armored personnel carriers, about seventy-five pieces of towed artillery of various sizes from 105 mm down to 75 mm, a few mortars and air-defense guns, and a small number of surface-to-air missiles.

Laos is a landlocked country whose only water access to the sea is via the Mekong River. On the river, there is a very small navy of some 500 men manning some twelve patrol craft, four medium landing craft, and about forty small river patrol boats.

The Lao air force has 3,500 men; its aircraft, which are rather old, include about thirty MiG-21s, about ten light transports, and one helicopter squadron of two Mi-6s and ten Mi-8s.

Besides the regular armed forces, Laos has a village "home guard" militia of about 100,000 men. The country has some trouble with internal opposition forces; about 2,000 insurgents in the United Lao National Liberation Front (ULNLF) oppose the present ruling group, and the Lao People's Revolutionary Party (LPRP), create incidents in the countryside, especially in the far northeast regions near Sam Neua, not far from the Vietnam border. The lack of security in this region makes it off limits to tourists, although a few adventurous visitors are willing to take the chance if the right kind of guide can be found. In the southern sector during the 1980s, occasional raids were coming across the Mekong River from Thailand.

The training of the Lao armed forces has come from various nations since 1975: the United States, the former Soviet Union, China, North Vietnam, and North Korea. The equipment is likewise of various origins. With a total armed forces strength of about 37,000, a little less than 1 percent of the five million population, the size of the national defense force could be called normal, about the same percentage of the population as the armed forces of the United States. Yet, as one of the poorest countries in the world, Laos has little money to spend on national defense. Outside military aid has largely disappeared. Until the late 1980s, the Soviet Union kept over 150 military advisers in Laos and provided various kinds of military hardware, but by early 1991 all the advisers were gone, and their departure probably meant the drying up of the military equipment pipeline. Most, perhaps all, of the Vietnamese advisers are gone, and although Laos maintains friendly relations with

Hanoi, Vietnam has problems of its own that leave little for expenditures in Laos.

By the late 1990s, the United States was assisting in at least two ways. During the Vietnam War, some two million tons of ordnance were dropped on Laos, and about one-third of the bombs did not explode. To help reduce the danger from this unexploded ordnance, Washington sent some thirty military trainers to Laos to teach the Laotians how to identify and safely remove the bombs. There is also help from the United Nations, private U.S. groups, Germany, and Britain. The U.S. Department of Defense Humanitarian Assistance Program sponsors a Civil Affairs Liaison Team in Laos conducting a variety of projects to help improve Lao national life: building schools, upgrading hospitals, installing irrigation, and even donating 30,000 sandbags to ensure that a disaster like the 1996 flood will not again threaten Laos's already meager food supply.

There is almost no armaments industry in Laos, and the government has little money for buying weapons. The Lao air force will have to make do with the Soviet MiG-21s it now has. Similarly, the army will likely have to be content with the tanks and artillery it now has, and with the modest levels of proficiency in training that its limited budget will allow. The small naval patrol will probably be sufficient for patrolling the Mekong River to control smugglers, and sometimes to prevent insurgents from crossing over from Thailand. The Thai armed forces formerly gave support to insurgent groups that crossed the Mekong into southern Laos, and even though Laos and Thailand are members of the Association of Southeast Asian Nations (ASEAN), some tension remains because Laos accuses Thailand of harboring thousands of hill tribe Hmongs at the Buddhist temple of Wat Tam Krabok, not far from the river.

## Conclusions

Because Laos is surrounded by countries with much larger armed forces, the obvious strategy for this vulnerable country is to make friends with all its neighbors. In the main, this is happening. Friendly relations result in help from neighbors, as, for example, in April 1994, when an agreement was signed for Malaysian training of Lao technicians to manage and service hydroelectric power stations. Laos's membership in ASEAN should add considerably to Laotian national security, because in recent years ASEAN has expanded its charter beyond the original economic linkage to include mutual security cooperation. In spite of some early alarm about foreign influences, the opening of Laos to the outside world is probably its best hope for security. If the former hermit nation becomes a crossroads of commerce and communications among its neighbors, and if foreign capital and expertise continue to flow into Laos, the overall benefits—economic, political, and military—will likely exceed the inevitable impacts on the culture and security of this historically vulnerable country. In the meantime, the country is benefiting from tourism, which is increasing every year, in spite of there still being some security risks if tourists stray too far into the hinterlands. The U.S. State Department advises some caution about tourism but does encourage businessmen to seek opportunities for investment in Laos.

## Suggested Readings

American Embassy, Vientiane, Laos. *Foreign Economic Trends: Laos*. 1993.

Far Eastern Economic Review. *Asia 1999 Yearbook*. Hong Kong, December 1998.

Karniol, Robert. "Agreement Confirms China's Link with Laos." *Jane's Defence Weekly*, June 11, 1994, p. 6.

Lintner, Bertil. "Ties That Bind." *Far Eastern Economic Review*, February 9, 1995, pp. 18–23.

Neher, Clark D. "Laos." In *Southeast Asia in the New International Era*. 2nd ed. Boulder, CO: Westview Press, 1994, pp. 231–44.

Thayer, Carlyle A. "Laos in 1998: Continuity under New Leadership." *Asian Survey*, January/February 1999, pp. 38–42.

U.S. Department of State. *Background Notes: Laos*. August 1998.

# 17
# Malaysia

*David G. Wiencek*

## Introduction

Like many of its neighbors, Malaysia was hit hard by the 1997 financial crisis that swept through the region. By 1998, the country had experienced a negative growth rate of –7.5 percent. But unlike its neighbors, Kuala Lumpur refused to follow calls to implement difficult economic reforms and austerity plans. Instead, the government of Prime Minister Dato Seri Dr. Mahathir bin Mohamed enacted controversial capital and currency controls on September 1, 1998, which froze foreign investments over a one-year period. These controls were designed to curb the Western financiers Dr. Mahathir had publicly blamed throughout 1998 as the main figures behind the country's economic collapse. Yet the controls also had the effect of protecting the economy from normal market forces and perhaps postponed the true economic pain to a later date.

In any event, the move led to a political crisis when the very next day Datuk Seri Anwar Ibrahim, the Deputy Prime Minister and Finance Minister, and a reform advocate and heir apparent to replace the long-serving Mahathir, was sacked and charged with corruption and indecent personal behavior. The high-level policy dispute between the two leaders took a bitter turn when Anwar was arrested a few weeks later and beaten by police. Photographs showing him with a black eye made headlines around the world.

In Kuala Lumpur, demonstrators numbering in the thousands and tens of thousands took to the streets in September and October 1998. Taking their cue from Indonesia, Mahathir's opponents launched a "Reformasi" (Reform) movement. Thus, Malaysia, a country that had known relative tranquility for decades, was suddenly gripped with domestic political turmoil.

The demonstrations eventually died out and short-term stability was restored,

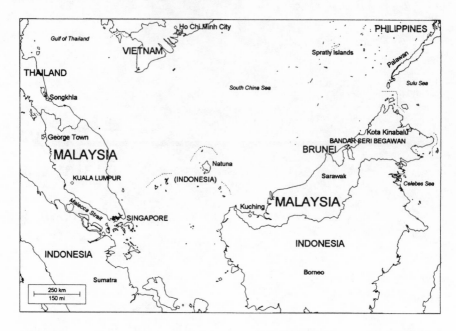

## Malaysia

particularly in the wake of the November 1999 elections giving a vote of confidence to Mahathir. But looking to the future, uncertainties remain because of Mahathir's questionable handling of the crisis and lack of genuine reform. In addition, the political opposition gained some ground in the recent elections. There appears to be a growing sentiment among the opposition, which favors a stronger emphasis on Islam in national policy—a potentially worrisome trend in this ethnically complex nation.

In the external security area, Malaysia continues to pursue a military modernization program, despite a temporary setback resulting from the financial crisis. A claimant to territories in the contested South China Sea, Kuala Lumpur has recently moved to upgrade its facilities on several remote islands, thus heightening tensions with its neighbors, particularly the Philippines. Otherwise, Malaysia generally faces a relatively calm external security environment and is on a course to procure the advanced military tools that will help maintain a high degree of security in coming years.

### Political Framework

Malaysia is a parliamentary democracy with a constitutional monarchical system. General elections are held every five years. The political scene has been dominated by the ruling United Malays National Organization (UMNO) party. UMNO has been in power in coalition with other parties since independence in 1957. In 1973, UMNO entered into a broad coalition with thirteen other parties known as the Barisan Nasional (National Front). The National Front has consistently won a two-thirds majority in the lower house of Parliament in the last few general elections, including the November 1999 elections. The two-thirds majority is important because it gives the ruling group the ability to amend the constitution if necessary. UMNO's power is said to be so pervasive that it reportedly is able to mobilize one party official to monitor each ten houses in every village in the country, ensuring that it has an accurate gauge of national political sentiment.[1]

The government is headed by the Prime Minister. Dr. Mahathir, 73, the leader of UMNO, has held the position of Prime Minister for the past eighteen years and, as such, is Asia's longest-serving elected leader. The head of state, known as the *agong* (king), is selected from among the sultans of the nine royal families. They rotate about every five years, making Malaysia the only country in the world with a rotating kingship. The king is apolitical and serves as a symbol of the state and a defender of Islam.

Over the years, Malaysia had devised a predictable political system under Prime Minister Mahathir's leadership. The stability created by this system resulted in a climate favorable to business and economic development. Malaysia experienced growth rates of better than 8 percent for over a decade, up until the Asian financial crisis broke in 1997–98. In the process, it attracted international investment and gradually transformed its economy from basic commodity producer (rubber and tin) to high-tech manufacturing center. Malaysia, for example, is the world's largest producer of semiconductor devices. It also now can boast the world's tallest buildings in the Petronas twin towers, a symbol of its economic successes. Standards of living also have consistently improved.

These political-economic achievements are considerable in light of the country's potentially fractious ethnic divisions. The population of 21 million is roughly split among three main ethnic groupings as follows: 62 percent Malays, Malay-related, and aboriginal; 28 percent Chinese; and 10 percent Indian. While there has been harmony among the groups for over a generation, there is a clear memory of previous communal violence. The most notable outbreak occurred in 1969, when deadly rioting took place in Kuala Lumpur. As one scholar recounted the episode:

> The precise death count will remain uncertain; but there can be no denying that, when Malay uneasiness was translated into mob action, scenes of horror followed. Kuala Lumpur, in particular, was stained with blood, most of it Chinese; lesser disturbances broke out elsewhere up and down [peninsular Malaysia]. Fearful that civil war would soon follow, if the Chinese struck in full retaliation against Malay attacks, the government ordered rigid curfews and put the country under a state of siege. For a time, rule by decree replaced parliamentary government.[2]

In the aftermath of these developments, the government implemented measures to boost the economic standing of ethnic Malays, who are known as *bumiputras* in the Malaysian language, and help put them on a more equal footing with the Chinese, who traditionally have controlled much of the economy. The government created business preferences for Malays through the New Economic Policy and later the New Development Policy. Under these programs, for example, 30 percent of corporate equity is reserved for Malays. During the economic boom years, high growth levels made it possible for all segments of society to expand their economic holdings. The Asian financial crisis, however, raised new pressures and increased the debt burden of many Malaysian companies. The New Development Policy, a ten-year program, is up for review in 2000, and its follow-on guidelines may include an easing of certain set-asides to make the economy more competitive again.

**The Anwar Affair**

The long-term stability enjoyed by Malaysia was put at risk with the Anwar affair. Prime Minister Mahathir has a reputation as a strong nationalist and frequent critic of the West. During the financial crisis, his contentious views came to the fore, when he blamed Malaysia's economic collapse on Western financiers, such as George Soros, and stated that there was an international plot to ruin Malaysia and that foreigners were attempting to "recolonize" the country.

Mahathir's approach contrasted sharply with that of Deputy Prime Minister and Finance Minister Anwar, 51, who was prepared to work with international authorities and implement reforms and austerity measures. Anwar's push for greater transparency and reform was apparently perceived by Mahathir as a direct challenge.[3] On September 2, 1998, Anwar was ousted. The man who was set to take over Malaysia, and who reportedly had a "father–son" relationship with the more senior Mahathir, was charged with corruption and immoral behavior. Anwar took his case to the people and was met with strong support. He led rallies in the capital and encouraged the government to undertake serious reforms. By the end of September, however, the government apparently had had enough and was not prepared to tolerate such political dissent. Anwar was arrested and sent to jail. He emerged briefly in court in the ensuing days and photographers captured the reality that the former leader had been badly beaten by police.[4] This outraged domestic and international opinion, and damaged Prime Minister Mahathir's standing and credibility.

Anwar was tried and received a six-year jail sentence on corruption charges; in August 2000, he received an additional nine-year sentence for immoral behavior.

The reform movement initiated by the Anwar affair was soon to be tested at the ballot box. Anwar's supporters, led by his wife Dr. Wan Azizah Wan Ismail, formed a new party, Parti Keadilan Nasional (National Justice Party), and linked up with other long-time regime opponents to form the Alternative Front. There was some question as to when the next election would be called, but the government announced that it would occur in November 1999. (Some believe the date was selected in order to avoid a large youth vote—likely in support of reform; some 680,000 young people were to be newly eligible to vote after January 2000.)[5]

## The November 1999 Elections

The building political drama came to a head with the November 29, 1999, elections. In the end, the opposition simply could not break UMNO's lock on power. The National Front recaptured power and retained its commanding two-thirds margin in Parliament.

Importantly, however, at the state level, the election saw the victory of the conservative Parti Islam Se Malaysia (Islamic Party of Malaysia, or Pas) in the resource-rich northern state of Terengganu. Pas, energized by the Anwar affair, now controls two states—Terengganu and Kelantan. Pas is known to favor an "Islamic development" agenda, and should its strength grow, it could feel emboldened to implement strict Islamic policies, which would have uncertain longer-term consequences for the broader non-Muslim community.

Finally, although Prime Minister Mahathir received a vote of confidence, the result may be a short-term victory. The Anwar affair exposed political fissures between those favoring reform and those favoring the status quo. At the same time, the crisis reopened the succession issue. Anwar had been groomed for years to take over the leadership of Malaysia. Within the next five years, the country will have to make a new judgment on who will succeed Dr. Mahathir, who will likely retire within this timeframe for either health or age reasons. Malaysians have known good living standards for some time and, as a result, it was difficult to vote against a leadership that had produced economic success. But the use of currency and capital controls may not be in the country's longer-term interest, and without deeper reforms, financial stability could be tested again soon.

## Risk Assessment

If current trends persist, Malaysia will continue to enjoy a relatively calm security environment. Internally, it will be important to guard against the rise of any Islamic fundamentalist tendencies that could put at risk the country's delicate ethnic balance. The memory of the 1969 race riots should not be forgotten as policymakers work to maintain a peaceful domestic order.

Externally, Malaysia's interests in the Spratly Islands in the South China Sea are an area of potential concern. Kuala Lumpur holds three of six reefs (Ardasier, Mariveles, and Swallow) in its claimed area of this disputed maritime region. Of the other three islands, Vietnam occupies two and the Philippines one. In 1991, Malaysia began construction of a resort and airstrip on Swallow Reef.[6] By 1999, after years of adopting a relatively low-key posture in the Spratlys, Malaysia began construction on another feature called Investigator Shoal, where it built a two-story concrete building and helicopter landing pad. It also may have occupied two additional nearby reefs. Prime Minister Mahathir described the new construction as follows: "We have built on our own zone and not outside the zone for climate research and marine life studies and also to prevent ship collisions."[7]

But these moves prompted complaints from the Philippines, which also claims Investigator Shoal as Pawikan Shoal (its Filipino name). In October 1999, Malaysian and Philippine aircraft reportedly came into contact without incident near Investigator/Pawikan Shoal. It is unclear why Malaysia has moved now to raise its profile in the Spratlys. It could be a response to events in the Philippines, where Washington and Manila have upgraded relations, although Manila still lacks the military capability to enforce its claims. It could also be part of a tacit understanding with China (see below) to try to move the dispute away from the multilateral realm into bilateral negotiations between Beijing and Kuala Lumpur. Whatever the rationale, the jockeying for outposts has heightened regional concerns, particularly with the Philippines, and in the process has helped raise inter-ASEAN (Association of Southeast Asian Nations) tensions.

In dealing with the external environment, Malaysia has relied on a number of elements, including good bilateral relations with its neighbors, the diplomatic framework afforded by ASEAN, and the Five-Power Defence Arrangement (FPDA) (Malaysia, Singapore, Britain, Australia, and New Zealand), a longstanding regional multilateral security pact. But in 1998, Kuala Lumpur froze its participation in FPDA exercises, mainly due to lack of funding as a result of the Asian financial crisis. By late 1999, it seemed that Malaysia would rejoin the grouping and continue its participation in FPDA training and exercises. Bilateral exercises also occur with Thailand, Indonesia, Brunei, and the United States.

In addition, in 1999 Malaysia appeared to upgrade its relations with China. In January 1999, the People's Liberation Army (PLA) Chief of Staff visited Kuala Lumpur. Then in May, Malaysia's Foreign Minister visited Beijing and endorsed a bilateral "Joint Statement on Framework for Future Bilateral Cooperation." Among other things, the Framework noted that the two sides would work to improve defense cooperation, including the exchange of information and intelligence, reciprocal personnel and ship visits, and training. Regarding the South China Sea disputes, the Framework indicates that the matter should be solved through "bilateral friendly consultations."[8] Malaysia's apparent willingness to resolve this issue through bilateral diplomacy is an important departure from previous ASEAN positions. In the past, the Spratly dispute had mainly been one of China versus ASEAN, and the smaller Southeast Asian nations were able to unite in an effective diplomatic posture against Beijing's maneuverings. It now appears, however, that those calculations may have changed and Malaysia may have reached some form of tacit understanding with China about the future of this important issue—an understanding that effectively undercuts ASEAN solidarity.

## Military Structure

Malaysia has been engaged in a defense modernization program for some time. This effort suffered a setback during the Asian financial crisis, when resources were constrained and funding for major projects—such as submarines, offshore patrol vessels, and tanks—was put on hold. With the crisis fading, it appeared that the main elements of the program have been restarted and will be funded in the 8th Malaysia Plan during 2001–2005.[9] Malaysia is acquiring state-of-the-art equipment that will help maintain a high degree of security in coming years. For example, in October 1999, it received the first of two UK-built *Leiku* class frigates. These advanced warships, designed for anti-surface and anti-submarine warfare, are equipped with high-performance Exocet MM40 anti-ship cruise missiles. They also have a hangar and flight deck for operation of a Super Lynx naval helicopter, six of which are on order. The Super Lynx will also be deployed on four Italian-built corvettes. Additional patrol vessels are on order, as is a training submarine and other naval capabilities. These assets will help Malaysia protect its national territory (peninsular Malaysia is separated by 500 miles from the eastern states on the island of Borneo), its Exclusive Economic Zone (EEZ), and other offshore resources, like oil and gas reserves.

In the air power arena, Kuala Lumpur has acquired Russian MiG-29 Fulcrums and British Aerospace Hawk 208 fighters, as well as American F/A-18D Hornets. The Russians have also transferred the capable AA-12 Adder air-to-air missile to Malaysia. Under the latest modernization plan, the Royal Malaysian Air Force (RMAF) is seeking to acquire more MiG-29s, as well as additional U.S. F/A-18D Hornets or new Russian Sukhoi Su-27 Flankers. The RMAF is also reportedly interested in the U.S. HAWK air defense system.

In terms of force structure, the Malaysian Armed Forces (MAF) are led by the Chief of Defence Force, who is appointed by the king. The MAF is being streamlined to make it a more effective force.

The MAF has been actively engaged in peacekeeping operations over the years. Recent deployments include Cambodia, the Iraq–Kuwait Observer Mission, and Bosnia.

## Conclusions

The Asian financial crisis tested Malaysia politically and economically. Results to date are mixed. Short-term stability has been restored, particularly in the wake of the November 1999 elections giving a vote of confidence to Prime Minister Mahathir. But looking to the future, uncertainties remain because of Mahathir's questionable handling of the crisis. Unlike its neighbors, Malaysia went against reformist trends necessitated by the financial crisis. For this reason, the political-economic battle is not over and will likely resurface at a later time, as reform-minded opposition forces grow stronger. At a minimum, there will be acute political tensions, particularly if conservative Islamic forces strengthen their base. Thus there is a potential for internal violence as the old order in Malaysia clashes with the new in this ethnically complex society. Externally, Malaysia's acquisition of advanced military capabilities will serve it well in the years ahead and help ensure that key national security missions are fulfilled.

## Notes

1. *Far Eastern Economic Review*, June 24, 1999, p. 11.

2. Lea A. Williams, *Southeast Asia: A History* (New York: Oxford University Press, 1976), p. 250.

3. See, for example, Ian Johnson, "How Malaysia's Rulers Devoured Each Other and Much They Built," *Wall Street Journal*, October 30, 1998, pp. A1 and A11.

4. See, for example, S. Jayasankaran and Murray Hiebert, "Bruised But Unbowed," *Far Eastern Economic Review*, October 8, 1998, pp. 19–20.

5. See Keith Richburg, "Malaysian Election Divides Generation: Opposition Attracts Younger Voters," *Washington Post*, November 28, 1999, p. A31.

6. Bradford L. Thomas and Daniel J. Dzurek, "The Spratly Islands Dispute," *Geopolitics and International Boundaries* (Winter 1996), pp. 305–306.

7. Quoted in "Mahathir Says Malaysia Owns Disputed Spratly Reefs," Agence France Presse, June 27, 1999, as translated by Foreign Broadcast Information Service (FBIS), June 28, 1999, FBIS-EAS-1999–0627. Also see Rigoberto Tiglao, "Seaside Boom," *Far Eastern Economic Review*, July 8, 1999, p. 14.

8. "PRC, Malaysia Sign Joint Statement," *Xinhua*, May 31, 1999, as translated by FBIS, May 31, 1999, FBIS-CHI-1999–0531.

9. Micol Brooke, "Malaysia's Armed Forces Dust Off Modernization Plans in Light of Regional Economic Upturn," *Armed Forces Journal International*, November 1999, pp. 38–44.

## Suggested Readings

Brooke, Micol. "Malaysia's Armed Forces Dust Off Modernization Plans in Light of Regional Economic Upturn." *Armed Forces Journal International*, November 1999, pp. 38–44.

Jayasankaran, S., and Michael Vatikiotis. "Wake-Up Call" [post-1999 election analysis]. *Far Eastern Economic Review*, December 9, 1999, pp. 16–17.

Suh, Sangwon, and Arjuna Ranawana. "Fighting Words." *Asiaweek*, April 2, 1999, pp. 28–29.

# 18
# Mongolia

## *Michael J. Mitchell*

The appearance of the sails off the Japanese coast of Kyushu on June 21, 1281, was not unexpected. The coastwatchers and lookouts had been waiting for the great armada to appear, and now it had arrived. As the day drew on, nearly nine hundred ships, with 25,000 soldiers and tens of thousand of sailors, began massing off the island in what was at that time the largest amphibious assault in the history of mankind.

The Mongols had arrived.

Kublai Yuan, the Great Khan, had finished subjugating China and Korea. His rule now extended across a full three-quarters of the known world. The Mongol armies—using speed, mobility, and a bow that was not only easy to handle on horseback, but powerful and accurate—had vanquished those who stood in their way. Europeans called them "The Storm from the East," while those in the Middle East referred to the Mongolians as the "Scourge from God." Now at its zenith, the Mongolian Empire stretched from Central Asia, through Central Europe, Russia, most of the Middle East, and much of Asia. And now, the Great Khan decided, Japan was next.

The Mongolians were furious with the Japanese emperor. Two delegations of Mongolian diplomats, each bearing terms for the emperor's surrender, had been executed and their heads impaled on stakes. This insult could not be tolerated.

As the battle raged and thousands of samurai threw themselves at the invaders, Japanese military leaders knew they were in trouble. Mongol reinforcements had arrived to support the attack. Across Japan, people turned to their gods and Shinto deities beseeching assistance and deliverance from the evil horde that had set upon their land. It was then that a great wind began to blow. For two days a tremendous storm battered the Mongolian fleet, sinking all but a handful of vessels. The invasion had been turned back, and the legend of the Kamikaze, or Divine Wind, was born.

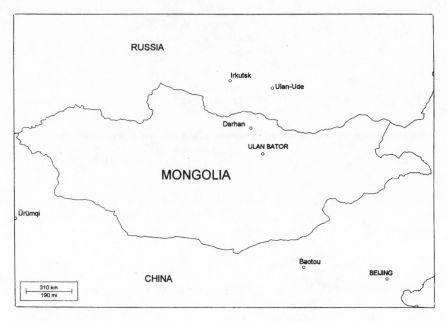

## Mongolia

Though Japan was saved, the Mongol Empire was not. Over time, their conquests began to wash away as rebellions and political upheavals took their toll. As fast as the Mongolian hoards rode across the world stage, they disappeared. Locked away in the harsh climate of Central Asia, it would take hundreds of years, several wars (including a Cold War), and the collapse of the Soviet Union for Mongolia to re-emerge and make a much less hostile encore presentation to the world community.

### A New Political Order

In 1990, Mongolia began to feel the rumblings of democratic activism that swept through Poland, the former Czechoslovakia, Hungary, and East Germany. Russian Glasnost and the liberal policies of President Mikhail Gorbachev served to embolden a group of students, who decided that communism had failed and the country needed to move quickly and establish a democratic state.

Their demonstration started as an oddity at first. A small band of students camped in the huge square, named Sukebaatar Square after General Damnidy Sukebaatar, the hero of Mongolia's independence movement. Looming over them stood the massive dull gray Parliament building. The students rolled out cots and began their protest by announcing they were on a hunger strike.

"We did not know what would happen, we only knew that this is what we had to do," stated Erdenine Bat-uul, a student leader and now member of Mongolia's Parliament (called the State Great Hural).[1] Within the space of a week, what had started as a small hunger strike suddenly blossomed into a full-scale political movement. People from all sectors of Mongolian society joined the hunger strikers and the hand-scrawled signs they brought to Sukebaatar Square stated their intention: "Democracy Now!" When the students asked for a public show of support, an estimated 400,000 people crammed the square, demanding that the politburo resign.

"That was the most dangerous time," Bat-uul stated. "Rumors were rampant that the military was going to be called out to clear the square and arrest us. The possibility for violence could not be discounted. Our peaceful protests were picking up momentum and you could feel the strength of the movement surging our way. Then we asked them [the politburo] to resign," he stated. Within days of the public ultimatum, the politburo announced that it had voted to legalize political parties and elections would select leaders to draft and ratify a new constitution. The politburo was dissolved. Without a shot being fired, without a Tiananmen Square, without tanks firing on demonstrators or on Parliament, without a single person being hurt, Mongolia moved from over sixty years of communist rule to a nascent democracy.

The first elections under Mongolia's new constitution in 1992 saw the Mongolian People's Revolutionary Party (MPRP), the former communist party, crush the new democratic parties in a landslide vote that was by all international standards free and fair. The Mongolian National Democratic Party (MNDP) and the Mongolian Social Democratic Party (MSDP) did not have the political infrastructure in place to compete in nationwide elections. The MPRP had the financial and people resources to reach into every corner of the country. They succeeded in winning seventy of Parliament's seventy-six seats. The MNDP won four and the MSDP earned two of the remaining seats.

During a four-year period, the MSDP and MNDP set about building a country-wide political apparatus. They raised funds and fine-tuned a message that would resonate with voters. As the election neared, party leaders decided to run as a coalition and formed the Mongolian Democratic Union. The coalition, taking a page from the script of Newt Gingrich's House Republicans in Washington, created the Contract with the Mongolian Voter. The coalition fashioned a list of over fifty action items they would change or implement if they were elected. These issues ranged from privatization of all state-run industries, to banking reform, to stimulating economic growth through engagement with the West and increasing foreign investment. Distributed via fax, mail, and riders on horseback, this document found its way to every single Mongolian of voting age throughout the country.

The candidates of the coalition and MPRP campaigned furiously prior to the July 1996 elections. The coalition, using modern campaign voter identification techniques and voicing a clear and convincing message, benefited from an economy that was in a severe depression.

The coalition's political battle plan worked. When the votes were finally tabulated, the coalition had won a staggering political victory. They now controlled fifty of seventy-six seats in Parliament. Shortly thereafter Mongolian television recorded a scene that was a historical first for Central Asia—the transfer of political power from one government to another through a democratic election.

## Between the Bear and the Dragon

Like any country, Mongolia's foreign policy and national security interests are a reflection of both internal politics and regional dynamics. History has been cruel to the Mongolians. For all their conquests, the country is landlocked between giants: Russia to the north and China to the south. Today, Mongolia is a country of 2.2 million people living in an area the size of continental Europe or the United States east of the Mississippi River. This vast land contains topography that varies from pancake-flat in the east to the Gobi desert in the south, and the steep Altai Mountains cut through the country in the west. A full one-third of the population is nomadic, moving their camels, goats, horses, yaks, and sheep to new pastures three times a year. Major industries consist of copper, livestock, cashmere, and wool. Some gold is mined in the country and a small quantity of oil is pumped for export to China via tanker truck. Mongolia's location is its greatest impediment to its economic development.

The country does boast regular flights to Europe, Russia, China, and South Korea. Air travel to Japan is scheduled during the prime summer tourist season. However, the only rail link in Mongolia is the Trans-Siberian Railroad, which bisects the country running north–south. There are no east–west rail links. Roads are unpaved and poor at best. It is a country with virtually no infrastructure outside the capital. Any international shipments moving by sea must transit either Vladivostok in Russia or Tanjing in China. The crime and disappearance of goods in Vladivostok is forcing Mongolia to depend more on the sea terminal at Tanjing.

The Russia–China dynamic has governed Mongolia's foreign policy since 1921. At that time a successful rebellion against China's Manchu dynasty forced the Chinese forces out of Mongolia while also defeating elements of the Czarist White Russian Army that had retreated into Mongolia. General Sukebaatar faced the cold, hard fact that it was only a matter of time before the Chinese would regroup and invade. Knowing he did not have the forces or the finances to repel a larger Chinese army, he played the only card available to him. Sukebaatar made a pact with the Bolsheviks: Mongolia would become a Soviet client state if Lenin guaranteed the independence of Mongolia. Shortly thereafter, Soviet forces moved into Mongolia and communism became the law of the land. Mongolia was now the second country in the world to adopt a communist form of government. The scheme worked. China dared not invade at the risk of provoking a war with the Soviet Union. During the fifties, sixties, and seventies, Mongolia was a buffer state to the giants during their sometimes tense on-again, off-again relationship. Today it still plays that role.

Despite the purges during Stalinist times, the Mongolians remain even more embittered toward the Chinese. Centuries of occupation have made Mongolians deeply distrustful of their Chinese neighbors. Many Mongols are convinced that

Chinese leaders will at some point seek to forcefully or economically assimilate their country into China. This view is reinforced by an occasional statement from a Chinese ministry in Beijing that refers to Mongolia as "greater China." In fact, Taiwan still officially recognizes Mongolia as part of China. This translates into domestic politics.

Debates on privatization and private property rights in Parliament featured many speeches warning of "wealthy Chinese businessmen buying up Mongolia." An example of how Mongolians can be almost xenophobic about the Chinese lies in a donation of trees made to the Mongolian capital of Ulan Bator (Ulaanbaatar) by Beijing as a gesture of goodwill. When many of the trees died from poor weather and disease, local officials feared that they had been deliberately contaminated with a blight that would kill Mongolian trees. This is the kind of fearful suspicion that underlies the veneer of good relations the two countries currently enjoy.

## The Third Neighbor

The cornerstone of Mongolian foreign policy is simple: Maintain good relations with both China and Russia. The keystone to this strategy is called "The Third Neighbor." As Mongolia moves in a careful diplomatic ballet between Russia and China, the country's leaders are looking to the West (and principally to the United States) as their "third neighbor" to strike a counterbalance between the giants on their borders. "Our goal is to build good relations with our neighbors," stated Prime Minister Amarjargal (Mongolians frequently use only one name). "We are in many ways a hostage to our geography, so we must break out by cultivating new diplomatic, cultural, and social relationships with Asian and western countries," he stated.[2]

Mongolia's political leadership has done this by selling itself as the most democratic state in Central Asia. Members of the U.S. Congress have rewarded Mongolia by supplying it with a steady stream of development assistance. At a time when international spending is decreasing, Mongolia's assistance numbers have actually climbed from US$8 million in 1996, to US$10 million in 1997, then jumped 20 percent in 1998 to US$12 million, where it is scheduled to remain until 2003. During a September 1999 visit to Washington, DC, Amarjargal made a series of high-level congressional visits stressing the success the coalition has made in wringing inflation out of the economy, cutting government spending, and dropping many trade tariffs, in addition to beginning the final round of privatization efforts aimed at selling off the country's largest state-run companies. He also reinforced a subtler point that has been used by supporters of Mongolia to demonstrate the importance of the country: it is extremely beneficial to have a vibrant democracy sharing a border that is thousands of miles long with China and Russia—both states that are under tremendous political stress.

"We have to look at our political and democratic process as regional selling points both from an international political view and business investment perspective," stated Jambaljmts Od, the former national security adviser to two prime ministers. "Demonstrating shared political values such as human rights, freedom of the press, transparent bureaucratic institutions, a commitment to private property rights, and contract law is the only way to set ourselves apart and make Mongolia relevant to the international community. It is the only way we can carry through on the 'Third Neighbor' policy," he stated.[3]

Mongolia has played a delicate balancing act with China. On the one hand it has sought to build stronger relations, but it also has not shrunk from what could be considered controversial actions. For example, the Dalai Lama has visited Mongolia several times. Each visit provokes a stern warning from the Chinese ambassador, but these are ignored as the country turns out en masse to worship with His Holiness. However, this is the exception and not the rule.

On July 16, 1999, Chinese President Jiang Zemin visited Mongolia for the highest-level official visit in five years. The Chinese president brought a pledge of some foreign assistance and a message of goodwill. However, according to officials, he skirted a point of pressing concern: a potential oil and gas pipeline that would run from Russian Siberia through eastern Mongolia into China. The energy pipeline has been talked about for years and what has Mongolian political leaders nervous is that, for the most part, they have been excluded from the discussions about the route. Mongolian officials fear they will be handed a fait accompli by their big neighbors and find themselves dictated to with regard to the route and, most important, royalty payments for transportation costs. A pipeline, if built, holds tremendous potential for opening a new revenue source for the cash-strapped country.

A pipeline, such as the one being discussed, would be able to bring badly needed clean fuel to China's populous northeastern region as well as to port locations, where it can be exported. The nearly bankrupt Russian government would have a critical opening to gain hard currency and expand into new markets.

"This is a national security issue of the highest order," stated Bat-uul. "We are not being included in these talks. We might find ourselves being blackmailed by the Chinese and Russian leadership. What can we do? When all is said and done, the fact that all our exports overseas must travel through a Russian or Chinese port is tremendous economic and political leverage."

What Mongolia has tried to do is inject U.S. and European involvement in their cause by requesting meetings with European and American engineering firms and development banks to discuss loan terms and construction costs. If Russia and China decide to move ahead with their project, the Mongolians want to be prepared to put a plan of their own on the table. The thought of thousands of Chinese and/or Russian workers on Mongolian soil makes many in Mongolian government circles uncomfortable. "We don't want to find ourselves being in a position where this pipeline comes through and everyone but Mongolia benefits," stated Od. Prime Minister Amarjargal agrees. "For our country this could be an incredible benefit, or an incredible curse," he said.

The United States has, since 1998, taken a more active role and become more involved in Mongolia. For example, in early 1999, U.S. Army special operations troops conducted a humanitarian exercise—aptly code-named "Magic Balance"—that included a parachute jump in the Gobi desert. Other small exchanges have also taken place. There was also a push within the U.S. Congress to include Mongolia in the Partnership for Peace (PFP) program. However, European leaders and many in the Clinton administration felt this would push too hard on China, and the idea has been shelved.

## A Regional Player? Mongolia and North Korea

Mongolia is also trying to play a role in regional politics. The relationship between Ulan Bator and Pyongyang is still strong, and Mongolian parliamentary delegations travel to the Hermit Kingdom for official visits, where they are received warmly. The Mongolians have also undertaken to provide a small amount of food assistance to the North and encouraged North Korean officials, rather unconvincingly, that the best option for the country is a peace agreement to formally end the war, liberalize their economies, and overhaul their political structures. "If nothing else," stated one American official, "the message comes from another Asian country and not the West. We appreciate their enthusiasm."

One interesting economic development plan that is being talked about on a sporadic basis is Mongolia hosting reunification flights between families living in the two Koreas. South Korean families would fly to Ulan Bator, where they would overnight and transfer to Mongolian-flagged international aircraft for the flight to Pyongyang. What makes Mongolia attractive for this venture is that South Korean airlines would not have to pay the high cost of gate fees they would incur if they flew into Beijing. Although considerable time has been spent developing this plan by Mongolian government officials, it is unlikely to be implemented until major progress has been made to reduce tensions and broker a peace deal on the Korean Peninsula.

## Conclusions

It is doubtful that Mongolian foreign policy will undergo any drastic changes in the near future. The key will be to continue the Russia–China balancing act while aggressively reaching out to the United States and Europe for trade, foreign investment, and at least a sense of security that engagement with them can provide. As Mongolia seeks to once again push outward, her political leadership is determined to use venues and forums such as, for example, the United Nations and the Association of Asian Nations to promote their interests and raise their visibility.

"We have a good story to tell," stated Prime Minister Amarjargal. "Our country is moving forward, we are walking down the path of democracy, political and religious tolerance are practiced, Mongolia is a stable country with a bright future if we can, economically and politically, move beyond our borders," he stated. As Mongolia reaches aggressively out to the world community the only question is whether anyone will reach back.

## Notes

1. During many trips to Mongolia between 1993 and 1999, the author spoke at great length with leaders of Mongolia's democratic movement. Bat-uul is recognized as one of the fathers of Mongolia's democratic transition. The author has drawn from his discussions with Bat-uul for the quotes in this chapter.

2. Amarjargal was named Prime Minister in June 1999. He was previously foreign minister. Amarjargal is an economics expert and was founder of a school dedicated to the study of business and economics immediately following Mongolia's transition to democratic rule. His comments in this chapter are taken from conversations and speeches he made during his visit to Washington, D.C., in late 1999.

3. Od is widely recognized in Western circles as one of the critical implementers of the "Third Neighbor" strategy. His statements were recorded during discussions with the author during his tenure as national security adviser from 1998 to 1999.

## Suggested Readings

Gonzalez, Michael. "Mongolia Gallops Toward Freedom." *Wall Street Journal*, May 27, 1997.

Interview with Nyamosor Tuya, Minister for External Relations. *Jane's Defence Weekly*, August 25, 1999.

Thayer, Nate. "In Mongolia, a GOP-Style Revolutionary Movement." *Washington Post*, April 6, 1997, p. A20.

Sanjaagyn, Bayar. "Mongolia's National Security Challenges." San Francisco: The Asia Foundation's Center for Asian Pacific Affairs (CAPA), September 1994, CAPA Report Number 16.

# 19

# New Zealand

## Bruce Vaughn

New Zealand is at a crossroads in defense and security. Years of decreasing defense budgets, when combined with looming bloc obsolescence, increased interoperability problems generated by the revolution in military affairs, continuing fragile relations with the United States, and a demanding peacekeeping agenda have drawn New Zealand's defense force down to a minimally credible level. New Zealand's defense forces will not be able to meet its self-defined defense and security objectives without the government's ongoing commitment to a defense modernization program. Further, given the increased instability in the Asia-Pacific region, New Zealand would be prudent to maintain a defense capability that could respond to possible over-the-horizon threats.

Labor Party leader Helen Clark's electoral victory over Prime Minister Jenny Shipley on November 27, 1999, may lead to reductions in defense procurement, as well as a shift in defense policy orientation. While tax and social issues were identified as the new government's top priority, Clark moved quickly to announce plans to review the air force modernization objectives of the previous Shipley government. This review of the F-16 program is to be headed up by Derek Quigley, author of the *Defence Beyond 2000* report. A comprehensive defense review may follow that could have negative ramifications for the Australia–New Zealand Agreement (ANZAC) frigate program.[1]

New Zealand perceives its defense posture through a strategic prism that is inspired by traditional security concepts as well as uniquely New Zealand notions of security. This prism is strongly influenced by New Zealand's geographic isolation, small population (3.8 million), value structures, history, traditions, economics, and trade patterns. To gain insight into this prism this inquiry into New Zealand's defense posture takes as its starting point the following questions.

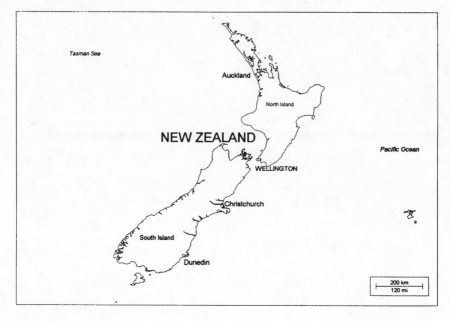

## New Zealand

1. What are New Zealand's self-described strategic interests?
2. Does New Zealand's defense policy adequately address those interests?
3. Can New Zealand sustain a force structure to meet its defense objectives?

Following a discussion of these questions, observations will be made on whether New Zealand's defense posture appears to be well suited for the evolving Asia-Pacific security environment. Insight into the above questions can be found through recent events. Most notable among these are the decisions associated with the *ANZAC* frigate program, the decision to lease F-16 aircraft, the interim report of the Foreign Affairs, Defence, and Trade Committee on *Defence Beyond 2000*, and the government's response to that report. A quick overview of the historical setting is also in order before delving into these questions in the contemporary context.

### The Historical National Security Setting

While New Zealand is strategically blessed with geographic isolation it has not been immune to invasion and armed conflict. The Polynesian Maori who first came to the uninhabited land found themselves unable to resist the onslaught of settlers from the British Empire during the nineteenth century despite their fierce martial traditions. The Maori fought much among themselves and made fighting into a highly developed art. The Maori believed that *mana* is acquired by assuming "the most dangerous position at the front of a phalanx."[2] Adept at hand-to-hand fighting and surprise attack, the Maori also developed hilltop fortifications known as the *pa*. The Treaty of Waitangi serves as the basis for peace between the Maori and more recent settlers of New Zealand. Today 12 percent of New Zealand's population are either Maori or of Pacific Islander descent. The Maori are also well represented in the New Zealand Defence Force today. Paradoxically, despite New Zealand's current low level of defense spending, New Zealanders—both Maori and Pakeha—have had a strong warrior tradition.

New Zealand defense thinking was intimately associated with British imperial defense from the outset. New Zealand's participation in British defense dominated the country's security outlook through World War II. New Zealand's participation in the United Kingdom's imperial strategy included the contribution of forces to many of its colonial conflicts. New Zealand was more reluctant than Australia to leave the imperial fold in the wake of World War II. During the colonial period New Zealanders did not view their involvement in Great Britain's wars as fighting other peoples' wars. New Zealand's loyalty to Britain and to the Commonwealth and notions of collective security, resistance to aggression, and the indivisibility of peace everywhere led New Zealand to make large contributions in proportion to its size.[3]

New Zealand's shared experiences with its fellow colony Australia led to a special defense relationship that was forged through the shared baptism of fire at ANZAC[4] cove during the Dardanelles campaign in World War I. New Zealand suffered an 87 percent casualty rate on the Gallipoli Peninsula during World War I. By the war's end 48 percent of New Zealand's male population between 19 and 45 had served, with an overall casualty rate of 58 percent.[5] While Gallipoli is commonly thought to be the first New Zealand–Australian joint combat experience, it is in fact predated by joint operations during New Zealand's Maori war. In 1863, 3,000 Australians volunteered to fight alongside New Zealand against the Maori.[6] In addition to the world wars, Australians and New Zealanders also fought together in the Boer War, the Korean War, the Malaya Emergency, the Confrontation in Indonesia, and Vietnam.

Conceptually speaking, the beginning of a separate New Zealand security identity can be traced to the Pacific Defense Conference in Wellington in 1939. At that time New Zealand questioned Britain's assurances that the Royal Navy could protect New Zealand from Japan. Following World War II, New Zealand security focused on collective security as well as regional self-reliance in association with Australia under the Canberra Pact. This pact built on ANZAC traditions and facilitated joint defense consultations, planning, exchange of officers, and intelligence. In 1951, New Zealand entered into the ANZUS (Australia–New Zealand–United States) alliance with the United States. After New Zealand's break with the United States in 1985 New Zealand has become more reliant on its bilateral relationship with Australia.

While New Zealand welcomed ANZUS it remained relatively more committed to the United Kingdom, while Australia increasingly looked to the United States for a security guarantor. New Zealand's most important defense relationship was with the British for thirty years after World War II. This was reflected in several ways.

1. Commitment of New Zealand forces to the Middle East in the event of crisis.
2. New Zealand forces in the Korean War fought in a Commonwealth Division.
3. In 1955 the Middle East commitment was converted into a contribution to the Commonwealth Strategic Reserve Force (CSRF) in Southeast Asia.
4. As part of the CSRF New Zealand contributed to the Malaya Emergency and the Indonesian "Confrontation."

The conflict in Vietnam and the British withdrawal from Southeast Asia marked the end of New Zealand's British-centric defense orientation. In this way it was one of the last states to recognize a geopolitical reality that began with the fall of Singapore at the outset of World War II.[7]

As New Zealand's ties to Britain faded, its association with the United States grew. This strategic shift was marked by three key events.

1. New Zealand joins ANZUS in 1951.
2. New Zealand joins the South East Asia Treaty Organization (SEATO) in 1954.
3. New Zealand contributes to the Vietnam War.

Even though New Zealand did not primarily look to the United States until after the final departure of the British from the region, the gradual reduction of British influence led to closer defense ties with Washington beginning in the 1950s.

In retrospect, it is not surprising that New Zealand pursued policies in the 1980s that defied the United States even though New Zealand had until that point in its history looked to great friends to guarantee its security. Because New Zealand's close association with Britain did not really dissipate until the 1970s it did not have the same sort of close association with the United States before the relationship was deeply tested by the nuclear issue. While the United States defense relationship began in earnest in the 1950s it was only the dominant relationship from the time of the Vietnam War through to 1984. From its outset this relationship was different from the security guarantee that New Zealand had enjoyed under the British. The announcement of the Guam Doctrine in 1969 under the Nixon administration had the effect of forcing New Zealand to begin to look to its own defense in a way that it had never had to do before that point. As a result of this series of events there was "little transference of positive sentiment to the United States" even though American power in the Pacific had been greater than Britain's since 1941.[8] The experience of the Vietnam War, the implications of the Guam Doctrine, and the beginnings of an independent security policy set the stage upon which New Zealand embarked on its anti-nuclear stance, which resulted in a degrading of its relations with the United States.

Table 12

**New Zealand's Defense Budget** (in billions of NZ$s)

|  | 1995 | 1996 | 1997 | 1998 | 1999 |
|---|---|---|---|---|---|
| Defense Expenditure Budget | $1.6 | $1.1 | $1.4 | $1.6 | $1.6 |
| US$1=NZ$ | $1.52 | $1.45 | $1.56 | $1.86 | $1.87 |

*Source:* International Institute for Strategic Studies (IISS), *The Military Balance* 1997/98 (London: Oxford University Press, 1997), p. 189.

## Military Structure

New Zealand's defense spending (NZ$1.4 billion)[9] is low in both absolute and relative terms. New Zealand defense spending has decreased 30 percent and personnel have been reduced by 25 percent over the past decade.[10] Measured per capita, New Zealand spends NZ$392 per annum, as compared to Japan NZ$507, Australia NZ$711, the United States NZ$1,588, and Singapore NZ$2,122.[11] This decline is exacerbated by a decline in the value of the New Zealand dollar as a result of the Asian financial crisis. Declining currency exchange rates have undermined New Zealand's ability to fund military modernization. Virtually all New Zealand's defense equipment has to be imported because the country has very little defense manufacturing capability.

Today New Zealand has a defense force of some 9,500 active armed forces with an additional 7,000 reserves. Army equipment includes: seventy-eight M-113 armored personnel carriers, forty-three 105-mm towed artillery, and fifty-one 81-mm mortars. The Navy has the *Waikato Leander* class and two *ANZAC* frigates, four *Moa* patrol craft and six support craft. The air force is replacing its nineteen A-4s with twenty-eight F-16 fighters. It also has a squadron of P-3K Orions and C-130 and 727 transport aircraft.[12]

Commander of New Zealand's Defence Force, Air Marshal Adamson, has described New Zealand's defense as at a crossroads. This is the result of declining budgets and the onset of bloc obsolescence. New Zealand released a White Paper in 1997 that lays out a plan for modernization.[13] How New Zealand will proceed with its modernization plan will be largely dependent on the outcome of the November 1999 election. The fate of any defense modernization plan, especially for the navy and air force, under a Labor government is less assured.

### Political and Economic Basis for National Security

In 1999 the National-led New Zealand government took the view that New Zealand must maintain a balanced force structure composed of air-, land-, and sea-based forces to be able to address New Zealand's defense needs. The Shipley government was of the opinion that the regional and global security situation is such that it is prudent to maintain existing military capabilities. In contrast, in the lead-up to the November 1999 election opposition Labor Party leader Helen Clark advocated a niche defense policy for New Zealand that would be based primarily on land forces. Such a policy would allow for further cuts in defense spending on expensive combat systems such as fighter aircraft or new frigates. Labor believes that New Zealand continues to enjoy a benign security environment that would allow such a cutback in defense.[14] Election rhetoric aside, it has been pointed out that New Zealand defense budgets have traditionally faired well under Labor governments.

New Zealand's strategic interests stem from its larger national interests, which are significantly shaped by the country's economy and values. In this way political will and economic prosperity—or economic decline—are the two key determinants that shape New Zealand's strategy and military posture. In recent polls, 70 percent of New Zealanders favored a "strong and effective national defense force," while 80 percent supported New Zealand's participation in international peace-keeping operations, and 54 percent supported the purchase of a third frigate.[15] Further, support for defense appears to be growing among New Zealand's younger generation. In 1996 only 56 percent under age 30 considered it "very important" or "fairly important" for New Zealand to have an effective defense force, while the figure rose to 67 percent in a 1998 poll.[16]

The most obvious examples of how national values impact the process is the New Zealand government's anti-nuclear posture and its support for international peacekeeping. A society's normative values are a national interest that the state's defense policy should uphold, support, and reflect. The political decision to make anti-nuclear policy more important than the alliance relationship with the United States demonstrates how national values can impact defense policy. The National Party and Labor Party differ in their approach to defense. In a relative sense, the National Party favors what appears to be a more traditional approach to security, while the Labor Party emphasizes peace support operations to a greater degree.

The national economic interest is another key determinant that shapes New Zealand's security posture. New Zealand is dependent on international trade for 60 percent of its gross domestic product (GDP). Further, 95 percent of its exports by value travel to their destinations by sea, with most traveling through the Asia-Pacific region.[17] This gives New Zealand an interest in the stability of the region and its seaways. New Zealand's economy did not benefit from the Asian financial crisis. It is estimated that despite a negative growth rate of 0.3 percent in 1998 New Zealand should return to its 1997 rate of 2.3–2.9 percent in 1999. Further, economic growth for 2000 is forecast to reach 3.2–3.8 percent. New Zealand also enjoys a US$18,500 per capita GDP.[18]

A New Zealand government-sponsored report on nuclear propulsion in 1994 tested the political climate to see if it was politically feasible to revisit the nuclear issue. Despite the report's findings that nuclear propulsion is safe, no decision to revisit the issue was taken despite the political cover that the report could give. It still appears that any attempt to revise New Zealand's nuclear stance would be considered political suicide. In addition, the Labor Party remains ideologically opposed to any change in nuclear policy.

## Strategic Interests and Defense Policy

New Zealand's strategic interests are strongly influenced by the fact that New Zealand is an isolated island state that enjoys a benign threat environment. New Zealand's nearest neighbor—3,000 km/1,860 miles away—is its ally Australia. Despite the distance, the countries enjoy a close relationship because of their similar values, cultures, and traditions. New Zealand's other neighbors in the Southwest Pacific are small, dispersed, and dependent island states and colonies. Within this region New Zealand's largest strategic concerns in recent years have been focused on opposing any nuclear presence in the region and peacekeeping.

New Zealand has also sought to patrol its Exclusive Economic Zone (EEZ) to protect its fishing resources. One of the key missions for the New Zealand navy is patrolling the EEZ and territorial waters. Any future direct threat to New Zealand would have to come across vast expanses of ocean. A more immediate security interest is the protection of the nation's ocean resources. To protect these resources New Zealand has to periodically deploy its frigates to stop illegal or unregulated fishing. New Zealand's Orion aircraft also contribute to this surveillance effort.[19]

New Zealand's anti-nuclear stance brought it into disagreement with France, as well as the United States. Opposition to French nuclear testing on Moruroa Atoll in the South Pacific reached a high point in the wake of French agents sinking the *Rainbow Warrior*, a Greenpeace anti-nuclear protest ship, in Auckland harbor in 1985. An activist was killed in the incident.[20]

New Zealand maintains close relations with the states of the Southwest Pacific. New Zealand has constitutional obligations for the defense of Tokelau, Niue, and the Cook Islands, and a Treaty of Friendship with Samoa. New Zealand also conducts military exercises with Fiji, Tonga, the Solomon Islands, and Vanuatu. New Zealand retains the capacity to provide search and rescue, fisheries protection, humanitarian assistance, disaster relief, and maritime surveillance assistance to the island states of the region. Former Prime Minister Bolger has referred to the Southwest Pacific region as "New Zealand's area of immediate strategic and political concern."[21]

Consistent with these strategic interests New Zealand's 1997 Defense White Paper, *The Shape of New Zealand's Defence*, articulates three elements of New Zealand's strategy. They are as follows:

1. Defend against low-level threats.
2. Contribute to regional security through defense relationships with Australia and the Five-Power Defence Arrangement (FPDA).
3. Be a good international citizen through collective security and peacekeeping.

Former Prime Minister Jenny Shipley has similarly identified the need to maintain surveillance over New Zealand's 200-mile maritime economic zone, the need to build New Zealand's peacekeeping capability, and to contribute to regional and international stability as key security objectives.[22]

Though New Zealand shares a general strategic outlook with Australia that emphasizes defense self-reliance, regional engagement, and good international citizenship, Wellington has made good international citizenship—demonstrated through peacekeeping—a relative priority. Such priority setting is required because New Zealand, as a small power, does not have the resources to pursue fully these three strategic objectives. Australia, as a middle power, has had the resources to meet these three objectives. New Zealand, which became self-governing in 1857, only assumed responsibility for its foreign policy in the wake of Britain's 1931 Statute of Westminster and Britain's decline following World War II. New Zealand now bases its strategy on the concept of "Self Reliance in Partnership." This policy framework was set out in the 1991 Defence White Paper and continues to be relevant today. As James Clad pointed out in the first edition of this book, New Zealand's security policy is "anchored to several berths: traditional small state diplomacy, alliance management, and internationalist and moral positions about security. . . ."[23]

As a small state New Zealand cannot easily separate its security from the security of its region, or of the world. This point is highlighted in *The Shape of New Zealand's Defence:*

> New Zealand hopes and expects to benefit from the globalizing trends in information, communications, commerce and technology. Those benefits can best be secured when there is an environment of peace, stability, and shared prosperity. For New Zealand this is particularly, but not exclusively, relevant in the Asia-Pacific region. Therefore our nation's foreign policy and our external security policies must continue to be internationalist, not isolationist. . . . New Zealand's continued prosperity will depend on the maintenance of stability and security in the Asia-Pacific region.[24]

## Alliance Relations

New Zealand has done much—given its small size and resources—to support its British, American, and Australian allies in war and through international peacekeeping and coalition activities. New Zealand dispatched expeditionary forces to the Boer War, World War I, World War II (with the United Kingdom), and to Korea, Vietnam, the 1991 Persian Gulf War, and with the Multilateral Interception Force monitoring UN sanctions against Iraq (with the United States), and to monitor peacekeeping in Bougainville (with Australia). Most recently New Zealand sent a contingent of 420 troops, a frigate, a supply ship, and aircraft to support peace operations in East Timor in 1999. It is a testament to its commitment to such overseas deployments that New Zealand was second only to Russia in per capita casualties suffered during World War I. New Zealand has also dispatched peacekeeping forces in conjunction with its American and Australian allies in such places as the Sinai, the Balkans, Haiti, and Bougainville. New Zealand is also a member of the FPDA, linking it with the United Kingdom, Australia, Singapore, and Malaysia.

It is in its relations with the United States that the two key themes of New Zealand's security policy collide with one another. New Zealand's idealistic stance against nuclear weapons and propulsion has driven a wedge between it and the United States in spite of New Zealand's desire to support the United States in numerous multilateral peacekeeping and security operations. This has had the effect of increasing New Zealand's reliance on Australia and of generally degrading New Zealand's capabilities because of lost intelligence, training, and exercise opportunities with the United States.

New Zealand's relations with the United States have been degraded since the mid-1980s dispute on nuclear policy. In 1985 Labor Prime Minister David Lange led New Zealand on a collision course with its American ally by pursuing a policy that banned nuclear weapons and nuclear-powered ships from New Zealand. This in turn led to then U.S. Secretary of State George Shultz's announcement in 1986 that the American security guarantee no longer extended to New Zealand and that official contacts above the level of Assistant Secretary of State were suspended. This cool state of affairs remained throughout the rest of the Cold War. Possibilities for a thaw were created by the Bush administration's 1991 decision to remove nuclear weapons from U.S. surface ships and by the Somers Report Commission of Enquiry into the safety of nuclear-propelled vessels. This chill thawed somewhat in the mid-1990s following a U.S. review of its policy toward New Zealand that restored some political and military contact but did not restore bilateral or multilateral exercises. Labor's electoral victory in November 1999 makes any resolution of the nuclear dispute between the two states unlikely in the foreseeable future.

Current United States policy precludes the full restoration of the New Zealand arm of the ANZUS alliance until New Zealand reverses its prohibition of nuclear-powered ships in New Zealand ports. Since that dispute, bilateral exercises between the United States and New Zealand have been blocked, as has New Zealand's access to U.S. training courses. The degree to which the ongoing dispute has detracted from the relationship is made evident from excerpts from the Pentagon's 1998 *United States Security Strategy for the East Asia-Pacific Region*. That document describes the relationship as only "generally positive" and reiterates U.S. policy to "prohibit exercises and place limits on other aspects of the bilateral defense relationship." The document does go on to state that the United States "appreciates the contribution of New Zealand to regional forums . . . humanitarian and peacekeeping missions . . . and its contribution to KEDO [Korean Peninsula Energy Development Organization]." The report concludes its discussion of New Zealand by stating that "the U.S. hopes that in the future conditions will allow full restoration of military cooperation with New Zealand."[25]

In recent years New Zealand has sought to find areas of cooperation with the United States that neither compromised its policies nor those of the United States. Former Prime Minister Bolger visited the United States in 1995 and Prime Minister Jenny Shipley visited in January 1999. These are the only two prime ministerial visits that have occurred since the 1985 rift. In March 1999 officials from the two countries discussed a package of thirty-two proposals that would allow New Zealand and the United States to work together on joint defense activities.[26] In August 1999, New Zealand Defence Minister Max Bradford, who had visited U.S. Defense Secretary Cohen in Washington in June 1999, described the relationship with the United States as "an awful lot better than a year ago." Bradford stated that defense discussions in 1999 "had very clear intentions on both of our parts and the result of that was we were able to announce an easing of a number of restrictions that stood in the way of a closer relationship." This included agreement on twenty-two new initiatives in such areas as staff exchanges, training, and contact, but fell short of multilateral exercises. The presence of New Zealand and U.S. troops in East Timor in 1999 provided another opportunity for forces from the two countries to operate together in ongoing operations.[27]

A further opportunity for high-level exchange was provided in September 1999 when New Zealand hosted the Asia-Pacific Economic Cooperation (APEC) organization meeting. In 1999 the issue of U.S. tariffs on New Zealand lamb threatened to become an area of contention. New Zealand, which has a population of 36 million sheep, suffers from U.S. tariffs of between 9 and 40 percent, depending on the volume of lamb exported. Prime Minister Shipley did not let this disagreement affect what she described as "a very warm relationship" despite the issue's importance to New Zealand. In her address to the state dinner Prime Minister Shipley thanked President Clinton for "your friendship in bilateral terms." Adding that "New Zealand and the United States have been able to make some very good progress over recent months . . . we have taken one or two very important steps forward."[28]

Evidence that there is at least the beginning of a thaw in relations was witnessed in 1998 and 1999 by the fruitful contacts at senior levels between New Zealand and American officials. New Zealand's continuing effort to stand alongside the United States in times of strife was most recently demonstrated by the deployment of a Special Air Service force and two P-3 Orions to Kuwait in 1998 during a flare-up of tensions with Iraq. This was recently reaffirmed by the deployments in conjunction with U.S. forces in East Timor in 1999.[29]

New Zealand would like to see various aspects of the relationship restored despite continued dispute over the nuclear issue. New Zealand's capabilities would benefit greatly from renewed training and exercises with U.S. armed forces. Given New Zealand's record of participation with American-led operations, there is a particular need to have interoperable equipment and procedures. The policy banning such arrangements will likely remain in place as long as New Zealand retains its present nuclear policy.[30] Despite this ban, sentiment seems to be growing in defense circles in Washington that at least some of the restrictions on military-to-military exercises should be lifted given that "U.S. and New Zealand Forces can stand side by side in the dark days of crisis."[31]

### Military Relationship with Australia

The weakening of New Zealand's ties to the United States has increased New Zealand's reliance on Australia. New Zealand and Australia are publicly committed to a mutually beneficial defense partnership. At an emotive level this is grounded in the shared ANZAC spirit. The partnership finds its formal expression through the 1944 Canberra Pact and the 1951 ANZUS Treaty and is reinforced by the two states' participation in the FPDA and the ASEAN Regional Forum (ARF). In recent years, there has been concern in Australia that New Zealand has not allocated sufficient resources to maintain a minimally credible defense force. In particular, Australia felt that New Zealand's decision in the 1997 White Paper to reduce from four frigates to three was in the words of Australian Minister for Defence McLachlan "disappointing to us."[32] Other interoperability issues continue to provide a bit of friction in the relationship.

New Zealand and Australia have periodically sought to reinvigorate their defense relationship. The vehicle used most recently to do this is known as Closer Defence Relations (CDRs). This concept was designed to complement the highly successful Closer Economic Relations Treaty between the two countries. CDRs seeks to serve as a forum to achieve better understanding of shared security interests and to harmonize major military acquisition programs, such as the ANZAC frigate, for mutual financial benefit. CDRs also seeks to enhance the ability to conduct combined operations and to facilitate interoperability, intelligence, support, and logistics. The guiding principles of the CDRs, as articulated in March 1998, are as follows:

- To work together for mutual security.
- The partnership is long-term and is focused on practical activities.
- The open defense relationship provides assurance that objectives are clear.
- Equity is measured in terms of outcomes.
- To develop and exploit the skills of personnel.
- To work together to achieve economic efficiency within the defense effort.[33]

New Zealand and Australia have agreed to meet at least annually at the Ministerial and Senior Officers level, known as the Australia–New Zealand Consultative Committee, to further the CDR process. In July 1999 Australian Minister for Defence John Moore and New Zealand's Minister for Defence Max Bradford reaffirmed the 1998 Joint Statement on Future Directions in Closer Defence Relations and reaffirmed their commitment to harmonize force development to increase interoperability and achieve savings.

Despite the strong ANZAC tradition New Zealand has shown some reluctance to engage fully in its defense relations with Australia. The New Zealand decision not to purchase a third *ANZAC* frigate is the most obvious recent example. New Zealand responded negatively to Australian Labor Party Shadow Defence Minister Arch Bevis's suggestion that a future Labor government in Australia would propose a fully integrated ANZAC battalion as a means of reinvigorating bilateral defense relations. New Zealand Defence Minister Max Bradford described the proposal as "an interesting idea, but not on our agenda."[34] More disturbing to Australia is the prospect that a future Labor government would move to a niche defense policy, which would make meaningful defense cooperation with Australia very limited.

Though a legacy of the period of decolonization, the FPDA may adapt to have a future. The FPDA is the third key alliance relationship for New Zealand. The Asian financial crisis limited Malaysia's ability to participate in joint exercises in 1998. Malaysia was expected to rejoin the exercises in 1999.

### Defence Procurement and Force Structure Planning

The New Zealand Defence Force (NZDF) has been making some progress in its attempt to re-equip the force. These decisions fall in line with the 1997 Defence Assessment, which committed NZ$663 million over five years to rebuild the force.[35] New Zealand has also been employing some unique solutions to get around budgeting difficulties. In particular, the NZDF is leasing several combat systems. Leasing has become an attractive option to initiating multiple costly procurement programs at a time when the New Zealand dollar has suffered as a result of the Asian financial crisis. The attractiveness of leasing is increased by a legal requirement that government departments pay for the depreciation of capital equipment annually.

The air force is leasing twenty-eight F-16 fighter aircraft (which were originally purchased by Pakistan) for NZ$362 million over the next ten years in two five-year contracts.[36] These are to replace the A-4Ks, which are to cease operations in mid-2000. New Zealand will have the option to buy the F-16 aircraft at the end of the lease for NZ$287 million. The future of the lease is in some doubt due to Prime Minister Helen Clark's opposition to the program. She has stated that the F-16 lease is "a complete waste of money."[37] If New Zealand terminates the agreement it will reportedly cost them a sizeable sum to break the contract. New Zealand is also considering leasing other combat systems. Plans include five to seven C-130J transport aircraft to replace its existing five C-130H aircraft. There is also a program under way to upgrade New Zealand's six P-3K Orion reconnaissance aircraft. The navy has also considered leasing an FFG-7 *Perry* class frigate to maintain a three-frigate navy.[38]

The 1997 White Paper concluded that the navy would have not less than three surface combatants. The option to purchase a third *ANZAC* class frigate was rejected by the government in November 1998. Options for replacing the HMNZS

*Canterbury*, which is to be decommissioned in 2005, were being considered in late 1999, with a final report due in early 2000. Operating two *ANZAC* frigates and one other frigate will present operational and support difficulties that would not be present if all three frigates were of the same class. The navy was also considering purchasing a military sealift ship and an SH-2G helicopter.

The army's modernization plans include twenty-four fire support vehicles and eighty infantry mobility vehicles to replace aging M113 armored personnel carriers and Scorpion light tanks. These purchases are to create a motorized battalion. In addition, the army is replacing its wheeled armored vehicles, buying new tactical communications equipment, grenade launchers, heavy machine guns, medium range anti-armor weapons, and reconnaissance vehicles.[39]

The added costs associated with modernization programs that will seek to begin to integrate technologies that are the result of the revolution in military affairs (RMA) will exacerbate existing pressures on resources for New Zealand. The impetus to integrate such technologies is driven to a significant extent by the desire to have forces that can operate in coalition with other like-minded countries. These RMA-inspired stresses on the defense budget come at a time when major platform replacement is already stretching thin defense budgets to the limit. These stresses in combination would seem to require either an increase in defense spending or a reordering of strategic objectives that is more closely in line with resources. Without such a decision, strategic objectives will increasingly become unobtainable, as force structures will be unable to support them.

**Peace Support Operations**

New Zealand is a strong supporter of the principle of collective security and an active participant in UN and multilateral peacekeeping and humanitarian operations. New Zealand has been involved in a plethora of peace support operations. The following is a list of recent activities:

1. East Timor
2. Peace Monitoring Group, Bougainville
3. United Nations Mission Observers in Prevlaka, Croatia
4. Stabilization Force, Bosnia
5. United Nations Truce Supervision Organization in Israel, Lebanon, and Syria
6. Operation Griffin in Kuwait with the Combined Joint Task Force
7. United Nations Special Commission on Iraqi Weapons of Mass Destruction
8. National Institute for the Removal of Explosive Devices, Angola
9. Mozambique Accelerated De-mining Program
10. Multinational Force and Observers, Sinai
11. Cambodian Mine Action Center
12. Unexploded Ordnance Program, Laos

13. United Nations Observer Mission, Sierra Leone
14. Kosovo Medical Deployment
15. United Nations Mission for the Referendum in Western Sahara.

In recent years New Zealand has also been involved in Haiti, Somalia, Rwanda, Bosnia, and the Persian Gulf. New Zealand also sent police to monitor the lead-up to the elections in East Timor and appears ready to sustain a long-term commitment to ongoing peace operations there.

New Zealand, which regularly meets its assessed dues, is concerned about several recent trends in peacekeeping. These concerns are as follows.

1. Only one in three peacekeepers today are serving under the UN (as opposed to regional arrangements such as NATO).
2. The UN Security Council is reluctant to authorize new operations.
3. The scope of operations is being reduced for budgetary reasons.
4. Some states (including the United States) continue to be in arrears in their UN payments, while others that have paid have yet to be reimbursed for their troop contributions.[40]

New Zealand also needs to continue to modernize its forces to be able to continue to make a meaningful contribution to such operations into the future.

New Zealand's commitment to make an effective contribution to international peacekeeping is being undermined by its inability to modernize its force in a way that will allow it to be interoperable with friends and allies abroad. This growing gap is being exacerbated by New Zealand's lack of funds to integrate innovations being generated by the ongoing revolution in military affairs. In the words of Defence Minister Bradford, "We all had a bit of a shock as a result of the Bosnian deployment and that we couldn't work adequately with the British because of the state of our equipment."[41]This reaffirms the need for the current government to continue to fund presently contemplated upgrades to the force.

Closer to home, New Zealand continues to play an important role in the peace process in Bougainville, where an estimated 10,000 to 15,000 people have died in a ten-year civil war between Papua New Guinea (PNG) and the secessionist Bougainville Revolutionary Army (BRA). New Zealand has been an active participant, along with Australia, Fiji, and Vanuatu, in the Peace Monitoring Group on Bougainville. Widespread violence on Bougainville subsided in the wake of the Sandline mercenary affair, which led to the ouster of the Chan government in the 1997 PNG elections.

Following the election a confidence- and cooperation-building conference was convened by New Zealand in order to bring various Bougainville factions to the bargaining table. The meeting was held at the Burnham army base outside Christchurch in the hope of restarting the all-Bougainville talks, which had been stalled since December 1995. A second round of talks at Burnham in October of 1997 included PNG representatives and produced a truce agreement aimed at securing future negotiations. This led to the 250-member truce monitoring force. A third round of talks was held at Lincoln University in Christchurch in January 1998. This produced an agreed framework, opened the way for United Nations involvement, and set a timetable for negotiations on Bougainville's future political status. On April 30, 1998, the truce monitoring force's mandate was extended as a peace monitoring force with the transfer of principal responsibility from New Zealand to Australia.[42]

On April 22, 1999, leaders of Papua New Guinea and Bougainville signed the Matakana and Okataina Understanding in Rotarua, New Zealand, in an attempt to further solidify the peace process. As part of the understanding New Zealand would be responsible for arms disposal. Because of the uncertainty of this latest attempt to consolidate the peace it appears that New Zealand will continue to be involved in Bougainville for some time.[43]

## Conclusions

Due to the increased complexity of combat systems, particularly those associated with RMA technologies, states can ill afford to wait until a threat is imminent or apparent before taking the decision to prepare for defense. This is especially so in a regional security environment that is increasingly destabilized. Long lead times between the decision to procure and the successful integration of weapons systems in an operational and doctrinal manner necessitate that states maintain at a minimum a core defense structure. This core can then act as the nucleus for a surge capacity should an identifiable threat emerge. Without such a core capability New Zealand's ability to build up a credible defense capability in time to address a future over-the-horizon threat comes into question. In short, unanticipated threats can emerge faster than defense capabilities can be developed.

In addition to such core defense needs there are the current ongoing interests to be looked after, both in the country's EEZ and in the extended security environment through peace operations and humanitarian support. These missions also dictate minimum force structure requirements. New Zealand appears to be at the minimum level of defense preparedness necessary to meet its present security interests. Deterioration of support for defense in New Zealand will put into question the country's ability to meet its security objectives.

New Zealand—having made its own distinct mark on its national security identity during the Cold War with its anti-nuclear stance—has retained an appreciation of its dependence on a stable international environment that can only be secured by larger, more powerful friends and multilateral bodies. Through its peacekeeping efforts and participation in coalitions New Zealand has been doing what it can to support world order considerations. While a belief that New Zealand could take its own path was stronger during the Lange government, Wellington has an appreciation of New Zealand's reliance on others. This balance is the result of an appreciation in New Zealand that the world is increasingly globalized—a message that is brought home by New Zealand's exposed vulnerability to the recent Asian financial crisis.

## Notes

The author would like to thank New Zealand's Military Attaché in Washington, DC, Lieutenant Colonel Alan Johnson, as well as Cathy Downes of the National Defense University, for their time and insights. In addition, Defense Attaché RADM Simon Harrington of the Australian Embassy in Washington, DC, deserves thanks for his comments. Any errors or omissions are of course those of the author. The views expressed in this chapter are those of the author alone and do not necessarily reflect official policy.

1. Russell Stout, "East Timor Jolts Kiwi Defence Thinking," *Asia-Pacific Defence Reporter*, December 1999, p. 10.

2. Keith Sinclair, *A History of New Zealand* (Auckland: Penguin Books, 1980), p. 24.

3. Report of the Defence Committee of Inquiry, July 1986, p. 8.

4. Here the term ANZAC refers to the Australian and New Zealand Army Corps, which was the unit into which Australian and New Zealand troops were grouped in Egypt prior to their landing at Gallipoli in World War I.

5. Barry Gustafson, "If You Ever Need a Friend, You Have One: Australia and New Zealand in War and Peacekeeping in the 20th Century," an address given at Georgetown University, Washington, DC, April 21, 1997, mimeo, p. 9.

6. J. Nockels, "Australian–New Zealand Defence Cooperation in the Asia-Pacific," in Desmond Ball, ed., *The ANZAC Connection* (Sydney: Allen & Unwin, 1985), p. 82.

7. Steve Hoadley, "New Zealand's Regional Security Policies," in Richard Baker, ed. *The ANZUS States and Their Region* (Westport: Praeger, 1994), p. 30.

8. Report of the Defence Committee of Inquiry, p. 11.

9. New Zealand Ministry of Defence Website, "Frequently Asked Questions."

10. John Roos, "Through Thick and Thin," *Armed Forces Journal*, July 1999, p. 16.

11. Max Bradford, Minister for Defence, "Government Committed to a Safe and Effective Defence Force," December 1, 1998.

12. IISS, *The Military Balance 1997/98*, p. 190.

13. Ministry of Defence, *The Shape of New Zealand's Defence: A White Paper*, November 1997.

14. New Zealand Government media release, "Labor Defence Stance Ignores History and Reality," April 16, 1999.

15. Max Bradford, Minister for Defence, Media Release, "New Zealanders Want an Effective Defence Force," November 17, 1998. See also Defence Committee of Inquiry, "Defence and Security: What New Zealanders Want," Wellington: Defence Committee of Inquiry, 1986.

16. Max Bradford, Minister for Defence, Media Release, "Support for Armed Forces Strong," June 3, 1998.

17. "Why Do We Need a Defence in Peacetime?" New Zealand Ministry of Defence Website.

18. "Economic Indicators," *Far Eastern Economic Review*, April 29, 1999, p. 73.

19. Max Bradford, Minister for Defence, "Frigate Te Kaha Sails for Southern Oceans," Media release, February 2, 1999.

20. M. King, *Death of the Rainbow Warrior* (Auckland: Penguin Books, 1986).

21. John Henderson, "New Zealand's Policy Towards the Pacific Islands," in Baker, *The ANZUS States and Their Region*, p. 94.

22. New Zealand Government Press release, "Maintain a Credible Defence Force for New Zealand," December 1, 1998.

23. James Clad, "New Zealand," in William M. Carpenter and David G. Wiencek, eds., *Asian Security Handbook: An Assessment of Political-Security Issues in the Asia Pacific Region* (Armonk, NY: M.E. Sharpe, 1996), p. 191.

24. Rt. Hon. J. Bolger Prime Minister, from the foreword to *The Shape of New Zealand's Defence*.

25. Secretary of Defense William Cohen, *United States Security Strategy for the East Asia-Pacific Region* (Washington, DC: U.S. DOD Office of International Security Affairs, November 1998), p. 27.

26. Cathie Bell, "U.S.–New Zealand Military Relations Could Warm," *Defence News*, March 8, 1999.

27. Cathie Bell interview with the Hon. Max Bradford, "From the Source," *Australian Defence Magazine*, August 1999, p. 53.

28. Transcript of President Clinton's and Prime Minister Shipley's Remarks at dinner, September 15, 1999.

29. Roos, "Through Thick and Thin," p. 16.

30. Philip Finnegan, "Closer Ties Sought with the U.S.," *Defence News*, May 10, 1999.

31. Roos, "Through Thick and Thin," p. 16.

32. Ian McLachlan, "The Spirit of ANZAC," address given at the Cook Hotel Wellington, NZ, Office of the Minister for Defence, March 25, 1998.

33. "Joint Statement on Future Directions in Closer Defence Relations," Office of the Minister for Defence, Parliament House, Canberra, ACT March 27, 1998.

34. New Zealand Government press release, "Aus/NZ Battalion Not on Our Agenda." September 14, 1998.

35. "Push Given to NZ Defence Equipment Program," *Australian Defence Business Review*, August 27, 1999.

36. Cathie Bell, "New Zealand Finalizes Deal with U.S. to Rent F-16s," *Defence News*, August 9, 1999.

37. Christopher Dore, "Jet Deal Blows Out to $57 M," *The Australian*, July 27, 1999.

38. Philip Finnegan, "In New Zealand the Weapon Plan Is to Fly Not Buy," *Defence News*, May 10, 1999.

39. Cathie Bell, "New Zealand Seeks Fast Vehicles for Motorized Battalion," *Defence News*, August 2, 1999.

40. Statement by New Zealand Permanent to the United Nations Mr. Michael Powles, March 25, 1999.

41. Bell interview with the Hon. Max Bradford, p. 53.

42. Karl Claxton, *Bougainville 1988–98* (Canberra: The Australian National University, 1999), pp. 18–9.

43. Greg Roberts, "Secessionists Warn of Civil War Unless NZ-Brokered Treaty Is Scrapped," *Sydney Morning Herald*, May 7, 1999.

## Suggested Readings

Address by the Chief of the Defence Force Air Marshal Carey Adamson. "New Zealand Defence Policy: In the Spirit of ANZAC." Centre for Australian and New Zealand Studies, Georgetown University, Washington, DC. 22 April 1999.

Baker, Richard, ed. *The ANZUS States and Their Region*. Westport: Praeger Publishers, 1994.

Government Response to the Interim Report of the Foreign Affairs, Defence and Trade Committee on Defence Beyond 2000. Government of New Zealand.

Ministry of Defence. *The Shape of New Zealand's Defence: A White Paper*. November 1997.

# 20

# North Korea

*Larry A. Niksch*

North Korea, officially the Democratic People's Republic of Korea (DPRK), came into being on September 9, 1948, following three years of military occupation by the Soviet Union. North Korea occupies the northern half of the Korean Peninsula. Its southern border with South Korea straddles the 38th parallel and is the armistice line established in July 1953 at the end of the Korean War. Most of North Korea's northern border is with China, with the Yalu and Tumen rivers as the boundary. A small strip in the northeast borders on Russia.

North Korea's total area is 47,399 square miles. The country's estimated population is 22 million, compared to over 46 million in South Korea. Nearly 70 percent of the population is urban. Pyongyang, the capital city, has an estimated two million people. The geography is predominately hilly and mountainous. Cultivable lowlands comprise less than 20 percent of the land area.

### Political Framework

The Soviet Union installed in the 1945–1948 period a political system in North Korea modeled after the Stalinist system of the USSR: a single party dictatorship of a communist party (the Korean Workers' Party); a supreme ruler, Kim Il-sung, a Korean communist leader who led a guerrilla band against the Japanese in the 1930s and who served in the Red Army from 1941 to 1945; and a collectivist socioeconomic structure based on mass participation in communist front organizations, state-controlled industries and trade, and Stalinist collective agriculture. Kim Il-sung also established, with Soviet aid, a powerful military, albeit under communist party control.

The system survived the Korean War and the collapse of the Soviet Union and other communist regimes at the beginning of the 1990s. Kim Il-sung held the titles

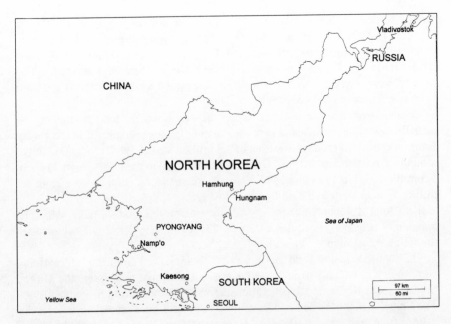

**North Korea**

of President and General Secretary of the Korean Workers' Party (KWP) until his death in July 1994. He was succeeded by his son, Kim Jong-il. Kim Il-sung began to extend power to his son in the late 1970s. By the mid-1980s, Kim Jong-il was believed to be making many key decisions within the government and the KWP. In 1992, he became Supreme Commander of the armed forces, the Korean People's Army (KPA).

Kim Jong-il appears to have managed the succession to supreme power, and he seems to have consolidated his authority. He has appointed large numbers of individuals of his generation to senior positions in the government, party, and military, thus effecting a generational change of leadership. In October 1997, he assumed the post of General Secretary of the KWP. He did not, however, assume the presidency. Instead, he amended North Korea's constitution to declare Kim Il-sung posthumously as "Eternal President" and to elevate Kim Jong-il's post of Chairman of the National Defense Commission to the most senior position in the government.

Kim Jong-il so far has been able to manage two challenges to the stability of his regime: (1) rapid economic decline and massive food shortages, and (2) uncertain relations with his military.

**Economic Decline and Famine**

North Korea's gross national product has fallen on the average by 5 percent annually since 1990. Food production has fallen by at least that much, producing famine conditions that may have killed up to three million people. North Korean factories in 1999 were estimated to be operating on the average at less than 30 percent of capacity; many are believed to have shut down. If unofficial cross-border trade with China is not counted, North Korea's foreign trade dropped by over 55 percent in the 1990s. Fuel is in short supply. Electric power outages have been frequent, even in Pyongyang.

South Korean and U.S. analysts report that North Korean food production, especially the staples of rice and corn, began to fall in the second half of the 1980s. From an estimated food grain output of 8.3 million tons in 1984, production fell to around 5.5 million tons in 1989. The decline continued in the 1990s, down to about 3.5 million tons in 1995 and 1996. Estimated demand, by contrast, rose from 6.4 million tons in 1990 to 6.8 million tons in 1996.

Kim Jong-il's economic strategy has focused on the food shortage, which he apparently believes constitutes a threat to his regime. His strategy has contained the following elements:

(1) Secure massive food aid and other financial aid from the international community, especially from North Korea's traditional adversary, the United States: North Korea first appealed for international food aid in September 1995. The United Nations World Food Program (WFP) has issued several appeals for donations from governments. Between January 1996 and the end of 1999, the United States responded with 1.47 million metric tons of food (mainly rice and corn), mainly through the WFP. The United States by far has been the biggest contributor to the WFP, for example, contributing 500,000 tons of the 600,000 tons distributed by the WFP in 1998. In 1999, the WFP provided enough food to feed 8 million North Koreans.

At the end of 1996, North Korea targeted the United States specifically for increased food aid. It used bilateral negotiations with the United States to demand ever increasing amounts of food aid in return for agreeing in late 1997 to the U.S.– South Korean proposal for four-party talks over a Korean peace agreement, agreeing to a meeting in October 1998 over North Korea's missile program, and agreeing to allow U.S. officials to visit a suspected nuclear site at Kumchangri in May 1999. Thus, U.S. food aid became more an object of negotiation between the United States and North Korea than strictly a humanitarian act of the United States. U.S. food aid along with massive shipments from China also were bulwarks of support for the North Korean regime during the critical period of the food crisis in 1997 and 1998.

Despite the massive nature of the international food aid program, North Korea limited the international presence inside the country. In 1999, the WFP had less than fifty monitors inside North Korea, most of them in Pyongyang. WFP monitors had access to 162 of North Korea's 211 counties, but even this access was limited and controlled by North Korean officials.

(2) Give priority to the military and communist party elite in the allocation of food and other economic resources: U.S. intelligence agencies have estimated that

since the late 1970s North Korea has allotted about 25 percent of its gross national product to the military. WFP officials acknowledged in 1997 that despite the fall in the daily ration to one hundred grams of food for an average citizen (below the subsistence level), military personnel were receiving 700 grams. Numerous reports from North Korea and from defectors described a rationing system that gave priority to residents of Pyongyang and other cities, which are populated largely by loyal communist party members and government officials. It was observed widely that the city residents were not experiencing the degree of hardship reported from locations away from the capital. In short, Kim Jong-il has manipulated the food allocation system to ensure adequate resources to the most politically strategic elements of the populace.

(3) Relax de facto (but not de jure) selective controls within the collectivist socio-economic system but reject any fundamental restructuring of the economic and collective farm systems: The North Korean government has responded to the economic crisis with several tactical economic moves, including promotion of double cropping, promotion of growing of potatoes, allowing the emergence of de facto private markets as the state food distribution system collapsed in many locales, emphasizing the role of small work teams on collective farms, and allowing South Korea's Hyundai Corporation to open a tourist project in North Korea. The regime, however, has rejected instituting the kind of fundamental economic reforms that China has encouraged it to do since the early 1980s, including dismantlement of collective farms, privatization of the retail trade and light industries, an end to price controls and production quotas, and adopting liberal policies to attract foreign private investment. Even the Hyundai tourist project requires Hyundai to make a payoff to the North Korean government of nearly US$1 billion over five years—the type of stipulation not likely to attract other foreign firms. The North Korean government refuses to acknowledge that the economic decline is the result of a failed economic system. Instead, it constantly cites uncontrollable factors, such as floods and droughts, the collapse of the Soviet Union, and U.S. economic sanctions.

## The Military

On paper, North Korea seems to have formidable, dangerous military capabilities; this perception is dominant in the United States. The KPA numbers 1.1 million. The numbers of tanks, armored personnel carriers, heavy artillery guns, and rocket launchers are impressive: 3,500 tanks, 2,500 armored personnel carriers, 10,600 artillery guns, and 2,600 multiple rocket launchers. Combat aircraft number over 500. These forces are concentrated heavily near the demilitarized zone facing South Korea.

In the 1990s, North Korea gave high priority to developing weapons of mass destruction. Unclassified estimates of North Korea's chemical weapons stockpile range from 1,000 to 5,000 tons. The Department of Defense believes that North Korea has the biotechnical resources to support a limited biological warfare effort. By the end of 1993, U.S. intelligence had calculated a better than even chance that

North Korea had produced one or two nuclear bombs from about 10–12 kilograms of plutonium it had acquired from its operating nuclear reactor at Yongbyon. Prior to 1994, North Korea was assembling a nuclear infrastructure that could have produced enough plutonium for dozens of nuclear weapons annually. In October 1994, North Korea and the United States concluded an Agreed Framework, which suspended operation of the known nuclear installations. Nevertheless, there are suspicions, including suspicions of the U.S. intelligence community, that North Korea is continuing a clandestine nuclear weapons program. An official of the South Korean Institute for Defense Analysis gave the startling estimate in November 1999 that North Korea possesses about 40 kilograms of plutonium—enough for ten small nuclear warheads. Japanese Foreign Minister Masahiko Komura stated in June 1999 that North Korea likely has "several nuclear weapons."

North Korea also in the 1990s gave high priority to developing long-range missiles capable of hitting targets in Japan and the United States. In 1996 or early 1997, North Korea began deploying intermediate-range No Dong missiles, which are capable of striking many areas of Japan. In August 1998, North Korea tested a Taepo Dong 1 missile, whose range could reach the U.S. territories of Alaska, Guam, the U.S. Commonwealth of the Northern Marianas, possibly Hawaii, and the Japanese island of Okinawa (home to 50,000 U.S. military personnel and dependents). The Taepo Dong-1 could be deployed as early as 2000. North Korea reportedly is working to develop a Taepo Dong-2 missile with full intercontinental range capable of hitting the continental United States.

The North Korean military threat thus has grown in terms of firepower and destructive capacity. However, in strategic terms, the threat has not grown and appears to be declining. The reason is the deterioration of North Korean conventional military forces, especially mobile forces like tanks, armored personnel carriers, infantry, and aircraft.

Weaponry has become obsolete since North Korea lost its major supplier, the Soviet Union, in 1991. A comparison of the 1985–86 and 1998–99 editions of the authoritative publication, *The Military Balance*, shows, after nearly fifteen years, few changes in the models of weaponry in the North Korean army and air force. This absence of upgrading is especially noticeable in mobile, offensive weaponry, which would spearhead a North Korean invasion of South Korea. Most of this weaponry is of 1970s vintage or earlier. This obsolescence factor was demonstrated in the naval clash between South Korea and North Korea in the Yellow Sea in June 1999; South Korean naval forces overwhelmed North Korea's navy, which fought using 1960s and 1970s technology.

North Korea's economic collapse has ruined the transportation system, created fuel shortages in the military, and lowered production capabilities in North Korea's defense industries. A detailed assessment of the U.S. Defense Intelligence Agency (DIA), which the publication *Defense Week* reported in January 1998, concluded that North Korea's military industries "will most likely undergo a major downsizing in the latter part of this century, forced to reduce under the weight of a bankrupt economy. It is likely that many, possibly most facilities will be dormant and not actively producing either military material or general purpose material and equipment." Food shortages have affected the nutrition of rank and file troops. Fuel shortages have resulted in the reported decline in the scope and duration of North Korean military exercises since 1994. Accounts from defectors and U.S. assessments describe growing corruption, lack of discipline, weakening morale, and physical deficiencies within the KPA.

In strategic terms, North Korea has lost the policy option of using the KPA to invade South Korea and attain North Korea's overriding strategic policy goal—reunification on North Korea's terms. This was the overriding threat that U.S. officials constantly warned against in the 1970s and 1980s. There is good evidence that the North Korean leadership is well aware of the situation. Top North Korean leader Hwang Jang-yop, who defected in 1997, has related that a North Korean military reassessment of 1992–1993 concluded that the KPA faced a long-term deterioration in capabilities. Kim Tok-hong, who defected with Hwang, related that a "senior officer" of North Korea's West Sea Fleet Command told him in April 1996 that within three years North Korea would lose the ability to fight a war due to shortages of equipment and parts.

In losing the invasion option, North Korea cannot use or threaten to use weapons of mass destruction to achieve militarily its great strategic objective. If Pyongyang's overriding strategic goal is no longer in reach militarily, North Korea has no realistic option to employ weapons of mass destruction against the United States and South Korea. The threat of these weapons thus is limited to (1) proliferation to other countries; (2) use as deterrence against a U.S. or South Korean military response to limited North Korean military and/or terrorist provocations; and (3) a threat to use them as an intimidation tactic in North Korean diplomacy.

## Policies Toward the United States and South Korea

North Korea in the 1990s followed the dual policy of seeking to draw the United States into higher-level, bilateral negotiations while shunning South Korea. By early 2000, North Korea was engaging diplomatically the United States, South Korea, Japan, and it considerably stepped up its diplomatic activities by participating in a summit meeting with South Korea in June 2000.

North Korea has sought high-level, bilateral negotiations with the United States since 1974; but in the 1990s, the focus of its policy objectives has shifted from the military to the economic. This reflects the economic crisis. North Korea thus has been willing to negotiate agreements with the United States regarding weapons of mass destruction in order to avoid U.S.-instigated international economic sanctions and secure U.S. economic benefits. Agreements reached are the U.S.–North Korean Agreed Framework of October 1994, the March 1999 agreement on U.S. access to the suspected nuclear site at Kumchangri, and the September 1999 Berlin agreement, in which North Korea promised no further tests of longer-range missiles. In these agreements, as well as North Korea's 1997 agreement to participate in four-party talks, North Korea has secured from the United States heavy oil, promised delivery of two nuclear reactors, expanding amounts of food aid, and a partial lifting of U.S. economic sanctions. In negotiations in the year 2000, North Korea pressed the United States to lift remaining economic sanctions and facilitate multi-billion-dollar direct financial aid.

North Korea has made concessions on weapons of mass destruction while continuing core weapons of mass destruction programs. It continually threatens to develop these weapons as an intimidation tactic in its diplomacy. The policy issue for the United States is whether it can succeed in using economic benefits to secure North Korea's agreement to shut down these programs. Related to this, North Korea's ever increasing financial price for its concessions is straining the U.S. ability to deliver and may force the United States to turn to Japan as a bankroller of future deals. Moreover, while North Korea has given its economic goals priority in negotiations, it has not abandoned its diplomatic objective of drawing the United States into negotiation of restraints on U.S. forces in South Korea and the withdrawal of U.S. forces. It holds open the option of interjecting this military agenda into future negotiations over its nuclear and missile programs.

## Suggested Readings

Council on Foreign Relations. *U.S. Policy Toward North Korea: Next Steps: Report of an Independent Task Force.* New York: Council on Foreign Relations, 1999.

Downs, Chuck. *Over the Line: North Korea's Negotiating Strategy.* Washington: The AEI Press, 1999.

Eberstadt, Nicholas. *The End of North Korea.* Washington: The AEI Press, 1999.

Kim, Samuel, ed. *North Korean Foreign Relations in the Post–Cold War Era.* Hong Kong: Oxford University Press, 1998.

Niksch, Larry A. *North Korea's Nuclear Weapons Program.* Washington: U.S. Congressional Research Service, CRS Issue Brief, November 1999 (updated regularly).

Oberdorfer, Don. *The Two Koreas.* Reading, MA: Addison-Wesley, 1997.

Pacific Forum–CSIS. *Managing Relations with North Korea: Where Should We Go from Here?* Honolulu, 1997.

Pollack, Jonathan D., and Chung Min Lee. *Preparing for Korean Unification: Scenarios and Implications.* Santa Monica: The Rand Corporation, 1999.

Shinn, Runn-sup. *South Korea: "Sunshine Policy" and Its Political Context.* Washington: U.S. Congressional Research Service, CRS Report, May 1999.

Snyder, Scott. *Negotiating on the Edge: North Korean Negotiating Behavior.* Washington: United States Institute of Peace Press, 1999.

U.S. House of Representatives, North Korea Advisory Group. *Report to the Speaker.* November 1999.

——————————— 21

# Pakistan

## *Samina Ahmed*

Pakistan's security dilemmas are both internal and external. For Pakistan's security managers, the main threat to Pakistani security is external, emanating from its powerful neighbor, India. A longstanding territorial dispute over Kashmir and three wars—as well as three near-war situations—in the past decade reinforce Pakistani perceptions of mistrust and hostility from India. Strengthening Pakistan's defense capabilities, conventional and nuclear, is a priority for Pakistani policymakers, given the glaring military asymmetry between the two states. At the same time, Pakistan uses all the means at its disposal, diplomatic and military, to undermine Indian security, including India's hold over the disputed territory of Kashmir. Pakistan also exploits its strategic position, neighboring on China and Iran and near the resource-rich Central Asian Republics and the Persian Gulf region to offset India's regional influence and to acquire external support for its rivalry with India.

While Pakistan's authoritative decisionmakers—composed of its powerful military as well as its civil bureaucracy—are primarily concerned about a perceived Indian threat, internal challenges threaten the security of a weak state. Pakistan faces a serious crisis of governance, rooted in a history of repeated military interventions and the absence of institutional, representative mechanisms for mediating intra-state disputes. Since political stability eludes the state, not only is the legitimacy of the state's institutions contested, but linguistic, regional, ethnic, and sectarian divisions threaten Pakistan's fragile national cohesion.[1] Pakistani policymakers, however, continue to focus on external security, allocating a disproportionate percentage of the state's scarce economic resources to defense, neglecting human resource development, and depriving an increasingly disillusioned citizenry of both economic development and political stability. In this atmosphere of heightened political, economic, and social polarization, Pakistan's externally driven security policies might just result in a complete rejection of state authority by its citizens.[2]

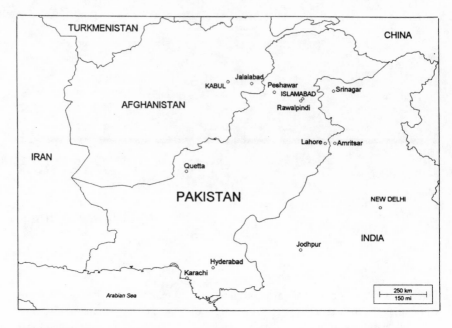

## Pakistan

### India-Centric Security

The Indian-centric focus of Pakistan's security policy can be traced back to the events accompanying the partition of Britain's Indian empire into two independent states in August 1947. The mass migration of Hindus and Muslims across the newly created India–Pakistan border resulted in hundreds of thousands of casualties. Differences over the divided economic and military assets of the British Indian empire and disputes over territory—particularly over the Muslim-majority state of Jammu and Kashmir, whose Hindu ruler opted for a merger with India—sowed the seeds of mutual hostility and mistrust between the two states.[3] In 1948–49, Pakistan and India fought their first war over Kashmir, a conflict in which India retained two-thirds of the disputed territory. Unsuccessful Pakistani attempts to challenge India's hold over Kashmir through the mediation of the United Nations heightened Pakistani animosity toward India. In 1965, Pakistan once again attempted to militarily challenge Indian control over Kashmir, resulting in an inconclusive war that reinforced the territorial status quo in the disputed territory.

As Pakistan enters the twenty-first century, the Kashmir dispute remains both a symptom and a cause of conflict between the two states. For Pakistan's principal decisionmakers, an aggressive and expansionist India has never reconciled itself to Pakistan's independence and has employed every conceivable tactic to destroy Pakistan and·to coerce her into subjugation. In their perceptions, India's objectives are to keep Pakistan weak—militarily, politically, and economically—so that it does not stand in the way of Indian aims and objectives in South Asia. The only way of meeting that threat is through the acquisition of the necessary military capability, conventional and nuclear.[4]

Although Pakistan devotes a considerable proportion of its budget to defense, given the resource gap between the two states their conventional asymmetries have increased over time. To offset this military imbalance and to counter India's nuclear weapons and ballistic missile capabilities, Pakistan also pursues a nuclear weapons program and develops or acquires nuclear-capable ballistic missiles. Pakistan's nuclear weapons program has the perceived advantages of prestige and the acquisition of a comparable regional standing with India. The resultant nuclear arms race enhances regional tensions and instability in South Asia.[5]

### The Option of Alliances

Pakistan also challenges India's claims to regional preeminence through external alliances. Alliance relationships are also pursued to reduce Pakistan's military asymmetry—conventional and nuclear—with India. At the height of the Cold War in the decade of the 1950s, Pakistan entered into a formal alliance relationship with the United States, joining a number of U.S.-sponsored security pacts, including the Southeast Asia Treaty Organization and the Central Treaty Organization. Although Pakistan ostensibly supported U.S. Cold War strategies of countering the global threat of communism, its alliance relationship with the United States was primarily aimed at countering the perceived Indian threat and India's regional standing.[6] As a result of the pacts, Pakistan became the beneficiary of considerable U.S. economic and military assistance, helping to create a large standing armed force to confront its regional rival.

Despite its membership in the anti-communist pacts, Pakistan also established close relations with the People's Republic of China (PRC), taking advantage of the hostility between India and China and the rift between China and India's external ally, the former Soviet Union. Pakistan's alliance with China paid dividends in the shape of military hardware and assistance. Pakistan's alliance relationship with China assumed a new importance as the United States imposed an embargo on defense cooperation with both Pakistan and India during their 1965 and 1971 wars—an embargo that had a far more serious impact on Pakistan's U.S.-equipped forces. U.S. neutrality in Pakistan's wars with India moreover contrasted with China's active support for Pakistan, especially during the 1965 war.[7]

Pakistan was anxious to resume its alliance relationship with the United States, hoping to regain preferential U.S. military assistance. Changes in the external environment in the post–Cold War era, however, posed new challenges for Pakistan's security planners. As Cold War security alliances became redundant, former allies such as Pakistan lost their strategic significance for the United States. At the same time, Pakistan's decision to match India's acquisition of nuclear weapons and ballistic missile capabilities introduced new tensions in U.S.–Pakistan relations.[8] Since the United States opted periodically to sanction Pakistan for its nuclear ambitions, China became a major source of nuclear and missile hardware and technology for Pakistan. Following the disintegration of the Soviet Union and an easing of tensions with India, however, China distanced itself from its Pakistani ally and appeared more accepting of U.S. pressures to end its nuclear and missile assistance to Pakistan. China's changed posture is reinforced by the May 1998 tests in India and Pakistan, underscoring Chinese perceptions of the threat posed to regional stability by two nuclear-powered neighbors with a long bilateral history of conflict.[9] New tensions also strain Pakistan's relationship with China, since Islamic religious extremism in China's Xinjiang province is linked with attempts by Pakistani religious parties to export their ideology beyond Pakistan's borders.

### Regional Policies and Internal Threats

This rise in religious extremism in Pakistan in turn has linkages with Pakistani policies toward neighboring Afghanistan. Ever since Pakistan inherited the north-west borders of the British Indian empire, its relations with Afghanistan have remained troubled over issues ranging from territorial and trade disputes to mutual accusations of internal intervention. To counter a perceived Afghan threat and to acquire regional influence over Afghanistan, Pakistan has provided moral and material support to chosen Afghan clients for decades. In the 1980s, Pakistani ambitions received a new impetus by the Soviet decision to intervene militarily to prop up a sympathetic Afghan regime at a time of enhanced tensions between the United States and the Soviet Union. Playing a major role in U.S.-led anti-Soviet operations in Afghanistan, the Pakistani military regime of General Zia-ul-Haq became the recipient of large-scale Western—in particular U.S.—military and economic assistance, enabling the regime to strengthen itself domestically and to gain international legitimacy.[10]

Although the Soviet withdrawal from Afghanistan put an end to U.S. military and economic assistance to Pakistan, the continued civil war in Afghanistan gives Pakistan a continued opportunity to intervene in Afghan affairs. Pakistani policymakers are motivated by the desire to establish a zone of influence in Afghanistan with perceived security benefits, as well as the potential for political and economic access to Afghanistan's resource-rich Central Asian neighbors.[11] With Pakistan's military and political assistance, its chosen Afghan allies the Taliban have captured more than two-thirds of Afghan territory. Pakistan's regional ambitions are, however, undermined by the denial of international recognition to the Taliban administration as the legitimate government of Afghanistan due to its extremist Islamic policies. Pakistan's relations with Iran have also deteriorated because of its backing for the Sunni Taliban movement, who pose a threat to the interests of Afghanistan's Shia minority. Since the Taliban support Islamic extremist movements in the region, Pakistan's relations with Russia and the Central Asian republics are strained. The

Taliban failure to defeat the remnants of the Afghan opposition also means a continuation of the Afghan civil war, adversely affecting Pakistan's prospects of gaining access via Afghan territory to the oil and gas resources of central Asian states such as Turkmenistan.[12]

Pakistan's internal security is also adversely affected by its interventionist policies in Afghanistan. Millions of Afghan refugees remain in the Pakistani bordering provinces of Baluchistan and the Northwest Frontier Province as the civil war continues in Afghanistan. Apart from the economic burden of sustaining a huge refugee presence when international assistance continues to decline, the presence of the Afghan Pakhtuns upsets the demographic balance between Pakistani Baluch and Pakhtuns in Baluchistan, fueling ethnic tensions as well as Baluch alienation against the central government.[13]

Pakistan's involvement in Afghanistan also fuels a flourishing cross-border traffic in drugs and arms that involves both Pakistani and Afghan elements. The trade in narcotics and arms undermines the security of Pakistan's citizens while it also deprives the state of its ability to control sub-state ethnic and sectarian violence. In Sindh, for example, inter-ethnic and intra-ethnic violence assumes an alarming proportion since all the contending parties are armed with sophisticated weapons that have entered Pakistani territory from war-torn Afghanistan. While tensions between Pakistan's Sunni majority and Shia minority result in sporadic incidents of violence, sectarian conflict has assumed serious dimensions due to the easy availability of arms from Afghan territory.[14] Attacks by Sunni militants on their Shia rivals, including Iranian citizens, in turn exacerbate tensions between Pakistan and Iran, while China is equally concerned about the linkage between its restive Muslim minority and Pakistan–Afghan religious militants.

Pakistani interventionist policies are not restricted to Afghanistan. Moral and material support is extended to anti-Indian dissidents in the disputed territory of Jammu and Kashmir.[15] This war by proxy is periodically accompanied by direct Pakistani military involvement. It is believed that such an interventionist policy serves Pakistani security interests since India is forced to pay a considerable military and economic price. Pakistani policymakers also stand firm in the belief that low-intensity conflict will remain confined to the disputed territory, ignoring the past consequences of their interventionist policies. In October 1947, Pakistan extended support to an anti-Indian tribal insurgency in Kashmir, sending regular forces into Indian-held Kashmiri territory, resulting in the first India–Pakistan war.[16] In 1965, General Ayub Khan's military regime sent in regular forces disguised as Kashmiri dissidents into Indian-administered Kashmir, calculating that the conflict would not extend beyond the disputed territory. India, however, opted to extend the conflict beyond the international border, resulting in the 1965 India–Pakistan war.[17]

Under General Zia's military regime, Pakistan again opted for a strategy of undermining Indian security through a war by proxy in Kashmir. By the late 1980s, Pakistan had acquired a nuclear weapons capability and its policymakers believed that nuclear deterrence would prevent the outbreak of conventional war. By 1990, when Pakistan's relations with India deteriorated to the brink of war as a result of the unrest in Indian-held Kashmir, implicit nuclear threats were made by Pakistan to persuade the United States to act as an intermediary. This successful strategy of nuclear bluff reinforced Pakistan's belief that it could conduct low-intensity conflict without risking open war, increasing the chances of a future conventional war which could escalate into a nuclear exchange.[18]

In May 1999, such a conflict almost occurred when Pakistan once again opted to conduct covert operations in the Kargil and Drass sectors of Indian-administered Kashmir, believing that Pakistan's nuclear weapons capability would prevent conventional war with India.[19] Accusing Pakistan of sending hundreds of regular forces and militants to forcibly alter the Line of Control and rejecting Pakistani denials that the fighters were Kashmiri Muslim militants, India launched a major military offensive, including thousands of troops and the use of helicopter gunships and jet fighters. A massive military buildup on both sides of the border, intensified shelling and artillery exchanges, and rising casualty figures signaled that the fighting could spiral out of control. During the fighting, as senior Pakistani and Indian officials implicitly threatened the use of nuclear weapons, the United States, concerned about the dangers of a nuclear exchange, interceded at Pakistan's request to end the fighting.[20]

Pakistan was forced to retreat, since its military intervention had almost resulted in a war in which India's conventional and nuclear superiority would have prevailed. The Kargil operation, however, cost Prime Minister Nawaz Sharif his office when his government was dismissed by the military on October 12, 1999, partly in response to Sharif's attempts to shift the blame of an inglorious Pakistani retreat onto the military high command. It is likely that the Kargil operation was initiated by Army Chief General Pervez Musharraf, who now heads the Pakistani military regime. The military high command had retained its control over sensitive areas of Pakistani security policy even after the restoration of democracy in 1988, following eleven years of direct military rule. Pakistani interventionist strategies in India and Afghanistan were directed by its military establishment, as was its nuclear weapons policy.

Since the memories of the 1971 defeat and India's role in the creation of Bangladesh still rankle, hostility toward India and perceptions of the Indian threat are rife within the Pakistani military. Because the military has also exercised direct or indirect control over the Pakistani state for most of its existence, all policy—internal and external—is dictated by the military's institutional preferences and interests. The stress on external security, for instance, with its focus on the Indian threat, emanates from and in turn reinforces the military's perceptions of the Indian threat. It also serves to bolster the corporate interests of the armed forces, since scarce economic resources are allocated to defense, sustaining a large standing military establishment and strengthening the military's political dominance.

The disproportionate emphasis on external security is, however, at the expense of human security.[21] At the same time repeated military interventions have deprived Pakistan's multi-ethnic population of representative and pluralistic avenues for bargaining and participation. The resultant economic underdevelopment and perceptions of alienation—especially among ethnic groups that are underrepresented in the armed forces—result in periodic outbreaks of inter-ethnic and intra-ethnic violence as well as violent challenges to the state's authority.[22] It was these perceptions of exploitation and alienation that fueled anti-state sentiments in East Pakistan. Underrepresented in the politically dominant military and thereby deprived of access to political power or economic resources, Pakistan's majority Bengali population in its eastern wing opted for secession following a bloody civil war. While Indian military intervention contributed to the outcome of the armed conflict, it was prolonged military rule that was primarily responsible for the dismemberment of Pakistan and the creation of Bangladesh in 1971.[23]

In post-1971 Pakistan, the military retains its political predominance, exercising direct or indirect control over the state. Pakistan's military high command has demonstrated time and again its ability to ward off all internal challenges to its political dominance, intervening at will and exercising a veto over all aspects of policymaking, internal or external. Each military intervention, however, creates new categories of challenges and threats. Authoritarian state structures and the absence of participatory mechanisms for accommodating ethnic and regional demands in a pluralistic society have transformed internal competition for political power and socioeconomic benefits into conflict between sub-state forces and between aggrieved internal actors and the state.[24] Pakistan currently stands at the crossroads. The perpetuation of authoritarian control or the institutionalization of democratic governance will determine the extent to which its citizens continue to accept the state's legitimacy.

## Notes

1. See Samina Ahmed, "Pakistan at Fifty: A Tenuous Democracy," *Current History* 96, no. 614, December 1997, pp. 419–24.

2. Samina Ahmed, "Pakistan: The Crisis Within," in Muthiah Alagappa, ed., *Asian Security Practice: Material and Ideational Influences* (Stanford, CA: Stanford University Press, 1998), pp. 361–62.

3. Pervez Iqbal Cheema, *Pakistan's Defence Policy 1947–58* (London: Macmillan, 1990), p. 24.

4. Stephen P. Cohen, *The Pakistan Army* (Berkeley, CA: University of California Press, 1984), pp. 145, 153–54.

5. Samina Ahmed, "Pakistan's Nuclear Weapons Program: Turning Points and Nuclear Choices," *International Security*, Spring 1999, p. 204.

6. H. Howard Wriggins, "The Balancing Process in Pakistan's Foreign Policy," in Lawrence Ziring, Ralph Briabanti, and W. Howard Wriggens, eds., *Pakistan: The Long View* (Durham, NC: Duke University Press, 1977), p. 311.

7. Anwar H. Syed, *China and Pakistan: Diplomacy of an Entente Cordiale* (Amherst: University of Massachusetts Press, 1974), pp. 114–15.

8. Hasan-Askari Rizvi, "Pakistan and the Post–Cold War Environment," in Craig Baxter and Charles H. Kennedy, *Pakistan 1997* (Boulder, CO: Westview Press, 1998), pp. 37, 45.

9. Samina Ahmed, "The (Nuclear) Testing of Pakistan," *Current History* 97, no. 623, December 1998, pp. 408–9.

10. Omar Noman, *The Political Economy of Pakistan 1947–85* (London: KPI, 1988), p. 121.

11. Barnett R. Rubin, "The Fragmentation of Afghanistan," *Foreign Affairs* 68, no. 5, 1989–90, p. 164.

12. Hasan Askari-Rizvi, "Pakistan in 1998: The Polity Under Pressure," *Asian Survey* 39, January/February 1999, p. 184.

13. Anita M. Weiss, "Pakistan: Some Progress, Sobering Challenges," in Selig S. Harrison, Paul H. Kreisberg, and Dennis Kux, eds., *India and Pakistan: The First Fifty Years* (Cambridge: Cambridge University Press, 1999), p. 143.

14. Ahmed, "Pakistan: The Crisis Within," pp. 340–41.

15. Robert Wirsing, "Pakistani Security in the 'New World Order': Going from Bad to Worse," *Asian Affairs: An American Review* 23, no. 2, Summer 1996, pp. 112–14.

16. See Sumit Ganguly, *The Origins of War in South Asia: Indo-Pakistani Conflicts Since 1947* (Boulder, CO: Westview, 1986), pp. 17–18.

17. Alastair Lamb, *Kashmir: A Disputed Legacy 1846–1990* (Hertingfordbury, Hertfortshire: Roxbury Books, 1991), pp. 259–64.

18. According to Pervez Hoodhboy, although "the facts seem to indicate that the alleged reports of nuclear movements [in 1990] were false, the belief that Pakistan's threat of nuclear devastation stopped Indian aggression dead in its tracks has become enshrined as an article of faith." Pervez Hoodbhoy, "Pakistan's Nuclear Future," in Samina Ahmed and David Cortright, eds., *Pakistan and the Bomb: Public Opinion and Nuclear Options* (Notre Dame, IN: University of Notre Dame Press, 1998), p. 71.

19. "The Indians cannot afford to extend the war to other areas in Kashmir, leave aside launching an attack across international borders," stated a Pakistani official, because of the "risk of nuclear conflagration." Quoted in Zahid Hussain, "On the Brink," *Newsline* (June 1999), pp. 24–5.

20. Pakistani Foreign Secretary Shamshad Ahmad, for instance, warned "We will not hesitate to use any weapons in our arsenal to defend our territorial integrity." Quoted in News Desk, "Pakistan May Use Any Weapons," *The News* (Islamabad), May 31, 1999.

21. Military expenditures, as a percentage of combined education and health, were 393 in 1960 and 125 in 1991. Weiss, "Pakistan: Some Progress," p. 137.

22. The higher ranks of the Pakistani officer corps are predominantly Punjabi and Pakhtun. Charles H. Kennedy, "The Politics of Ethnicity in Sindh," *Asian Survey* 31, no.10, October 1991, p. 946.

23. Hasan Askari-Rizvi, *The Military and Politics in Pakistan* (Lahore: Progressive Publishers, 1974), pp. 231–32.

24. Noman, *Political Economy*, p. 194.

## Suggested Readings

Ahmed, Samina, and David Cortright, eds. *Pakistan and the Bomb: Public Opinion and Nuclear Options*. Notre Dame, IN: University of Notre Dame Press, 1998.

Askari-Rizvi, Hasan. *The Military and Politics in Pakistan 1947–86*. 3rd ed. Lahore: Progressive Publishers, 1986.

Baxter, Craig, and Charles H. Kennedy, eds. *Pakistan 1997*. Boulder CO: Westview Press, 1997.

Lamb, Alastair. *Kashmir: A Disputed Legacy 1846–1990*. Hertingfordbury, Hertfordshire: Roxbury Books, 1991.

Noman, Omar. *The Political Economy of Pakistan 1947–85*. London: KPI, 1988.

Symonds, Richard. *The Making of Pakistan*. 2nd ed. Lahore: Islamic Book Service, 1987.

# 22

# The Philippines

*David G. Wiencek*

## Introduction

The Philippines consolidated its democratic form of government and improved its economic performance in the latter half of the 1990s. The country is well positioned to build on these recent political-economic successes as it enters the new millennium. National defense capability remains an important outstanding concern that needs to be addressed. External security challenges, particularly with regard to the country's South China Sea possessions, are real and growing. Internal armed opposition groups, meanwhile, have obtained a new lease on life after several years of declining membership and reduced operational effectiveness. Entrenched poverty and lack of real job opportunities, not ideology, motivate many new recruits in rural areas, thus contributing to an environment of continuing internal security threats.

Two consecutive successful presidential elections have reinforced the country's commitment to democracy. In 1992, Fidel Ramos was elected president. His tenure in office witnessed a return to political stability and the beginnings of economic growth. In 1998, current President Joseph Estrada won office, and he has guided the Philippines on a steady political course. The economic growth initiated during the Ramos years suffered a setback due to the 1997 Asian financial crisis. After two years of better than 5 percent growth, the country's gross domestic product (GDP) shrank to −0.5 percent in 1998. Even so, the Philippines fared better than other Southeast Asian economies, such as Malaysia, Thailand, and Indonesia, who were much harder hit by the financial crisis, experiencing economic contractions in 1998 of −7.5, −9.4, and −13.2, respectively. But Manila has rebounded. Positive growth rates of 3–4 percent are forecast for 1999 and 2000.

The political stability and economic growth of the late 1990s stand in sharp

## The Philippines

contrast to the turbulence of the recent past. The long, troubled years of Marcos's rule gave way in 1986 to Cory Aquino's "People Power" revolution. While President Aquino will be remembered for a commitment to democratic principles and putting in place a foundation for economic revival, her term in office was marked by seven coup attempts, major problems with the communist insurgency, severe energy shortages, staggering natural disasters, and a profound change in the country's relationship with its main ally, the United States.

From that time until recently, the relationship between the United States and the Philippines in the so-called "post-bases era" was essentially moribund. But by 1999 the two sides had revived their ties. In May 1999, the Philippine Senate approved the Visiting Forces Agreement (VFA), a measure that updated previous agreements governing the legal status of U.S. forces and provided a basis for the U.S. military to begin operating again in conjunction with Philippine forces for training and exercises. Beyond its provisions, the VFA signaled that the two long-time allies were prepared to go forward into the new millennium as security partners working to rebuild deterrence in Southeast Asia, demonstrating their determination not to allow Beijing a free hand to destabilize the region.

The Philippine military, known collectively as the Armed Forces of the Philippines (AFP), has adapted to the realities of the post–Cold War, post-bases security environment. For decades, the AFP's principal mission was internal security, focused on combating the communist and Muslim insurgencies. The U.S. security umbrella afforded a hedge against any potential external threats. In the mid-1990s, with the insurgencies winding down and the U.S. military no longer present, the situation changed. AFP leaders began speaking of developing a more conventional-oriented force with a focus on external defense and protection of the country's maritime interests and long coastlines.

This shift in posture was formally recognized in legislation known as the AFP Modernization Act (Republic Act No. 7879), signed by then-President Ramos in February 1995 and officially endorsed by Congress in December 1996. This Act sets forth the guidelines for a 15-year military modernization program, which will help upgrade capabilities in the areas of air defense, maritime surveillance, command and control, protection of offshore territories, intelligence, and logistics support. Budgetary constraints, however, will be a major impediment to credible force modernization for the foreseeable future. Thus, maintaining positive overall national economic growth is essential to the success of the AFP's much-needed modernization initiatives.

At the same time, Philippine leaders have recognized the need to combat other threats, such as terrorism, drug trafficking, arms smuggling, and maritime piracy. These concerns are now receiving more coordinated policy attention, although additional resources will be required in these areas as well to ensure mission success.

The future trend in the Philippine military is therefore toward a more well-rounded force able to meet a broader array of potential security threats. The revitalized link with the United States is important for rebuilding deterrence, maximizing training opportunities, and helping allow Manila to focus on its most demanding priorities without having to spread scarce resources simultaneously over many competing defense and security requirements.

## Political Framework

The Philippines is one of Asia's most vibrant democracies, with freedom of speech, press, and other civil liberties guaranteed by the 1987 constitution; yet within this context, a relatively small group of elites dominate the political process and, despite efforts to curb it, corruption is a problem. Under the constitution, the president, elected by direct popular vote, is the head of government and is the commander-in-chief of the armed forces. National security policy formulation occurs at the cabinet level through the National Security Council and at the agency level through the Department of National Defense headed by the Secretary of National Defense—by law a civilian. The Secretary of National Defense supervises the country's National Defense Program and exercises executive control over the AFP. The Chief of Staff commands the AFP and serves as the president's chief military adviser. The military is organized into five unified area commands (Northern Luzon, Southern Luzon, Visayas, Western, and Southern).

The Philippine National Police (PNP) formerly had the lead role for counterinsurgency operations. But in 1998, the government shifted counterinsurgency and internal security responsibilities from the PNP back to the military, which had this role in years past. The shift was an apparent recognition that insurgent and rebel groups were regaining strength after a period of decline. The shift was also made to ensure the PNP's commitment to its primary public safety and law and order missions in order to help combat growing threats from organized crime, kidnapping for ransom, and drug trafficking.

### Relationship with the United States

The Philippines remains allied with the United States under the 1951 Mutual Defense Treaty. Military-to-military relations were substantially affected by the Philippine Senate's historic vote on September 16, 1991, rejecting an agreement that would have provided for continued U.S. use of Subic Bay Naval Base for ten years. With that decision, the Senate brought to a close almost a century of major U.S. military presence in the Philippines.

As a result, meaningful defense cooperation between the two sides ground to halt. It was not until the mid-1990s that the situation began to change. This shift was spurred in large measure by China's aggressive moves in the South China Sea. In particular, China seized Mischief Reef in 1995. Sensing Manila's exposed strategic position after the U.S. departure, China acted to stake its bold territorial claim to the entire South China Sea. It occupied an outpost on Mischief Reef in the Spratly Islands, nearly 1,000 miles from the Chinese mainland. Yet Mischief Reef is only 150 miles west of Palawan Island, in the heart of Philippine-claimed waters and well within Manila's 200-mile exclusive economic zone.

This takeover touched off a diplomatic crisis between Manila and Beijing, with the Philippines in the end having to back down in the face of a much more formidable political-military opponent. It also led to a reevaluation of security trends in Southeast Asia. By 1998, Washington and Manila had concluded the VFA, the first step in revitalizing their defense ties. The VFA provides legal protection for U.S. military personnel participating in exercises on Philippine territory, and as such updates a previous Status of Forces Agreement, which had lapsed by 1996, effectively suspending bilateral military exercises. The Philippine Senate officially endorsed the VFA in 1999, paving the way for resumed military contacts, ship visits, and exercises, and helping breathe life back into the Mutual Defense Treaty.

The two sides are currently engaged in discussions aimed at identifying the Philippines' most urgent defense requirements, as well as identifying excess U.S. defense articles and equipment that can be quickly transferred to Manila at low or no cost. Thus, passage of the VFA signals a new era in bilateral relations and shows that the two democratic allies are back on track in what has been a close historical relationship with deep ties and friendships.

### Other Relationships

The Philippines maintains close contacts with neighboring Association of Southeast Asian Nations (ASEAN) militaries. It conducts joint exercises and training with Singapore; carries out exercises, patrols, and information exchanges with

Malaysia; and operates a border patrol and intelligence exchange with Indonesia. The Philippines also has a Memo of Understanding in place with Australia covering defense and technical cooperation and training, and has other cooperative agreements with France and South Korea. In the multilateral arena, Manila sent a force of some 600 troops, mainly medical and engineering personnel, to East Timor in 1999 to support UN peacekeeping operations there.

**Risk Assessment**

The Philippines has been fortunate in that it has encountered no real external threat since the Japanese invaded in World War II. The principal security threat facing the country since then has been internal communist-inspired rebellions, first in the form of the Huks in the late 1940s and early 1950s and, since 1968–69, that movement's successor, the Communist Party of the Philippines (CPP) and its military wing, the New People's Army (NPA). CPP-NPA activity reached its zenith in the mid- to late 1980s, when the NPA reportedly fielded upward of 26,000 cadres and exercised control in about 20 percent of Philippine villages. With the demise of the Soviet Union, the communist model lost its legitimacy and accelerated internal CPP disputes, leading to a de facto breakup of the Philippine communist movement. Taking advantage of a strategic opening, President Ramos moved early in his term to reconcile with the insurgents; he legalized the CPP and offered an amnesty program to the rebels. While rebel activity dropped sharply, an unfortunate by-product of the downfall of the movement was an increase in crime, marked by a shift to banditry and kidnap-for-ransom operations by some former members, particularly in metro Manila and central Luzon.

Since then, the rebels have used the ceasefire period to regroup somewhat. Membership is slowly growing again, as is the number of villages affected by the communist remnants. This increase in CPP-NPA activity has coincided with the economic downturn the country suffered during the Asian financial crisis. It is a recognition that in hard times the rebels offer many peasants their only real employment opportunity. Thus, positive future national economic growth is vitally important for combating the sputtering leftist rebel movement in the Philippines.

With regard to the country's other long-running insurgency, Muslim secessionists in Mindanao have continued low-level military operations, shunning government peace initiatives. They are also engaged in kidnapping and banditry, posing serious threats to businesses and others in the southern Philippines. The Abu Sayuf Group (ASG), a small splinter faction of the Moro National Liberation Front (MNLF), has emerged as a new terrorist force beyond the control of more mainstream Muslim groups. The size of this group is unknown, but estimates vary from 200 to over 1,000 members. To date, the ASG's operational base fortunately has for the most part been restricted to the southern Philippines, but it also has some capability to carry out activities as far away as Manila. There have been increasing reports that the ASG is receiving weapons and funding from foreign sources.[1] ASG reportedly has forged links with such international extremist groups as Hamas and Hezbollah in the Middle

East, and may have received support from notorious international terrorism financier Osama bin Laden. In addition to bin Laden, other key terrorist personalities, such as Ramzi Yousef, mastermind of the 1993 U.S. World Trade Center bombing, have carried out attacks in or from the Philippines. Indeed, in 1994, Yousef threatened to conduct attacks there using chemical weapons.

### External Security Environment

Renewed interest in external defense in recent years has been sparked mainly by Chinese maneuvers in the South China Sea. Starting in 1995 with the seizure of Mischief Reef, these activities have raised serious concerns for Philippine defense planners. The 1995 Mischief Reef I episode highlighted the vulnerability of Manila's claims in and near the Spratly Islands. It also dramatically exposed the country's defense weaknesses and shortcomings. In late 1998 and early 1999, with the region distracted by the Asian financial crisis, additional Chinese construction was observed on Mischief Reef. This Mischief Reef II activity resulted in new permanent, multi-story structures on concrete platforms (see photograph) and raised additional worries in Manila. The new structures are manned by Chinese military personnel, are able to mount anti-aircraft guns, and are large enough to serve as landing pads for military helicopters.

Located in the southern reaches of the South China Sea, the Spratlys are claimed by China, Taiwan, and Vietnam; Malaysia and Brunei, meanwhile, assert small claims, although in 1999 Kuala Lumpur increased activities on its Spratly possessions. According to the Center for International Relations and Strategic Studies at Manila's Foreign Service Institute, the Philippines claims 53 islands and islets in the South China Sea as the Kalayaan (Freedomland) Island Group (KIG), administratively part of the Province of Palawan and not considered by the Philippines to be associated with the Spratly archipelago. The Philippines currently occupies eight islands in the KIG and has stationed troops on some of them since the early 1970s; the largest, Pag-asa (Thitu) Island, reportedly has the largest garrison and a 1,300–1,800 meter airstrip.

The developments in Mischief Reef dramatically underline China's strategic push into the South China Sea. This Chinese activity is part of a calculated move by Beijing to expand its sphere of influence and ultimately, perhaps, dominate the vital sea-lanes of Southeast Asia. The cumulative objective of these Chinese activities is to develop strategic waypoints in the Paracel Islands in the northern portion of the South China Sea (particularly Woody Island) down through the Spratlys. This Chinese strategy is closely linked with its enunciated goals of moving away from a coastal defense orientation and more toward a blue water navy capable of power projection and dominating the so-called First Island Chain, which runs from the Spratlys up to Taiwan and the Ryukyus, and then eventually extending to the Second Island Chain, which Chinese strategists see as running out to the Marianas, Guam, and Palau.

All these developments have raised serious concerns in Manila, which is now

**New Chinese Structure on Mischief Reef, March 1999** *(Courtesy of the Armed Forces of the Philippines, Manila.)*

extremely wary of China's "creeping invasion." The situation remains tense. The Philippines has been overflying Mischief Reef on a regular basis. In 1998, it also reportedly ordered its patrol craft to fire warning shots across the bow of any "enemy ship" that closed within five nautical miles. In late November 1998, the Philippines arrested some twenty Chinese fishermen and seized six boats operating in the vicinity of Mischief Reef. In May 1999, two Chinese naval ships allegedly pointed their guns at a grounded Philippine supply ship. Subsequently, a Philippine navy patrol boat pursued three Chinese fishing boats near Scarborough Shoal, firing warning shots and sinking one of the fishing boats after colliding with it several times. In October 1999, meanwhile, Vietnamese troops in the Spratlys fired at a Philippine plane during an overflight, and Malaysian and Philippine aircraft came into contact without incident near Investigator Shoal.

These incidents illustrate how a crisis could develop between the disputants, sparking a confrontation that could affect the entire region. Manila's current lack of credible military options limits its capability to respond effectively or protect its interests in the South China Sea. All parties to the dispute remain committed to arriving at some sort of peaceful resolution, but diplomacy has yet to yield any concrete solutions to this protracted and complicated territorial dispute.

The Philippines has periodically raised the possibility that a military encroachment on its territories in the South China Sea would invoke a U.S. response under the Mutual Defense Treaty. United States authorities, however, have not endorsed such an interpretation and have stated that the treaty would not trigger an automatic response but rather consultations in accordance with "constitutional processes" (per Article IV of the treaty). In short, the United States has emphasized that ambiguity is important as a deterrent to an act of aggression in the Spratlys. But this cautiously neutral U.S. stance is outdated and should be reconsidered in light of China's recent moves against a longtime democratic ally. Washington cannot permit China to dominate the South China Sea, nor should the United States watch passively as Chinese threats to Philippine interests grow.

### Internal Security Environment

The internal security environment has shown signs of improvement in recent years. But the Asian financial crisis dealt the country a setback in its efforts to get the economy moving, thereby increasing economic opportunities for the country's poor and helping alleviate the need for segments of the population to turn to crime or terrorism. Hopefully, authorities can keep internal security problems at a manageable level while the economy slowly gains momentum following the 1997–98 crisis.

By the end of 1999, police reports indicated the NPA was regaining strength. Membership in 1999 was believed to be in excess of 9,500, an increase over the previous year's estimate of approximately 8,900. These numbers compare with a membership level of about 6,000 during the mid-1990s.

The NPA has managed to retain an identity despite the breakup of worldwide communism. Ideologically, the group appears to have strengthened its alignment with the Chinese communist leadership, one of the last bastions of inspiration still available. Interestingly, CPP-NPA propaganda now decries the former Soviet leadership as "revisionist" and closet capitalists during their time. Theoretically, the NPA still advocates a Maoist strategy of protracted armed struggle. In practice, NPA members have been reduced to such mundane crimes as kidnapping and extortion to support the movement.

The CPP-NPA celebrated its 30th anniversary in 1998–1999. While not a spent force, the group no longer poses a strategic threat to the country. Having said that, it would be unwise to discount the continuing internal security problems this group presents to the Philippines, particularly in hard economic times. The group has access to new tools, such as the Internet, to get its message out. It also practices coercion in its recruiting, particularly among young people, to keep its ranks filled and its operational capability intact. A group that has survived for thirty years will likely find a way to keep going for many more.

The situation in Mindanao where there has been talk recently of a potential Kosovo-like ethnic crisis between Muslims and Christians also remains problematic. The country scored an important victory in 1996, when the government signed a formal agreement with the MNLF ending its 24-year rebellion. Under the agreement, the MNLF was demobilized and rebel fighters began to be integrated into the PNP and the military. An autonomous Muslim region was established in

Mindanao and MNLF leader Nur Misuari was elected governor of that region. While political progress has been made, economic development in the area has been limited.

In addition, the government's efforts to rein in a smaller rebel faction—the Moro Islamic Liberation Front, or MILF (with about 11,000 members in 1999), bent on establishing an independent Islamic state in the southern Philippines— have sputtered. The two sides agreed to a ceasefire in 1997, but armed confrontations persist and a peaceful settlement remains elusive. The MILF is currently assessed to dominate about one-tenth of the island of Mindanao.[2]

Aside from rebel threats, the Philippines faces other internal security concerns, in particular threats from kidnapping, organized crime, illegal drugs, and maritime piracy.

Official data suggest that the situation with regard to kidnapping is improving somewhat. Sources in Manila report that key kidnap gangs have been rolled up, thanks in large measure to the sustained efforts of President Estrada's Presidential Anti–Organized Crime Commission and Task Force.

Organized crime gangs, meanwhile, continue to operate in the Philippines. They are engaged in kidnapping, drugs, gun running, illegal immigration schemes, and trafficking in Filipino women. Chinese triads and the Japanese yakuza are among the criminal syndicates operating in the country. In 1999, President Estrada established the Philippine Center on Transnational Crime (PCTC) to provide better policy, law enforcement, and intelligence coordination against organized and transnational crime concerns.

Illegal drugs in particular are a growing concern. The Philippines is a producer, exporter, and consumer of cannabis. The country is slowly becoming a significant source of herbal cannabis, with supply lines to Europe, and possibly into the United States, particularly through Hawaii. China is a significant source of illicit drugs intended for the Philippines, while Hong Kong and Taiwan remain staging points of Chinese Triad gangs smuggling multi-kilo shipments of methamphetamine hydrochloride (known locally as "shabu") to the Philippines.

## Military Structure

The Philippine military is attempting to gradually shift its primary focus away from an army-dominated counterinsurgency strategy and toward a more broad-based self-defense capability, within the confines of budgetary realities. The new outlook places greater emphasis on the navy and air force. In particular, there is a need for these services to protect the country's territorial waters and marine resources from encroachment, and deter maritime piracy, fish poaching, and drug running and other smuggling activities.

The navy is badly in need of upgrading and is slowly seeking to replace its small World War II vintage fleet with modern craft. The initial emphasis is on patrol (fast attack craft) and coastal combatants. So far only three ex-*Peacock* class offshore patrol vessels have been procured; these were purchased from the British in 1997 following their departure from Hong Kong.

Air defense and airlift capabilities are other priorities that are currently sorely lacking. The air force continues to make do with a limited force of ten F-5A fighters and a sole F-5B two-seat trainer. Five of the F-5As were delivered in 1998 from South Korea after being declared surplus by Seoul. Plans to procure additional combat aircraft have remained stalled for years. A consensus seems to be emerging in Manila that the air force should move to an interim capability, such as the venerable A-4 Skyhawk, rather than jump to top-of-the-line multi-role fighters that would be too expensive and too difficult to absorb from a training and maintenance standpoint.

But most of the discussions about force modernization and equipment upgrades remain theoretical at this time. Budget restrictions have simply sapped the life out of Manila's planning process. Military shortcomings are pervasive. One commentator bleakly summarized force deficiencies as follows:

> . . . obsolete jet fighters, practically no air interdiction or air to air capability, no maritime surveillance capability, obsolete and not so well maintained naval platforms, no missile of any type, dilapidated transports, unreliable radios and communication equipment, very limited night and limited visibility fighting equipment, old and inaccurate artillery pieces, etc.[3]

Clearly, the Philippine military faces major modernization challenges. The AFP Modernization Act set forth important guidelines for future procurements within the confines of an overall spending program originally targeted at US$12–13 billion. But cutbacks and the effects of a currency crisis have reduced the value of the plan's spending to less than US$4 billion. The government's inability to find the funds for defense modernization continues to contribute to an exposed defense posture. It is also taking a toll on military morale and personnel retention.

Military professionalism is much improved over the Marcos and Aquino years. Yet continuing training and education are essential ingredients to maintaining a professional force. Further development of leadership, doctrine, and new skills required for information-age warfare will be required in the future.

### Armaments Industry

The Philippines has for some time had a limited indigenous arms manufacturing capability, producing small arms, such as the M-16 rifle, and other equipment. The AFP implemented a Self-Reliant Defense Posture program in the early 1970s to enhance its efforts in this area.[4] One recent program of note involved the production of Simba light armored vehicles. A factory was set up by GKN Defence, a unit of British automotive and industry group GKN Plc, in a joint venture with local Asian Armoured Technologies Corporation. The AFP ordered 150 Simbas; eight of which were delivered fully built, and the remaining 142 were assembled in the Philippines under a countertrade arrangement.

## Conclusions

The link between economic security and national security is a key feature of the post–Cold War international security landscape. This nexus is particularly noticeable in the Philippines. Sustained economic growth is an important contributor to national security, while lack of growth directly impacts internal instability and undercuts Manila's ability to develop a credible external defense capability.

Today, in the aftermath of the Asian financial crisis, Manila is well positioned to build on its recent political-economic successes and create the foundations for strong and sustained growth. The prospects are also good that political stability will continue through the Estrada administration into the next presidential election period in 2004. Yet policymakers in the Philippines need to summon more political will in the intervening years to ensure that the necessary resources flow to the AFP, even in a tight budget environment, to help build defenses against both internal and external threats.

In the meantime, the country will likely face continuing challenges from China vis-à-vis the South China Sea situation. The United States and other Asian friends and allies need to do more to help build deterrence in Southeast Asia and ensure that China is not permitted to dominate the vital sea-lanes in the South China Sea. With this type of assistance, the Philippines can gradually accumulate the capabilities for self-defense, and at the same time address its other important internal priorities.

## Notes

1. See Merliza M. Makinano, "Terrorism as a Threat to National Security." Manila: Office of Strategic and Special Studies, Armed Forces of the Philippines, May 1997. Also see generally Mark Turner, "Terrorism and Secession in the Southern Philippines: The Rise of the Abu Sayaff," *Contemporary Southeast Asia* (June 1995), pp. 1–19.

2. James Hookway, "Philippine Islamic Resistance Resurfaces," *Wall Street Journal*, June 22, 1999.

3. Captain Rene N. Jarque, "Defending the Philippines at the Dawn of the 21st Century: Challenges for the Armed Forces." Manila: Office of Strategic and Special Studies, Armed Forces of the Philippines, May 1997, p. 11.

4. For a discussion, see Carolina G. Hernandez, "Arms Procurement and Production Policies in the Philippines," in Chandran Jeshurun, ed., *Arms and Defence in Southeast Asia* (Singapore: Institute of Southeast Asian Studies, 1989), pp. 125–51.

## Suggested Readings

Buss, Claude A. *Cory Aquino and the People of the Philippines.* Stanford, CA: Stanford Alumni Association, 1987.
Center for International Relations and Strategic Studies, Foreign Service Institute. *The Philippines and the South China Sea Islands: Overview and Documents.* Manila: Foreign Service Institute, December 1993.

Dolan, Ronald E., ed. *The Philippines: A Country Study*. 4th ed. Washington, DC: U.S. Government Printing Office, 1993.

Fisher, Richard D., Jr. "Rebuilding the U.S.-Philippine Alliance." Washington, DC: The Heritage Foundation, February 22, 1999, Backgrounder No. 1255.

Jarque, Captain Rene N. "Defending the Philippines at the Dawn of the 21st Century: Challenges for the Armed Forces." Manila: Office of Strategic and Special Studies, Armed Forces of the Philippines, May 1997.

Makinano, Merliza M. "Terrorism as a Threat to National Security." Manila: Office of Strategic and Special Studies, Armed Forces of the Philippines, May 1997.

Wiencek, David. "Reviving an Asian Alliance." *Washington Times*, May 27, 1999, p. A18.

# 23

# Singapore

*William M. Carpenter*

## Introduction

Probably the most fortuitous event in Singapore's recent history was its separation from Malaysia in 1965 to become a fully independent city-state. Given internal self-government by Britain in 1959, Singapore had then become part of the newly formed Malaysia in 1963. It was a union not to be, however, because of fundamental differences with the regime in Kuala Lumpur; by 1965, separation was necessary. Since that time, Singapore has prospered at a more rapid rate than it would have by remaining a small part of Malaysia. Strategically located to be an influential entrepôt of foreign trade, it has in addition built up a strong industrial base and has seen annual economic growth rates sometimes better—sometimes not as high— as in the East Asian economic recession of the late 1990s. But overall, Singapore is one of the strongest economies in East Asia. Per capita gross domestic product (GDP) was $29,000 in 1997. Economic prosperity enables Singapore to afford a respectable armed force for its own protection, and importantly, for the security of the sea-lanes in and near the critical Malacca Strait.

## Political Framework

Shortly after independence in 1965, Singapore became a republic headed by a president, but in fact it was led from that time until 1990 by the strong leader of the People's Action Party (PAP), Prime Minister Lee Kuan Yew. On November 29, 1990, Lee handed over the prime ministership to Goh Chok Tong, but Lee remains a potent force in the government as a senior minister. Goh took a surprising risk in 1992 by resigning his seat in Parliament to contest a by-election—he won by a large majority. The leading party, the PAP, seems to be in no danger of losing its governing role,

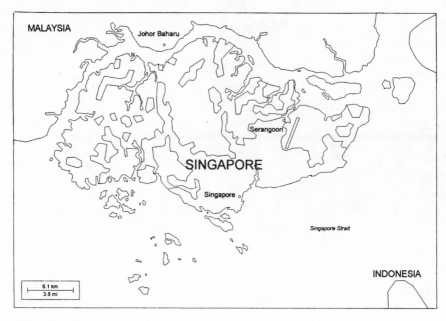

## Singapore

even though in the 1993 presidential election the people gave 41 percent of the vote to a relatively unknown candidate who ran against the PAP's candidate, Ong Teng Cheong; Ong went on to become Singapore's first executive president.

The two main opposition parties, the Chinese-based Singapore Democratic Party and the Workers' Party, are struggling with financial and organizational problems and seem not yet to be serious threats to the PAP's tenure. In 1981, the Workers' Party was the first opposition party to elect a member of parliament in fifteen years, but as late as 1997 there were only two MPs out of 81 seats in the legislature. Nevertheless, the PAP has lost some of its power; between 1980 and 1997, the PAP share of the popular vote dropped from 78 to 65 percent.

### Risk Assessment

Most observers of the East Asia region would agree that the risk of invasion of Singapore by a foreign power is negligible. The threat situation has not changed significantly since characterized in 1993 by Singapore's former defense minister, Yeo Nong Hong, who said: "The prospects for peace and stability in the Asia-Pacific are better today than they have been for a long time . . . but . . . there are elements of uncertainty which make the longer-term future of the Asia-Pacific more unpredictable." The future is certainly unpredictable, but it is one of the anomalies of the ASEAN (Association of Southeast Asian Nations) nations that although it would be hard to make a case for the probability of invasion of any one of them, they were all—until the economic downturn of the late 1990s—taking steps toward greater self-armament, buying the latest air defense aircraft and sophisticated naval ships, as well as modern tanks and helicopters for their ground troops. Singapore is the only nation pressing ahead with a military buildup. It has purchased eighteen F-16 fighters from the United States, and is leading ASEAN in a naval expansion and modernization program. Singapore bought two diesel submarines from Sweden and expects to buy two more. Crews are being trained for twelve fast-attack craft being built in a Singapore shipyard; they will be equipped with state-of-the-art electronics. Modern mine-hunting craft will be bought from Sweden, and there is a plan to buy a 3,000-ton frigate.

Granted that the risk of invasion is low, the defense planners of Singapore do have security threats to consider, and one of the primary concerns is the safety of the sea-lanes. Pirates are on the prowl in a new and menacing mode. Today ships operate with very few crew members and they carry highly valuable and resalable cargo, making them attractive targets for the modern-day "robbers of the sea." About one-third of the worldwide incidents of piracy (228 in 1996, 247 in 1997, and 202 in 1998) have occurred in or near the South China Sea. Typically, armed bands of pirates board ships at sea at night, take over the bridge watch and then the entire crew, and either take a quick haul of cash and valuables, or steal the entire cargo. To the credit of Singapore, and with the cooperation of Malaysia and Indonesia, piracy in the Strait of Malacca has been substantially eliminated. The keys to deterring the pirates have been more frequent naval patrols and increased aerial reconnaissance. The threat continues, however, as the pirates have shifted from the Strait, increasing the number of attacks in the South China Sea. Singapore is building up its air force; an important capability will be maritime surveillance, for which the force will introduce new maritime patrol aircraft.

The South China Sea is a cockpit of tension. Singapore is not directly involved in the territorial claims and counterclaims over islands in the sea (mainly the Spratlys), but any conflict that may arise in that important body of water will have some impact on Singapore; if nothing more, it will interrupt the sea-lanes, immediately affecting port calls in Singapore. The issue underlying the South China Sea tension is the potential of huge oil deposits under the Spratlys and possibly elsewhere in the sea. China claims the entire sea, defying the claims of Malaysia, Indonesia, Brunei, the Philippines, Taiwan, and Vietnam.

## Military Structure

The military establishment of Singapore is headed by the minister of defense, who promotes the national defense strategy of total defense—a concept that commits every Singaporean to the nation against all threats. Total defense has five parts: social, economic, psychological, civil, and military. Singapore has made the decision to continue strong government support for its expanding economy, and thus has balanced the competing demands of the military and the economy by placing heavy reliance on the citizen armed force. All male citizens and permanent residents must serve in the military for two or two and one-half years—the length of service depends upon the rank attained. Most inductees serve in the Singapore Armed Forces (SAF); the remainder serve in the Singapore Police Force. On completion of service, all remain in the reserves until age forty.

The total strength of the military forces is 70,000, with a conscript quota of 33,800. The SAF has succeeded in integrating the service branches into a capable and unified force. The total of regulars and reserves is 263,000 fully equipped servicemen. Perhaps by tradition the army is the largest force, with a strength of 55,000, augmented by substantial reserves. It is equipped with some 60 main battle tanks and 350 light tanks, as well as towed artillery, mortars, and anti-aircraft guns and missiles. Although they have key roles in Singapore's defense plans, the navy and air force are much smaller than the army: 9,000 in the navy and 6,000 in the air force. Besides providing for air defense and reconnaissance, the air force supports the ground force with close air support and helicopters. Singapore defense forces engage in joint training with all ASEAN members, and with the United States, Australia, New Zealand, Taiwan, and India.

## Conclusions

Singapore, like its ASEAN neighbors, does not have the military force to cope, by itself, with an attack by a major power such as China or Russia. This city-state sees two factors as essential for its security: the continued strategic presence of the United States, and the preservation of the Five-Power Defence Arrangement (FPDA—Singapore, Malaysia, Australia, New Zealand, and Britain). The British maintain that the FPDA is still relevant and useful for maintaining security and stability, and is not likely to change. The U.S. Department of Defense issued a position paper in 1998, which reaffirmed U.S. intentions to maintain forward deployment of forces in East Asia and the Western Pacific region; further, the paper stressed the strengthening of bilateral alliances, while also seeking multilateral security dialogues. This strategy includes U.S. Air Force deployments to Singapore and builds on access arrangements negotiated after the U.S. departure from its bases in the Philippines. In particular, Singapore has offered the United States access to its long-planned new pier facility at Changi, which can accommodate an aircraft carrier.

Given the prospect of confidence in the American presence and the retention of the FPDA, Singapore's military structure should be adequate for the country's security needs for some years to come. This nation of 3.7 million people (77 percent Chinese, 14 percent Malay, and 7 percent Indian) had a GDP of US$96 billion in 1997 and spent about US$5 billion on defense (about 6 percent of GDP, which is half of the government budget). Given the strength of the economy, and in spite of the economic slowdown of the late 1990s, this level of defense expenditure should be manageable.

## Suggested Readings

Lee Kuan Yew. *Memoirs: The Singapore Story*. Singapore: Prentice Hall, 1998.

Lee Lai To. "Singapore in 1998: The Most Serious Challenge Since Independence." *Asian Survey*. January/February 1999, pp. 72–79.

"One on One: Su Guaning, Singapore Deputy Secretary of Defence for Technology." *Defense News*, 20–26 April 1998.

U.S. Department of State. *Background Notes: Singapore*. October 1998.

# 24

# South Korea

*Victor D. Cha*

## Introduction

Assessing the security of the Republic of Korea (ROK) without reference to North Korea is akin to telling half of a story. One cannot be understood without the other; indeed, since the establishment of the two countries in 1948 until only very recent developments, including the 2000 North-South summit, each has defined its security and national identity in juxtaposition to the illegitimacy of the other. In spite of this research handicap, three factors stand most prominently when looking at ROK security at the beginning of the twenty-first century exclusive of the North Korea problem: the 1997 Asian financial crisis and its aftereffects on ROK defense; the resiliency of the U.S.–ROK alliance; and future South Korean force modernization plans. In this chapter, I attempt a synthetic analysis of these factors, arguing that South Korea's economic crisis, while putting short-term material constraints on national security and modernization plans, is not likely to have a long-term impact. Indeed, the inelasticity of ROK demand for a robust and modern defense capability in spite of spending cuts elsewhere attests to the importance attached to the programs. More interesting, however, are the secondary and tertiary consequences of the economic crisis and force procurement on the U.S.–ROK alliance. Government officials in Washington and Seoul state unequivocally that the alliance will remain intact even after the peninsula's security stabilizes. Yet at the same time, the ROK exhibits a clear preference for building more autonomous defense capabilities in the future. Certain activities in pursuit of this goal fit well with the alliance's natural evolution away from its asymmetrical dependent origins. At the same time, other activities cut against the grain of the alliance. Insights from strategic culture offer one way of understanding these contradictory trends and deducing propositions for the future.

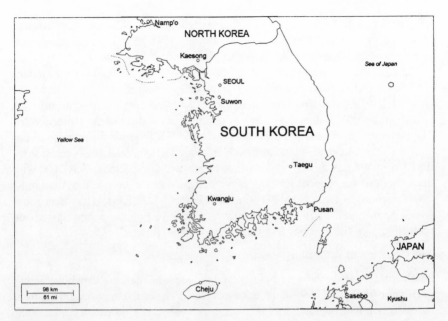

## South Korea

## Overview of Defense Plans

South Korean defense still rests on the principles of Yulgok ("rich nation/strong army") established in 1974 under the Fourth Republic of Park Chung Hee.[1] Areas of modernization that have drawn the most attention in recent years are missile defense, next generation aircraft (KFX), submarines, and destroyers. The ROK navy is in the midst of completing the first stage of the KDX Destroyer Program, which entails development of 3,200-ton destroyers (KDX1) to replace old *Gearing* class ships acquired from the U.S. Navy in the 1960s and 1970s. There are also plans for construction by 2006 of nine 4,300-ton destroyers (KDX2) with an operating range of 4,000 miles; and eventually, acquisition of state-of-the-art *Aegis* class destroyers (KDX3) starting in 2010. An active submarine program is also under way. The ROK's first submarine program started in 1987 and will produce twelve new 1,200-ton 209-class diesel submarines (a joint venture of Daewoo and Germany's HDW) by 2001 (nine completed). The new SSU program plans include acquisition of six 1,500- to 2,000-ton submarines by 2002. This would be followed by indigenous production of 3,000-ton submarines in the future. The Korean fighter program (KFP) started in 1994 with twelve F-16s purchased from Lockheed Martin. Samsung has assembled thirty-six planes pursuant to this transaction. Production plans are under way for an additional seventy-two under licensing arrangements (US$5 billion) to replace F-14 Phantoms and F-5 Freedom Fighters with 120 KF-16s. The KFX is the ROK's next generation fighter program estimated at 8 trillion won. Currently under consideration for this program are the French Dassault, F-15E Boeing, SU-35 Russian Sukhoi, and Eurofighter Typhoon (a British–Spanish–German–Italian venture).

Regarding missile defense, South Korea's SAM-X program aims for a modern air defense system that covers South Korean cities, government offices, and military installations, and is designed to replace Nike Hercules surface-to-air missiles (which are terribly outdated systems originating in the days of the Korean War). The government has allotted thus far some US$1.7 billion for the purpose of developing capabilities to defend against North Korean Scud missiles. A decision by the ROK on the missile defense system to be pursued is expected in July 2000 with the actual purchase slated for 2003. Potential candidates include the Russian S-300 (Rosvoorouzhenie), SAMP-T (Eurosam/France), U.S. Patriot (Raytheon), and Israeli Arrow. U.S. Patriot systems currently deployed on the peninsula provide protection only for U.S. bases in Osan, Kunsan, and Suwon.

## The Question of Intentions

South Korea's goal is a more modern and autonomous defense capability; however, the causal variable for force improvement is *not* the security threat from North Korea. Instead, the FIPs (force improvement plans) indicate a gradual shift in focus from traditional ground-based contingencies to regional ones. Recent developments, including the ROK's "sunshine" or engagement policy and the 2000 summit with the DPRK have reinforced this trend, but the military's widened focus to more regional concerns predated the recent detente and reflects a deeper change in strategic thinking. Some argue that the primary contingency Korea is preparing for is conflict with Japan. Others see Korea's place in the region rooted in armed neutrality.[2] In either case, the emphasis on naval capabilities and moderate power projection is clear. In 1995 a South Korean trading firm purchased two *Kiev* class aircraft carriers from Russia, ostensibly for scrap metal purposes, but many believe for the technology for future domestic development (the navy has talked about developing a 12,000-ton transport ship that could serve as a small aircraft carrier by 2010). Other programs include the planned purchase of four Airborne Warning and Control (AWACS) early warning aircraft from the United States by 2010 at a cost of US$1.7 billion; CN-235 transport planes (from Spain and Indonesia); in-flight refueling capabilities; and development of a longer-range fighter plane (KTX 2).[3] The ROK plans to put its first military satellite in orbit in 2005 (at a cost of US$168 million).

## The 1997 Economic Crisis and Security

Contrary to much of the academic literature on the causes of the arms buildup in Asia, the economic crisis that hit Korea in late 1997 has not had major effects on the overall direction of force improvement plans.[4] Rather, Seoul's persistence in terms of maintaining a suitable allocation of resources for force improvement in spite of the financial constraints is testament to its demand inelasticity on such matters. Of course, the immediate effect of the crisis was an overall flattening out of defense spending. While the defense budget grew by as much as 10–12 percent annually until 1997, the budget increase for 1998 was only 0.1 percent, and 1999 registered the first-ever decrease (0.4 percent) since the founding of the Republic.[5] Moreover, because of the rapid devaluation of the won, budget items denominated in foreign currency became prime targets of spending cuts. As a result, the 1999 budget cut dollar-based purchases of foreign weaponry by an astounding 50 percent. These included major FIP planned purchases of early warning aircraft (four by 2010); a US$1.7 billion missile defense system (discussed below); and naval force improvement, in particular, the downsizing of the KDX 4,500-ton destroyer program and SSU 1,500-ton submarine program.[6]

However, a distinction needs to be made between severe material constraints on a country that force a revision and reshaping of the underlying preferences that inform FIPs, and material constraints that do not. In the first case, budget cuts would be accompanied by a scaling down and/or changing of the strategic vision. For South Korea, the crisis undoubtedly imposed on the Ministry of National Defense (MND) short-term material constraints, but this did not force a revision or reshaping of preferences. First, the 1999 decrease in defense spending proved to be the aberration rather than the new post-crisis norm, as the projected 2000 budget calls for spending increases on the order of 12–13 percent. Second, the ununiform nature of defense spending cuts enacted by the government—favoring procurement in relative terms—again attested to the value placed on FIP.[7] This trend was also evident pre-crisis, when most of the military budget was being subjected to post–Cold War paring down, but portions dedicated to force improvement increased between 1996 and 1997.[8] Third, the primary changes to FIP as a result of the crisis took the form of postponements rather than outright cancellation of programs. The most prominent of these was the postponement in early 1998 of the AWACS purchases and the decision on the missile defense (SAM-X) purchases (but as best can be determined, nothing was canceled). Finally, as further testament to the resilience of the ROK's FIP visions, two programs that were initially cut back in early 1998—the destroyer and submarine modernization programs—were reinstated only months later in supplementary budgets.[9]

## The Alliance

How do South Korean force improvement plans affect the United States? Both Washington and Seoul have been unequivocal in public statements supporting the current and future (i.e., post-DPRK threat) resilience of the U.S.–ROK alliance. Seoul maintains that its military modernization complements, not replaces, the U.S. defense umbrella. While there is no reason to doubt these statements, the ROK's FIP priorities in conjunction with the economic crisis produce second- and third-order effects that do test the resiliency of the alliance. Thus the importance of the economic crisis on security in Korea is deceiving. On the surface, the effect appears minimal, as the material constraints imposed by the crisis affect neither core deterrence and defense capabilities nor the basic contours of the FIPs (albeit affecting the timing). However, if one moves beyond the simple causally linear analysis, a host of interesting tertiary effects materialize because FIP visions interact with economic imperatives and produce unintended consequences for the alliance.

### Host Nation Support (HNS)

For example, many believed that the economic crisis might lead to deterioration of the U.S.–ROK alliance. First-order challenges posed by the crisis were primarily in the areas of cost-sharing and host nation support—both politically sensitive issues for the alliance. In the former case, South Korea, in response to U.S. burden-sharing pressures, started contributing in the early 1980s to the maintenance cost of joint facilities, reaching annual contributions of US$45 million by 1989. Thereafter, a new formula was introduced where South Korea contributed at annual 10 percent increases over the base year of 1995, amounting to US$399 million annually by 1998. While the rates of increase in ROK contributions have been substantial, they still pale by comparison with the total cost of United States Forces Korea (USFK)/year (US$1.33 billion), and with comparable Japanese (US$6 billion per year) and German contributions (US$1.4 billion per year).

At the outset of the crisis, MND made early statements suggesting the need for relief from the anticipated US$440 million contribution for 1999. However, this did not become an issue of contention. In a Special Measures Agreement for 1999–2001 negotiated at the Security Consultative Meeting (SCM), Seoul and Washington agreed to a substantial decrease in the ROK's 1999 contribution (6 percent rather than 10 percent), with US$40 million deferred to 2000.[10] Moreover, the two governments reached this compromise with almost no political fallout. Instead, they emphasized these changes as temporary adjustments due to the ROK's unusual circumstances, couched in the language of "helping friends in need," and thereby turned a potential problem into an opportunity for strengthening the relationship.

### Russia

While the HNS issue and the economic crisis resulted in a positive dynamic for the alliance, there are a number of developments that do not. One is alternative sources of military procurement. The basic problem here is that traditional modes of acquisition are proving less adequate for ROK needs and priorities. The ROK traditionally transacted the majority of its military modernization with the United States, usually through the Foreign Military Sales (FMS) program. However, Seoul's FIP priorities on autonomy, technology, and cost increasingly clash with the FMS program (i.e., government–government sales without the transfer of technology). Moreover, the economic crisis has heightened these priorities not only in terms of buying at better prices, but also in terms of technology transfer for local job creation.[11]

The result is that the ROK increasingly searches out alternative suppliers for its modernization plans. In the KFX fighter and the SAM-X missile programs, for example, Seoul is entertaining European, French, and Israeli alternatives to the American F-15E and Patriot. The ROK's first military satellite, scheduled for deployment in 2005, relies heavily on French technology. This trend has been most prominent recently in relations with Russia. Soviet–South Korean normalization in 1990 was accompanied by a massive US$3 billion loan, which Moscow subsequently demonstrated a clear inability to repay. Seoul suspended the second half of this loan program and in August 1994 consented to an arrangement in which Russia would partially repay the debt with military hardware.[12] This largely consisted of small arms and logistic equipment, but the volume was large enough that the ROK created in October 1996 an infantry division outfitted with Russian-made equipment.[13]

This could be an inexpensive way to modernize the ROK military under continued fiscal austerity. Russia, through its state-run arms firm, has offered an array of sophisticated weaponry to fulfill South Korean FIP needs. The most well-known of these are the Sukhoi SU-35 fighter for the KFX program; *Kilo* class diesel submarines for the SSU program, and the S-300 surface-to-air missile (S-300 PMU-1 [SA-10 Grumble] and S-300V [SA-12A/B] Gladiator/Giant) for the SAM-X program. On the surface, these are all cheaper than their American counterparts (e.g., the S-300 is 30 percent cheaper than the Patriot 3 missile defense system). In addition, the liquidity requirements are further minimized because of Russian willingness to allow the ROK to debit up to 50 percent of costs from Russia's outstanding debt (e.g., *Kilo* class submarines could be purchased 50 percent in cash and the remainder credited as debt repayment). Moreover, in accordance with ROK FIP priorities, the Russians are extremely liberal with regard to transferring core technologies (e.g., SU-35, SU-37, and S-300 PMU-1 or S-300V).[14]

But unlike small arms, these higher-technology weapons, if acquired by Seoul, would pose major problems in terms of systems integration with existing U.S. systems.[15] Russian weapons also suffer from poor maintenance records and nonexistent servicing in some cases. Nevertheless, because of the fiscal constraints, technology needs, and desire for greater autonomy, South Koreans talk as if they are proactively seeking out the Russian alternative. MND has made a point of explicitly noting that the Russian S-300 has as much chance of being the mainstay of SAM-X missile defense as the Patriot, which prompted a less than enthusiastic response from U.S. Secretary of Defense William Cohen at the April 1997 SCM meetings.[16] The ROK established a cooperation agreement on military technology transfer.[17] In May 1999, MND announced a plan to purchase three *Kilo* class submarines for US$1 billion (a decision that was later postponed). These activities are currently minor and pose no threat to the alliance. However, if economic austerity puts increasing pressure on the Koreans to demand cheap weapons as well as core military technologies with which they can create domestic jobs, and procurement purchase decisions over the next few years fall in the direction of the Russians, these could bring acute problems to the alliance.

**Arms Transfers**

Another potential problem for the alliance that sits at the nexus of military modernization and the economic crisis is third party arms transfers. In particular, one area of tension may be in missile technology transfer. The ROK has sought to move away from a 1979 agreement with the United States that restricts South Korean missile ranges to 180 km.[18] Seoul wants greater independence from the United States in terms of an indigenous missile program capability and membership in the Missile Technology Control Regime (MTCR), which would enable the ROK to develop missiles with a range of up to 300 km. North Korea's Taepo Dong test flight in August 1998, demonstrating missile ranges and technology far more advanced than the ROK's, also made the missile competition issue one of extreme nationalism in the zero-sum prestige game with the North. To the surprise and unease of Americans, the ROK test-fired a surface-to-surface missile some eight months later, demonstrating both the capabilities and determination to develop a more advanced and independent missile deterrent. (Analysts maintain that the South Korean missile already violates the 1979 limits but was deliberately underfueled to deflect accusations by the U.S.) In addition, U.S. intelligence reports cite evidence of clandestine ROK activities indicative of an effort to develop longer-range missiles.[19] Tentative agreement had been reached on extending the range for production and deployment to 300 km, but in the July 1999 Clinton–Kim summit meetings, Seoul proposed a new agreement allowing South Korean research, development, and testing of missiles up to 500 km and payload launch vehicles for civilian use without limits. South Korean officials also would prefer translucency rather than complete transparency requirements on future missile programs.

A prolonged economic downturn would add acute pressures to this delicate issue in the alliance. One of the ways out of the current economic situation is to grow out of it through boosting exports rather than domestic demand, and one of the areas where this argument may gain increasing appeal in South Korea is in security. In particular, the second-order problem of a sustained economic crisis is ROK's desire to grow exports through arms transfers. An MND report to the National Assembly in October 1997 complained about the growing deficit of US$24 billion in arms purchases with the United States because the ROK could not export arms or technology. From an American perspective, changes in current arrangements on ROK missile ranges raise all sorts of precedent-setting questions regarding American efforts to secure nonproliferation commitments from other countries. On the other hand, inflexibility could reinforce South Korean inclinations to seek these technologies from alternative suppliers, particularly Russia.[20]

*Theater Missile Defense (TMD)*

Another potential problem for the alliance arising out of military modernization and economic austerity is theater missile defense. The South Korean government has expressed decided disinterest in participating in a U.S.-led TMD initiative in the region. One of the primary rationales given for this decision is that the cost and technology requirements for participation are beyond the South's current means. Strategically, Seoul argues that TMD is unnecessary given that the primary DPRK threat is artillery, not ballistic missiles. In addition, ROK officials informally state that China's strongly expressed antipathy to TMD is another major reason for Seoul's policy. Beijing has publicly applauded the ROK decision not to participate, and even made clear the implicit quid pro quo at assistant minister talks on Northeast Asia disarmament and nonproliferation issues in Seoul in early June 1999 when China's Director General for Disarmament Sha Zukang reiterated support for Seoul's decision to refrain from joining the TMD program and made concurrent statements about the need for the DPRK to sign on to the chemical and biological weapons conventions. In short, Seoul argues that TMD is too expensive, upsetting to others, and irrelevant to ROK security needs. Depending on the degree to which support for TMD deployment becomes a defining characteristic of the American alliance network in the twenty-first century in Asia (i.e., anti-TMD bloc led by China, and pro-TMD with Japan, Taiwan, and Australia behind the United States), this could be a major source of contention for the United States and Korea.

## Strategic Framework and Korea's Future

What are we to make of Korea's force modernization and its implications? Do they reflect a grand strategy quite different from Korea's Cold War identity? Do FIP-related issues like missile ranges or the Russian arms trade indicate Korean intentions to move out from under the U.S. umbrella? Do they indicate that Korea–Japan peer competition will be a new axis of conflict in the region, rendering irrelevant the traditional U.S.–Japan–Korea trilateral network that undergirded security throughout the Cold War? Finally, is Seoul's ambivalence to TMD symptomatic of an evolving Korea–China continental accommodation that many see as the "natural order" of things in Asia?[21]

There are, of course, no simple answers to these questions. However, Korea's strategic culture, despite globalization rhetoric and some policy initiatives to the contrary, is fundamentally grounded in what Alastair Johnston calls a *parabellum* or hard realpolitik view of security.[22] At the center of the paradigm that defines Korean strategic choice are certain immutable geopolitical traits. As a border state for the major powers and a relatively weak power in relation to its immediate neighbors, Korea's history has been one characterized by the bitter experience of foreign penetration by outside in the nineteenth century; the loss of sovereignty in the early twentieth century; and then division by war. Even in the post–Cold War era, its strategic situation is characterized by proximity to a hyper-realist state in North Korea and a neo-realist state in China. The combination of historically definitive experiences in a security-scarce region naturally makes balance of power politics the primary template for the Korean strategic mindset, even in the face of the 2000 North-South summit.

In addition, the history of pre-modern and modern international relations on the peninsula provides the lesson that only one orientation—*bilateralism*—works best for Korean security (as opposed to unilateralism or multilateralism). The reasons for this again derive from geopolitics and past systems of order in the region. Korea, even when unified, remained the "shrimp" in Northeast Asia, dwarfed by the relative power of its neighbors ("whales") in China, Japan, and Russia. In addition, past forms of order in the region have always centered on one of two arrangements: great power competition or great power concerts—both of which tend to operate in ways that exploit or exclude the smaller powers. Under such conditions, bilateralism with a great power was Korea's primary form of power accretion. In short, it was the only way Korea could survive.

If one accepts this interpretation, then two points emerge regarding Korea's future. First, the moderate push discussed above for more self-reliant defense capabilities, autonomy, and alternative military suppliers found in Korean FIPs are a perfectly natural response to the uncertainties of the post–Cold War era. In good realist tradition, Seoul operates under the assumptions of self-help and therefore must develop capabilities to hedge against the future dissolution of the alliance. The political imperative here is to manage this process in a transparent way such that FIPs hedge against such an outcome rather than actually contributing to it.

Second, while substantial friction may surface between the United States and the Republic of Korea over elements of force improvement, suppliers, technology transfers, and even TMD, this will always be bounded at the outer edges (on the Korean side at least) by the inclination for bilateralism over unilateralism. And given the foundation laid since 1950 with the U.S. alliance (reinforced by similar economic and political values), the most likely partner of choice will remain the United States. Thus, if ROK military modernization initiatives ever push severely against the edges of the alliance, the former will most likely adjust to the latter rather than vice versa.

## Notes

1. Force improvement in the 1970s focused largely on growth in numbers, while that of the 1980s focused on quality improvements. For historical background, see Victor Cha, *Alignment Despite Antagonism: The United States–Korea–Japan Security Triangle* (Stanford, CA: Stanford University Press, 1999), chapter 3; and Ministry of National Defense (MND), *Defense White Paper 1998* (Seoul 1998), pp. 155–60.

2. Arguments in these two veins are found in "ROK Navy Pursues Blue Water Navy," *Korea Times*, November 12, 1995; *Wall Street Journal*, January 17, 1995; *Joongang Ilbo*, January 23, 1995; Kent Calder, *Pacific Defense* (New York: William Morrow, 1996); and Aidan Foster-Carter, *Korea's Coming Reunification: Another East Asian Superpower?* Economist Intelligence Unit, Special Report no. M212 (London: Economist Intelligence Unit, 1992).

3. On these points, see MND, *Defense White Paper 1997–98*; "Defense Ministry Pushes Destroyer Plan," *Korea Herald*, June 8, 1998; Myung-ho Moon, "Debate on a Blue Water Navy," *Munhwa Ilbo*, April 8, 1997; "Military Concerned About Defense Budget Cuts," *Korea Herald*, February 7, 1998; Charles Morrison, ed., *Asia-Pacific Security Outlook* (Honolulu: East-West Center, 1997); "Major Military Procurement Projects to Be Delayed or Canceled," *Korea Times*, January 8, 1998; "South Korea to Buy Eight CN-235 Indonesian Military Aircraft," *Korea Herald*, November 20, 1997; *Korea's Seapower and National*

*Development in the Era of Globalization* (Seoul: Sejong Institute, 1995); Yong-sup Han, "Korea's Security Strategy for 21st Century: Cooperation and Conflict," *Korea Focus* 5.4 (July–August 1997); Joon-ho Do, "Security Strategy for 21st Century," *Wolgan Choson*, November 25, 1993; and Seo-hang Lee, "Naval Power as an Instrument of Foreign Policy," *Korea Focus* 5.2 (March–April 1997).

4. This literature generally posits a direct causal link between the region's economic growth and the accelerated pace of military modernization and defense spending. Representative works include Michael Klare, "The Next Great Arms Race," *Foreign Affairs* (Summer 1993), pp. 136–52; Paul Bracken, *Fire in the East* (New York: HarperCollins, 1999); and Calder, *Pacific Defense*.

5. Cuts in spending did not affect core deterrence and defense capabilities. For example, the 1999 budget still included increases for programs to maintain and upgrade K-1 tanks (80.5 billion won) and a 61 billion won increase for soldier morale and welfare and KTX1 training aircraft.

6. *Korea Herald,* June 8 and September 15, 1998.

7. For example, in the 1999 budget the one program conspicuously featuring continued expenditure increases was force procurement. Force improvement costs for 1999 comprised 30.1 percent of the 1999 budget and were scheduled to increase by 1.5 percent from 1998 *(Korea Herald,* September 22, 1998, and ROK Ministry of National Defense, personal interviews, Washington DC, July 8, 1998).

8. The actual increase was marginal (from 28 percent to 28.9 percent of the budget), but the ROK Defense Ministry highlighted this in their annual report as being a significant turnaround *(Defense White Paper 1997–98,* pp. 191–192).

9. The revised budget included funds for the KDX2 and SSU programs, subject to approval by the National Assembly in September 1998; see "Defense Ministry Pushes Destroyer Plan," *Korea Herald,* June 8, 1998; and *Xinhua News Agency,* June 7, 1998.

10. This arrangement, incorporated into a new Special Measures Agreement for 1999–2001, allowed an ROK contribution of US$333 million for 1999, representing a 6 percent rather than 10 percent increase (of which US$40 of $80 million previously earmarked for construction was deferred to 2000, bringing the actual total for 1999 down to US$290 million). See *Choson Ilbo,* December 22, 1998; and *China Daily,* December 23, 1998.

11. Bryan Bender, "ROK to Choose New Naval Defence System," *Jane's Defence Weekly,* August 18, 1999.

12. For a detailed treatment of this topic, see Tae-Hwan Kwak and Seung-ho Joo, "Military Cooperation Between Russia and South Korea," paper presented at the 1999 American Political Science Association meeting, Atlanta, GA, September 4–5, 1999.

13. This included BMP-3 armored fighting vehicles, T-80U tanks, anti-aircraft missiles and anti-tank missiles. MND's supplemental rationale for the Russian arms was for training purposes (as much DPRK equipment is Russian in origin, see ibid., p. 7)

14. For details, see Kwak and Joo, "Military Cooperation," pp. 5–9.

15. Russians cite the example of Greece—where Russian and U.S.-made SAMs are both employed—to rebut these claims, but most military experts see severe compatibility problems for an ROK military that has been so heavily dependent on U.S. systems to this point.

16. *Korea Herald,* September 15, 1998.

17. *Korea Times,* September 4, 1998.

18. The quid pro quo for the voluntary limit on ROK missile ranges was U.S. technology for the ROK's NHK-2 missile. See *Korea Times,* November 13, 1998; and *Hanguk Ilbo,* November 10, 1998.

19. One prominently reported revelation in this vein was the discovery of South Korean rocket motor testing sites that had not been made public to the United States. See *New York Times,* November 14, 1999.

20. In this vein, in early 1999 ROK officials actively sought Russian missile technology worth about US$200 million for the M-SAM program; see Kwak and Joo, "Military Cooperation," p. 13.

21. See Robert Ross, "The Geography of Peace," *International Security* (Spring 1999); and Victor Cha, "Engaging China: Seoul–Beijing Detente," *Survival* (Spring 1999).

22. Alastair Johnston, *Cultural Realism* (Princeton, NJ: Princeton University Press, 1995), p. 61.

## Suggested Readings

Cha, Victor. *Alignment Despite Antagonism: The United States–Korea–Japan Security Triangle.* Stanford, CA: Stanford University Press, 1999.

Council on Foreign Relations. *Managing Change on the Korean Peninsula.* Task Force Report, 1998.

Moon, Chung-in, and David Steinberg, eds. *Kim Dae-jung Government and Sunshine Policy: Promises and Challenges.* Seoul: Yonsei University Press, 1999.

Oberdorfer, Don. *The Two Koreas.* Reading, MA: Addison-Wesley, 1997.

# 25

# Sri Lanka

*M.A. Thomas*

## Introduction

Sri Lanka, the small teardrop country located off the southern coast of India, is a tropical paradise mired in a protracted ethnic conflict. The island nation is often overshadowed in world affairs by its larger and more prominent South Asian neighbors, India and Pakistan. The major controversial issues in Sri Lanka today include strained relations between the majority Sinhalese and minority Tamil communities, the question of regional autonomy for Tamils, and the ongoing civil war between the Sri Lankan government and the Liberation Tigers of Tamil Eelam (LTTE) terrorist organization.

## Sinhalese–Tamil Discord

Traditional antagonisms between the Sinhalese and Tamil communities have psychological implications that bear on the present-day state of relations between the two largest ethnic groups in Sri Lanka. Even prior to independence, the distribution of jobs on the basis of ethnic patronage divided the two communities. As a colonial power, the British elevated Tamils, who constituted a minority in Sri Lanka (then known as Ceylon), over the majority Sinhalese to prestigious positions within the bureaucratic administration.

Since independence in 1948, the Tamil community has been vulnerable to the Sinhalese domination of Sri Lanka's politics. Both major Sinhalese political parties, the United National Party (UNP) and the Sri Lanka Freedom Party (SLFP), have competed with each other to further Sinhalese nationalism, which often meant discriminating against Tamils in education and employment. Additionally, the Tamil-dominated area of the Northern Province has suffered from lack of infrastructure due to poor development schemes by the central government.

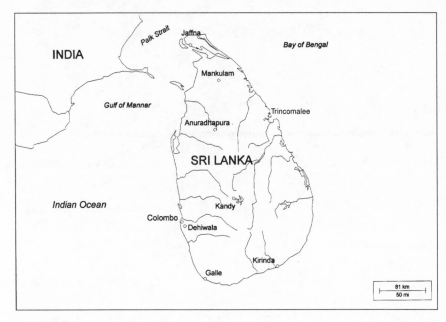

## Sri Lanka

The demand by moderate Tamils for regional autonomy, i.e., an autonomous Tamil linguistic state within a federal union of Sri Lanka, has further divided the two ethnic groups. Perceiving themselves as having limited opportunities owing to the Sinhalese domination of Sri Lanka, moderate Tamils view regional autonomy as the only practical way to preserve their identity. Sinhalese nationalists, however, are skeptical of Tamil intentions, and view regional autonomy as the first step toward the country's fragmentation. Perceptions of being victimized, as well as increased unemployment among youths, led Tamils to become more militant in their approach to rectifying the inequities between the two communities.

Sri Lankan society is further polarized by fears that ethnic majorities will dominate positions of influence and repress the religious, linguistic, and cultural systems of minorities. Such fears profoundly affect the way the Sinhalese majority in Sri Lanka is perceived by the Tamil minority. Perhaps more surprisingly, such fears also intrude deeply on the thoughts of the Sinhalese vis-à-vis the Tamils, for even though the Sinhalese are the majority in Sri Lanka, they are intimidated by the large Tamil population in nearby India, which, with the Sri Lankan Tamils, significantly outnumbers the Sinhalese.

### Political Framework

Sri Lanka has maintained a relatively stable democratic tradition since its independence from Great Britain in 1948. In its search to find the best form of democracy to suit its polity, the country has experimented in the past with a British Westminster type of parliamentary government with both bicameral and unicameral legislatures. Currently, Sri Lanka has a French quasi-presidential form of government with a unicameral legislature. This type of government, in turn, is likely to change in the not so distant future, regardless of which political party is in power.

## Politics in Sri Lanka

Sri Lanka's politics have been dominated by the two major Sinhalese political parties: the SLFP, led by President Chandrika Banderanaike Kumaratunga, and the UNP, led by Ranil Wickremansinghe. The SLFP—which is the largest party within the ruling People's Alliance (PA) coalition—and the UNP have for decades engaged one another in an intense rivalry. Traditionally, the UNP has been stigmatized as a Westernized, elite, free-market party. The SLFP, on the other hand, traditionally has been regarded as a socialist party attempting to incorporate Buddhist culture into politics. Though the SLFP has abandoned many of its socialist principles in favor of economic reforms, it continues its rivalry with the UNP on the basis of partisan political issues rather than on ideological grounds.

In the past, the rivalry between the two parties has inspired deep distrust of the political system by the Tamil community. As previously mentioned, the UNP and the SLFP competed to see which party could better suppress the Tamil community (and hence further Sinhalese nationalism). Today, the rivalry between the two parties often weakens the functioning of the government by causing political gridlock. For example, even though the UNP may accept the PA's devolution proposal (discussed below) in principle, it officially rejected the controversial package in August 1999 because of partisan jealousies and personal animosities.

The Janatha Vimukthi Peramuna (JVP—People's Liberation Party) is the third largest political party, which has suddenly reemerged due to its increasing support base of students, laborers, and peasant farmers. The radical Sinhalese group, which is based on a mixture of Maoist ideology, class politics, and confrontational methods, has been known for its two violent insurgencies in the past twenty-five years. Attempting to overthrow the government and replace it with a socialist state, the JVP used aggressive military force and guerrilla tactics in 1971 and from 1988–90 to disrupt the government. The JVP has pledged to adhere to the democratic process.

### Regional Autonomy and the Devolution Proposal

At times the Sinhalese-led government has debated federalism for Sri Lanka. However, differing views on the specifics of a federal union have resulted in a stalemate on the issue. For example, Tamil groups have advocated the merging of the Tamil-dominated Northern Province with the Eastern Province to increase Tamil representation. On the other hand, opponents of this concept claim that, in addition to Tamils, the Eastern Province is inhabited by roughly equal numbers of Sinhalese and Muslims, who would resist being merged into a Tamil-dominated autonomous region.

Ultimately, with no progress on the issue, some Tamil groups elevated their demand from regional autonomy to an independent homeland, referred to as Tamil Eelam ("Precious Land"). In addition, these groups, abandoning constitutional procedures for attaining their goals, began to adopt a militant posture.

In an attempt to improve relations with the Tamil community, as well as reform the political system in general, President Chandrika Kumaratunga officially released her "devolution package" in August 1995. The issue of devolution has revived the debate on federalism and regional autonomy for Tamils.

The devolution package calls for transforming Sri Lanka into an "island of regions." It advocates devolving powers from the central government to the proposed regional councils over matters such as law enforcement, land administration, procurement of foreign aid, and development. In effect, Sri Lanka would have a federal type of government. However, President Kumaratunga is careful not to use the word "federal" in her rhetoric, due to sensitivities exhibited by Sinhalese nationalists, who feel that devolution is the first step toward Tamil secession.

Unresolved issues concerning devolution include the relationship between the central government and the regions, and whether the Eastern Province should be united with the Northern Province to fall under Tamil dominance. The devolution package was formally rejected in the parliament by the opposition UNP in August 1999. The government put the controversial issue on the back burner until after the December 1999 presidential elections.

Intransigence on the regional autonomy issue by previous Sinhalese-led administrations has left the government with a vulnerability. It is open to charges of blatant discrimination against Tamils. President Kumaratunga, on the other hand, has decided to tackle the issue directly with her devolution proposal. This has strengthened her image with the international community, as well as with Sinhalese and Tamil moderates, who are tired of the drawn-out ethnic conflict.

President Kumaratunga won the December 21, 1999, presidential elections. Ironically, the LTTE, which unsuccessfully attempted to assassinate her during a campaign rally, may have contributed toward her reelection due to a sympathy vote.

## Security Environment

Externally, Sri Lanka enjoys cordial relations with all its South Asian neighbors, as well as with a number of countries throughout the world. Sri Lanka particularly enjoys excellent political and military bilateral relations with the United States. The Sri Lankan government continues to win favor with the United States by considerably improving its human rights record among its security forces, as well as by proposing measures to find a solution to the seventeen-year-old conflict with the Tamil insurgents.

Internally, all of Sri Lanka's defense resources are geared toward combating the LTTE terrorist organization. The island's ethnic insurgency developed gradually from the aforementioned longstanding tensions between the Sinhalese and

Tamil communities. The year 1983 is considered a turning point in the ethnic insurgency because of the sudden escalation of enmity that resulted from an LTTE ambush of a military convoy in July of that year. The attack killed 15 soldiers and triggered a backlash against the Tamil community when Sinhalese mobs attacked innocent Tamils inhabiting Colombo and other Sinhalese-dominated areas, destroying their businesses, homes, and other property while the government's security forces looked on. The country was further polarized after these events prompted an increased migration of Tamils to the north and the movement of Sinhalese away from Tamil-dominated areas.

Within a matter of a few years, the LTTE was transformed from an organization that engaged in isolated terrorist incidents to one that could readily confront the Sri Lankan armed forces. By 1986, the LTTE had virtual control of the Jaffna Peninsula. After the government launched a major offensive against the LTTE, driving them from Jaffna city into the jungles, political pressure brought India into the conflict.

After a series of negotiations, in 1987 India and Sri Lanka signed the Indo-Lanka Accords, which proposed regional autonomy for Tamils in the Northern and Eastern Provinces within the framework of a unitary state. The Accords were unacceptable not only to Sinhalese nationalists but to the LTTE, which demanded nothing short of an independent homeland. As a result, the LTTE fought the Indian Peacekeeping Force (IPKF) sent in to supervise the disarming of Tamil militants. Though the IPKF was able to oust the LTTE from Jaffna city, it was unable to overcome the LTTE's superior guerrilla warfare tactics in the jungles.

After the IPKF pulled out of Sri Lanka in 1990, hostilities resumed between the Sri Lankan armed forces and the LTTE. In the renewed fighting, both sides were equipped with more sophisticated and lethal military hardware than ever before. Since 1995, the armed forces have had some military successes against the LTTE, leading to the expulsion of the Tigers from Jaffna city once again. However, the LTTE remains a significant threat because of its expertise in guerrilla warfare and its ability to conduct terrorist campaigns.

## The Tamil Tigers (LTTE)

The LTTE, or the Tamil Tigers as they are commonly known, is considered one of the most ruthless terrorist organizations in the world. Established in 1972, the group went underground three years later after assassinating the mayor of Jaffna city. The LTTE is known for its network of contacts with various terrorist groups around the world.

The militants' choice of the tiger as their symbol represents not only the ferocity of the animal but also a deliberate contrast with the lion, which has traditionally been a symbol of the Sinhalese people and is depicted on the Sri Lankan flag. The organization has an elite squad known as the Black Tigers, who conduct suicide missions against military and civilian targets. The Black Tigers have assassinated not only prominent political leaders in Sri Lanka but also the former prime minister of India, Rajiv Gandhi.

Previously, the LTTE was viewed by most Tamil civilians as the legitimate defender of the Tamil cause. Much of its funding came from Tamil expatriates, as well as the Indian government. However, in recent years, the LTTE has lost much support from Tamil civilians and has resorted to tactics that instill fear in order to control the Tamil community. External support from Tamil expatriates and the Indian government has also waned and, as a result, the LTTE has engaged in drug trafficking to finance its operations.

Ideologically, the LTTE has at times employed Marxist rhetoric to characterize its struggle. However, irrespective of ideology, the creation of an independent Tamil state has remained the movement's only goal. In pursuit of this objective, the LTTE has been prone to use direct and violent action rather than formulating principles on which the independent state would operate.

The leader and founder of the LTTE, Velupillai Prabhakaran, is often described as a megalomaniac. He is practically worshiped by Tiger cadres, who have been instilled with Tamil nationalist propaganda. Prabhakaran has insisted that all LTTE soldiers wear a cyanide capsule around their neck, maintaining that it is better to commit suicide than be captured alive by the enemy.

**Military Structure**

For most of Sri Lanka's modern history, the armed forces have played a mainly ceremonial role, previously in support of British forces. As a result, the armed forces were largely unprepared for and untrained to contain the Tamil insurgency. After increasing defense expenditures and soliciting external assistance, the Sri Lankan government has provided the armed forces with the means to better combat the LTTE, whose position has been weakened by recent government military successes on the Jaffna Peninsula.

Sri Lanka's armed forces are subservient to the country's civilian leadership. However, divisive issues periodically arise between the armed forces and the civilian leadership. For instance, military leaders resent civilian leaders when the latter initiate military operations for self-serving political motives that run counter to the sound tactics advocated by military experts. Civilian decisionmakers who are driven by parochial political dynamics are regarded as unnecessarily placing the lives of soldiers at risk.

The armed forces, especially the army, are vulnerable to charges of committing human rights abuses not only against Tamils but also against Sinhalese (during the JVP insurrection). The issue of human rights has drawn both domestic and international criticism of Sri Lanka's government and armed forces. It has tarnished the image of the government and earned sympathy for the LTTE.

In recent years, the government has attempted to reduce the propensity of the armed forces to commit gross human rights abuses, which have been directed predominantly against Tamil civilians. The government has succeeded to some extent, with the establishment of a human rights commission, human rights training within the armed forces, and punishment of those soldiers who continue to commit human rights abuses. Tamil civilians, who have suffered the most, remain disenchanted with the Sri Lankan military.

## Conclusions

The ethnic insurgency has taken its toll on both the Sinhalese and Tamil communities in Sri Lanka. Sinhalese civilians have had their family members and friends in Sri Lanka's armed forces killed and maimed by the ruthless Tigers. They have also been the victims of terrorist attacks. These conditions have hardened the attitudes of many Sinhalese against the Tamil people in general. As a result, many Sinhalese have found it difficult to sympathize with Tamil demands. Likewise, Tamil civilians have witnessed the torture and death not only of Tamils in the LTTE but also innocent Tamil civilians who were caught in the line of fire or suspected of being militants by the armed forces or the IPKF. Many Tamils question the basic intentions of the Sinhalese people.

The actions of the government are questioned by both communities: The government is vulnerable to charges by the Sinhalese that it is needlessly sending soldiers to their deaths; many Tamils view the government's sincerity in resolving the conflict as suspect. The government is also vulnerable to accusations by both the Tamil and international communities of gross human rights violations perpetrated by the armed forces against Tamil civilians.

Until recently, most Tamil civilians genuinely lent their support to the LTTE, which was seen as the legitimate champion of the plight of Tamils, who were discriminated against in a Sinhalese-dominated society. However, the tide began to turn when the LTTE was perceived as protecting its own interests rather than those of the Tamil people. As support by Tamil civilians slowly waned, the LTTE resorted to fear tactics to control the Tamil population, further alienating its support base.

Though a significant number of Tamils continue to support the LTTE, a larger number find themselves alienated from both the LTTE and the Sri Lankan government. They fear the repercussions of betraying the LTTE as well as the brutality of the Sri Lankan armed forces. Friendly overtures from the PA-led government have changed the minds of a portion of Tamils, who would accept some form of the devolution package as a solution to the ethnic conflict.

## Suggested Readings

Dissanayaka, T.D.S.A. *The Agony of Sri Lanka*. Colombo, Sri Lanka: Swastika (Private) Ltd., 1983.

Gunaratna, Rohan. *International and Regional Security Implications of the Sri Lankan Tamil Insurgency*. Colombo, Sri Lanka: Taprobane Bookshop, 1997.

———. *Sri Lanka's Ethnic Crisis and National Security*. Luton, England: South Asian Network on Conflict Research (SANCOR), 1998.

Narayan Swamy, M.R. *Tigers of Lanka*. Colombo, Sri Lanka: Vijitha Yapa Bookshop, 1994.

Ram, Mohan. *Sri Lanka: The Fractured Island*. New Delhi: Penguin Books, 1989.

# 26

## Taiwan

*Dennis Van Vranken Hickey*

In recent years, the Republic of China (ROC, or Taiwan) has experienced an extraordinary metamorphosis. It has managed to transform itself from a backward, authoritarian state into a multi-party democracy and an economic powerhouse. But Taiwan also has alarmed Beijing by appearing to move closer to formal independence from China. These fears have escalated with the election of Chen Shui-bian, a former independence activist, as ROC president in March 2000.

### Political Framework

In 1949, the ROC government retreated from mainland China to Taiwan. From that time until his death in 1975, Chiang Kai-shek ruled the island with an iron fist and promised to take back the mainland by force. Opposition parties were banned, dissidents were jailed, the press was muzzled, and parliamentary elections were restricted to a small proportion of the seats. In short, the ROC was an authoritarian regime.

In 1987, the Generalissimo's son, President Chiang Ching-kuo, lifted martial law and paved the way for the democratization of Taiwan. Shortly after this move, lawmakers legalized opposition parties and elections were held to choose a new legislature and National Assembly (a body that amends the ROC Constitution). Restrictions on the broadcast and print media also were lifted. With its first direct presidential election in 1996, Taiwan completed its transition from an authoritarian, one-party state to a full-fledged democracy. The ROC is now described officially by the U.S. Department of State as a "multi-party democracy."

According to Article 36 of the ROC Constitution, the President of the ROC has "supreme command of the land, sea and air forces of the whole country." But day-to-day administration of the military is carried out by the Ministry of National Defense (MND) under the Executive Yuan. Within the MND is the Minister of National Defense (who must be a civilian by law) and the General Staff Headquarters (GSH). Under the GSH are the various services—the army, navy, air force,

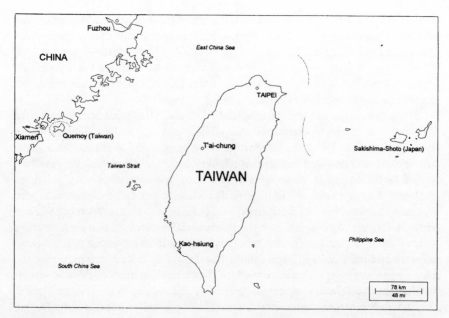

## Taiwan

Combined Services Force (a logistical command), Armed Forces Reserve Command, the Coast Guard Command, and the Military Police Command. The GSH is headed by a Chief of the General Staff. In 1998, legislation was passed to resolve the ambiguous power relationship between the Minister of National Defense and the Chief of the General Staff. The new law stipulates that the Defense Minister is in charge of all affairs concerning national defense and that the Chief of the General Staff serves as the most senior military adviser to the president.

For more than four decades, questions and concerns pertaining to Taiwan's security remained shrouded in mystery. With the lifting of martial law, however, questions began to be raised about Taiwan's security. It is now a common practice for Taiwanese to discuss and debate *all* of the major defense issues confronting Taiwan. These include questions about (1) military strategy; (2) relations with the United States; (3) the need for costly new weapons systems; (4) a proposed theater missile defense system; (5) conscription policies and exemptions from traditional military service; (6) sexual harassment; (7) political warfare classes; (8) efforts to launch ROTC programs on college campuses; (9) efforts to "depoliticize" the military; (10) armed forces morale; (11) the possible establishment of confidence-building mechanisms with the mainland; and (12) Taiwan's *de jure* independence from China.

### *Risk Assessment*

On May 1, 1991, President Lee Teng-hui terminated the Period of National Mobilization for Suppression of the Communist Rebellion. This move formally signified the ROC's willingness to renounce the use of force to achieve the unification of China. Taipei now professes a desire to ultimately unify the country peacefully through a three-stage unification process outlined in the *Guidelines for National Unification*. Despite President Clinton's pledge not to scrap the *Guidelines*, the People's Republic of China (PRC) suspects that Taiwan's leaders actually support permanent separation from China.

Throughout most of the 1990s, official ROC policy held that both sides of the Taiwan Strait should be considered as "political entities." In July 1999, however, President Lee Teng-hui stunned the world when he appeared to abandon this vague terminology and declared instead that relations between Taiwan and the mainland should be considered as "state-to-state" or at least "special state-to-state" relations. Following Lee's remarks, one ROC official proclaimed that, "We feel there is no need to continue using the 'one China' term." Although Taiwan authorities later sought to reassure Beijing, Washington, and the international community that these remarks did not signify a change in policy, the statements led to an escalation in cross-Strait tensions and bolstered PRC perceptions that Taiwan is indeed inching closer and closer to de jure independence from China. These developments could hold serious implications for Taiwan's security and for peace and stability in the Western Pacific.

Although Taipei has renounced the use of force to unify China, Beijing has not reciprocated. The PRC has long embraced, as a basic policy, the position that it may use all means necessary, including military means, to achieve unification. Consequently, ROC military authorities assert that the PRC is the greatest menace to Taiwan's security.

Most security specialists agree that the prospects for armed conflict across the Taiwan Strait will remain fairly low unless Taipei provokes Beijing. PRC authorities have outlined a number of conditions that might lead the mainland to use force against Taiwan. Most recently, they include the following:

- Independence of Taiwan
- Foreign occupation of Taiwan
- Taiwan's development of nuclear weapons
- Taiwan's refusal to negotiate unification with China for a prolonged period of time

Taiwanese security analysts also have identified various situations that might lead Beijing to resort to military action. They contend that the PRC would employ force against the island under the following circumstances:

- If Taiwan declared independence
- If massive disturbances break out in Taiwan
- If the comparative fighting strength of Taiwan's military weakens significantly
- If foreign forces interfere in Taiwan's affairs
- If Taiwan continues to reject reunification talks
- If Taiwan develops nuclear weapons

Some have warned that an attack would be most likely between the years 2005 and 2010—after China has completed its military modernization program and before the deployment of America's theater ballistic missile defense system (TMD) in East Asia. But others caution that recent developments in Taiwan have led the PRC to consider using force against the island sooner.

Should the PRC opt to use force against Taiwan, the MND believes it would resort to one of three actions:

- A sea and/or air blockade of Taiwan
- A raid on Taiwan's outlying islands
- A full-scale assault on the island

The ministry believes that these moves could be undertaken independently, sequentially, or simultaneously.

Most defense analysts suspect that a paralyzing blockade intended to bring Taiwan to its knees would be Beijing's most likely form of military action. In order to achieve this objective, the PRC might employ missile tests (it has deployed hundreds of M-9 missiles in coastal provinces facing Taiwan), mines, submarines, and surface ships to blockade certain shipping routes and/or announce that waters surrounding Taiwan are in an area in a state of civil war. Any of these moves could lead many foreign ships to steer clear of Taiwan, making shipping prohibitively expensive. Hence, Taiwan's navy and air force purchase equipment and conduct exercises with an eye toward busting any possible blockade the PRC might attempt to impose on the island.

In addition to the longstanding PRC military threat, Taiwanese officials express strong concerns about the financial turmoil that swept much of the region in the late 1990s. For Taipei, the impact of an economic crisis could be devastating. For instance, the ROC depends heavily upon foreign arms for its security. An economic slowdown could hamper Taipei's ability to purchase new weapons systems at a time when archrival Beijing is acquiring Russian-built *Kilo* class submarines, Su-27 strike fighters, and *Sovremenny* class destroyers. The economic crisis forced Taipei to pare or defer several planned military purchases and seek short-term relief from the U.S. Defense Department.

A financial crisis could undermine Taiwan's security in numerous other ways. Perhaps most alarming for Taipei is the fact that it is the one state that simply cannot afford to slip into an economic quagmire. Unlike Thailand, South Korea, Indonesia, and other countries, it cannot even hope for an International Monetary Fund (IMF) bailout. The ROC was banished from that organization in 1980.

## Military Strategy

Dramatic transformations in Taiwan's armed forces have accompanied the sweeping economic and political changes that have occurred on the island. For roughly three decades, the ultimate goal of the ROC military was to take back by force the Chinese mainland. Military planners concentrated on building an army capable of fielding forty or more divisions. The structure of the armed forces reflected this mission: the ROC maintained one of the world's largest land armies. But this policy has changed.

According to official MND documents, the ROC military's current strategy might best be described as "strong defense and effective deterrence." The ROC hopes that its military strength will deter an attack on its territory. Should deterrence fail, however, the military is prepared to defend the country. In order to achieve these objectives, the island maintains a formidable military force and a close relationship with the United States.

### A Formidable Military

Taiwan hopes that its military muscle will help deter PRC aggression. Weapons systems are being upgraded to cope with the mainland's growing military might. Primary emphasis is being placed on building a more effective navy and air force. At the same time, the armed forces are being reorganized and downsized into a smaller defensive force.

Current plans call for downsizing the ROC military into a defensive force of roughly 400,000 troops by 2001. A majority of these cuts will affect the army—it will be downsized from 268,000 to 200,000 troops. But at these levels, the army will continue to make up approximately 50 percent of Taiwan's total armed services (the navy and air force will each comprise 25 percent). According to unconfirmed reports, a second-stage downsizing program is being planned that will lead to additional cuts in force levels.

The ROC army's current mission is "focused on defending the territory and ensuring the security of the ROC on Taiwan."[1] Although intended primarily to serve as a fighting force, Taiwan's military also helps farmers harvest their crops and provides relief and rescue operations during natural disasters. In keeping with the Chingshih project—a military reorganization plan that was adopted in 1997—army combat units are being both modernized and restructured. Traditional army divisions will ultimately be turned into "joint-branch brigades."[2]

Weapons systems in the ROC army's inventory include M48 and M60H tanks, M109 and M110 self-propelled artillery, M113, V-150, and CM-21 armored personnel carriers, UH-1H helicopters, Kung-feng 6A rocket systems, TOW-type anti-tank guided weapons, Chaparral SP, Hawk, Tien-kung (Sky Bow) and Tien-chien (Sky Sword) air defense missile systems, vehicle-mounted Avenger missiles and man-portable Stinger missiles, and Hsiung-feng I and Hsiung-feng II anti-ship missile systems. There are also unconfirmed reports that Taiwan plans to produce surface-to-surface ballistic missiles in response to China's provocative 1995 and 1996 missile tests. These missiles—which could be armed with conventional or nuclear warheads—would be capable of striking targets in southern and southeastern China. (Although Taiwan does not possess nuclear weapons it admits that the MND has the capability to produce them.)

During peacetime, the ROC navy "is responsible for carrying out missions such as surveillance and sea patrol, the transportation of supplies to the offshore islands, and the escort of ships."[3] It also provides aid to Taiwanese fishing boats requiring assistance. If attacked, the ROC navy will play a critical role in the island's defensive strategy. According to Taiwan's *1998 National Defense Report*, the navy "is expected to take part in joint operations together with the army and air force to conduct counter-blockade at sea, the surface warfare in the area, and the interdiction against the invading enemy."[4] Like other branches of the ROC military, the navy is being restructured and streamlined. The number of admirals reportedly will be cut and it is likely that the mission of the elite marine force—whose training focuses largely on seizing beachheads as the vanguard of an invasion force—will be revised.

Taiwan's navy is acquiring technology and equipment designed to enhance its ability to engage in warfare at three levels—air, sea, and below the ocean surface. It also has formed an anti-submarine command to study ways to counter a possible PRC blockade. In order to enhance its naval forces, Taipei has purchased American minesweepers, anti-submarine helicopters, *Knox* class destroyers, Mk-46 torpedoes, and Harpoon anti-ship missiles. It also has acquired *La Fayette* class frigates from France and a variety of domestically manufactured frigates, fast-attack craft, and sophisticated missiles.

Finally, Taiwan is putting more muscle into its air force. In January 1994, the armed forces began to take delivery of 135 domestically manufactured Indigenous Defense Fighters (IDF), a new warplane designed originally to replace Taiwan's aging stock of eighty Lockheed F-104G and over 300 Northrop F-5E/F aircraft. Perhaps most significant, Taiwan has acquired 150 F-16A/B warplanes from the United States and sixty Mirage 2000-5 fighters from France. It also has purchased four American-built Grumman E-2T Hawkeye early warning planes.

### American Military Support

With the abrogation of the U.S.–ROC Defense Treaty in 1979, the United States terminated its formal security commitment to Taiwan. However, the United States continues to play a critical role in Taiwan's defensive strategy. American military equipment, technological assistance, and an informal or tacit alliance augment the island's defenses.

According to the Taiwan Relations Act (TRA)—the legislation that guides official American policy toward Taiwan—the United States will "make available to Taiwan such defense articles and defense services in such quantity as may be necessary to enable Taiwan to maintain a sufficient self-defense capability." Recent sales of American-built military equipment have included missiles, advanced fighter aircraft, sophisticated anti-submarine helicopters, and the Patriot anti-missile system. Taiwan also has entered into negotiations on the purchase of several *Aegis* class cruisers from the United States and it has agreed to study the possibility of participating in the proposed TMD system for East Asia. As might be expected, the PRC opposes the arms transfers and officials warn that Taiwan's inclusion under the TMD would be the "last straw" in Sino-American relations. Perhaps responding to PRC pressure, the United States announced it will not sell *Aegis* warships to Taipei at this time, and it is unclear how Taiwan will fit into plans for TMD.

In addition to arms sales, the United States has transferred critical technologies to Taiwan. This technological assistance has enabled Taipei to domestically manufacture a range of military hardware—including advanced warplanes, missiles, warships, and tanks. The United States also shares intelligence with Taiwan, and despite the lack of formal diplomatic ties U.S.–ROC military-to-military contacts remain intact.

The U.S. security commitment to Taiwan is discussed in the TRA and three joint communiqués with the PRC. Some argue that the TRA mandates an American military response to a PRC attack. But these individuals are mistaken. The TRA provides the United States only with an *option* to defend Taiwan; it does not necessarily commit the United States to Taiwan's defense. Nevertheless, as a 1998 *National Defense University* study observed, "any U.S. administration would come under significant pressure to defend Taiwan were conflict to occur, *no matter the cause.*"[5] Both sides of the Taiwan Strait agree that the prospect of American intervention has long played a key role in Taiwan's defense.

## Conclusions

The ROC military has abandoned its past strategic objective of having a massive military that—beyond defending Taiwan and the offshore islands—would also be capable of liberating mainland China. Military strategy now focuses almost exclusively on defense and deterrence. In order to achieve these objectives, the ROC is seeking to streamline its military and acquire a new generation of military forces based on the principles of smaller force levels, higher-quality weapons systems, and enhanced operational capabilities. The ROC also is seeking to strengthen its military ties with the United States. In addition to the acquisition of arms and technology, Taipei is interested in enhancing military exchanges with the United States.

It is likely that these moves will bolster Taiwan's security. They help keep the cost of a PRC invasion prohibitively high. In the final analysis, however, more than military equipment and U.S. support will be needed to protect Taiwan. As one U.S. official explained, "in the end, stability in the Taiwan Strait will be contingent on the ability of the two sides of the strait to come to terms with each other on a political basis."[6]

## Notes

1. ROC Ministry of National Defense, *1998 National Defense Report: Republic of China*, p. 61.

2. Ibid, p. 63.
3. Ibid, p. 64.
4. Ibid.
5. Institute for National Strategic Studies, National Defense University, *Strategic Assessment 1998: Engaging Power for Peace* (Washington, DC: U.S. Government Printing Office, 1998), p. 46.
6. Jay Chen and Sofia Wu, "Roth Reaffirms U.S. Commitment to Taiwan's Security," Central News Agency, June 19, 1998.

## Suggested Readings

Copper, John F. *Taiwan: Nation-State or Province?* 3rd ed. Boulder, CO: Westview Press, 1999.
Hickey, Dennis Van Vranken. *Taiwan's Security in the Changing International System.* Boulder, CO: Lynne Rienner, 1997.
———. *The United States and Cross-Strait Rivalry: Strategic Partnership and Strategic Ambiguity.* Washington, DC: Atlantic Council of the United States, May 1999.
ROC Ministry of National Defense. *1998 National Defense Report: Republic of China.* Taipei: Li Ming Cultural Enterprises, 1998. Translated from the Chinese by Yang Lien-chung and Chien Wu-nan.
U.S. Department of Defense. *The Security Situation in the Taiwan Strait.* Washington, DC: The Pentagon, February 26, 1999.

# 27
# Thailand

*David G. Wiencek*

## Introduction

The Asian financial crisis of 1997 was triggered when Bangkok devalued the baht after a decline in exports and in the stock market. Suddenly, the country with one of the world's highest growth rates over the previous decade went into an economic tailspin that eventually had an impact around Southeast Asia and throughout the global economy. The economic crisis touched off a political crisis, with demonstrators taking to the streets of Bangkok. Political stability was restored after a new Prime Minister, Chuan Leekpai, assumed office in November 1997. At the same time, Thailand's ambitious defense modernization program ground to an immediate halt. The country's recently acquired small aircraft carrier, a symbol of the apparent economic success Thailand had achieved, was forced to spend most of its time in port because the navy lacked the funds to put it to sea; eventually it wound up as a part-time tourist attraction. As Thailand enters the new millennium, therefore, it continues to confront major challenges associated with getting its economy back on track. The nation's security concerns are now mainly economic in nature: assure economic growth in order to avoid internal political or labor turmoil. Tensions with Burma over border issues, which are also tied to illegal narcotics trafficking, remain acute and are likely to be a key focus of Thai defense planners, particularly now that major military modernization efforts have slowed in light of inadequate resources to engage in any form of military power projection to protect the country's broader regional interests.

## Economic and Political Framework

Thailand averaged better than 9 percent economic growth from the mid-1980s to mid-1990s, making it one of the world's best economic performers. But the foun-

## Thailand

dation for this economic success was a weak one. By 1997, rampant building in Bangkok had led to an oversupply of hotels and offices. Lax oversight and regulation and a corrupt banking system compounded this type of speculative development. Once the crisis came in 1997, these systemic flaws were exposed and international authorities had to intervene to help stabilize the situation. Some fifty-eight finance companies were closed down, and the economy experienced a 9.4 percent contraction in 1998. Eventually, the International Monetary Fund (IMF) pledged US$17 billion in emergency loans. By 1999, positive growth had been restored. Yet banks are still awash in debt, and reforms are being implemented slowly. Unemployment, somewhat difficult to measure due to the sizeable portion of the workforce involved in agriculture, also has risen sharply. At the same time, crime levels have surged, especially armed robberies and various forms of business-oriented violence, including assassinations. In one high-profile case in 1999, an Australian auditor for an international accounting firm was murdered while investigating an indebted company. It will likely take years for Thailand to recover fully from the wide-ranging effects of the crisis of the late 1990s.

Events in the economic arena also spurred political change, and may, in the long run, end up actually having strengthened Thailand's democracy. The steep decline in living standards brought pressure on the government of then-Prime Minister Chavalit Yongchaiyudh. Thousands of students and workers took to the streets of Bangkok in October 1997 to protest against Chavalit's handling of the economic crisis and political corruption. But unlike 1992, when an army crackdown on pro-democracy protesters led to hundreds killed, the situation was different this time. The protesters were left alone and the Chavalit administration ultimately conceded, turning power over to widely respected reformer Chuan Leekpai.

Chuan's coalition government has worked responsibly with international authorities to gradually put needed reforms into place and clean up corrupt political practices. The political stability established by the Chuan government has helped solidify Thailand's multi-party democracy. The days of the coups—the military staged seventeen between 1932 and 1991—are likely over. The military now appears to be working within the system.

Thailand remains a constitutional democracy, with the current monarch, King Bhumipol, now having ruled for half a century. The king has little direct power under the constitution but is a symbol of national identity and unity. He has subtly exercised authority in past political crises and his influence will be missed when he eventually passes from the scene.

### Risk Assessment

For over a decade, Thailand has employed a broad interpretation of its security interests and it is one that has been in large measure driven by economics.[1] The country continues to pursue an economics-oriented security policy designed to foster and protect economic growth, and this focus has only likely become more crucial given the economic downturn of the late 1990s. In a current formulation, Lt. General Teerawat Putamanonda of the Royal Thai Army has characterized the military's security outlook as follows: "From Thailand's perspective, potential conflicts or threats seem to be more internal, nonmilitary threats that stem from economic, social, or environmental problems. There are no major threats from our immediate external environment."[2] Another senior military leader, Royal Thai Navy Commander-in-Chief Admiral Thira Haocharoen, echoes this threat assessment by concluding:

> Our assessment is that there will be no threat of a major war in the next 10 years. There might be minor skirmishes for some resources. No country wants to give up its resources. In the current hard economic time, all countries want to feed themselves rather than go to battle. Regarding threats from the countries surrounding us, we cannot specifically say which country will become a threat. We will monitor weapon buildup by every country and try to achieve a balance with it.[3]

This outlook reflects a marked change from the 1980s when Vietnam's intervention in Cambodia's civil war dominated Thai security concerns. Today, the military helps strengthen internal stability by contributing to rural development programs, working with other governmental agencies to defuse nonmilitary threats, and assisting local authorities with border security.

Perhaps the most critical externally driven security concern facing Thailand today stems from the activities of drug trafficking groups along the border with neighboring Burma. In recent years, trafficking in amphetamines has increased, with Burma's rebel United Wa State Army (UWSA) identified as the region's biggest amphetamine trafficker. Amphetamines are targeted mainly at the Thai market, where the drug is known as "mad medicine" and is widely used by young people and workers.

In August 1999, Thailand shut down a main Wa border crossing point used to funnel drugs into Thailand. In response, Burma closed a separate border point, disrupting legal economic activity and trade between the two countries.[4] The group essentially has been given a free pass by Burma's ruling military junta to continue dealing drugs. The Burmese military has no troops in Wa territory and the Wa have indicated that they will not make their territory opium-free until 2005.[5]

According to recent reports, the UWSA may now be employing ultra-light, hang glider type aircraft to ferry drugs across the Thai border.[6] Meanwhile, the Thai military has restricted overflights of the area due to indications that the UWSA possesses Russian-made SA-7 anti-aircraft missiles procured from local arms dealers and possibly acquired from Chinese sources.[7]

The narco insurgency of the Wa will likely continue unabated for years, contributing to major instability with Thailand and resulting in the sustained flow of illegal narcotics to Europe and the United States.

## Southern Separatists

In the south, meanwhile, low-level violence continues in the provinces along the Malaysian border. In 1997, Muslim separatists carried out a series of bombings and other attacks. In 1998, members of the New Pattani United Liberation Organization (PULO) conducted more bombings. (New PULO was formed in 1998 after the arrest of leading PULO members.) But authorities launched a counteroffensive and, with substantial assistance from Malaysia, where PULO members had traditionally sought refuge, were able to restore calm to the region. The movement is today a shadow of its former self, with active fighters estimated to number less than 100, down from the 1,000 members of twenty years ago. The movement appears to be more crime-oriented now, and less bent on establishing an independent Islamic state. A situation may in fact exist where local criminals and bandits are committing acts of violence using the cover of separatist forces. In any event, Thai authorities are working to provide amnesty to former fighters and reabsorb them into southern society.

## Military Structure

The military employs a Total Defense Concept aimed at assuring internal stability and deterring external aggression. With the economic crisis, however, internally oriented missions are of necessity receiving priority. Indeed, many forms of exercises, patrols, and training with an external security orientation were cut, with some units being forced back into the classroom in an attempt to keep proficiencies up. The emphasis today seems to be focused on dealing with illegal drugs and refugees penetrating Thai territory. The defense budget, once geared to major acquisitions for power projection and regional security missions, including submarines, frigates, armored fighting vehicles, and even military satellites, took an immediate hit, with a 25 percent reduction mandated under IMF aid plans. Military reform is being facilitated by the fact that Prime Minister Chuan also assumed the Defense Minister's portfolio—one of the few times a civilian has held the post and a sure sign that business as usual in military procurement has come to an end.

The military chain of command is also being restructured. In the future, the Defense Permanent Secretary and the Supreme Commander of the military will be on the same level. The Supreme Commander will have the authority to order troops into combat.[8]

The Royal Thai Army force structure includes "seven infantry, two armor-cavalry, two special force, one artillery, one air defense, and one engineering division."[9] But the financial crisis has necessitated a force downsizing. The 190,000-man army will likely be cut by 40,000 over then next ten years. The 73,000-man navy and the 43,000-man air force will face similar reductions.[10]

No program cutback was more widely discussed than the purchase from the United States of eight F/A-18 Hornet combat aircraft. The Thais had already paid some US$74 million out of a total deal worth over US$300 million. But the sale was canceled after President Clinton intervened on behalf of the cash-strapped Thais and helped them obtain a refund. By late 1999, however, Bangkok was expressing an interest in acquiring up to twenty refurbished surplus F-16A/B fighters from Washington for about US$100 million. Earlier in 1999, the Royal Thai Air Force also decided to purchase fifty used Dassault/Dornier Alfa Jet light ground-attack fighters and trainers from Germany that had been retired by the Luftwaffe several years ago. The Alfa Jets were reportedly acquired for the low price of US$27,000 each, but each aircraft will require over US$1 million in refurbishments to assure airworthiness.[11]

In the naval area, Bangkok became the first Southeast Asian nation to possess a sea-based air power system when it acquired the small aircraft carrier *Chakri Naruebet*, a symbol of Thailand's previous economic wherewithal. This US$336 million vessel, built in Spain, displaces 11,500 tons; it has a ski-jet flight deck with two aircraft elevators and can carry some four helicopters and six short takeoff/vertical landing aircraft, useful for force projection, search and rescue, and humanitarian missions. But no sooner did the Thais acquire this vessel than they found themselves unable to support its costly operation when the economic crisis hit. The *Chakri Naruebet* reportedly was only able to be deployed about once a month and spent most of its time in port as a part-time tourist attraction. The Thai press dubbed the ship the "Thai-tanic" because it was such a white elephant. By June 1999, only one of its Sea Harrier jump jet aircraft was in service.[12]

Thailand has taken an interest in peacekeeping operations and deployed 1,500 troops and provided the deputy commander in support of the international force in East Timor in 1999.

## Relations with the United States

U.S.-Thai security ties derive from a 1962 communiqué signed by then U.S. Secretary of State Dean Rusk and Thai Foreign Minister Thanat Khoman. The Rusk–Thanat arrangement obligates Washington to come to Thailand's aid if attacked. The two allies thus have strong military ties dating back decades. Although the United States maintains no bases in Thailand, Bangkok regularly grants the United States important air transit rights and quietly provides other logistical support to American forces. In the current environment, military-to-military relations are built on a vigorous joint training program and, in particular, the annual Cobra Gold exercise, which is the largest joint training opportunity in Southeast Asia.

U.S.-Thai relations suffered some setbacks during the financial crisis of the late 1990s. Many in Thailand perceived that Washington was not providing enough assistance to a friend during a critical moment. Indeed, the Chinese stepped in with US$1 billion in aid, a move that was seen as an attempt to enhance long-term Chinese influence, possibly on key security issues, such as attempting to gain Thai support for Beijing's positions in the South China Sea dispute.

## Conclusions

Thailand suffered a major economic reversal in the late 1990s. All efforts are focused today on getting the economy back on track and creating a more transparent business and political climate. Political stability has been restored under the reform-oriented Chuan administration, which has held power for over two years. The effects of the financial crisis hobbled the military and its horizons are severely limited. It will have to concentrate on internal security concerns and close-to-home missions for the foreseeable future. The military's role in politics has been significantly reduced and new reforms are helping ensure a more streamlined procurement process. These are steps that will go a long way toward safeguarding Thailand's now vibrant democracy.

## Notes

1. For further discussion, see the analysis in the first edition of this book by Professor M. Ladd Thomas in "Thailand," in William M. Carpenter and David G. Wiencek, eds., *Asian Security Handbook: An Assessment of Political-Security Issues in the Asia-Pacific Region* (Armonk, NY: M.E. Sharpe, 1996), pp. 240–248.

2. See Teerawat Putamanonda, "The Strategy of Conflict: A Royal Thai Army Perspective," in Frances Omori and Mary A. Sommerville, eds., *Strength Through Cooperation: Military Forces in the Asia-Pacific Region* (Washington, DC: National Defense University Press, 1999), p. 234.

3. "Interview with Navy Commander Admiral Thira Haocharoen," *Bangkok Daily News*, January 2, 1999, as translated by Foreign Broadcast Information Service (FBIS), January 5, 1999, FBIS-EAS-99–005.

4. "Burma Closes Northern Crossing," *The Nation* (Thailand), August 19, 1999; and Don Pathan, "Govt Watches New Border Problem with Unease," *The Nation* (Thailand), September 5, 1999.

5. U.S. Department of State, *International Narcotics Control Strategy Report, 1998.*

6. "Drug Traffickers Use 'Ultra-light' Planes to Evade Thai Crackdown," Deutsche Presse Agentur, August 20, 1999.

7. "Thai Police Seize Missile Planned for Sale to Burma's Wa Army," *The Nation* Website, 9 September 1999, as monitored by BBC, September 9, 1999; and "Airmen Told to Beware Wa Missiles—Threat Linked to Drug Suppression," *Bangkok Post*, September 11, 1999.

8. Micool Brooke, "Wide-Open Market: U.S. and Russian Arms Firms Square Off in Pacific Rim as Thailand Resumes Military Modernization," *Armed Forces Journal International*, October 1999, p. 70.

9. Putamanonda, "The Strategy of Conflict: A Royal Thai Army Perspective," p. 233.

10. Philip Finnegan, "Thai Military Regroups for Changing Roles," *Defense News*, November 29, 1999, p. 3.

11. Geoffrey Thomas, "Russians to Top Bill at Malaysia's LIMA," *Aviation Week & Space Technology*, November 22, 1999, p. 40.

12. Brooke, "Wide-Open Market," p. 68.

## Suggested Readings

Cole, John M., and Steven P. Sciacchitano. "U.S.-Thai Relations: Gradually, Two Long-time Allies Are Settling into a New Relationship." *Armed Forces Journal International*, July 1998, p. 12.

Fisher, Richard D., Jr., and Robert P. O'Quinn. "The United States and Thailand: Helping a Friend in Need." Washington, DC: The Heritage Foundation, March 12, 1998. *Backgrounder* No. 1164.

Putamanonda, Teerawat. "The Strategy of Conflict: A Royal Thai Army Perspective." In Frances Omori and Mary A. Sommerville, eds., *Strength Through Cooperation: Military Forces in the Asia-Pacific Region.* Washington, DC: National Defense University Press, 1999, pp. 233–238.

# 28
# Vietnam

*Lewis M. Stern*

## The Political Framework

The momentum of economic reforms put in place in Vietnam in the mid-1980s made it more difficult to wage politics in accordance with old rules and formulas. Though the Vietnamese Communist Party (VNCP) continued to play a leadership role in economic reforms, it had to share center stage with increasingly vocal and organized interests. The military has had to argue aggressively for its portion of an inelastic national budget. Since at least the mid-1990s the social and economic changes generated by the reforms initiated in the early and mid-1980s have led to serious discussions of the importance of an independent judicial system, recognition of the need for a clear legal framework to guide both the economy and the polity, and more efficient activities within the National Assembly—all of which have had fairly widespread support in the system.

The locus of foreign policymaking power shifted and remained fluid beginning in the early 1990s, in part as a result of the leadership changes put in place by the Seventh National Party Congress in mid-1991. The Foreign Ministry remained without a Politburo-level vote following Nguyen Co Thach's "retirement" from that body in late 1991 until January 1994 when his successor, Nguyen Manh Cam, was given a seat on the Politburo. Foreign Minister Cam became part of a well-orchestrated system of redistributed power that evolved rather quickly following Thach's retirement. Under Thach, the Foreign Ministry had at times been clearly competitive with and capable of standing up to the Defense Ministry. After the Seventh National Party Congress, and until Cam's promotion to the Politburo in January 1994, the system began to resemble a troika, in which the Foreign Ministry was the "junior partner," and Defense and Interior had a mandate to function more in concert with one another. Up to the Seventh National Congress, foreign policymaking and national de-

## Vietnam

fense strategy formulation relied on the strength of personality of the foreign minister, and on personal friendships and party alliances. Under Do Muoi, the foreign and security policy players acted more as components of a complex bureaucracy with inter-agency dimensions, and formalized reporting requirements that mandated sharing information, discussing views, and organizing staff work.

Potentially important changes in the manner in which Vietnam made and implemented foreign policy took place during the tenure of the Eighth Central Committee. General Secretary Muoi and his successor, Le Kha Phieu, became involved in the management of important foreign relations, including sensitive and potentially lucrative bilateral links with Association of Southeast Asian Nations (ASEAN) states, in a manner that exceeded the involvement of their predecessors. The party's External Relations Department became central to the foreign policymaking process, acting as the party's conscience on affairs of state and providing foreign policy advice to the Central Committee. The Department assumed responsibilities for thoroughly coordinating position papers intended to galvanize discussion throughout the party and the government. The National Assembly had come to demand more responsiveness from the Foreign Ministry, as well as other elements of the system. The External Relations Department of the Foreign Ministry's party organization found itself reporting and reviewing policies, and contributing to Foreign Ministry efforts to answer questions from legislators. That necessitated more systematic communication between the VNCP's External Relations Department and its Foreign Ministry counterpart.

## The External Security Environment

Throughout the tenure of the Eighth Central Committee of the VNCP—from the mid to the late 1990s—foreign policy was based on the "principle" of diversification, making friends with many countries, and pursuing memberships in multilateral organizations. Hanoi's foreign policy placed a primacy on mending and improving ties with China, continuing the normalization of relations with the United States, expanding contacts with the European Community, and becoming a responsible participant in ASEAN. Vietnam's foreign policy also aimed at consolidating ties to the remnants of the Soviet Union as well as "renovating" ties with the new countries in the Russian Federation, and improving ties with South Asia, the Middle East, Africa, and Latin America. Finally, during the latter part of the 1990s, Vietnam was acutely conscious of the need to nurture relations with immediate neighbors. Hanoi periodically revived the loaded locution "special relationship" to describe links with Laos; remained concerned with the special problems that Cambodia represented for Vietnam and for the region; and remained conscious of the potential for growth in bilateral relations with Thailand.

Throughout the 1990s Vietnam's foreign policy concerns ranged from the health of socialism in the aftermath of the breakup of the Soviet Union, to the conditions for regional stability, the meaning of Vietnam's integration into ASEAN, and the fundamental policy assumptions behind the effort to broaden bilateral relations on a global basis. Vietnam remained concerned with the "contradictions" that could exert potentially destabilizing influences in the region, including the emergence of tensions involving economic and political competition between the region's larger players and imperialist powers, and between developing countries and the United States, as well as Japan.

## Internal Security Concerns

Vietnam acknowledged that a foreign policy strategy based on widened relations presented any number of emerging forces with the opportunity to undermine political security, social order, and culture. Through the tenure of the Eighth Congress, Hanoi remained concerned with "outside forces" that had "stepped up their activities of peaceful evolution, attempting to mate rebellion and subversion," and stressed the need to confront Western propaganda aimed at undermining popular confidence in the party, discrediting the regime's standing and preventing the government from doing its job. By the mid-1990s, though, some subtle distinctions emerged between external forces of subversion and internal threats to stability. By 1994–1995, party documents began to speak of a "number of hostile forces" that persisted in threatening peace and fomenting rebellion, suggesting that a consensus had emerged that acknowledged that certain internal forces and potential circumstances that sowed division, eroded the regime's economic reforms, and undermined the institutions managing modernization were as much a menace to the regime as outright enemies operating from foreign shores.

## Vietnamese-Cambodian Relations

Since the United Nations supervised elections in 1993, and the formation of the Royal Cambodian Government, Cambodia represented one of Hanoi's most pressing and immediate security concerns. For example, in December 1995 the Cambodian government complained that a Vietnamese military unit had transgressed the border. Phnom Penh gradually elevated their concerns over this incident, and raised serious questions about the management of violations of the joint communiqué signed by the prime ministers of the two countries in mid-January 1995. Another problem that complicated the relationship was the activities of ethnic Vietnamese anti-Hanoi activists affiliated with an organization called "Free Vietnam" alleged to have operated from Cambodian soil since late 1994. In early 1996 the Cambodian government deported three ethnic Vietnamese leaders of this organization to Vietnam.

Vietnam campaigned publicly for the immediate induction of Cambodia into ASEAN, beginning soon after the July 1998 election. Hanoi's vocal efforts to win support for Phnom Penh's case suggested to many in the region that Hanoi sought leadership over what could in effect become an Indochina voting bloc in ASEAN. In mid-1999, at a moment when the region was preoccupied with China's efforts to drive the South China Sea issue, Hanoi sought to mend fences with select ASEAN friends, including Cambodia. Hanoi made notable investments in the relationship with Phnom Penh, perhaps in the hope of being able to develop a united Indochina position on the "Eastern Sea" in the context of ASEAN activities on the disputed territories issues. In late May 1999, Vietnam and Cambodia conducted a round of border negotiations. Vietnam endorsed the bilateral agreements that had emerged in 1992 and 1995 on land and sea borders with Phnom Penh. National Assembly President Norodom Ranarith (Ranariddh) visited Vietnam in late May. The Prince was well received, and the visit was hailed in the Vietnamese media as a positive step forward in bilateral relations. In the immediate aftermath of Ranarith's visit, in what was clearly an effort to get beyond the single most troublesome issue that had complicated relations in 1995, the Cambodian police undertook an investigation of the five groups that existed under the umbrella organization called the Free Vietnam Revolutionary Government. A report on this investigation was publicized in a pro-FUNCINPEC (United Front for an Independent, Neutral and Peaceful Cambodia) newspaper in early June. In early June 1999 General Secretary of the Vietnamese Communist Party Le Kha Phieu traveled to Cambodia for meetings that were hailed in the Vietnamese party–controlled press as historically significant events. In language generally reserved for important foreign policy achievements, the public accounts suggested that Phieu's meetings with senior Cambodian officials underscored the continued relevance of the relationship, and resulted in a critical agreement to resolve bilateral border issues.

Cambodia continued to represent a potentially complicated foreign policy problem for Vietnam. Cambodia was conspicuous by its absence from the recitation of foreign policy achievements contained in the April 1996 draft of the Political Report to the Eighth National Congress of the VNCP, perhaps because relations had soured temporarily over border issues and lingering problems associated with ethnic Vietnamese residents of Cambodia, who had been the subject of organized violence several times since the end of the Cambodian conflict. However, Cambodia was restored to the list of countries of focus in the final Political Report, though not as a relationship of "special solidarity" as Laos was described, but merely as a country with which Vietnam had "built better relations," a reference to the 1996 joint agreement, which supported the promotion of bilateral cooperation in trade, transport, and communications; the conduct of a third round of talks on the status of Vietnamese residents in Cambodia; the signing of a consular agreement; and the continued work of the experts working group on border issues.

## Vietnamese-Lao Relations

The Lao-Vietnamese "special relationship" was born of long years of sustained military presence, close political coordination through the Indochina Federation, intertwined party histories, and intimate leadership relationships. That link shifted to a new footing with the gradual Vietnamese military disengagement from commitments to Cambodia and Laos, the refocusing of Vietnamese attention on internal economic development and institutional reform in the mid-1980s, and the gradual erosion of the strong ties and habits of Lao subservience toward the late 1980s, as the region experienced fundamental political and economic change.

Laos has spent the last dozen years immersed in an economic reform effort, dating from the 1986 introduction of the "New Economic Policy." Market-based trade and business activity have attracted the activism of international donor organizations, invigorated intercourse with neighbors, and enabled Laos to profit from its status as a major producer of hydroelectricity for export. Moreover, Laos entered ASEAN in 1996, and has assumed a role as an active participant in key ASEAN groups on water resources and ASEAN Mekong Basin development cooperation. In this context, Vietnamese-Lao relations have been proper, cooperative, and symbolically and rhetorically correct, though issues such as the flow of illegal Vietnamese immigrants into Laos seeking to profit from opportunities for economic enrichment, border demarcation issues, and other housekeeping matters impact on the relationship.

Vientiane's management of its own close relationship with China has probably nettled Hanoi from time to time, especially as the Chinese footprint deepened through larger investments in aid and assistance. Vietnam is also attentive to the close economic links and essentially comfortable friendship between Laos and Thailand, the shared interests based on ethnic affinities and proximity, and Thailand's periodic aspirations to draw Laos more closely into its "orbit," as was the case during Chatchai Chunhawan's tenure as prime minister in the early 1990s, in the context of Chatchai's thinking about a "Golden Peninsula" alliance of modernizing, economically robust relationships.

## Vietnamese-Thai Relations

Thailand's relationship with Vietnam has been positive and productive, helped along by Vietnam's entrance into ASEAN in 1995. The Thai saw opportunities for bilateral co-development of petroleum resources, potentially lucrative trade relations, and stable, friendly diplomatic links with Hanoi. Vietnam has been receptive to Thai initiatives to manage some of the trouble spots in the bilateral relationship, including periodic conflicts over fishing in areas adjacent to territorial waters, and the residual consular problems surrounding the ethnic Vietnamese resident in northern Thailand since the 1950s. In 1998 the government of Thailand awarded citizenship to third generation Vietnamese residents of Thailand, a significant break with longstanding Thai citizenship policies that had for decades kept the Dien Bien Phu refugees and their offspring in a limbo of legalities and without critical entitlements and access to important social services. In early June 1999 Thailand's Deputy Foreign Minister visited Hanoi and announced the establishment of a consultative mechanism to sustain policy discussions, as well as the signing of a visa exemption agreement.

Thailand and Vietnam continue to have foreign policy differences, not on the order of magnitude that characterized the frigid relationship during Bangkok's support for the Non Communist Cambodian Resistance efforts against the presence of Vietnamese military forces in Cambodia, but of significance in the context of ASEAN's foray beyond economic and social cooperation and into regional security issues and conflict resolution. For example, in the aftermath of the July 1998 election in Cambodia, Thailand approached the issue of Cambodian membership in ASEAN cautiously, preferring to wait until the government that was seated as a result of negotiations that followed the July 1998 election could achieve some stability and coherence. Cambodia's unpredictability—especially since the July 1997 unseating of Prince Norodom Ranarith by Hun Sen, and Hun Sen's ire at ASEAN for deferring membership for Cambodia in the aftermath of his acts against his coalition partner, plus the level of domestic uncertainty, pre-election violence, as well as the troubled formation of a post-coup coalition—prompted Bangkok to side with Singapore and the Philippines in the judgment that Cambodia's entry into ASEAN should wait a decent interval.

Hanoi's coolness toward the Thai notion of a more activist though selective intervention by ASEAN into domestic affairs that threatened to undermine regional goals of peace and prosperity, and Hanoi's periodic efforts to generate anti-China sentiment over South China Sea issues, suggested to Thailand, and others, that Vietnam was unwilling to formulate decisions on the basis of organization-wide consensus, and that Hanoi was inclined to encourage a trend toward factions in the enlarged regional association. Thailand's concern for the ASEAN tradition of consensual politics is likely to emerge as a salient issue in bilateral relations with Vietnam.

## Sino-Vietnamese Relations

Throughout the mid and late 1990s, though Vietnam acknowledged the critical importance of effective, friendly relations with China, Hanoi felt a high level of frustration about the relationship. Senior party officials continued to describe the bilateral link as positive and correct, but privately lamented Beijing's haughty approach to the relationship. Vietnamese officials saw the relationship as being primarily characterized by a one-sided trade equation that redounded to China's favor; Beijing's efforts to turn Vietnam into a "dumping ground"; Chinese attempts to control cross-border trade in a manner that struck Vietnam as organized, state-supported smuggling; and calculated Chinese efforts to gain access to regional markets and trade routes through formal agreements on road, rail, sea, and air transportation with Hanoi. Senior party officials believed that the relationship was an unbalanced one, but that stability was so necessary to Beijing's plans to modernize and develop its economy that China was therefore prepared to consolidate its relationship with Vietnam premised on the peaceful resolution of disputes. Nevertheless, through the late 1990s Vietnamese officials believed that China would approach the resolution of bilateral problems in its own way, on its own schedule, and with little regard for Hanoi's equities. Indeed, progress in the second half of the 1990s was slow. After striking an agreement in 1991, it took until 1996 before China and Vietnam restored rail links that were disrupted in 1979 when China attacked Vietnam in reaction to Hanoi's actions against Democratic Kampuchea. There was some minor, technical progress in expert level land border talks in the late 1990s. Discussions on the Tonkin Gulf had yielded less progress.

In 1997, during his visit to China, then General Secretary Do Muoi had pressed for a bilateral agreement in principle to resolve the border demarcation issues by the year 2000, a point that was strongly reiterated during General Secretary Le Kha Phieu's February–March 1999 visit to China. China continued to take exception to Vietnam's map of claims in the Gulf, and to Hanoi's argument that Chinese-occupied strong points along the shared land border were properly Vietnamese territory. Through mid-1999 there was still no agreement on the principles for joint delineation of the borders and for resolution of the claims to offshore islands and territorial waters in the Tonkin Gulf. However, Beijing and Hanoi had agreed to continue the work of the "experts group" in maritime and land border issues, and to work together at the highest levels to manage bilateral issues.

## Disputed Territories and Border Issues

The Vietnamese government and military have remained concerned with how China responds to Vietnam's efforts to define its stake in conflicted territories in the Eastern Sea (or the South China Sea, as Beijing refers to it) and lingering land territorial claims and border issues. Vietnam's response to two issues—disputes over sovereign claims to Spratly Archipelago areas (Truong Sa) and challenges to Vietnam's sovereignty over special economic zones and continental shelf areas (Tu Chinh)—has been to hold, in the first instance, that disputes should be resolved on the basis of international law, and in the second instance to demand the cessation of oil and gas exploration activities in what Hanoi argued was uncontested continental shelf area, while invoking international law as the basis for proceeding with the peaceful resolution of conflicts over joint ventures in that area. The Defense Ministry continues to be closely attentive to these developments and has raised the issue of "Chinese provocations" with third countries, including the United States, in order to extract statements that could be construed as supportive of Vietnamese claims.

Since the early 1990s, China has taken several dramatic steps to stake out these claims. In February 1992, the National People's Congress passed the Law on Territorial Waters and their Contiguous Areas, which held that the Spratly Islands were part of Chinese territories. The law authorized the use of military force to settle claims issues. ASEAN responded by issuing a declaration at their annual meeting that urged restraint, called upon the claimants to settle the territorial disputes peacefully, and supported economic development efforts in the South China Sea while sovereignty issues were being negotiated. In 1995, China initiated construction of guard posts in the vicinity of Mischief Reef, 135 miles from the Philippine Island of Palawan, prompting vigorous complaints from Manila and a strong statement from Washington to the effect that any South China Sea conflict that interfered with the freedom of navigation would prompt the U.S. Seventh Fleet to provide escort services aimed at protecting the international rights of free passage.

In the 1990s, the confrontation between Beijing and Hanoi over this issue has so far been confined to diplomatic jousting, though the potential for escalated action remains distinct; the brief naval fighting between China and Vietnam in 1988, as each country maneuvered military forces in an effort to reinforce claims in the Spratlys, remains a distinct memory in both capital cities. The Chinese Foreign Ministry has issued statements protesting against Vietnam's dispatch of armed forces to occupy submerged reefs of the Spratly Archipelago, and demanded that the Vietnamese withdraw their forces and dismantle the facilities. Vietnam has reiterated their sovereignty over the Spratly and Paracel Islands, citing the usual historical and legal accounts that, from Hanoi's perspective, affirm this claim. The February 1999 statement by Vietnam posited that the facilities mentioned in Chinese complaints are civilian economic-scientific-technological service stations. In general terms, Hanoi's position is that the stations in question are on the Ba Ke submerged reef area, which is not part of the Spratly Islands. Vietnam generally invokes the 1982 United Nations Convention on the Law of the Sea in arguing that the activities of such stations are in accordance with international laws governing normal civil operations.

From Hanoi's perspective, there has been about ten years of high-level bilateral diplomacy aimed at resolving the border issue. In 1991, Vietnam and China agreed to develop the shared border into a "peaceful and friendly frontier" and to settle outstanding territorial issues through negotiations. In 1993, Vietnam and China signed the "Agreement on the Fundamental Principles for Resolving the Border Issue." That agreement provided for regular negotiations at the "government and experts" levels to settle issues associated with the land and sea borders between Vietnam and China, including the Tonkin Gulf. During Do Muoi's 1997 visit to Beijing, and again in 1999 during General Secretary Le Kha Phieu's visit, both countries agreed to sign a land border agreement before 2000 and an agreement on the Tonkin Gulf by the year 2000. Though that agreement has suffused foreign policy statements by both countries with a certain amount of optimism, Vietnamese senior officials appear to hold a distinctly realistic attitude toward the likelihood of achieving a resolution to the South China Sea dispute, given Beijing's record of intransigence, and its unwillingness to move far from the starting points for discussion that have dominated China's thinking on these claims since the late 1980s. Nevertheless, in recent incarnations of the dispute, the Vietnamese have noted that both China and Vietnam have agreed to "maintain the existing mechanism on negotiations" on sea issues, persist in peaceful negotiations to find "a fundamental and long-term solution acceptable to both sides," and to refrain from actions that could complicate or widen the dispute.

### U.S.-Vietnamese Relations

Following normalization in July 1995, the Vietnamese placed a priority on negotiating a trade agreement in order to secure the extension of Normal Trade Relations (formerly called Most Favored Nations status), which would facilitate Vietnamese exports to the United States at prevailing tariff rates. The benefits that would accompany economic normalization were important to Vietnam, and included Export–Import Bank loans to U.S. corporations to support exports to Vietnam; provision of Overseas Private Investment Corporation (OPIC) insurance to U.S. companies to support investment in Vietnam; the granting of Generalized System of Preference status; specialized Commodity Credit Corporation support; Agency for International Development (AID) programming; and the opening of a U.S. Foreign Commercial Office in Vietnam. In view of its status under U.S. law as a so-called "Jackson–Vanik" country, Normal Trade Relations could not be extended until Vietnam was certified by the president as having a free and fair immigration policy, or until a waiver on national interest grounds was in place.

In May 1997, Vietnam concluded a bilateral copyright agreement and a debt agreement, and in April 1997 Treasury Secretary Rubin visited Hanoi. These were critical steps. On March 10, 1997, President Clinton granted a waiver of the Jackson–Vanik amendment under Section 402 of the Trade Act of 1974, and in June the president transmitted a determination to Congress stating that continuation of the waiver for Vietnam would substantially promote the freedom of emigration objectives of the amendment. In late June 1997 the House of Representatives voted down House Joint Resolution 120, a resolution to disapprove the presidential waiver of the Jackson–Vanik amendment. Nevertheless, before a trade agreement could be signed Vietnam would have to take positive steps toward a more transparent set of economic practices in line with world standards in trade, intellectual property rights, market access, and investment policy.

Since the lifting of the embargo, Vietnam had been generally discouraged about the prospects for a trade agreement; reluctant to make changes in its economic system, including concessions on trading rights, elimination of non-tariff measures, creating a single law governing domestic and foreign investment; and suspicious of Washington's motives. In early 1999, Hanoi responded in a constructive way to the draft text of a trade agreement that the United States put before the Vietnamese in late 1998. However, Vietnam continued to believe that the United States harbored ulterior motives that transcended the development of normal relations in the areas of trade, economics, cultural exchange, and scientific cooperation. In part, this explains why it took until July 2000 to get Vietnam's signature on the bilateral trade agreement. Significant elements of the Vietnamese leadership believed the core goal of normalization for the United States revolved around a democratization and human rights agenda, to which Hanoi took strong and vocal exception. This was apparent in the views expressed by the Vietnamese military establishment, and had a major impact on U.S. efforts to develop a modest and slow-paced defense relationship.

From the perspective of the Defense Ministry, following the lifting of the American embargo, the United States had introduced democracy and human rights issues into the dialogue with Vietnam, shifting the emphasis of normalization discussions from the practical dimensions of managing entry-level relations in the economic and trade sphere to sorting out the political problems involved in engaging with Washington on sensitive "international" issues. Since late 1996, when the possibility of a formal and proper military-to-military relationship was first broached with the Vietnamese, the Vietnamese were at best ambivalent about a defense relationship with the United States. The Defense Ministry was of the view that the relationship was a good thing, but managing the interaction was potentially complex for them, especially in light of Sino-Vietnamese relations. Various departments within the Defense Ministry had differing views. The influential Social Policy Department was more strident and did not see the strategic advantages, largely because it focused on issues such as Agent Orange and Vietnamese MIAs. The External Relations Department regarded the relationship with Washington as important, but was inclined toward an extremely incremental process of furthering the relationship. The Foreign Ministry was more inclined to endorse programs, including the controversial demining training offered to—but initially rejected by— the Defense Ministry. The result was an only partial inclination on the part of the Vietnamese military to "engage" fully.

It is important to recognize that by mid-1998, the Defense Ministry had come to see some real improvements in the overall bilateral relationship with Washington. The Defense Ministry was pleased with the March 10, 1997, decision by President Clinton to grant Vietnam a waiver of the Jackson–Vanik amendment under section 402 of the Trade Act of 1974, and the Presidential Determination, forwarded to Congress on June 3, 1998, stating that continuation of the waiver for Vietnam would substantially promote the freedom of emigration objectives of the amendment. The Ministry recognized that these positive developments could establish an appropriate environment for "enhanced" military-to-military contacts. The Defense Ministry took certain modest steps that signaled a willingness to "expand" the defense relationship, in decidedly modest but symbolically important ways.

However, the Vietnamese remained tepid about defense relations. Twice, in 1997 and again in 1999, the Defense Ministry walked back from agreements on military-to-military activities. The 1999 decision to reject initiatives aimed at nudging the relationship forward, and to curtail high-level delegations, suggested that the Vietnamese were (1) nervous about China's reaction to any steps forward in the defense relationship with the United States, (2) still not prepared to accept the argument that establishing normal and annual routines in terms of working level contacts represented an appropriate step, and (3) seized by lingering concerns regarding Defense Department motives and goals. However, a visit by Secretary of Defense Cohen in 2000 represented a breakthrough and eased the concerns of Vietnamese military leaders regarding defense relations with the United States.

**Military Structure**

The Vietnamese army stands at about 580,000 troops today, about half of the force strength that existed during the height of the Third Indochina War—the period of Vietnam's occupation of Cambodia. The military of today is a much slimmer force preoccupied with modernizing its arms inventories, rationalizing all aspects of military education, and altering strategic thinking to reflect post–Cold War defense requirements. The military has been focused on maritime border issues and the problems in the South China Sea, and has sought to contour strategic thinking in a manner that reflects the need for an expanded coastal defense. The military has attempted to integrate into its thinking a new way of looking at neighbors and regional players. People's Army of Vietnam (PAVN) senior officers have visited counterparts throughout southeast and northern Asia, and worked to establish constructive relations with ASEAN militaries. Hanoi retains a close relationship with the Indonesian military, has worked to make contacts with Royal Thai Armed Forces counterparts, and sought to sustain what once were close links with the military in Cambodia. Vietnam and China have maintained regular military contacts through routine consultations and senior-level visits, and PAVN has played a role in the various border issue discussions with China.

Vietnam's military leadership preserved its relevance and status in the national political leadership as part of the equation of Politburo and Central Committee memberships. The military took three Politburo seats, two more than in 1991. Then Defense Minister Doan Khue and then Director of the General Political Department General Le Kha Phieu were joined by Lieutenant General Pham Van Tra, Deputy Defense Minister and Director of the General Staff Department, who was ranked 11th and subsequently replaced the ailing Khue, who died in January 1999. In effect, the military's share of influence as a percentage of total Politburo seats went from 8 percent in 1991 to 12 percent in 1994, as a result of the election of four additional Politburo members (including Phieu) at the January 1994 interim party conference, and then to 16 percent in 1996.

It is important to look at the issues that the military raised in the context of preparations for the National Party Congress, because those matters represent a useful public inventory of the key security and defense concerns that dominated the 1990s, and promised to linger as policy concerns through the next national party meeting. During the process of debating the draft documents that would become the basis for the Eighth Party Congress Political Report and other key documents, PAVN was very blunt about the failure of military party organizations to grasp basic economic concepts, and the "significant number" of party members in the military who had been captured and corrupted by the allure of money. The military warned that two main threats confronted the nation: economic backwardness and a degenerated ruling party. Party organizations within the armed forces focused on conventional military issues: readiness, defense requirements in view of the situation in the South China Sea, training needs, and the development of technical military capabilities. Most of the senior echelons of military party committees emphasized local military development projects, "peaceful transformation" as a threat to security, the strengthening of provincial armed forces, and perfecting local militia organizations. Many views spoken at these meetings criticized the theory that a strong economy engendered a vigorous defense on the basis of the observation that economically strong countries did not necessarily have matching security, though it was stipulated that independence and stability were generally the product of modernization and industrialization.

From the mid-1990s to the latter part of the decade, the armed forces remained focused on readiness issues, requirements springing from the South China Sea situation, and training needs. Service-specific party committee inspections focused on training levels and performance. Provincial-level military units and party committees spoke to the issues of developing local forces, perfecting local commands, recruiting and retaining party committee and youth union members from the services, and developing specialized, educated cadre. Training, readiness, defense capabilities, technological levels, and national and local defense strategies remained concerns for the provincial and regional military party committees through the late 1990s.

The biggest issue that remained unresolved at the time of the convening of the National Party Congress in 1996 was the party's responsibility in creating regional defense forces in the northern zone. Another potentially controversial issue was the matter of combining military region-level troops with local party organization assets, provincial administration personnel, and minority group representation to establish credible regional forces. At the same time the senior echelons of military party committees emphasized local military development projects, and military involvement in local socioeconomic development. Delta area military regions confronted economic difficulties when trying to stabilize border areas and fulfill local defense duties. National-level meetings of the Defense Ministry placed a primacy on creating an environment in which industrialization and modernization of defense production could take place in tandem with overall national economic developments. These issues clearly remained agenda items for PAVN through 1998 and into 1999.

The single most important formulation of Vietnam's defense and military preoccupations during the late 1990s was contained in the Defense Ministry's 1998 white paper, *Consolidating National Defense, Safeguarding the Homeland*, which made clear that Vietnam's concept of national defense envisioned a countrywide capability of coping with security requirements—an "All People's National Defense." That concept tied defense and security to Vietnam's economic development plan: Economic well-being and progress were one indispensable form of guaranteeing security and providing for the common defense. The white paper painted a picture of a future well-equipped and technically proficient Vietnamese army, fitted for defensive purposes, able to provide the military's weapons and equipment on the basis of indigenous production capabilities, wise procurement planning, and "selective cooperation" with a range of countries and militaries.

The white paper underscored Vietnam's efforts to reduce active duty troop strength, and to develop a reserve force, to achieve a level appropriate to the peacetime situation. As a whole, according to *Consolidating National Defense*, the armed forces needed to train officers and technical personnel for the tasks that a modernized military would have to confront. That meant ensuring a university level education for all officers, major improvements in the system of army schools, and specialized training for career officers in economics, law, production, technology, and management. The military would have to focus on developing a national defense industry in an intensive manner that would keep pace with more sophisticated technical military requirements. *Consolidating National Defense* also suggested the need to modernize Vietnamese military science to keep abreast of worldwide revolutionary developments in defense doctrine and strategic thinking. Vietnam's command system, challenged by developments in communications and information science, had to begin to reflect these changes.

The Vietnamese military is still adjusting to a rapidly moving environment in the midst of significant political change, economic reform, and regional transition. PAVN has an increasingly prominent role in formulating internal security policies, border and coastal defense strategies, and a real impact on significant aspects of the economic reforms by virtue of the military resources deployed in support of modernization and industrialization. Nevertheless, there is still a thick veneer of old-style thinking in the military—fealty to international communist goals, concern with the survival of national liberation movements, suspicions regarding neighbors, strong objections to interventions and actions by big powers, and continued recognition of debts owed to old friends. All that, however, coexists with military awareness of changing regional and global diplomacy and intensified economic interconnectedness. PAVN is straddling the old world and the new, and is struggling to make sense of its national role.

## Note

This chapter is adapted from a monograph, "Vietnam's Security, Defense and Foreign Policies in the 1990s," prepared for the Center for Naval Analyses in April 1999.

The views expressed in this chapter are those of the author alone and do not represent the positions of the U.S. Department of Defense or any part of the United States government.

## Suggested Readings

Brown, Frederick Z. *Second Chance: The United States and Indochina in the 1990s*. New York: Council on Foreign Relations, 1989.

The Institute for International Relations. *Asia Pacific's Changing Environment and Its Impact on Vietnam–U.S. Relations*. Hanoi: Statistical Publishing House, 1998.

Marr, David. *Vietnam Strives to Catch Up*. New York: Asia Society, 1995.

Ministry of Defense, Vietnam. *Consolidating National Defense, Safeguarding the Homeland*. Hanoi, 1998.

Morley, James W., and Masashi Nishihara, eds. *Vietnam Joins the World*. Armonk, NY: M.E. Sharpe, 1997.

Sidel, Mark. *The United States and Vietnam: The Road Ahead*. New York: Asia Society, 1996.

Simon, Sheldon W. "The Economic Crisis and Southeast Asian Security: Changing Priorities." National Bureau of Asian Research Analysis, vol. 9, no. 5, December 1998.

The Stanley Foundation. *Emerging from Conflict: Improving U.S. Relations with Current and Recent Adversaries*. Iowa: The Stanley Foundation, 1998.

Stern, L.M. *The Vietnamese Communist Party's Agenda for Reform: A Study of the Eighth National Party Congress*. North Carolina: McFarland and Company, 1998, pp. 69–102.

Vu Khoan. "Keynote Address." In *East Asia at the Crossroads: Challenges for ASEAN*. Hanoi: Ministry of Foreign Affairs, Institute for International Relations, November 1998.

# Epilogue

## William M. Carpenter and David G. Wiencek

This book has identified and assessed a wide range of political-security issues facing the Asia-Pacific region. Our point of departure has been to analyze the key factors and country-specific settings that will have an important bearing on the region's future stability. At the dawn of the new century, the situation remains very dynamic and fluid, and, as our authors have pointed out, there are a number of worrying security trends as we look to the future.

In the early 1990s, positive regional developments created a sense of optimism in many quarters; important economic successes clearly were achieved. It then appeared that economic growth rates would remain high in the years ahead, but the end of the 1990s saw a disappointing downturn throughout the region. By 2000, the worst seemed to be over, but economic recovery may be painfully slow and uneven among the nations of the region. It will take time for the long-term positive economic trendline to be reestablished.

Meanwhile, the economic downturn had many complex causes, among them corrupt political and business practices and a lack of financial transparency. Politically speaking, the crisis could end up as a positive force if the democratic tendencies and financial reforms it brought to the surface are able to establish deeper roots in the countries that were affected the most, such as Indonesia, Thailand, and South Korea. Democracy can be messy but it is a crucial ingredient to future economic success and long-term political stability.

The financial crisis of the late 1990s also had a major impact on defense modernization programs. Many states had to freeze or cut ambitious plans to upgrade their defense forces. This has helped create something of a vacuum, in that China pushed ahead with its aggressive military buildup as its neighbors in many cases simply could only watch and wait for their economic recovery—and rebuilding effort—to get back on track. For its part, Taiwan, one of the nations least affected by the financial crisis, was hit by a major earthquake in September 1999. The cleanup from this disaster was expensive and is bound to have an impact on Taiwan's defense spending.

At the same time, many militaries remain committed to international peace-keeping efforts, such as occurred in 1999 in East Timor. But peacekeeping is expensive and, as East Timor shows, the nations of the region simply lack the resources to play an active role; those who wanted to contribute, for example, had no real way to get their forces to where they were needed. In the end, the United States and Australia were the only nations in the region with any real transportation, logistics, and support capabilities. This lack of mobility must be seen as a net negative today among the military forces of the region.

More broadly, the Cold War continues to cast a long shadow in Asia, even as the rest of the world has in many ways benefited from the demise of the former Soviet Union and communist bloc. The Korean Peninsula and Taiwan Strait remain historical prisoners of the previous half-century of conflict and tension. In our assessment, these two locations will remain political-military flashpoints for the foreseeable future. Other security challenges in the form of weapons of mass destruction proliferation, maritime piracy, and illegal narcotics trafficking, as described in the preceding pages, are also shaping the Asia-Pacific security setting in new and important ways. Likewise, internal conflicts have not gone away, and in some cases have intensified. Indonesia, the Philippines, Thailand, Burma, Sri Lanka, Kashmir, and other locations will continue to feel the impact of separatist and/or terrorist movements.

The region's overall security structure remains unclear. The United States continues to play a leading role, but China's power is growing and a long-term competition is shaping up between these two great powers. Other nations, such as India, are building their political-military capacities and could exert greater influence in the years ahead.

In sum, as we noted at the outset of this book, Asia is a region of great potential —and potential danger. In the years ahead, the region's policymakers will face many challenges as they try to maintain political stability and fashion a durable and balanced regional security setting.

# Glossary of Abbreviations and Acronyms

| | |
|---|---|
| ABRI | Angkatan Bersenjata Republik Indonesia (Indonesian Armed Forces) |
| ADF | Australian Defence Forces |
| AFP | Armed Forces of the Philippines |
| AFTA | ASEAN Free Trade Area |
| AID | Agency for International Development |
| AIDS | Acquired Immunodeficiency Syndrome |
| ALH | Advanced Light Helicopter |
| ANZAC | Australia–New Zealand Agreement |
| ANZAC | Australian and New Zealand Army Corp |
| ANZUS | Australia–New Zealand–United States |
| AOSIS | Alliance of Small Island States |
| APEC | Asia-Pacific Economic Cooperation organization |
| ARF | ASEAN Regional Forum |
| ASCM | Anti-Ship Cruise Missile |
| ASDF | Air Self Defense Force |
| ASEAN | Association of Southeast Asian Nations |
| ASEM | Asia-Europe Meeting |
| ASG | Abu Sayuf Group |
| ASW | Anti-Submarine Warfare |
| ATV | Advanced Technology Vessel |
| AUSMIN | Australia–United States Ministerial |
| AWACS | Airborne Warning and Control aircraft |
| BJP | Bharatiya Janata Party |
| BLDP | Buddhist Liberal Democratic Party |
| BMDO | Ballistic Missile Defense Organization |
| BRA | Bougainville Revolutionary Army |

| | |
|---|---|
| CCP | Communist Party of China |
| CDR | Closer Defence Relations |
| CINCPAC | Commander-in-Chief, Pacific |
| CPP | Cambodian People's Party |
| CPP | Communist Party of the Philippines |
| CRPP | Committee Representing the People's Parliament |
| CSCAP | Council for Security Cooperation in the Asia Pacific |
| CSRF | Commonwealth Strategic Reserve Force |
| CTBT | Comprehensive Test Ban Treaty |
| DFAT | Department of Foreign Affairs and Trade |
| DIA | Defense Intelligence Agency |
| DOD | Department of Defense |
| DPP | Democratic Progressive Party |
| DPRK | Democratic People's Republic of Korea |
| DRDO | Defense Research and Development Organization |
| DSP | Defense Support Program |
| EEZ | Exclusive Economic Zone |
| EU | European Union |
| FIP | Force Improvement Plan |
| FMS | Foreign Military Sales |
| FPDA | Five-Power Defence Arrangement |
| FUNCINPEC | United Front for an Independent, Neutral, and Peaceful Cambodia |
| GATT | General Agreement on Tariffs and Trade |
| GDP | Gross Domestic Product |
| GPS | Global Positioning System |
| GSDF | Ground Self Defense Force |
| GSH | General Staff Headquarters |
| HIV | Human Immunodeficiency Virus |
| HNS | Host Nation Support |
| IAEA | International Atomic Energy Agency |
| ICBM | Intercontinental Ballistic Missile |
| IDF | Indigenous Defense Fighters |
| IMB | International Maritime Bureau |
| IMF | International Monetary Fund |
| IMO | International Maritime Organization |
| IPKF | Indian Peacekeeping Force |
| IRBM | Intermediate-Range Ballistic Missile |
| JIOG | Joint International Observer Group |
| JSF | Joint Strike Fighter |
| JVP | Janatha Vimukthi Peramuna (People's Liberation Party) |
| KEDO | Korean Peninsula Energy Development Organization |
| KFP | Korean Fighter Program |
| KIG | Kalayaan (Freedomland) Island Group |

| | |
|---|---|
| km | Kilometer |
| KMT | Kuomintang Party |
| KPA | Korean People's Army |
| KWP | Korean Workers' Party |
| LACM | Land-Attack Cruise Missile |
| LCA | Light Combat Aircraft |
| LOS | Law of the Sea Treaty |
| LPRP | Lao People's Revolutionary Party |
| LTTE | Liberation Tigers of Tamil Eelam |
| MAF | Malaysian Armed Forces |
| MBT | Main Battle Tank |
| MIA | Missing in Action |
| MILF | Moro Islamic Liberation Front |
| MIRV | Multiple Independently targetable Reentry Vehicle |
| MND | Ministry of National Defense |
| MNDP | Mongolian National Democratic Party |
| MNLF | Moro National Liberation Front |
| MPRP | Mongolian People's Revolutionary Party |
| MRBM | Medium-Range Ballistic Missile |
| MSA | Maritime Safety Agency |
| MSDF | Maritime Self Defense Force |
| MSDP | Mongolian Social Democratic Party |
| MTCR | Missile Technology Control Regime |
| NAFTA | North American Free Trade Agreement |
| NATO | North Atlantic Treaty Organization |
| NEC | National Election Commission |
| NGO | Non-Governmental Organization |
| NLD | National League for Democracy |
| NMD | National Missile Defense |
| NPA | New People's Army |
| NPT | Nuclear Non-Proliferation Treaty |
| NSC | National Security Council |
| NSR | National Security Review |
| NWS | Nuclear Weapons State |
| NZDF | New Zealand Defence Force |
| OHR | Over the Horizon Radar |
| OPIC | Overseas Private Investment Corporation |
| OSCE | Organization on Security and Cooperation in Europe |
| OTI | Office of Transition Initiatives |
| PAP | People's Action Party |
| PAVN | People's Army of Vietnam |
| PCTC | Philippine Center on Transnational Crime |
| PFP | Partnership for Peace |

| | |
|---|---|
| PLA | People's Liberation Army |
| PNG | Papua New Guinea |
| PNGDF | Papua New Guinea Defense Force |
| PNP | Philippine National Police |
| PRC | People's Republic of China |
| PSB | Public Security Bureau |
| PULO | Pattani United Liberation Organization |
| RCAF | Royal Cambodian Armed Forces |
| RMA | Revolution in Military Affairs |
| RMAF | Royal Malaysian Air Force |
| ROC | Republic of China |
| ROK | Republic of Korea |
| RPC | Regional Piracy Center |
| SAF | Singapore Armed Forces |
| SAM | Surface-to-Air Missile |
| SAR | Special Administrative Region |
| SBIRS | Space-Based Infra-Red System |
| SCM | Security Consultative Meeting |
| SDF | Self Defense Force |
| SEATO | Southeast Asia Treaty Organization |
| SLBM | Submarine-Launched Ballistic Missile |
| SLFP | Sri Lanka Freedom Party |
| SLOC | Sea Lines of Communication |
| SLORC | State Law and Order Restoration Council |
| SLV | Space Launch Vehicle |
| SPARTECA | South Pacific Regional Trade and Economic Cooperation Association |
| SPDC | State Peace and Development Council |
| SPNFZ | South Pacific Nuclear Free Zone |
| SRBM | Short-Range Ballistic Missile |
| START | Strategic Arms Reduction Treaty (U.S.–Russia) |
| TMD | Theater Missile Defense |
| TNI | Tentara Nasional Indonesia (Indonesian Armed Forces) |
| TRA | Taiwan Relations Act |
| UCD | Union of Cambodian Democrats |
| ULNLF | United Lao National Liberation Front |
| UMEH | Union of Myanmar Economic Holdings |
| UMNO | United Malays National Organization |
| UN | United Nations |
| UNAMET | United Nations Mission in East Timor |
| UNCLOS | United Nations Convention on the Law of the Sea |
| UNP | United National Party |
| USFK | United States Forces Korea |

| | |
|---|---|
| UWSA | United Wa State Army |
| VFA | Visiting Forces Agreement |
| VLCC | Very Large Crude Carrier |
| VLF | Very Low Frequency |
| VNCP | Vietnamese Communist Party |
| WFP | World Food Program |
| WMD | Weapons of Mass Destruction |
| WTO | World Trade Organization |

# Appendix

This appendix shows in table form comparative data on the countries surveyed in this book. The data provide a snapshot and summary of key geographic, population, political, and economic indicators.

| Country | Total Geographic Area (sq km) | Population and Population Growth Rate[1] | Labor Force | Government Type | Economy: Gross Domestic Product (GDP), Real Growth Rate and Product Per Capita (Purchasing Power Parity, U.S. Dollars) | Military Manpower Availability Males Ages 15–49 Those Fit for Military Service | Military Expenditures (U.S. Dollar Figure/ Percent/ of GDP) |
|---|---|---|---|---|---|---|---|
| Australia | 7,686,850 | 18,783,551 0.9% | 9.2 million (Dec. 1997) | democratic; federal-state system recogniz- the British monarch as sovereign | $393.9 billion, 4.5%, $21,200 (1998 est.) | 4.8 million males 4.2 million fit | $6.9 billion 1.9% (FY97/98) |
| Burma | 678,500 | 48,081,302 1.61% | 18.8 million (FY95/96 est.) | military regime | $5.61 billion, 1.1%, $1,200 (1998 est.) | 12.4 million males and 12.2 million females; 6.6 million males fit; 6.5 million females fit | $3.904 billion 2.1% (FY97/98) |
| Cambodia | 181,040 | 11,626,520 2.49% | 2.5–3 million | multiparty liberal democracy under a constitutional monarchy est-ablished in Sept. 1993 | $7.8 billion, 0%, $700 (1998 est.) | 2.5 million males 1.4 million fit | $85.3 million 2.4% (1998) |
| China | 9,596,960 | 1,246,871,951 0.77% | 696 million | communist state | $4.42 trillion, 7.8%, $3,600 (1998 est.) | 361 million males 198 million fit | $12.608 billion NA% (FY99) |
| India | 3,287,590 | 1,000,848,550 1.68% | NA | federal republic | $1.689 trillion, 5.4%, $1,720 (1998 est.) | 269 million males 158 million fit | $10.012 billion 2.7% (FY98/99) |
| Indonesia | 1,919,440 | 216,108,345 1.46% | 87 million | republic | $602 billion, –13.7%, $2,830 (1998 est.) | 61 million males 35.8 million fit | $959.7 million 1% (FY98/99) |

| Country | Area | Population / growth | | Government | GDP | Military manpower | Military expenditure |
|---|---|---|---|---|---|---|---|
| Japan | 377,835 | 126,182,077 0.2% | 67.72 million | constitutional monarchy | $2.903 trillion, −2.6%, $23,100 (1998 est.) | 30.6 million males 26.4 million fit | $42.9 billion 0.9% (FY98/99) |
| Laos | 236,800 | 5,407,453 2.74% | 1–1.5 million | communist state | $6.6 billion, 4%, $1,260 (1998 est.) | 1.2 million males 648,087 fit | $77.4 million 4.2% (FY96/97) |
| Malaysia | 329,750 | 21,376,066 2.08% | 8.398 million | constitutional monarchy | $215 billion, −7%, $10,300 (1998 est.) | 5.5 million males 3.3 million fit | $2.1billion 2.1% (1998) |
| Mongolia | 1,565,000 | 2,617,379 1.45% | 1.115 million (mid 1993 est.) | republic | $5.8 billion, 3.5%, $2,250 (1998 est.) | 702,141 males 457,270 fit | $20.3 million 2% (1997) |
| New Zealand | 268,680 | 3,662,265 0.99% | 1.86 million | parliamentary democracy | $61.1 billion, −0.2%, $17,000 (1998 est.) | 943,624 males 793,814 fit | $562 million 1.05% (FY97/98) |
| North Korea | 120,540 | 21,386,109 1.45% | 9.615 million | communist state, one-man dictatorship | $21 billion, −5%, $1,000 (1998 est.) | 5.7 million males 3.4 million fit | $5–7 billion 25–33% (1997 est.) |
| Pakistan | 803,940 | 138,123,359 2.18% | 37.8 million[2] | federal republic | $270 billion, 5%, $2,000 (1998 est.) | 33.4 million males 20.5 million fit | $2.48 billion 4.4% (FY98/99) |
| The Philippines | 300,000 | 79,345,812 2.04% | 31.3 million | republic | $270 billion, −0.5%, $3,500 (1998 est.) | 20.2 million males 14.2 million fit | $995 million 1.5% (1998) |
| Singapore | 647.5 | 3,531,600 1.15% | 1.856 million | republic within commonwealth | $91.7 billion, 1.3%, $26,000 (1998 est.) | 1 million males 757,940 fit | $4.244 billion 5.1% (FY98/99) |
| South Korea | 98,480 | 46,884,800 1% | 20 million | republic | $584.7 billion, −6.8%, $12,600 (1998 est.) | 13.9 million males 8.8 million fit | $9.9 billion 3.2% (FY98/99) |

*(continued)*

| Country | Total Geographic Area (Sq km) | Population and Population Growth Rate[1] | Labor Force | Government Type | Economy: Gross Domestic Product (GDP), Real Growth Rate and Product PerCapita (Purchasing Power Parity, U.S. Dollars) | Military Manpower Availability: Males Ages 15–49 / Those Fit for Military Service | Military Expenditures (U.S. Dollar Figure/Percent/of GDP) |
|---|---|---|---|---|---|---|---|
| Sri Lanka | 65,610 | 19,144,875[3] 1.37% | 6.2 million | republic | $48.1 billion, 4.7%, $2,500 (1998 est.) | 5.2 million males / 4.0 million fit | $719 million 4.2% (1998) |
| Taiwan | 35,980 | 22,113,250 0.93% | 9.4 million | multiparty democratic regime headed by popularly elected president | $362 billion, 4.8%, $16,500 (1998 est.) | 6.5 million males / 5 million fit | $7.446 billion 2.8% (FY98/99) |
| Thailand | 514,000 | 60,609,046 0.93% | 32.6 million | constitutional monarchy | $369 billion, −8.5%, $6,100 (1998 est.) | 17.4 million males / 10.5 million fit | $1.95 billion 2.5% (FY97/98) |
| Vietnam | 329,000 | 77,311,210 1.37% | 32.7 million | communist state | $134.8 billion, 4%, $1,770 (1998 est.) | 20.4 million males / 12.9 million fit | $650 million 9.3% (1997) |

*Source:* Adapted from U.S. Central Intelligence Agency, *The World Factbook 1999,* available at Website, www.cia.gov/cia/publications/factbook/index.html.
1. Western analysts believe that China's real defense spending is several times higher than the official figure because several significant items are funded elsewhere.
2. Extensive export of labor, mostly to the Middle East, and use of child labor.
3. Since the outbreak of hostilities between the government and armed Tamil separatists in the mid-1980s, several hundred thousand Tamil civilians have fled the island; as of late 1996, 63,068 were housed in refugee camps in south India, another 30,000–40,000 lived outside the Indian camps, and more than 200,000 Tamils have sought political asylum in the West.
NA – Not Available

# About the Editors and Contributors

## The Editors

**William M. Carpenter** is a Senior Consultant to SRI International in Arlington, Virginia, on international security affairs. He was for many years Assistant Director of the Strategic Studies Center of SRI International. A retired Navy captain, he has served in command and staff assignments at sea and in Japan in three wars, and also in planning and policy offices in Washington before extending his career into the research field of international security studies with a specialty in East Asian affairs. He has made many visits to East Asian countries and is the author of books, studies, and articles on international affairs. He is a 1940 graduate of the United States Naval Academy. His most recent publications are: *The America That Can Say No* (translated into Japanese and co-authored with Stephen P. Gibert), and *America and Island China: A Documentary History* with Stephen P. Gibert (revised edition forthcoming).

**David G. Wiencek** is Director of Research and Information Services with ArmorGroup/Parvus International Corporation, an international security and risk management company in Washington, DC. He previously operated his own consulting company, International Security Group, Inc., specializing in international political risk assessments, East and Southeast Asian political-security affairs, weapons of mass destruction and proliferation studies, and terrorism issues. His articles have appeared in *The Washington Times*, *Jane's Intelligence Review*, *Defense News*, and *Global Defence Review*. His recent publications include: *Dangerous Arsenals: Missile Threats in and from Asia* (Centre for Defence and International Security Studies [CDISS], Lancaster University, UK, 1997). Mr. Wiencek holds B.A. and M.A. degrees in international affairs from American University, Washington, DC.

## The Contributors

**Samina Ahmed** is a Fellow at the Belfer Center for Science and International Affairs, Kennedy School of Government, Harvard University. She is a political scientist who specializes in nuclear proliferation, regional security, and ethnic conflict in South Asia. She has previously worked in the Institute of Regional Studies, Islamabad, and the Pakistan Institute of International Affairs, Karachi. Dr. Ahmed has a master's degree in International Relations and a Ph.D. in Political Science from the Australian National University, Canberra. She has been the recipient of a number of research grants and awards and has worked as a visiting Fellow at Oxford University, a Visiting Researcher at the Stockholm International Peace Research Institute, and a Visiting Scholar at the Cooperative Monitoring Center, Sandia National Laboratories, Albuquerque, New Mexico. Dr. Ahmed is the author of several book chapters and articles in academic journals. Her latest publications include "Pakistan's Nuclear Weapons Program: Turning Points and Nuclear Choices," *International Security* 23, no. 4 (Spring 1999); a co-edited book, *Pakistan and the Bomb: Public Opinion and Nuclear Options* (Notre Dame, Indiana: University of Notre Dame Press, 1998); and "Centralization, Authoritarianism and the Mismanagement of Ethnic Relations in Pakistan," in Michael E. Brown and Sumit Ganguly, eds., *Ethnic Management in Asia and the Pacific* (Cambridge, Massachusetts: CSIA Studies in International Security, The MIT Press, 1997).

**Henry S. Albinski** is Visiting Professor of Government and International Relations at the University of Sydney and Emeritus Professor of Political Science and of Australian and New Zealand Studies at the Pennsylvania State University. His professional interests, and substantial publications, have focused on Australian foreign and defense policy, Australian politics and Australian studies, as well as on New Zealand, Canada, Pacific Basin affairs, and the United States in the Asia-Pacific context. He has held numerous private and public sector consultancies, participated in a broad range of task forces, lectured worldwide, and held numerous visiting appointments, primarily in Australia. He was the founder of, and for 16 years directed, the Australia–New Zealand Studies Center at the Pennsylvania State University.

**Maureen Aung-Thwin** is director of the Burma Project of the New York–based Open Society Institute, part of the network of foundations created and funded by philanthropist George Soros. A graduate of Northwestern University, Ms. Aung-Thwin serves on the boards of Human Rights Watch/Asia and the Burma Studies Foundation, which oversees the Center for Burma Studies at Northern Illinois University in De Kalb, Illinois. She has served on the staff of the Asia Society in New York, has worked as a journalist based in Hong Kong, and has contributed articles on Burma to such publications as the *Christian Science Monitor*, the *Far Eastern Economic Review*, *Foreign Affairs,* and *Ms Magazine.*

**John C. Baker** is a technology policy analyst at RAND, Arlington, VA, where he focuses on the political and security implications of space technologies, including commercial observation satellites. Previously, he was a senior staff member at George Washington University's Space Policy Institute. He directed the Institute's South China Sea Remote Sensing Project, which brought together a team of multidisciplinary experts to assess the usefulness of higher-resolution commercial satellite imagery for enhancing regional transparency and mitigating the risk of conflict over the disputed Spratly Islands. He has also been a staff member with the International Institute for Strategic Studies (IISS), Pacific–Sierra Research Corporation, and the Brookings Institution. He holds a M. Phil. in Political Science from Columbia University.

**Victor D. Cha** teaches in the Department of Government and School of Foreign Service, Georgetown University, Washington, DC. He is the author of *Alignment Despite Antagonism: The United States–Korea–Japan Triangle* (Stanford: Stanford University Press, 1999, and East Asian Institute, Columbia University), which won the Masayoshi Ohira Memorial Prize for best book on East Asia. He has also authored numerous articles on international relations and East Asia appearing in such scholarly journals as *Survival, International Studies Quarterly, Journal of Peace Research, Asian Survey, Asian Perspective, Korean Journal of Defense Analysis,* and *Korean Studies.* Professor Cha is a recipient of numerous academic awards including the Fulbright (Korea), and MacArthur Foundation Fellowships. He spent two years as a John M. Olin National Security Fellow at Harvard University's Center for International Affairs and as a postdoctoral fellow at the Center for International Security and Arms Control, Stanford University. Dr. Cha has served as an independent consultant and lectured to various branches of the U.S. Department of Defense and the Department of State. He has appeared as a guest analyst on various media services including *CNN,* Associated Press TV, Fox-TV, *Voice of America,* Australian Public Radio, National Public Radio, *New York Times, Washington Post, Reuters, Mainichi Shimbun, Japan Times, Asia Times, Choson Ilbo, Sisa Journal,* and *Korea Herald.* In 1999, he was the Edward Teller National Fellow for Security at the Hoover Institution on War, Revolution, and Peace at Stanford University and a recipient of the Fulbright Senior Scholar Award.

**James Clad** has more than two decades of experience in Asia as an analyst, diplomat, journalist, and lawyer. Currently Director of Asia Pacific Energy at Cambridge Energy Research Associates, Clad concentrates research for clients on investment risk, domestic political and economic trends, and strategic issues in Asia. Concurrently the Henry Luce Foundation Professor of Southeast Asian Studies at Georgetown University, he has also served as a *Far Eastern Economic Review* correspondent in South, Central, and Southeast Asia, and was Senior Associate for Asian Affairs at the Carnegie Endowment in Washington, DC. Trained as a barrister in the British legal system, Professor Clad served in the New Zealand diplomatic service in South and Southeast Asia from 1977 to 1983. His book *Behind the Myth: Business, Money and Power in Southeast Asia* (HarperCollins, 1991) critiqued the fundamentals behind Asia's growth well before the onset of the 1997 financial crisis. His most recent book is *After the Crusade: American Foreign Policy for the Post-Superpower Age* (University Press of America, 1995). He often testifies before congressional committees and is a frequent media commentator on Asian affairs.

**Paul C. Grove** is the Regional Director of the International Republican Institute's (IRI) Asia and Middle East Division, Washington, DC. In addition to strategic programmatic development and outreach, he is responsible for the overall management and implementation of IRI's programs in Burma, Cambodia, Indonesia, Mongolia, Morocco, the People's Republic of China, Thailand, Vietnam, and the West Bank. Prior to becoming Regional Director, he served for two years as IRI's Director of China Programs and Deputy Regional Director of the Asia and Middle East Division. From 1994 to 1996, Mr. Grove served as IRI's Chief of Delegation in Phnom Penh, Cambodia, where he created, managed, and implemented over 200 political development programs throughout the country. He provided technical assistance to leaders of both elected and non-elected political parties and the National Assembly. From 1989 to 1994, Mr. Grove served as a Legislative Aide and Legislative Assistant to U.S. Senator Mitch McConnell (R-KY). He advised the Senator on defense and foreign policy issues, and implemented the Senator's legislative agenda for health care, telecommunications, education, transportation, and science and technology. Mr. Grove received his B.A. from Bates College and studied two terms at the London School of Economics and Political Science.

**John B. Haseman** retired from the U.S. Army in 1995 with the rank of colonel. He served three tours of duty in Indonesia, most recently as Defense and Army Attaché from 1990 to 1994. Colonel Haseman had 18 years of duty in Asia and spent most of his 30-year military career dealing with Southeast Asian issues. Besides Indonesia, Colonel Haseman served in the Republic of Korea, the Republic of Vietnam, Thailand, and Burma, and had Army Staff duties dealing with political/military policy in Asia. A linguist in the Burmese, Indonesian, and Thai languages, Colonel Haseman has published five books and book chapters, and more than five dozen articles and book reviews on Asia in a variety of professional journals. He is the Indonesia correspondent for the respected London publication *Jane's Defence Weekly*. Mr. Haseman lives in Colorado and works as a consultant on Asian affairs.

**Dennis Van Vranken Hickey** is Professor of Political Science and University Fellow in Research at Southwest Missouri State University. His publications include articles in *Asian Affairs, Asian Survey, The Journal of Contemporary China, Orbis,* and *Pacific Review*. Professor Hickey has also published two books: *U.S.–Taiwan Security Ties: From Cold War to Beyond Containment* (Praeger, 1994) and *Taiwan's Security in the Changing International System* (Lynne Rienner, 1997), and has contributed op-eds to a variety of newspapers, including *The Wall Street Journal* and *The Los Angeles Times.*

**Peter R. Lavoy** is Director for Counterproliferation Policy in the Office of the U.S. Secretary of Defense, Washington, DC. Dr. Lavoy is on leave from the Naval Postgraduate School in Monterey, California, where he is an Assistant Professor of National Security Affairs. Dr. Lavoy has published numerous journal articles and book chapters on the proliferation of weapons of mass destruction (WMD) and on South Asian political and military issues. He has two forthcoming books: *Learning to Live with the Bomb? India and Nuclear Weapons, 1947–1999,* and *Planning the Unthinkable: Military Doctrines for the Use of WMD,* co-edited with Scott Sagan and James Wirtz (Cornell University Press, 2000). Dr. Lavoy received a Ph.D. in Political Science from the University of California, Berkeley.

**Satu P. Limaye** is the Director of the Research Division, Asia-Pacific Center for Security Studies, Honolulu, Hawaii. He received his Ph.D. in international relations from Oxford University (Magdalen College) where he was a Marshall Scholar. He graduated magna cum laude and Phi Beta Kappa from Georgetown University in 1985 with a Bachelor of Science in Foreign Service degree. He previously was an Abe Fellow at the National Endowment for Democracy's International Forum for Democratic Studies. From 1993 to 1996, Dr. Limaye was Research Fellow and Head of Program on South Asia at the Japan Institute of International Affairs. His publications include the book *U.S.-Indian Relations: The Pursuit of Accommodation* (Westview Press, 1993), and articles in *Contemporary South Asia, Studies in Conflict and Terrorism, The Nikkei Weekly,* and *The Asian Wall Street Journal.* Dr. Limaye has contributed to Oxford Analytica, Ltd. *Daily Brief,* a consulting service based in Oxford, England, and was the Washington correspondent for *Business South Asia* (published by the Economist Intelligence Unit). In 1994, he was rapporteur for the Asia Society Study Group on "South Asia and the United States After the Cold War." He subsequently served as a member of the Society's Study Group on "Preventing Proliferation in South Asia." Dr. Limaye has taught at Georgetown University and Sophia University's Faculty of Comparative Culture (Tokyo). He has been a consultant to the Ford Foundation, the National Endowment for Democracy, and the Friedrich-Naumann-Stiftung.

**Robert A. Manning** is currently a Senior Follow and Director of Asian Studies at the Council on Foreign Relations. Previously he was a Senior Fellow at the Progressive Policy Institute, and a Research Associate at the Sigur Center for East Asian Studies of George Washington University. He is author of *The Asian Energy Factor: Myths and Dilemmas of Energy, Security and the Pacific Future* (St. Martins, 2000). He has also written "Back to the Future: Towards a Post-Nuclear Ethic—The New Logic of Nonproliferation," Progressive Foundation, 1994. From 1989 until March 1993, he was Advisor for Policy to the Assistant Secretary for East

Asian and Pacific Affairs, U.S. Department of State. He was involved in policy planning and public diplomacy of a wide range of policies, including those toward Korea, Japan, China, political-military affairs and Asian security, Asia-Pacific economic cooperation, Vietnam, and Cambodia. Previous to that, he was diplomatic correspondent for *U.S. News and World Report* (1985–87) and prior to that, he was a Washington correspondent for the *Far Eastern Economic Review*. He has written widely on international affairs, with articles appearing in *Foreign Affairs, Foreign Policy, Survival, Washington Quarterly, World Policy Journal, The New York Times, The Wall Street Journal, The Washington Post, Los Angeles Times* (regular contributor to the Sunday "Opinion" section), *The New Republic, International Herald Tribune, Le Monde Diplomatique, Asahi Shimbun, Sankei Shimbun, Chuo Koron, Sin Dong-A* (Korea), and other publications.

**Sean M. McDonald** completed his Ph.D. in geography at the University of Glasgow in Glasgow, Scotland. A former International Trade Specialist with the U.S. Department of Commerce, he is currently an Assistant Professor of Geography and Director of the International Cultures and Economy Program at Bentley College, Waltham, Massachusetts.

**Michael J. Mitchell** is Vice President at the Mercury Group, Washington, DC, and specializes in assisting a wide-ranging client list in crisis communications and media strategies. He previously was Senior Program Officer at the International Republican Institute (IRI), Washington, DC, where he specialized in Asian affairs. During the Bush administration, he was director of congressional relations for the Department of State's Office of International Narcotics and Law Enforcement Affairs. He also served as a special assistant to Senator Mitch McConnell (R-KY) on the Senate Foreign Relations Committee's Terrorism and Narcotics Subcommittee. Mr. Mitchell holds an M.A. in International Trade from George Mason University, and a B.A. in Communications from Clarion University of Pennsylvania. He is the author of several articles on Burma's democracy movement. He has spoken to a wide variety of civic, political, and corporate groups, and is a guest lecturer at the U.S. Army's JFK Special Warfare School, Fort Bragg, North Carolina.

**Larry A. Niksch** is a Specialist in Asian Affairs with the Congressional Research Service of the Library of Congress, Washington, DC. He received a B.A. in history from Butler University, an M.S. in foreign service from Georgetown University, and a Ph.D in history from Georgetown University. Dr. Niksch specializes in U.S. security policy in East Asia and the Western Pacific region, internal political conditions in the countries of the region, and foreign policy developments within the region. In addition to his reports published by the Congressional Research Service and congressional committees, Dr. Niksch has written articles for a number of journals and newspapers in the United States and Asia-Pacific countries. He has contributed to several books, most recently a chapter on "North Korea's Negotiating Behavior" in *North Korean Foreign Relations* (Oxford University Press, 1998). He has spoken at numerous conferences in the United States and abroad. He has lectured at the Army War College, the Naval War College, the Air War College, and the U.S. Pacific Command. He is interviewed frequently by East Asian and U.S. media outlets and by the Voice of America. Dr. Niksch is a Senior Adviser on East Asia to The PRS (Political Risk Services) Group. Dr. Niksch served as a member of the U.S. presidential observer group to the Philippine presidential election in February 1986.

**William J. Olson** is the Staff Director for the U.S. Senate Caucus on International Narcotics Control. Before joining the Caucus, Dr. Olson was a Senior Fellow at the National Strategy Information Center (NSIC), a think tank in Washington, DC. He is the co-author of two recent NSIC studies: *International Organized Crime* and *Ethnic and Religious Nationalism*. Formerly, Dr. Olson was Deputy Assistant Secretary of State in the Bureau of International Narcotics Matters at the Department of State. Prior to this position, he was Director and served as Deputy Assistant Secretary (acting) for Low Intensity Conflict in the U.S. Department of Defense. His published works include over fifty articles and books on light forces, U.S. strategic interests in the Persian Gulf, the Iran–Iraq war, the Soviet invasion of Afghanistan, guerrilla warfare, the war on drugs, conflict management, and most recently studies on international organized crime. He is the editor of a book series on regional conflict through Harper-Collins, founded the *Journal of Small Wars and Insurgencies*, edited a special volume for the *Annals of Political Science* on small wars, served on the editorial board of *Parameters,* and is co-author and editor of *Trends in Organized Crime*. Dr. Olson has lectured extensively to civilian and military audiences on drug policy and other foreign policy and security issues. He holds a Ph.D. from the University of Texas at Austin.

**Lewis M. Stern** has been the Director for Indochina, Thailand, and Burma in the Office of the Assistant Secretary of Defense for International Security Affairs, U.S. Department of Defense, Washington, DC, since 1988. He is the author of *Renovating the Vietnamese Communist Party: Nguyen Van Linh and the Program of Organizational Reform, 1987–1991* (Singapore: Institute of Southeast Asian Studies, 1993), *Imprisoned or Missing in Vietnam: Policies of the Vietnamese Government Concerning Captured and Unaccounted for United States Soldiers, 1969–1994* (North Carolina: McFarland and Company, 1995), and the *Vietnamese Communist Party's Agenda for Reform: A Study of the Eighth National Party Congress* (North Carolina: McFarland and Company, 1998).

**Robert Sutter** specialized in Asian and Pacific Affairs and U.S. foreign policy with the Congressional Research Service of the Library of Congress from 1977 to 1999. In his government service of over 30 years, Dr. Sutter has held a variety of analytical and supervisory positions with the Central Intelligence Agency, the

Department of State, the Senate Foreign Relations Committee, and the Congressional Research Service. He received a Ph.D. in history and East Asian languages from Harvard University. He teaches regularly at Georgetown and George Washington Universities and the University of Virginia. He has published 11 books and numerous articles dealing with contemporary East Asian countries and their relations with the United States.

**M.A. Thomas** has been a research analyst for the U.S. Department of Defense since 1993. His area of responsibility is South Asia, focusing particularly on Sri Lanka and India. Mr. Thomas is also an instructor of South Asia Area Studies at Campbell University in North Carolina. He received his B.S. degree from Loyola College, Baltimore, and his M.A. degree from the University of Pennsylvania in South Asian regional studies and international relations.

**Bruce Vaughn** completed his Ph.D. in political science at the Australian National University and is currently Senior Defense Analyst at the Embassy of Australia in Washington, DC. He has published articles on South Asian security issues in *Intelligence and National Security*, *Central Asian Survey*, *The Indian Ocean Review*, *Strategic Analysis*, and the *Strategic and Defence Studies Centre Working Papers* series. Before beginning his Ph.D., he worked on foreign and defense policy issues for the Senate Democratic Policy Committee, the Senate Treaty Review Support Office, and the Senate Select Committee on Secret Military Assistance to Iran and the Nicaraguan Opposition.

# Index